P9-DTL-390

# DATE DUE

| | | | |
|---|---|---|---|
| | | | |
| | | | |
| | | | |
| | | | |
| | | | |
| | | | |
| | | | |
| | | | |
| | | | |
| | | | |
| | | | |
| | | | |
| | | | |
| | | | |
| | | | |
| | | | |
| | | | |
| | | | |
| | | | |
| | | | |
| | | | |

DEMCO 38-296

# INNOVATION EXPLOSION

*Using Intellect and Software to
Revolutionize Growth Strategies*

JAMES BRIAN QUINN
JORDAN J. BARUCH
KAREN ANNE ZIEN

THE FREE PRESS

*New York   London   Toronto   Sydney   Singapore*

Riverside Community College
Library
4800 Magnolia Avenue
Riverside, California 92506

HD 56 .Q56 1997

Quinn, James Brian, 1928-

Innovation explosion

THE FREE PRESS
A Division of Simon & Schuster Inc.
1230 Avenue of the Americas
New York, NY 10020

Copyright © 1997 by James Brian Quinn, Jordan J. Baruch,
and Karen Anne Zien
All rights reserved,
including the right of reproduction
in whole or in part in any form.

THE FREE PRESS and colophon are trademarks
of Simon & Schuster Inc.

Manufactured in the United States of America

10  9  8  7  6  5  4  3  2  1


**Library of Congress Cataloging-in-Publication Data**

Quinn, James Brian, 1928–
     Innovation explosion : using intellect and software to
  revolutionize growth strategies / James Brian Quinn, Jordan J.
  Baruch, Karen Anne Zien.
        p.  cm.
     Includes bibliographical references and index.
     ISBN 0-684-83394-8
     1. Innovation management.   2. Creativity and organizations.
3. Technology strategy.   4. R&D management.   5. National science
and technology strategy.   6. Software engineering.   I. Baruch,
Jordan J.   II. Zien, Karen Anne.
III. Title.
HD56.Q56   1997
658.4'063—dc21                                              97-22960
                                                                CIP


ISBN 0–684–83394–8

*To Our ~~Spouses~~ "Spice" for Life*

# Contents

*Acknowledgments* ix

Introduction: Knowledge and Innovation     1

1. Executive Overview: Intellect, Innovation, and Growth     20

## PART I: SOFTWARE REVOLUTIONIZES INNOVATION

2. Software-Based Innovation     45

3. Managing Software-Based Innovation     74

## PART II: NEW ORGANIZATION FORMS

4. Beyond Teams: Independent Collaboration     107

5. Motivating Creativity Toward Markets     141

## PART III. TOP MANAGEMENT'S ROLE

6. Vision, Leadership, and Strategic Focus     163

7. Creating "Best in World" Capabilities     187

## PART IV: MIDDLE MANAGEMENT ISSUES

8. Matching Strategies, Structures, and Incentives          219

9. Middle Management Issues: The Basics                     244

## PART V: NATIONAL STRATEGY CONSIDERATIONS

10. The Politics of Science: The Nature of Scientific Knowledge   265

11. National Technology Competitiveness: Government-Industry
    Strategies That Work                                    279

12. National Technology Strategies: Creating Public Markets   314

13. National Technology Strategies in a Services and
    Software World                                          343

    *Notes*   387
    *Index*   409

# Acknowledgments

A book of this size and scope has many contributors. We wish it were possible to list them all. However, we must give special acknowledgment to certain people who gave so freely of their time and efforts.

We are especially lucky to have access to probably the finest business-technology research library in the country, the Feldberg Library at Amos Tuck School of Business Administration at Dartmouth College. Chief librarian James Fries and his talented reference librarians, Bette Snyder, Karen Sluzenski, and Janifer Holt, contributed endless hours of skilled library search and helpful documentation on the extensive literature underlying this work. At the Polaroid Corporation Library, reference librarians Michael Fournier and Rebecca Kenney contributed similarly. This book would have been impossible without them.

At critical junctures Philip Anderson, Sydney Finkelstein, and Charles Hutchinson of the Tuck and Thayer Schools at Dartmouth provided helpful reviews of early draft chapters and made many important content contributions, especially in the software and organization chapters. Professor Anderson was especially helpful in developing the "Beyond Teams" arguments, and those concerning the "Velcro ball" concepts of object-oriented design and human interaction. John Ehlers (Ensar, Inc.), Bart Patel (Fluent, Inc.), Brad Quinn (computer validation consultant), Goodloe Suttler (Analog Devices), and Brian Walsh (Spectra, Inc.) generously contributed days of their time to developing the software chapters and provided many of the useful examples they contain. James F. Quinn (Division of Environmental Studies, University of California, Davis) was a major contributor to the software and structure of science chapters.

Sheldon Buckler, chairman, Commonwealth Energy System and former vice chairman, Polaroid Corporation, Teresa Amabile, Dorothy Leonard-Barton, Steven Wheelwright of Harvard Business School, and Thomas Hustad of the Graduate School of Business, Indiana University, provided many days of generative thinking and discussion during early conceptual stages. Margaret Wheatley and Myron Kellner-Rogers' Berkana Dialogue groups (and further dialogues convened with Tom Guarriello, Dick Knowles, and Nancy Margulies) are sources as to the characteristics of self-organizing systems and organizations: information, relationships, and identity.

The process of developing this book extends over many years and involved interviews with literally thousands of people in several hundred organizations. We cannot list them all, although our gratitude extends to all. In terms of contribution to this book, we especially acknowledge the following people, listed in alphabetical order by the companies they represent:

Roger Appeldorn, Stefan Babirad, James Biesecker, Peter Jamieson, Ronald Kubinski, Roger Lorenzini, Sumita Mitra, Sankar Narayan, Paul Pankow, and Mark Sorlien, 3M; Joshua Weston, ADP Services, Inc.; John Loewenberg, Aetna Life; Roger Ballou and Wendy Brown, American Express Company; Douglas McLean, Apple Computer, Inc.; Terry Neill and Robert Elmore, Arthur Andersen Worldwide; Martin Stein, Bank of America; Dennis Lee, Bell Corp.; Dennis Allen, BellSouth; Scott Beck and Lawrence Zwain, Boston Market; William Barker, CBS/Fox Company; Robert Burnside, Nancy Dixon, Stan Gryskiewiez, and Chuck Palus, Center for Creative Leadership; Raymond Caron, Janet Duchaine, Melvin Ollestad, and Edward Hanway, CIGNA Corp.; Craig Goldman, Earl Dawson, and Douglas Williams, Chase Manhattan; Walter Wriston, Daniel Schutzer, and Henry Lichstein, Citicorp; José Aliel and Jean-Louis Pello, Club Méditerranée; Thomas Sawyer, Dayton Hudson Corporation; Fred Smith and Thomas Oliver, Federal Express Corporation; Lew Veraldi, Charles Gumushian, and David Fossett, Ford Motor Company; Fred Middleton, Herbert Boyer, and Robert Swanson, Genentech; J. Edward Muns, Don Bollinger, Larry Cattran, Maureen Conway, Jack Dupre, Mark Halloran, Ned Kuypers, Dan Pearce, Joseph Raffa, and Jim Stimple, Hewlett-Packard Company; Nobuhiko Kawamoto, Yasuhito Sato, T. Yashiki, and F. Kikuchi, Honda Motor Company, Ltd.; James Alles, Declan Barry, Alan Cook, David Davidson, Mike Harding, Phil Heyworth, Joe Howard, Ian Hudson, Tak Kawamura, Trevor McNeilly, Rich Purgason, and David Sodeberg, ICI; Marv Patterson,

Innovation Resultants International; the late Robert Noyce, Gordon Moore, and Andrew Grove, Intel Corporation; David Evans, J. C. Penney, Inc.; Michael Miller, Peter Miller, and Peter Woicke, J. P. Morgan, Inc.; Hirachi Tanaka, Yuji Nishie, and Hachiro Saito, Japan Railways Institute; Christopher Macmanus, Johns Hopkins Hospital; James Ford and Paul Heuber, Kmart Corp.; Mori Tamura and Shoichiro Eguchi, Kenwood; Richard Bere and Michael Heschel, Kroger Company; Deborah Krau, Lahey Clinic; Dennis Smith, Loew's Corp.; Mitchell Blaser and Jerry Maskovsky, Marsh & McLennan; Richard Leibhaber, MCI; Jon d'Alessio and David Malmberg, McKesson Corporation; Theodore Gerbracht and Howard Sorgen, Merrill Lynch; Eric Vogt, Micromentor; Peter Neupert, Robert Muglia, Paul Maritz, Michael Murray, and Nathan Myhrvold, Microsoft Corporation; Patrick Campbell, NationsBank; James Barksdale, Netscape; Arthur H. Sulzberger, Sr., Arthur H. Sulzberger, Jr., and Warren Hoge of *The New York Times;* Hiroshi Yamauchi and Howard Lincoln, Nintendo Company; John Foster and Timothy Foster, NovaCare, Inc.; Pascal Charropin, Jean-Pierre Dupont, Jean-Paul Villot, Océ; Ralph Sarich, Orbital Engine Company; Roger Clapp, Richard Collette, Maarten de Haan, Mark Durrenberger, Jim Fesler, Harvey Korotkin, Dianne Lathrop Law, Pennell Locey, Tadaaki Masuda, Gianfranco Palma, Joe Parham, Len Polizzotto, Gustav Schötz, Keith Shoneman, Kunito Okamura, and Henny Waanders, Polaroid Corporation; Len Pomata and Cora Carmody, PRC, Inc.; Calvin Massey, Scripps Clinic; Robert Ferkenhoff, Sears Merchandise Group; Paul England, Smith-Kline Beecham Pharmaceuticals; Masaru Ibuka, Akio Morita, Norio Ohga, Nobutoshi Kihara, Makato Kikuchi, Heitaro Nakajima, Akira Suzuki, Yoshinori Tanaka, Katsuaki Tsurushima, Kenji Wada, and Toshiyuki Yamada, Sony Corporation; Marshall Carter and David Sexton, State Street Bank and Trust Company; H. S. Smith III, Super Valu Stores; Lawrence Pulliam and Richard Seigel, Sysco Systems; Peter Fritz, TCG Ltd.; Joseph Ripp, Time Inc.; Takeshi Okatomi, Kiichi Hataya, and Toshio Yajima, Toshiba Corporation; Lawrence Bacon, Travellers Companies; Donald Karmazin and Lafayette Ford, United Airlines; Klaus Nielson and Rino Bergonzi, United Parcel Service; Michael Eisner and Sharon Garrett, Walt Disney Company.

We owe enormous gratitude to all of these contributors.

In addition, we are indebted to the over 150 corporate executives and academics who hammered out, over many months, the President's Domestic Policy Review on Industrial Innovation. Theodore Schell, formerly of the U.S. Department of Commerce and now at United

Telecommunications, was critical to that process. Those discussions and recommendations are reflected throughout this book.

Unfortunately, a project like this must be financed. Fortunately, there are very kind, helpful, and generous people who made this project possible. Our major sponsors have included John Foster, CEO of No-vaCare; Robert Clements, CEO of Marsh and McLennan; Peter Koster, president of William M. Mercer Companies; Roger Ballou, president, U.S. Travel & Related Services, American Express Company; Thomas Doorley, senior partner, Braxton Associates; Peter Lengyel, vice president, Bankers Trust; Donald Frey, CEO, Bell & Howell; Charles Zoi (at that time president of Bell Atlanticom). Special assistance for foreign interviews was provided by Hiroshi Murakami, secretary general of the International University of Japan, and by Allen Taylor, Warren Bull, and James Gannon, respectively CEO, senior vice president–strategic planning, and vice president–human resources, the Royal Bank of Canada.

Especially instrumental in sponsoring Karen Anne Zien's 1993-94 studies were Sheldon Buckler and Carole Uhrich, executive sponsors, and Ed Chao, Patrick Flaherty, David Hinds, Suzanne Merritt, Phil Norris, Leigh Shanny, Michael Zuraw, and cultural anthropologist Barbara Perry, members of the research team for Polaroid's Invention and Innovation Research Project.

We all appreciate the genuine help and intellectual support of the team at the Free Press. Bob Wallace has been the main champion, counselling, editing, mentoring, and arguing persuasively for structural changes—and an exciting title. His associate editor, Julie Black, copy editor, Beverly Miller, and outstanding production editor, Loretta Denner, also provided thoroughly professional, rapid response, and cheerful help whenever it was needed. They are a superb team.

The efforts of those who conceive and even write a book like this pale beside the enormous work of competent research associates, secretaries, and professionals who undertake the major burden of production. At the Amos Tuck School, the major research contributors were Evan Sotiriou and Penny Paquette. At Polaroid Corporation and at Apogee: Sustainable Innovation Systems, the major research contributors were Danielle Gryskiewicz and Carolyn Sullivan. Special professional consultation was provided by Bill Eidson, Rob Faust, Danielle Kennedy, and Judith Nast. Suzanne Sweet and Tammy Stebbins worked and reworked the endless drafts of the book and its outlines from early 1995 through mid-1996. At that time Nancy Harber and Kristy Legace took over this complex task. They all performed with amazing charm, good humor, and thorough professionalism.

" In April of 1978, President Jimmy Carter asked the Secretary of Commerce, 'What actions should the Federal Government take to encourage industrial innovation?' It was the first time that a President of the United States had recognized the role of industrial innovation in enhancing the well-being of the nation. It was also the first time that one had recognized that the policies and practices of the federal government could positively influence a process that had often been considered random even in the private sector.

"Although one of the authors (Baruch) was charged with managing the ensuing study, specific thanks are due to Stuart Eizenstat, the president's senior domestic policy advisor; Dr. Frank Press, his Science and Technology Advisor; Juanita Kreps, Secretary of Commerce, and Theodore Schell, special assistant in the Office of Productivity, Technology and Innovation. Special thanks are due to the 180 representatives from industry, eighteen government agencies, and academe who stepped away from their outside responsibilities and brought their intellects and their experience to bear on forging a set of recommendations to the President. Those recommendations, as they have been adopted over the years, have forged many of the policies that still influence the government's role in industrial innovation. Without their efforts this might have been a very different book about a very different country.

"I am also grateful for the opportunity to thank Dr. Leo L. Beranek for his mentoring over the early days of my career and for steering me into broadening my scope from engineering to management.

"Lastly, my gratitude to my wife, Rhoda Baruch, who, for over fifty years, has shared her intellect and love with me, constantly encourages me, helps me up when I stumble, cheers my successes and makes it all worth while. "—Jordan J. Baruch

" Four people have contributed most to my care to integrate my 'life-work with my work-work,' as represented by this book: my husband, Jim Zien; my daughters, Rebecca Kathleen and Jennifer Kristin; and my favorite author, Timothy L. Smith, AKA 'Dad.'" —Karen Anne Zien

There is one person we all clearly recognize as absolutely crucial to this book. She is Allie J. Quinn, mentor, researcher, friend, spouse, and gourmet cook extraordinaire. Supporting all of the authors, she researched, edited, shaped, and did the production work for all aspects of the book. Without her remarkable efforts, there simply would be no book. Working from many locations in the United States and throughout the world, she provided our intranet to each other and to the major resources of the Tuck School. She became a familiar figure passing through the airports of the world with skis or surfboards under one arm and a computer under the other, but with a smile that lit up the world wherever she went.

To all of the above, we express our deep gratitude.

# Introduction:
# Knowledge and Innovation

Intellect and innovation are the sources of virtually all economic value, growth, and strategic edge today. Unfortunately, despite much popular discussion about "knowledge creation" and "managing knowledge assets," few managers systematically understand the basic interrelationships among intellect, professional knowledge, technology, and innovation.[1] For example:

- What are the critical classes of professional and creative knowledge? How do they interrelate?
- What are the relevant characteristics and repositories of knowledge or intellect within the firm? How can managers leverage these for maximum value?
- Through what processes is technological knowledge actually created?
- How do invention, innovation, and diffusion relate to these processes?
- How can enterprises structure their organizations to leverage their intellectual and innovative resources most effectively?

Unless managers understand such basics fully, they are unlikely to gain full advantage from their knowledge or innovation systems. This introduction examines certain key relationships, determining how various aspects of knowledge, intellect, science, innovation, and technology interrelate to create value, and how successful enterprises can best

1

leverage and organize around these processes for competitive advantage. Later chapters develop each element in depth.

## PROFESSIONAL KNOWLEDGE

The knowledge of an enterprise—in order of increasing importance—encompasses (1) *cognitive knowledge* (or know what), (2) *advanced skills* (know how), (3) *system understanding* (know why), (4) *motivated creativity* (care why), and (5) *synthesis* and *trained intuition* (perceive how and why).[2] (See the box for definitions.) A primary locus of such knowledge is clearly inside the enterprise's human brains. But the first three levels can also exist in the organization's software, systems, databases, or operating technologies. If properly nurtured, intellect in each form is both highly leverageable and protectable. *Cognitive knowledge* is essential, but usually far from sufficient for economic success. Many may know the rules for performance—on a football field, piano, laboratory bench, or accounting ledger—but lack the higher skills necessary to make money at it in competition.

Some people may possess *advanced skills* but lack *system understanding.* They can perform selected tasks well but do not fully understand how their actions affect other elements of the organization or how to improve the total entity's effectiveness. Similarly, some people may possess both the knowledge to perform a task and the advanced skills to compete, but lack the will, motivation, or adaptability for success. Highly *motivated* and *creative* groups often outperform others with greater physical or fiscal endowments, as do those with finely honed *intuitions,* especially in the arts. Intuition may be the highest form of trained intellect: the capacity to integrate uncodifiable knowledge about many subtle and complex interactions one has never encountered in the same way before.

### Software Leverages for Knowledge

Software is the key factor in developing, leveraging, and diffusing all levels of intellect. Such software includes databases, analytical and modeling software, service processing software (like accounting routines), operations software (guiding physical machines and processes), systems software (interrelating multiple processes or operations), and network software (intermittently interconnecting multiple locations and systems). Each form can extend human capacities in new ways: (1) capturing knowledge more rapidly and accurately than ever before, (2) en-

# KEY DEFINITIONS

*Intellect* is knowing or understanding: the capacity to *create* knowledge, the capability for rational or highly developed *use* of intelligence. Intellect includes in ascending order of importance: (1) cognitive knowledge (or know what), the rules and facts of a discipline; (2) advanced skills (know how), the capacity to perform a task sufficiently well to compete effectively; (3) system understanding (know why), understanding the interrelationship and pacing rates of influences among key variables; (4) motivated creativity, discovery, or invention (care why), the capacity to interrelate two or more disciplines to create totally new effects; (5) intuition and synthesis (perceive how and why), the capacity to understand or predict relationships that are not directly measurable. Intellect resides not just in human brains; it can also be captured in an organization's systems, databases, or operating technologies.

*Science* seeks increased understanding about natural phenomena. Its output essentially consists of factual statements or theories that can be verified by observation or reproducible experiments. Scientific results tend to be widely available and shared in the open literature or on networks.

*Technology* is knowledge systematically applied to useful purposes. When science is utilized in an orderly way for practical purposes, it generally becomes part of technology. However, systematic understanding in other spheres—such as management, health care, or environmental studies—may also constitute technologies. One may not be able to predict outcomes with mathematical precision, but they can be predicted probabilistically or in scenario terms. Technology generally involves a significant component of know-how, not available in public references.

*Invention* or *discovery* involves the initial observation of a new phenomenon (discovery) or provides the initial verification that a problem can be solved (invention). The patent law stresses invention as the fabrication of something new and useful—not obvious to one skilled in the art—the result of study, thought, or experimentation.

*Innovation* consists of the social and managerial processes through which solutions are first translated into social use in a given culture. Technological innovation involves a novel combination of art, science, or craft employed to create the goods or services used by society.

*Diffusion* spreads proved innovations more broadly within an enterprise or society.

abling analysis of more complex problems than humans can handle alone, (3) controlling physical processes under harder conditions and more accurately than humans can, (4) allowing remote monitoring of physical and intellectual processes without human intervention, (5) searching a broader range of information sources and interconnecting far more human minds—enabling creative solutions that would otherwise be impossible, and (6) diffusing knowledge more widely, efficiently, and effectively than any other means.

Software is radically changing every element in innovation, from basic research, to needs analysis in the marketplace, to design of virtually all products and services, to model building and prototyping, through initial and mass production, to distribution, marketing, and post-sale service. It enables innovators to work together in new modes: in virtual laboratories, virtual skunk works, remote independent collaborations, and tightly integrated worldwide experimentation and production to simultaneously achieve greatest intellectual advance, highest quality, greatest flexibility, and lowest cost. Its software systems are now an integral part of any enterprise's organization, culture, and innovation-value creation system. Software is a form of intellect—and often the most valuable single intellectual asset a firm has, yet few enterprises have learned to manage it as such. A major focus of this book is to analyze and present ways to integrate human and software systems to maximum advantage in innovation.

## Characteristics of Intellect

The value of a firm's intellect increases markedly as one moves up the scale from cognitive knowledge toward motivated creativity and trained intuition. Training programs and software can facilitate intellectual resource development at all levels. Yet, in a strange and costly anomaly, most enterprises reverse this priority in their training and systems development expenditures, focusing virtually all their attention on basic (rather than advanced) skills development and little or none on systems, motivational, creative, or perceptive capabilities (see Figure I.1). The result is predictable: mediocrity and loss of profits. The best-managed companies avoid this grim fate by exploiting certain critical characteristics of intellect at both the strategic and operational levels.

*Exponentiality.* Properly stimulated, knowledge and intellect grow exponentially. All learning and experience curves have this characteristic. As knowledge is captured or internalized, the available knowledge base itself becomes higher. Hence a constant percentage accretion to the base becomes exponential total growth, as documented by many studies and in the common use of organizational learning and experience curves as tools.[3] Economic effects markedly accelerate as higher levels

**FIGURE I.1**
**Skills Value versus Training Expenditures**

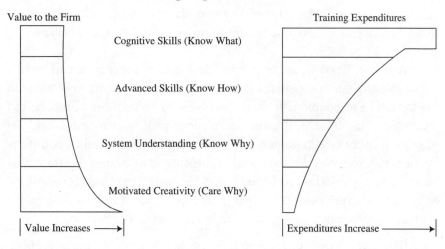

of knowledge allow an organization to attack more complex problems and to interrelate with other knowledge sources it earlier could not access. For example, Microsoft has moved from single "operations" systems or applications programming to an environment in which it must integrate all "applications" into a uniform graphics-based environment and interactively hook many different problem modules together across a variety of computing platforms. Pharmaceutical firms have had to move from blind screening of chemicals into the understanding of complex biotechnical interactions at both the submicroscopic and systems levels. Brokerage houses like Merrill Lynch have had to move from simple execution of purchase and sale orders for customers into complex data gathering and analysis of a variety of new financial instruments and influences on a worldwide basis. To meet these challenges, Microsoft's, Merck's, and Merrill Lynch's knowledge bases and levels of intellect have had to expand exponentially in the past decade.[4]

The strategic consequences of exploiting exponentiality are profound. Once a firm obtains a knowledge-based competitive edge, it becomes ever easier to maintain its lead and harder for competitors to catch up. The most serious threat is that through laziness, bureaucracy, or complacency, intellectual leaders may lose their knowledge advantage. This typically occurs when they fail to adapt rapidly enough to changing external conditions, particularly new concepts that obsolesce their earlier skills—as software prototyping is making physical model building in autos or architecture obsolete and molecular design techniques are superseding blind screening in pharmaceuticals today. This is why the highest levels of intellect—self-motivated creativity and synthesis through intuition—are so vital. Firms that nurture "care why" and "perceive how and why" thrive on rapid change and simultaneously refresh their cognitive, advanced skills, and systems-knowledge bases.

**Best Attracts Best.** Because a firm has leading intellect, it can attract better talent than competitors can. The best people want to work with the best. These people can then perceive and solve more complex and interesting customer problems, make more profits as a result, and attract even more talented people to work on the next round of complexity. Recruiting, developing, and capturing individuals' exponential knowledge capabilities has been the key to strategic success for most intellectual enterprises—from Bell Labs, JPL, or Intel, to Microsoft, McKinsey, Morgan Stanley, and the Mayo Clinic. For example:

• Microsoft, realizing that software design is a highly individualistic effort, interviews hundreds of candidates to find the few most suited to write its advanced operating systems.[5] It then places its new members directly onto small teams of three to seven people under experienced mentors to design complex new software systems at the frontier of user needs. (Chapter 3 describes Microsoft's system more fully.) Starting with excellent talent, Microsoft's culture drives everyone with the unstated expectation of sixty- to eighty-hour weeks on intensely competitive projects and creates a work environment that supports this level of commitment. The best commercial programmers seek out and stay with Microsoft largely because they believe "Microsoft will determine where the industry moves in the future," they enjoy its informal atmosphere, and they can share the excitement and rewards of being at that frontier. Each Microsoft success builds its experience base and recruitment attractiveness for the next wave of challenges.

***Sharing and Embedding.*** Knowledge is one of the few assets that grows most—also usually exponentially—when shared. Communication theory states that a network's potential benefits grow exponentially as the nodes it can successfully interconnect expand numerically. As one shares knowledge with other units, not only do those units gain information (linear growth), but they share it with others and feed back questions, amplifications, and modifications, which add further value for the original sender, creating exponential total growth. Proper leveraging through external knowledge bases—especially those of specialized firms, customers, and suppliers—can create even steeper exponentials. There are, nevertheless, some inherent risks and saturation potentials in this process. Determining what knowledge should be concentrated and protected, what may be decentralized and shared, and how to share and sift knowledge from data are critical elements in intellectual strategies. Chapters 4 through 9 develop a number of practical approaches for this. However, one example can make the general point explicit.

• The core intellectual competency of many financial firms (e.g., Fidelity Securities, State Street Boston, and Aetna) lies in the human experts and the systems software that collect and analyze the data surrounding their investment specialties. Access to the critical algorithms in these powerful software systems is tightly limited to a few specialists working at headquarters. Here they share and leverage their own specialized analytical skills through close interactions with other financial experts, highly talented modelers, and the massive access the organization has to worldwide economic and transactions data. These companies leverage their systems' outputs as broadly as possible through their extensive brokerage outlets, which in turn feed back more information for use in the central system. Nevertheless, the structure of sharing must be carefully controlled. For security and competitive reasons, sales brokers cannot have access to their corporate system's analytics, and corporate analysts must be kept out of brokers' individual customer files. Yet for maximum impact, the system itself must capture and manipulate data aggregates from both sources. The detail in which this sharing can occur without compromise is a major source of competitive edge, as is its integration into the software and support systems of the firm. The latter provide the key to converting intellect into a proprietary asset.

Intellectual synergies and proprietary protection derive from sharing and embedding the firm's crucial knowledge capacities in its systems and culture so that isolated elements of the firm's intellect lose significant value if detached from the organization's other competencies.[6] For example, when the trust department of a major bank developed a unique set of analytics to support the mortgage-backed securities market, a rival lured away the key programmers who had developed the system. The competitive loss turned out to be minor, however; in a different corporate culture with different management styles, databases, support systems, and customer relationships, the pillagers were unable to implement their elegant analytics effectively.

***Expandability.*** Unlike physical assets, intellect increases in value with use, tends to have much underutilized capacity, can be self-organizing,

is greatly expandable under pressure, and generates its greatest val
when leveraged in users' hands. How can a company systematically exploit these characteristics? Sun Microsystems, implementing its motto,
"The system is the computer"—both externally through Java and its
equipment designs and internally through 230 servers on its 22,000-
workstation Sun network—presents one example. As another, Arthur
Andersen Worldwide (AAW) offers some interesting insights for leveraging expandability.

• Andersen Worldwide attempts to electronically interlink 82,000
people in 360 offices in 76 countries. Its ANET, a T-1 and frame-relay
network, connects 85% of Andersen's professionals through data, voice,
and video interlinks. ANET allows AAW specialists, by posting problems
on electronic bulletin boards and following up with visual and data contacts, to self-organize instantly around a customer's problem anywhere
in the world. It thus taps into otherwise dormant capabilities and vastly
expands the energies and solution sets available to customers. The capacity to share in AAW's worldwide variety of problems and unique solutions is strengthened through centrally collected and carefully indexed
subject, customer reference, and resource files accessible directly via
ANET or from CD-ROMs, distributed to all offices. These, in turn, expand the intellectual capabilities AAW field personnel have available to
add value for both existing and future customers. The key intellectual
asset is not AAW's database per se. What matters most is its ability to
motivate use of the knowledge, which depends more on AAW's unique
training, culture, mentoring, and worldwide customer base. Many of
the files could be duplicated, but the dynamics permitting their effective
extension internally and through client use could not.

Effective managers of both professional and innovative intellect
consciously harness all these characteristics. The processes they use re-
semble successful coaching more than anything else. The critical activities are (1) recruiting the right people and encouraging them up the
experience curve as rapidly as possible, (2) stimulating them to internalize and share with others the information, knowledge, skills, and attitudes the firm needs for success, (3) creating systematic software,
technological, and organizational structures to capture, focus, and
leverage intellect to the greatest possible extent, (4) demanding and rewarding top performance from all players, and (5) guiding them toward
a clear, exciting vision. Easier said than done. But much can be learned
from how successful (and failing) practitioners have handled these issues. Conclusions in this book draw on an extensive literature search,

hundreds of personal interviews throughout the world, and numerous published case studies of leading professional and innovative companies in the United States, Europe, and Japan.[7]

## CREATING SCIENTIFIC AND TECHNOLOGICAL KNOWLEDGE

Business managers can quickly recognize, internalize, and conceptualize the ways in which professional knowledge can be managed. Many of the same principles apply to scientific and technical knowledge. However, because executives and policymakers have less familiarity with scientific and technological processes—and because of some very misleading concepts about how scientific knowledge and innovations are generated—they are more tentative about managing these forms of knowledge. Unfortunately, their lack of understanding frequently leads to terrible mismanagement in corporations, educational institutions, and national policy circles.

### Creating New Knowledge

Processes for *creating totally new knowledge or effects* build on and then go beyond those involved in developing deep professional skill. They cluster around the fourth level in the knowledge process: motivated creativity. This state is at the heart of this book, and its processes are often quite disorderly. Creative processes demand a degree of interactiveness, cultivation of differentness, external contact, and freedom of action that professional or routine activities do not. And they defy management concepts that rigidify, routinize, or control individual behavior.

Where creative activities are located in the firm's architecture and how they can best relate to the other three levels of basic knowledge in the firm—cognitive, advanced, and systems knowledge—are crucial in organizing a knowledge-generating enterprise. In the past, in order to enhance efficiencies, most enterprises formed their organizations around specialized management functions, skill sets, product clusters, dominating process investments, customer classes, or geographical needs. These clearly optimized the capacity of power holders to direct and control the organization. However, the varying demands of customers, the unwillingness of creative professionals to work in such hierarchical situations, their rigidity and lack of responsiveness, and the extended capabilities new technologies present for managing highly disaggregated organizations require entirely new organizational concepts.

These new concepts focus not on maximizing control for power holders but on developing and deploying intellectual assets to create maximum customer value.

Effectively attracting, harnessing, leveraging, and disseminating intellect also calls for some entirely new leadership styles. The combination leads to some very unusual, disaggregated, and fluid organizational structures—and sometimes to no formal organizational structure at all. The new forms include, among others, circular, lattice, inverted, starburst, network, and independent collaborative organizations. Later chapters develop each in detail. Each of these new forms develops intellect in a different way and should be used only for the particular purposes it handles best. The organization's software system becomes an actual component in these new structures, determining much of the language, interaction style, and indeed the culture of the enterprise. Not only is no single organizational approach to innovation a panacea, but many different structures can be used to advantage in the same company. Because they are also useful for certain purposes, hierarchies will doubtless continue in many situations. But we foresee continually greater use of the kinds of highly disaggregated, interactive organizations set forth in Chapters 4 through 9. In each, software is central to effectiveness.

## Organizing Around Intellect

All of these forms share certain characteristics. All tend to push responsibility outward to the customer contact point. All flatten the organization and remove layers of hierarchy. All seek faster, more responsive action to deal with the customization and personalization that affluent and complex marketplaces demand. All require breaking away from traditional thinking about chains of command, one-person-one-boss structures, the center as a directing force, and management of physical assets as keys to success. But each differs substantially in its purposes and management and each requires different nurturing, balancing, and support systems to achieve its performance goals. The key determinants in choosing among the various forms are:

- *Primary locus of intellect.* Where the deep expertise in the firm's particular core competencies and deep knowledge skills primarily reside.
- *Locus of customization.* Where the intellect is converted into novel solutions for customers or the system.

• ***Direction of intellectual flow.*** The primary direction(s) in which value-adding knowledge flows.

• ***Method of leverage.*** The primary way in which the organization leverages its intellect, usually through software, hard technology, focused interactiveness, or human development.

Some practical examples will make the relevant points clear:

• Some companies create their competitive advantage through developing large-scale systems—for example, multiple-product chemical complexes, energy distribution grids, large logistics systems, telecommunications networks, large aircraft or space vehicles, and financial and brokerage systems. Most of the advanced technical, management, and creative skills to innovate across these systems must lie at the enterprise's center. The enterprise may tap the creative skills of many external sources through outsourcing components or subsystems, yet all elements must be coordinated from the center; and no system changes can be made unilaterally at the decentralized nodes. Adaptation of the output for individual customer's needs may occur at the nodes in the hands of professionals. But the information system is centralized, and the primary flow of intellect for the system is from the center to the nodes. The leverage of intellect grows arithmetically, varying directly with the number of nodes.

• Inverted organizations—in which the personnel in contact with customers give orders to what would ordinarily be the line hierarchy—are superb when individual experts embody most of the organization's knowledge, when they do not have to interact with each other to solve problems, and when these same people customize their knowledge at the point of contact with customers. Health care institutions, client-partner situations, and field design teams in civil engineering are typical examples. The primary flow of knowledge is from the nodes to the center, and the leverage grows both arithmetically (depending on the number of experts) and exponentially (depending on their training and the way the software system captures and distributes their knowledge). Such systems—exemplified by NovaCare, SAS, Bechtel, and Rubbermaid, all described in detail later—are extremely empowering and effective when used in the right setting. In these organizations the contact people literally give orders to the intermediate hierarchy of specialists and staff support personnel, creating rapid innovation responses to customer needs.

• Innovations in advanced physics, materials, biotechnology, consulting, real estate development, minerals exploration, ecology, weather, entertainment, and certain financial services or software situations require high interactiveness among widely dispersed individual experts and organizations, all working in their own self-interest. The locus of intellect and customization is at the nodes, but the experts must interact frequently to achieve significant innovative results. Such innovations are best accomplished with virtually no formal organization other than the software databases, networks, models, and market interactions necessary to facilitate independent collaboration. Knowledge must flow freely among the nodes through software. In these situations, the software becomes the organization. And leverage grows exponentially with the numbers of nodes participating. This is a genuine network, or "spider's web," organization and is very powerful when used properly. Nevertheless, as many have discovered, it can be frustrating and ineffective when proper support structures are not in place.

In between the above are a variety of situations where everything from individual inventors, through focused teams, to hard-driving hierarchies can produce best results. We encountered over twenty-five different base strategies in our studies. A broad sampling of these options and prescriptions for their use appear in Chapters 4 through 9.

The keys to organizing and managing creative intellect lie in understanding the innovative process itself, where that process is best lodged for specific strategic purposes, and how to interconnect and motivate it for optimum results. Software capabilities have profoundly changed the very nature of the innovative process and the organizational options available to support it effectively. Software can now find new needs, discover new scientific phenomena, make or improve inventions, coordinate and shorten innovative processes, assist in introducing and modifying new products, decrease risks of failure, and accelerate product introductions and paybacks in entirely new ways. How to integrate these technological potentials with innovative human capabilities to optimize economic and societal outcomes is the core of this book's message. Their interaction is radically changing all of our concepts of economics, management, and organization. Effective implementation of these new potentials depends on a real understanding of the nature of the innovative process itself.

## ESSENTIAL CHARACTERISTICS OF INNOVATION

A strong research-based literature about innovation and diffusion processes sets forth the essential, but often forgotten, characteristics of innovation processes that need to be considered and managed in all strategies for continual innovation. Successful company and government innovation practices intimately mirror the way classic studies have suggested that innovation, knowledge, and technology tend to develop over long periods of time. One may in fact be the cause of the other. Many key relationships were developed in our 1976-1980 and 1993-1994 studies[8] and verified in simultaneous and later studies by independent researchers.[9] All our action conclusions reflect such research-based observations. These show innovation as:

## Probabilistic

Because innovation involves first reduction to practice in a social system, no one can predict whether a particular solution will work, how well it will work if successful, whether customers will accept it if it works, or how customers will use it once they have it. The first use of major innovations is often in unexpected markets, and traditional market research is often wildly wrong. Hence the most successful companies in our studies used multiple parallel development approaches to increase their probabilities of success. They also tended to utilize continuous, fast, empirical, and flexible test-and-respond systems connected directly to the marketplace. In low-probability systems, wider networking becomes an imperative to increase the likelihood of finding a workable answer at all. Probabilities that a project will lead to commercial success generally vary from one in hundreds for basic or early applied research, through one in twenty to one in five for later applied and early developmental projects, to nine in ten for later developmental projects. Any deterministic structure or innovation process not designed specifically around these probabilistic characteristics will tend to increase long-term development costs.

## Complex

Few important innovations today are carried through entirely by single individuals or within single disciplines.[10] Most require multiple skilled contributors. In each discipline, probabilities of success and potential value-added improve if the innovating individuals and teams have close to best-in-world capabilities. (If properly motivated and interconnected best-in-world talents cannot achieve a result, who can?) This is why venture capitalists give such inordinate attention to the technical, motivational, and integrative qualifications of their technological entrepreneurs. Many different individuals are usually required to generate and integrate the detailed expert knowledge needed for a significant enough advance to convince today's sophisticated customers to take introduction risks or to change their existing use patterns. Yet everyone's expertise is rarely required for the full innovation cycle. Contributors must be extremely specialized in order to understand their technological (or professional) fields at best-in-world levels. At the same time they must focus these skills intensively on a totally new problem that also calls for other experts' knowledge. Hence, the most innovative organizations tend to operate in adhocracies that bring together groups of experts from a variety of disciplines for the intensive short-term interactions and close communications briefly required in most innovations—yet otherwise leave them in discipline-based, product, or functional centers to increase their expertise.[11] Software is the key to managing these dynamic, disaggregated, information intensive collaborations.

## Time-Consuming

Components, subsystems, systems, and physical disciplines interact in such seemingly unpredictable ways and with such asynchronous timing that each potential interaction must be checked carefully, experimentally, and repeatedly.[12] Time schedules are rarely met precisely. If they are met, there may be a trade-off in experimental thoroughness or end-result quality. A corollary to Murphy's law says, "If you anticipate it, you will design for it. So the unexpected is what always happens." Given this predictable unpredictability and likelihood of delay, the progress rate on an innovation is best measured by the number of successful and relevant experiments one can make per unit of time. Hence, there is a strong need to shorten cycle times and increase interaction rates with customers and other technical experts. The combination usually calls for multiple groups of experts with different talents trying different approaches and interacting with each other and users in as much of an interactive skunk works environment as possible. As we will show, software can take over and discipline many of the data finding, analytical, experimental, product or service design, visual rendering, tool creation, process coordination, and product introduction steps that formerly slowed innovation. It can also facilitate the human interaction processes necessary to bring the needed diverse intellectual skills to bear jointly on a complex problem. Hence the capacity to develop and manage software has become a core skill for generating innovation.

## Spurts, Delays, and Setbacks

All major studies of innovation show that innovation progress is rarely linear.[13] Innovation occurs in spurts, with setbacks and unforeseeable delays interspersed with random interactions that lead to uneven progress. Unexpected costs always occur, and overruns are common. Ambiguity is high, as are active antagonism and resistance to change. Hence there is a need for the wide-ranging, ad hoc, boundary-less, boot-legging, coalition, and external networking behaviors that facilitate innovative problem solving, lower measured costs, and allow innovators to work in unplanned spurts and to bypass resisters if necessary. Innovative organizations recognize this necessity and create allowable ways to break their normal operating rules in order to ensure lateral interactions and stimulate exchanges with outside parties. Such innovative structures are directly contrary to power-centered, discipline-oriented, functional, or formal matrix organizations. They require behavior, measurements, and reward systems that are totally different from the commonly used appraisal techniques designed for more bureaucratic command-and-control structures. Although there has been much chatter about the need for more disaggregated interactive structures, very few company or government systems have actually restructured around the imperatives of managing innovative intellect. We will suggest how to do this without losing the strategic focus and efficiencies good managers demand.

## Need Oriented

Classical studies say that about 70% of all major innovations are driven by a recognizable market need rather than by a new concept, technique, or technology seeking a need.[14] Further, over half of all innovations in many industries are made by customers either guiding or adding value to a producer's innovation.[15] Customers with a genuine need also tend to be more tolerant and helpful in handling the uncertainties inherent in being lead customers for innovations. Inventors rarely forecast customers' reactions well. They tend to look at their task as being to "do the technical job better," without thoroughly understanding the subtleties of consumer interactions. As a consequence, increasing early interactions with customers substantially improves probabilities of payoff, learning and innovation by both parties, experimental cycle times, and time-to-market. Properly designed software can contribute substantially to these benefits. Software now facilitates much higher levels of information exchange, more direct and continuous customer-innovator interactions, and greater creation of value for customers during design and implementation. Interactiveness decreases both the risks of creating the wrong output and the probability of overlooking secondary consequences or multipliers important to customers.

## Resistance Creating

Because there is an inherent risk in adopting any new technology and because any significant innovation will attack existing power structures, there is always antagonism and resistance to change both inside and outside the firm. Even 3M, which claims an ability to predict technical outcomes correctly 95% of the time, says that 50% of its unrelated products or new-to-the-world innovations fail, largely within the firm. Gillette expects only one market success resulting from three entering the market, derived from one hundred earlier technical investigations. Sony's marketing project leader on CD development said he spent 75% of his time overcoming internal resistances to change as the firm moved from vinyl-analog to digital-optical CD technologies.[16] Adopters will accept a new technology only if its benefits substantially exceed their perceived risks. Mansfield has shown that the rate of diffusion for technologies varies directly with the perceived benefits to its users.[17]

Many innovations fail not because they lack potential value to society or even to customer institutions but because they do not match the incentives specifically surrounding the customers' decision makers.[18] Such innovations do not answer the basic question, "What's in it for me?"—called the WIIFM ratio (of personal benefits versus costs) for these decision makers. A classic example is government agencies' (or other bureaucracies') resisting productivity-enhancing computers because they would decrease the number of personnel reporting to the decision maker and hence decrease that person's salary. Similarly, unless internal customers' specific incentives for adopting a technology are significantly greater than their perceived personal risks or their unit's already projected profits, they too will resist despite the technology's benefit to the overall enterprise. Yet few enterprises consciously set up measures and rewards in ways that would increase the WIIFM ratio for key decision makers. Opposition to innovation is not just passive. An innovation actively creates opposition by destroying the plans, power, and wealth of those who are already doing things differently.[19] Successful innovation policies must proactively overcome incentives for the status quo. Chapters 6 through 9 illustrate how leading innovative firms do this.

## Intuition and Tacit Knowledge

Because innovations move so rapidly at times, and because the sought-after result (by definition) has never been achieved before, it is almost impossible to rely on codified explicit knowledge for innovation. Much information must inevitably come from personal knowledge and individuals' intuitive insights which go beyond carefully documented past sources. In fact, the patent law requires that an invention *not* be an extension obvious to one skilled in the art. Consequently, true inventors often think in terms of metaphors and analogies to their problems, seeking solutions in a very nonlinear fashion.[20] Discovery and invention are themselves largely nonrational processes where the subconscious suddenly associates one matrix of ideas with others that have never intersected before. This "eureka" phenomenon is critical to most true inventions and step-function innovations.[21] Successful innovation systems therefore tend to consciously intrigue and frustrate innovators with intense needs (through close user interactions), then release the innovators into informal or unstructured circumstances (adhocracies) where subconscious thought—and the greater stimulus of high intellectual interaction rates with others (network interactions)—can take over.

## Fanatics or Champions

Numerous studies note that dedicated fanatics or innovation champions are needed to overcome the frustrations, ambiguities, time delays, and resistances inherent in the process.[22] As several of these studies note, true champions can rarely be appointed. They must be psychologically committed to the innovative concept itself and must emerge for personal reasons; typically they are people who initially identified the opportunity, created the invention, or found it could help them satisfy their own strong needs for personal recognition. Given the high expertise other contributors generally must have, champions tend to lead largely through their own charisma or referent authority, not delegated authority. Because bureaucratic layers discourage such independence and relationships, champions emerge best in organizations that are flat and largely "voluntary."[23]

## ANALYTICS AND ADHOCRACIES

All these characteristics of the innovation process are well documented. Each poses problems for rational, corporate, organizational, and individual innovation strategies. Later chapters will deal with solutions to each in detail. Because the characteristics of adhocracies map onto this process so well, this organizational form tends to be dominant in innovative organizations. Our studies suggest that the most continually innovative companies emphasize both (1) analytical structures that provide the targeting information, broad vision, success criteria, and high degree of focus that coordinated innovation requires, and (2) the kinds of ad hoc organizations and nonbureaucratic systems that shorten cycle times, increase learning, decrease risk, and consequently improve the probability and potential value of innovation outputs. Such coupled concepts work because they match the needs of the innovation process. Rather than installing systems that run counter to the process or try to change the process into a more orderly, controllable form, successful managers accept and try to manage within the essential chaos of the process itself.[24]

As we will show, the form of innovative adhocracies can differ enormously. Each specific innovation strategy calls for different group sizes, skill mixes, management styles, incentives, planning horizons, innovation approaches, pricing strategies, supporting policies, and reward systems. Because of complexity and enhanced software capabilities, innovation increasingly is being performed not by formal teams, but by collaborations of independent units in entirely different organizations and locations. All technological strategies—whether at the national, corporate, or micro-organizational level—need a sophisticated balance between a set of clearly structured and highly motivating goals and some very independent (yet interdependent) organizational modes specifically adapted to the particular problems at hand. This is the subject of Chapters 4 through 9. Properly implemented, these two concepts do not conflict; rather, they support each other. Neither is as effective alone as in combination. This is as true at the national level as in private organizations, in small as in large organizations, and in nonprofit as in profit-seeking endeavors.

The same conclusions obtain for managing scientific—as opposed to technological—endeavors. Although many think of science as the epitome of rational, orderly thought—indeed the term *scientific* is used in the vernacular this way—the history of scientific advance does not support this view. Chapter 10 discusses the highly disorderly, nonlinear, and quite surprising way scientific knowledge actually develops. This process amplifies the need not to rely on the fallacious, linear, deterministic models of scientific and technological progress so often used by those who would like to "control" the process or make it more "efficient." Academia is making a serious error in emphasizing only one aspect of the scientific process: testing hypotheses through controlled experiment. The other processes—careful observation, database construction, taxonomy building, technology development, synthesizing, and diffusion—need more balanced emphasis. As a society, and as managers, we need to understand the truly chaotic way in which science, innovation, and technology develop and learn how to manage in this chaos rather than attempt to convert the process into something it will never be: orderly and predictable. We need to concentrate more on effectiveness than efficiency for profits and societal benefits.

## SUMMARY AND CONCLUSIONS

Knowledge building, innovation, and scientific-technological advance are the critical ingredients for economic growth and competitive advantage today. But few managers have a clear idea of how such processes actually occur. Their misunderstandings have often led to poor national policy and mediocre business results. Knowledge-building processes, especially in science and technology, tend to be tumultuous, complex, interactive, and nonlinear.[25] Yet our internal organizations and management practices generally reflect assumptions of orderliness and control that are invalid. Professional knowledge building is somewhat more orderly but needs to be understood and managed in greater depth than it usually is. Professional knowledge managers need to understand and better exploit the five levels of useful knowledge—cognitive, advanced, systems integration, creative, and intuitive—and to design training programs, management practices, organizations, and performance measurement schemes appropriate to the kinds of knowledge desired. Integrating these into innovative processes can be especially fruitful. Later chapters explain how to develop, organize, and manage such intellect among each of these five major levels to support innovation most effectively in a strategic context.

As we will demonstrate, software has emerged as the dominating new tool in managing these processes; it lowers costs, investments, risks, and innovation cycle times by orders of magnitude while simultaneously increasing the probability and value of innovations by connecting them better to both the scientific and user worlds. Software makes it much easier to manage within the essential chaos of research and innovation, especially if managers will break away from their old hierarchical and newer "team" concepts and embrace some even more powerful, flexible, and empowering processes. The effects on all aspects of innovation, organization, and competition can be profound.

# 1

# Executive Overview:
# Intellect, Innovation, and Growth

With rare exceptions, the economic and producing power of a modern corporation or nation lies more in its intellectual and systems capabilities than in its hard assets of raw materials, land, plant, and equipment. Intellectual processes create most of the competitive edge for companies and value-added in all sectors of the economy. This is especially true for the large services industries—software, medical care, communications, education, entertainment, accounting, law, publishing, consulting, advertising, retailing, wholesaling, and transportation—that provide 79% of all jobs and 76% of the gross national product (GNP) in the United States today.[1] (See Table 1.1.) In manufacturing as well, intellectual activities—such as research and development (R&D), process design, product design, logistics, marketing, market research, systems management, and technological innovation—generate the preponderance of value-added. Management and innovation in all these fields will be software dominated. By the year 2000, McKinsey & Company estimates, 85% of all jobs in America and 80% of those in Europe will be knowledge, software, or technology based. Germany's Ministry of Labor estimates that by 2010 only 10% of all German jobs will be in manufacturing trade skills.[2]

The results of this changing economic landscape are profound for both corporate and national policymakers for the next two decades.

• *Intellectually based services* will account for almost all the job growth in the world's advanced and rapidly emerging countries, in both

20

the services industries and manufacturing. (See Figures 1.1 and 1.2.) Managing intellect and services effectively in worldwide competition will pose some of the decade's most serious management challenges.

• *Overcapacity* will exist worldwide for virtually all raw materials, foods, manufactures, and physical goods, holding average returns on these items close to cost of capital. The exceptions—other than a smattering of cartels and cyclicalities—will be those companies and countries that can add value through unique development of their intellectual, innovation, or services capabilities.

• *Software* will emerge as the core element in innovating, managing effectively, and creating competitive edge in the new economy. It will decrease innovation times, costs, and risks by factors of ten while increasing value in customers' hands even more. Managing innovation and software will be the two most critical management skills of the new decade, yet few companies know how to exploit this interface to achieve its full potentials.

• *New highly disaggregated organizational* forms, flexible innovation structures, and fast-response intellect-leveraging capabilities—enabled by software—provide benefits well beyond those that "teams" can offer. Much advanced innovation will be done through "independent collaborative" approaches featuring virtual laboratories, virtual skunk works, and software modeling techniques that will allow companies to leverage their human and fiscal resources in ways never before imagined.

• *Global outsourcing* and services trade will occur on a scale dwarfing past practice. Intellectually based services dominate the value chains of virtually all comapnies. And new technologies have decreased traditional scale and location advantages for everyone. Disaggregation, global sourcing, and dealing with the lateral competition of best-in-world specialist service suppliers have become strategic imperatives of the new era.

As the bimillenium approaches, nations and enterprises that hope to be successful in world competition need to understand, integrate, and manage their intellectual, technological, and innovation resources in a dramatically different fashion. Providing guidance for this process is our goal.

## STRATEGIC FORCES IN THE NEW ECONOMY

Certain powerful forces are compelling enterprises and governments to change the ways they conceptualize and implement their technology and growth strategies.

**TABLE 1.1**
**U.S. National Income:**
**Contribution and Employment by Industry, 1996**

|  | National Income ($ billions) | Employment (millions) |
|---|---|---|
| Total economy | 6,153.9 | 121.6 |
| *Goods Sector* | | |
| Agriculture, forestry, fisheries | 114.1 | 1.9* |
| Mining and construction | 325.9 | 6.1 |
| Manufacturing | 1,069.1 | 18.2 |
| **Total goods sector** | **1,509.1 (24.5%)** | **26.2 (21.5%)** |
| *Services Sector* | | |
| Finance, insurance, real estate | 1,037.0 | 7.0 |
| Retail trade | 506.6 | 21.6 |
| Wholesale trade | 351.2 | 6.6 |
| Transportation and public utilities | 322.9 | 6.3 |
| Communications | 148.5 | } 34.4 |
| Other services | 1,444.1 | |
| **Total private services** | **3,810.3** | **75.9** |
| Government and Government enterprises | 843.1 | 19.5 |
| **Total services sector** | **4,653.4 (75.6%)** | **95.4 (78.5%)** |

Source: *Survey of Current Business* (April–May 1997). *1995 data

*The services industries are large, technologically oriented, and capital intensive. Services account for 78.5 percent of all jobs and 75.6 percent of all value-added (as measured) in the United States.*

## Intellectually Based Services

Services are a dominant and growing economic activity in the United States and all other major advanced economies (see Figures 1.1 and 1.2). The most useful definition of services is that used by the *Economist:* "Services are anything sold in trade that could not be dropped on your foot." Globally, services trade expanded 56% faster than merchandise trade from 1980 to 1992. In addition to the services industries, intellectually based services like R&D, product design, process design

**FIGURE 1.1**
**Employment as a Percentage of Total Labor Force**

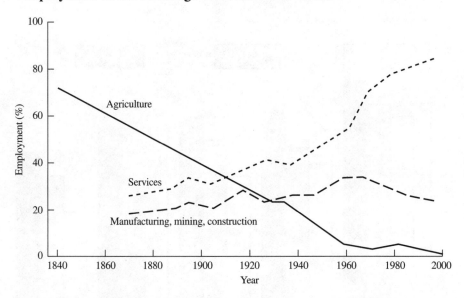

Source: Bureau of Census, *Historical Statistics of the U.S.: Colonial Times to 1970* and *Survey of Current Business 1971–1997.*

*Services jobs have always exceeded those in manufacturing and have provided virtually all job growth in this century .*

logistics, management information systems (MIS) marketing, sales, distribution, accounting, and human resources development dominate the value chains of product producers. Virtually all new product innovations are made in software and embody intellectual intangibles. None of the official trade figures on services reflects either these values or the huge transaction volumes of asset exchanges handled by software and services entities worldwide (see Table 1.2).

Software usually provides the most valued functionalities for information technology (IT) hardware or other heavy investments (e.g., computer and communication infrastructures, print or copy generation, materials handling, and transportation facilities) that support services outputs. Service innovations have certain unique characteristics. They tend to be continually and interactively developed between the producing and using parties. Rapid diffusion and limited proprietary protection are common in service innovations. Both service innovations and service outputs move across borders and boundaries easily. Most service outputs are customized in some way for each user. And in a competitive services environment, most output benefits accrue to the using, not the innovating, country or enterprise.

24   *Innovation Explosion*

**FIGURE 1.2**
**Employment in Services: Competitor Nations**

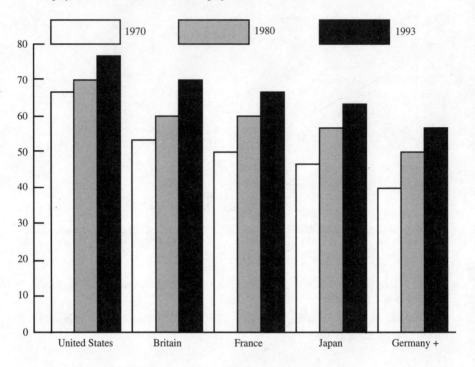

Employment in services as % of total employment

Sources: OECD; national statistics. Reproduced by special permission from "Schools Brief: The Manufacturing Myth," *Economist*, March 19, 1994, p. 91.

*Major advanced countries' economies depend increasingly on services.*

Developing intellect, innovation, technology, and services—not managing physical resources—is the key to growth for most companies, as well as industries and nations. A major management shift is necessary at the enterprise level from a focus on managing ROA (return on physical assets) to managing a new form of ROI (return on intellect). At the enterprise level, this means that recruiting, developing, challenging, capturing, and measuring intellect need as much—or more—attention than buying, maintaining, improving, or exploiting physical assets and products. (Chapters 2 through 9 develop practical management approaches in depth.)

Both business managers and national policymakers need to shift their thought processes away from traditional hard product and manufacturing concepts and toward a software, innovation, and services

**TABLE 1.2**
**Transaction Values in Services**

|  | Value ($ trillions) |
|---|---|
| Foreign exchange | 320 |
| FedWire | 220 |
| Treasury bonds | 65 |
| Custodial accounts | 14 |
| Swaps and derivatives | 13 |
| Mutual funds | 3 |
| U. S. credit card volume | 0.7 |

*Transaction volumes in financial services exceed GNP and trade volumes by factors of thirty to fifty times.*

focus. Traditional modes of stimulating innovation and protecting intellectual property often break down in this environment. For nations, it means first providing meaningful, accessible, and challenging educational opportunities and, second, strengthening the knowledge, skill base, and information infrastructures of the society. At the policy level it means a decreased focus on massive capital expenditure programs and an increased emphasis on creating incentives, new technological and work opportunities, market-driven demand systems, and public support infrastructures that encourage people to learn, to apply their skills, and to excel in useful activities.

Sadly, few nations or enterprises have handled this shift well. Nevertheless, companies like Sun Microsystems, GE, IBM, Ford, Orbital Engines, Nintendo, Argyle Diamonds, AT&T, and all surviving publishers suggest the benefits of doing so. The book analyzes and presents multiple examples of practical success and failure models at the enterprise and national levels.

## Worldwide Overcapacity

For the next several decades, overcapacity worldwide will exist for virtually all physical goods, raw materials, foods, and manufactures. For over a century, almost all raw materials and manufactures have dropped in cost relative to real wages, and food production per capita has increased

## FIGURE 1.3
## The Availability of Raw Materials: Price Relative to Wages

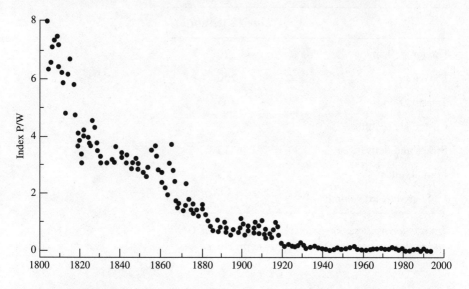

Sources: 1800–1980: Julian Simon, *The Ultimate Resource,* "The Scarcity of Copper: Price Relative to Wages." Copyright 1981. Reprinted by permission of Princeton University Press.

1980–present: U.S.Department of Commerce, *Survey of Current Business,* Govt. Printing Office, Washington, D.C. (various dates).

*Almost all raw materials prices (in this case, copper) have dropped continuously relative to real wages, indicating an increasing surplus of raw materials.*

for decades (see Figures 1.3 through 1.5). If latent demand (where need exists) could be converted into effective demand (where purchasing power exists), producing sufficient goods would now present few problems with available technologies. Ultimately, unchecked population growth could destroy all possibilities of raising average wealth. For the near term, however—both worldwide and within the United States— the key issue is likely to be more one of distribution than production. The resulting problems are tragically large. Goods now pile up and are thrown away in mountainous heaps by the rich, while the poor suffer devastating shortages. In the longer term, improved education and increased services trade may assist in greater worldwide wealth distribution and help decrease population growth. For the next several decades, however, where adequate incentives exist the primary economic problems worldwide will be managing production overabundance, wealth distribution, and the impacts of overpopulation on natural systems.

From an input viewpoint, not only are materials abundant; today's electronic capabilities can also convert worldwide intellect into an es-

**FIGURE 1.4**

**Trends and Cycles in Prices of Commodities and Manufactured Goods**

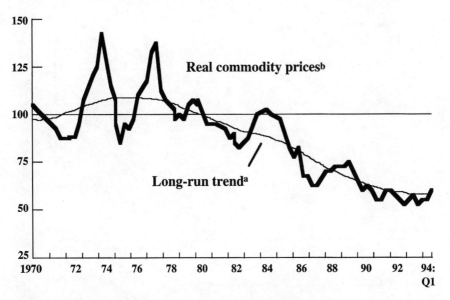

Source: International Monetary Fund, World Economic Outlook, Washington, D.C. (October 1995).
[a] Derived from the Hodrick-Prescott filter.
[b] Commodity prices deflated by the price of the manufacturers.

*Manufacturer and commodity prices continue to drop, indicating technological advances and greater availability.*

sentially infinite resource. If intellect is the dominant value-producing component of capital, there is no shortage of such capital, except in the sense of stimulating it to work on future versus current consumption projects. Since intellectual capital can constantly be generated or amplified through learning, the key element in capital for productive purposes is infinitely expandable. The real problem is in creating incentives and mechanisms to *generate* intellect and *connect* it to present and future market demands. Hence the preeminent economic resource issue from a national viewpoint is how to create maximum useful learning and distribution of knowledge. Paradigms focused on allocating limited capital and physical resources are increasingly questionable. Unfortunately, all of our development and economic concepts are based on scarcity, emphasizing efficient resource use. We need new paradigms at both the national and corporate levels that move from efficiency in resource use and toward effectiveness in value creation. Only as people become more affluent and better educated will they stop the population pressures that could become world destroying. This shift in issues calls for radical

**FIGURE 1.5**
**World Food Production and World Population Trends**

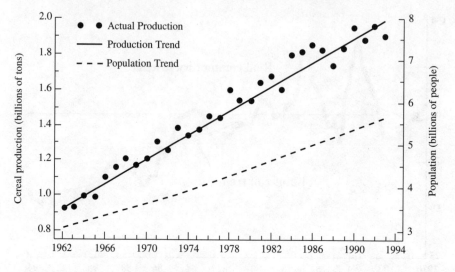

Source: United Nations, *Statistical Yearbook*, relevant years.

*For over three decades, per capita food supplies have grown. Advanced countries could produce much more if wealth were distributed differently worldwide.*

changes in traditional economic, social, and management approaches focused on exploiting physical assets. We will outline some important approaches emphasizing management of intellect, conservation, and innovation that are both feasible and most promising.

## Software

Software is central to virtually all sophisticated innovation and management activities. It facilitates all stages of value creation and innovation processes, from initial problem identification and basic research stages to product design, process design, prototyping, flexible production, market analysis, new product presentation, effective marketing and distribution, logistics management, iterative adaptation of products and services to customer needs, and postsale service. Needs are often first sensed in software from system models or online customer databases. Most basic and applied research is performed using electronic databases and electronic models. Most major products and constructions—ships, aircraft, automobiles, machine tools, tunnels, buildings, resource exploitation systems, roads, city designs, circuits, molecule designs, industrial processes—are now first conceived, rendered, and prototyped in software. Frequently designs move directly from software to production through the media of CAE/CAD/CAM.[3]*

Often the end product itself or the highest-value component in that product—as in computer, entertainment, communications, advertising, logistics, and financial services outputs—is software. This is true in many of the fastest-growing industries. Increasingly, financial services, product design, entertainment, publishing, marketing, databases, scientific discoveries, network services, and software create many millionaires, while hardware production generates only a few. Microsoft has a gross margin of 85%; Compaq, the leading hardware manufacturer, makes 23%. As many of the intermediate steps in innovation become compressed into software, the structures, risks, costs, time delays, leverage points, organizations, and research systems for innovation in both software and hardware all change dramatically. (This is the subject of Chapters 2 through 9.) Improved management of software and its utilization to support new innovation and organizational capabilities will be the crucial factors in almost all future corporate and national growth strategies.[4] Both corporations and nations now need genuine strategies for these purposes. Few have them.

## Beyond Teams: Radically Disaggregated Organizations

To compete successfully in this vastly changed economy, management styles and organizations must change radically. Staying ahead requires that enterprises have both greater depth in intellectual resources and greater capacity to integrate these resources for rapidly changing customer needs. This calls for personnel with T-shaped skills—deep vertical knowledge and strong lateral associative skills—and for highly disaggregated, interactive, yet strategically focused organizations. Adhocracy is not enough. Disaggregated groups must be stimulated to outperform the world's best competitors toward focused strategic goals. Creative groups cannot be driven to such ends; they must be led. They must see themselves as active participants in the company's vision, genuine resources in its strategy, and drivers toward "figure of merit" targets that *define winning*—not just "benchmarks", which mean *competitive equality* and eventual mediocrity. Strategies need to focus resources on those few in-

---

*Computer-assisted engineering (CAE), computer-assisted design (CAD), and computer-assisted manufacturing (CAM).

tellectually based core competencies that will ensure best-in-world capabilities. How to do all this is the subject of Chapters 2 through 9.

Radically disaggregated organizations are not just teams in a new guise. Market and technological complexities often force innovative structures beyond the limits where teams can operate effectively. Software-based innovation sometimes demands "non-organizations," independent collaborations, and virtual labs and skunk works, where experts and customers can work independently, asynchronously, and with urgency toward goals of compelling interest to all. In other cases, it permits decentralized, market-focused groups to innovate separately but effectively with highly centralized technical experts, production facilities, or resource bases that must stay together for efficiency or strategic reasons. Software creates permeable boundaries for organizations and allows experts to work together in new modes that do not require expensive organizational reconfigurations or co-location. Knowledge, not people or things, moves across boundaries. Software-based innovation cuts cycle times, investments, and risks by factors of ten and increases impacts even more by providing software "hooks"—open interfaces and capabilities through which customers (and their customers) can further modify the service or product output for their own purposes. These outsiders voluntarily become contributors to the enterprise's innovative success.

The software system becomes an integral part, and often the essence, of these enterprises' organization and culture. It determines the language, rules, feasibility, and limits of communication. In companies like Kao, Merrill Lynch, Boeing, NovaCare, Wal-Mart, Sharp, Ford, American Airlines, Silicon Graphics, Sun Microsystems, Microsoft, and Bechtel, it allows unending possibilities for fast responsive future innovations. Over time, organizations often migrate toward a circular "three-level" form (see Chapter 4) that best represents and accommodates the swirling interactiveness such innovation requires. Totally new inverted, infinitely flat, lattice, starburst, and weblike structures come into being and call for new leadership, coordination, incentive, and performance measurement techniques. Practical adaptations of these organizational forms and their supporting management structures have forever changed innovation practice. Chapters 4 and 5 discuss in detail these new organizations and the opportunities and problems they pose.

## Globalization, Outsourcing, and Knowledge Diffusion

Globalization and knowledge diffusion affect all markets, raw materials, parts, and services competition and sourcing. Because the dominant

**FIGURE 1.6**
**World Trade in Services**

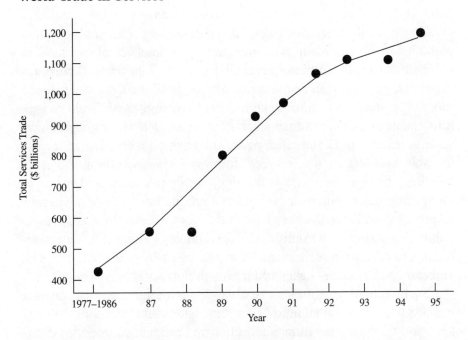

Sources: Coalition of Service Industries, *The Service Economy,* Vol. 10, No. 3, 1996, Washington, D.C. (based on data from U.S. Department of Commerce, Bureau of Economic Analysis; U.S. Department of Labor, Bureau of the Census).

*Even with the limitations of current measurements, services trade has grown 300 percent in ten years—56 percent faster than merchandise trade—and may help stimulate wealth redistribution.*

competitive resource is intellect—and intellect can be shipped across borders instantly and tariff free—remote locations no longer imply remoteness from marketplaces. Research, design, advertising, financial, software, data entry, and other services can be produced anywhere. And through software, innovations are instantly available and accessible anywhere else in the world. (See Figure 1.6.) Large distribution chains, the Internet, and global outsourcing allow innovators to link their concepts immediately to international needs and to leverage their innovations quickly into the most advanced markets in the world. Each company is now in competition with all the world's inventors trying to subvert, replace, or improve each element in its value chain anywhere in the world. Innovation is forever foreshortened and changed.

By exploiting intellect as the dominant resource for economic development, it is possible for less developed countries (and innovators in them) to vault over or shorten—as Japan, Israel, Korea, Singapore, and parts of India have—many of the heavy-investment or basic-industry building steps that were long considered essential for technological exploitation or development. By concentrating on intellectual and services trade (domestically and internationally) individual innovators, corporations, and societies can also leverage the value of their resources much more extensively than traditional models have suggested. Technologies now enable and demand such leveraging on a much wider geographical scale to achieve their full efficiencies. Information technologies are not the sole enablers in this respect. Improved transportation, materials handling, storage, producing, farming, communication, and management technologies enhance the potential production and sale of virtually all products and services anywhere in the world. Research, design, agricultural, logistics, environmental, biotechnology, financial, entertainment, and education technologies can also be easily produced, diffused, and exploited globally—expanding growth potentials everywhere.

Such technology diffusion tends to generate far greater economic benefits than the original innovation. Extensions into international markets, and the future potential intellectual and product sources this diffusion taps, can create gigantic benefit multiples beyond those of the domestic markets toward which innovations are usually initially targeted. Corporate or national policies that do not concentrate on such diffusion leverages, as most do not, forgo the most promising rewards from knowledge and innovation. Through associated technological multipliers, the benefits of diffusion usually vastly overwhelm the profits made on the original innovation, as did the worldwide sales of TVs, camcorders, tapes, movie rentals, audiovisual systems, and myriad software and service enhancements that sprang off Sony's videotape recorder (VTR) innovation or MITS's (Altair) and Apple's (personal computer) innovations. Corporate and national strategies should reflect this reality.

## Chaos and Hypercompetition

Market chaos and hypercompetition are the result of these new forces.[5] Since any element in a company's value chain can be produced by an independent external party specializing in that activity, companies no longer compete just with other companies in their "industries." They must compete laterally with the best-in-world producer of that activity, wherever that producer may be. Everyone is competing with everyone else; for example, banks, airlines, telecommunications, retailers, overnight delivery services, and auto companies all compete in the financial services and transportation businesses. Thus innovations that appear in one sector or country constantly affect many others. To deal with this, wholly new strategies—focusing on core competencies, strategic outsourcing, alliances, and highly disaggregated organizations—now link enterprises and nations in new ways. All center on developing, managing, and leveraging intellectual capabilities much more effectively. How to approach this new environment strategically is the subject of Chapters 6 through 9.

These forces have created a much faster-moving, more chaotic, and more competitive environment than ever before. Both corporate executives and national policymakers have found that highly centralized, command-driven systems no longer work well. More interactive, incremental, and decentralized strategies are replacing them. But most institutions need to move much more radically and quickly than they have. The rapid replacement and customization potentials that software-based innovation imposes make this an urgent imperative. At both the national and enterprise levels, the problem for managers is how to maintain the clear benefits of careful analysis and choice in guiding their enterprises, while at the same time dealing with the essential chaos, irrationalities, and unknowns that technological innovation and diffusion processes entail. A rapid, proactive, targeted, but flexible innovation system—designed around a few intellectually based core competencies developed in great depth—may be the only strategy that can continually win in this tumultuous hypercompetitive world. Chapters 2 through 9 develop a number of new, tested approaches to such innovation.

## CHANGING TRADITIONAL ECONOMIC PARADIGMS

It now seems clear that intellect, innovation, and technology are central to economic growth. Yet, for years, economists did not acknowledge the special role of these factors in economic growth. Technology was considered "a residual," providing only 0.1 to 0.5% of all growth.[6] Innovation and the intellectual assets supporting it were largely ignored or subsumed as mere components in the capital and labor factors of economic equations. Today, neither intellect, innovation, nor technology is explicitly included in most macroeconomic models or clearly measured in the elaborate output statistics collected by the U. S. Department of Commerce, Census Bureau, Organization for Economic Cooperation and Development (OECD), United Nations, and other macroeconomic measurers.

## Breaking with Tradition

Determining the impact of technology and innovation on growth is very difficult.[7] Schumpeter was perhaps the first major economist to break with the historic tradition and focus on entrepreneurial forces.[8] But his work had little initial impact on the macroeconomic measuring community. In the mid-1950s, studies by Abramovitz, Kendrik, Solow, Kindelberger, and Dewhurst began to accord technology its proper role: not just as one aspect of growth but the central one for many societies.[9] Kuznet's and Solow's studies suggested that some 70% of all growth in the mid-1900s was due to technological innovation, and perhaps 80 to 90% of all productivity gains were technologically based, under the broad definition of technology used here.[10] Finally, Robert Solow won the 1987 Nobel Prize for his work on the interactions of technology as a factor in economic growth. On close analysis, technology turns out to be the vital growth component in each of the four more traditional economic input factors: land, labor, capital, and education (see the box).

There was almost no growth in living standards or per capita wealth until technology enabled the industrial revolution. Prior to that time, the situation of most people living on farms or in cities had changed little for centuries. Suddenly the application of technology enabled the value of people's outputs to significantly exceed their living cost. Earnings could fulfill more than bare necessities. Wealth could be *accumulated,* providing the capital for future investment, growth, and efficiency improvements. Now the information revolution may, for the first time— without coercion—allow the effective *distribution* of wealth, which is essential to a more humane and peaceful world.

## Technology for Quality of Life, Not Just Productivity

Technology is now the greatest single driver of quality of life for most of the world. It enhances quality and choice in foods, housing, transportation, jobs, entertainment, health care, water quality, and so on. Most societies would like to exploit these benefits further. But, ever more urgently, new and stronger policy and social concepts are needed to deal with technological change's negative by-products, like job displacement, pollution, new human health problems, aging populations, terrorism, alienation, or misuses of the technologies themselves.

# TECHNOLOGY IN TRADITIONAL ECONOMIC FACTORS FOR GROWTH

*Land,* and the natural resources it represents, can contribute little to growth unless technology is applied to unlock its riches. The great "heavy crude" reserves of Venezuela or the Athabasca Tar Sands of Canada are worthless without technologies to exploit them but immensely valuable with technology.[11] Technology can convert the desert wastes of Israel or the minerals in Siberia's frozen interior into a great growth stimulus. Properly applied, it can allow the world's arable land to support a population of 30 billion people or convert a worthless gram of sand into a powerful computer.[12]

*Labor's* contribution to growth is limited without the application of intellect and technology. Over two-thirds of all labor income derives from investments in these factors.[13] Social reorganizations can, of course, increase the percentage of people usefully employed, and transferring labor from less to more productive sectors can add a further increment. Once usefully employed, however, workers' physical capacities quickly limit to about 30% the increased output they can achieve by more rapid performance of the same task. Once workers have learned their tasks and are motivated to perform them, technology and innovation become the critical factors in providing an estimated 80 to 90% of all increased output value per person-hour and hence workers' real contributions to wealth, as well as workers' capacities to earn higher real wages.[14] Intellect and innovation, not more physical effort by workers, are the critical factors in achieving higher output from work processes. Together they provide both the real impetus for higher standards of living and the knowledge bases that create wealth for the next generation.

*Capital* makes several important contributions to growth. It provides the resources that allow higher-level technological choices. It helps create and maintain desired aggregate demand levels. It provides a basis for aggregating and allocating outputs for future versus present consumption. But it is the utilizable technology in a capital investment, and not the fact of the investment, that makes the major contribution to growth. Capital investment in political or religious monuments or in unused military hardware does not offer nations continuing economic gains. It is the capital invested in expanding technological intellect— the systematic knowledge and skills to satisfy needs—that creates human capital's most important economic contributions.[15] Once a nation's savings level drops to just equal the capital it consumes, its growth is limited almost completely to the technology and knowledge improvements it can absorb. How capital is invested is as important as the level of investment. Japan saves (invests) far more per capita than the United States, and Germany invests 40% more on plant and equip-

*(continued)*

## TECHNOLOGY IN TRADITIONAL ECONOMIC
## FACTORS FOR GROWTH *(continued)*

ment, but because the capital is less efficiently used, their GDP per person is lower than America's.[16]

Capital provides its greatest growth stimulus when invested in technological or intellectual infrastructures such as education and training, information or auto highways, communications or health care systems, or intellect-incorporating software and machines that increase productivity or the value-added to raw materials.[17] Effective investments continue to produce useful outputs year after year for many people. Increasingly, the embodiments of capital expenditures do not need to be physical things. Databases, educational systems, legal structures, software, and human know-how have similar effects. Software often is critical to the output of both physical and intellectual systems, makes new output options possible, or (as in financial service products, advertisements, TV programs, movies, or games) becomes the value-creating output itself. In many cases, without software, hard asset investments would be useless. But most of our corporate or national capital accounts do not even show software investments as assets.

*Education and training* are critical input factors for growth. Many economists are now studying the relationship between human capital and growth.[18] It turns out that education too has a technological component. Increased education in mythologies (like astrology) or training in tea ceremonies or scientology will contribute negligibly to growth in human well-being. On the other hand, increasing students' capacities to understand human or physical relationships and apply such knowledge to human-technical systems can help society create, produce, and distribute all its products and services much more effectively. These are the elements of education that relate most directly to economic growth, although other aspects of academic training (like the arts) may offer important benefits in terms of creativity or quality of life. A recent study showed that raising the average level of employee education by even one year correlated with improved productivity of 8.5% in manufacturing and 13% in services.[19]

Progress on these issues is rapidly becoming the limiting factor in how quickly nations and private companies can apply technology to improve life quality.—hence our focus on national policy issues (in Chapters 10 through 12) as well as private innovation (in Chapters 2 through 9).

Despite the enormous and demonstrable contributions technology makes in all these respects, the economic models used to generate and test policy at the national level neither measure nor separate the special contributions of technology. As a result, technology receives a much lower priority in political and economic discussions than it generally warrants. (See Chapter 11.)

## Technology Multipliers

One major failure is that the powerful multipliers technology creates never enter into discussions. The Keynesian multipliers that capital investment produces are widely recognized. These operate by creating higher levels of demand through the multiple expenditures caused by an incremental investment infusion; capital goods producers pay monies to employees, suppliers, and shareholders, who then purchase more goods and services from retailers, who distribute the sums to their employees and suppliers, who then purchase more products and services, employing more retailers, wholesalers, and producers, and so on. Such infusions are at the heart of deficit spending policies in recessions. Under proper conditions, Keynesian multipliers of three to six are not uncommon.

But there are classes of technological innovation (like Edison's light bulbs or power generators) that can induce a matrix of change and progress in other sectors that are thousands of times the Keynesian multipliers of the investment in the original innovation. For example, when installed and diffused in a regional power network (like the Tennessee Valley Authority or Rural Electrification Agency), these innovations essentially create a whole new economy. They permit new manufacturing and service enterprises that otherwise could not exist, allow the use of modern technology and equipment in these facilities, widen the service areas available to achieve scale economies for support industries, raise expectations and hence latent demand levels, and ultimately create home appliance, light fixture, communication, electrical equipment, component, entertainment, and service demands that otherwise could never exist. More dramatically, relatively tiny investments in innovating the first microprocessors, radios, spreadsheets, hybrid corns, personal computers (PCs), antibiotics, the Internet, and scientific selective breeding have created economic multipliers millions of times greater than their original investments.

## Direct and Indirect Multipliers

A single innovation may directly affect an entire industry's concept of that product's use by customers (as Intel's development of the microprocessor did) and cause sales, profitability, employment, and value-added growth all out of proportion to the innovator's initial expenditure. Ted Hoff's almost intuitive initial innovation of the microprocessor directly enabled others to create today's $156 billion PC and software support markets. In addition, such innovations can have even greater "indirect multiplier" effects on other enterprises and sectors. The National Aeronautics and Space Administration officially estimates the effects of these indirect multipliers as fifteen times its programs' actual cost, probably low in terms of their computer and satellite contributions alone.[20] Silicon Graphics' customers have made thousands of times its profits by exploiting its products. As microprocessors, biotechnology, and cellular phones have, new technologies often enable other innovators to create cost savings, new industries, new services, or quality improvements that were previously unimaginable. In addition to the profits that microprocessors make for semiconductor and PC manufacturers, whole segments of the $3.6 trillion service and $1 trillion manufacturing industries depend on this technology. Many derivative industries, including the robust software, smart components, and work-at-home industries, have sprung up. For example:

• As an adjunct of the microprocessor's development, Nintendo (with the largest installed base of microcomputers in the world) largely created the video games industry and became the highest-volume user of chips and producer of creative interactive software in Japan. Its suppliers then utilized these new capacities to provide both more sophisticated hardware components and other software at higher quality and lower costs for other customers, opening totally new options for the suppliers themselves and a secondary wave of entire new industries (based on 32- and 64-bit systems) in Japan and abroad. Nintendo's software suppliers in Hokkaido, Russia, and India quickly became important pockets of economic growth and progress in their societies.

*In stimulating long-term growth through innovation, policymakers need to understand that the primary driving force is neither the initial investment nor innovation itself but the technological multipliers that technological innovation and diffusion achieve.* An incremental $1 billion invested in a federal building may increase national income *one time* by some small factor (two to three times). The same $1 billion invested in an effective technology could create $100 billion *each* year *over many years* in employment opportunities and profits, *plus* the Keynesian multipliers the supporting investments achieve.

## Rationally Picking Winners?

All of this appears terribly rational. Why not just pick those technologies which have the highest technological, economic, and sociological multipliers and support those? In part, this became the command-and-control model of early national R&D, and later technology strategies.[21] Business managers also attempted a similar approach in their strategies: analyze and identify markets with the greatest potentials and allocate resources toward those. Such approaches worked reasonably well at both the national and corporate levels when there were shortages in most markets, as was the case during the Great Depression and after World War II. Several examples will make the point at the national level.

• In the post-World War II era the French National Plan successfully stimulated basic industries' technologies and quickly rebuilt public infrastructures destroyed by the war.[22] Israel successfully targeted its education and technology strategies toward the problems of military survival and absorption of a huge inflow of immigrants—many from devastated or relatively underdeveloped countries—with neither savings nor particular skills. And Japan focused on high-investment, labor-intensive, mass-production industries, with high export potentials and possibilities for great technological leverage. Japan supported this strategy through financial policy mechanisms that discriminated against current consumption, encouraged savings, and lowered capital costs.[23] The combination enabled Japan to employ its huge displaced labor force after World War II, export in sufficient volume to meet its needs for raw materials and energy imports, and develop the high technologies that could use its superb educational system in the second generation of its growth strategies.

Although it is now popular to deride such policies as nonproductive, the United States successfully stimulated growth through similar approaches for many decades. For two hundred years, the government invested heavily in canal, dam, railroad, highway, and airline infrastructures, developing and linking the nation's geographically dispersed markets. It created the Rural Electrification Agency to bring electricity to all farm homes, provided tax incentives for oil, gas and natural resource development, and diverted a massive percentage of many rivers' flows for urban and agricultural development. And it developed the world's best public education and health systems.

## The Impacts of Scale and Affluence

But all such strategies broke down as shortages disappeared, affluence grew, overcapacity became manifest, and customization of products became important. Many national programs and laboratories became bu-

reaucratized, inefficient, corrupted, or irrelevant.[24] Even private enterprises found that the rules appropriate for management and policymaking changed as economies moved from eras of shortages to those of
plenty. Managers discovered that command-and-control allocation
techniques—which had been very useful for R&D in the post-World
War II era when the main problem was to apply available technologies to
demonstrable customer demands—grew increasingly slow and ineffective as customers became more specialized, fragmented, demanding,
and custom oriented. Market research often did not predict customer
responses well in new concept or upscale markets as new products from
xerography, to microcomputers, to Zap Mail, automatic teller machines
(ATMs), video games, Post-it Notes, or the Internet clearly demonstrated. Corporate executives also made large errors. They found that
products which seemed highly beneficial when used in niche markets
could become enterprise destroying when unanticipated (and unin-
tended) counterforces began to interact in larger-scale uses or in mass
markets. Asbestos, DDT, interuterine devices, supersonic transports,
silicone breast implants, chlorofluorocarbons, Thalidomide, fission
power reactors, and consumer packages that allowed cyanide inserts
provided some of the more bizarre interactions and consequences. All of
these have led to new approaches to public intervention and private innovation.

## OUTMODED ECONOMIC MEASURES AND MODELS

National policies also faltered as outmoded economic constructs, measures, and incentives began to distort reality and lead to wrong conclusions.[25] Most experts agree that services' $4.4 trillion output and $770
billion worldwide trade figures are massively understated, especially
when one considers the value of embedded software and design, informational, financial transaction, and intracompany intellectual exchanges not captured.[26] Services especially require new measures
reflecting changes in service quality and the benefits captured by customers. Chapters 11 through 13 suggest some important approaches.

While significantly understating services contributions, the national
accounts identify as additions to GNP the extra taxi fares and gasoline
usage of people caught in automobile-induced traffic jams, as well as
the "new sales" value of appliances, houses, component parts, and service incomes required to repair or replace things that fail because of
poor quality. Simultaneously, the increased asset values of better educational systems, more highly trained people, more extensive access to li-

braries or databases, and better-quality health care or environmental systems appear nowhere. The national accounts distort these public economic values at three levels: (1) the real costs of existing environmental or lifestyle degradation (from pollution, inadequate education, police protection, or health care) are not recognized in public accounts; (2) the positive values (cleaner rivers, higher land prices, better trained people, and longer lives) generated by public expenditures to correct these degradations are never credited to the activities that created them; and (3) the market values (of the outputs, jobs, and supplier industries) created by these expenditures are perversely considered solely as costs in national analyses and in the public mind. The results are poor policy, wasted national resources, a less efficient market economy, and fewer growth opportunities for jobs and entrepreneurship. Chapters 10 through 13 develop some better approaches to these issues.

Major changes in our conceptual structures, approaches, and outcome measures are needed to improve both the efficiency of resource use and the total benefits society achieves from their deployment. Key among these is developing a framework of efficient "public markets" for goods and services people desire, but whose markets cannot be created directly by individuals or private firms. The aggregate of individual decisions and individual wealth does not determine the aggregate wealth of a country. Public wealth—including parks, water resources, information bases, educational, waste handling, legal, and defense institutions—goes well beyond the sum of individuals' wealth and is crucial to future quality of life. These assets also determine much of the nation's future wealth-generating potential. Developing and measuring these real wealth capabilities need much higher priority than they have been accorded in most economic constructs and public discussions. Public markets are natural extensions and facilitators of private markets. Chapters 10 through 13 show how these public markets can be created effectively to generate giant new growth and innovation opportunities. The challenge is great. So are the opportunities.

## SUMMARY

Intellect, science, technology, innovation, and knowledge diffusion are the crucial growth forces in any modern economy or corporation. Intellectually based services provide 79% of all jobs, 76% of GNP, and almost all of the value-added in the economy and in individual companies, including manufacturers. Meanwhile overcapacity in virtually all product and commodity markets is decreasing their prices and profits relative to real wages and forcing average returns toward cost-of-capital levels. Unfortunately, many of our corporate practices, economic and accounting measurements, and national policies reflect an earlier materials- and product-based economy—and waste inordinate resources.

Software has enabled disaggregation of organizations and outsourcing on a scale never seen before. These forces have created a hypercompetitive world, where each enterprise must compete against best-in-world competitors on each element in its value chain. The key factors for corporate success and economic growth, with few exceptions, have shifted from managing physical resources toward managing knowledge creation, innovation, and diffusion. Software has become the key element in managing and leveraging intellect. It is revolutionizing all steps in the innovation process, creating totally new strategies and organizational options for corporations and forcing a review of all past concepts for stimulating national economic growth. Nations and companies that win will be those that use the new capabilities to implement new knowledge-based growth strategies, disaggregated yet focused organizational structures, software-based innovation techniques, and more appropriate performance and incentive measures in this new era. These are the focal points of this book.

# PART I

# SOFTWARE REVOLUTIONIZES INNOVATION

# 2

# Software-Based Innovation

There is a genuine revolution under way today. Increasingly, innovation occurs through software. Software is a set of instructions designed to modify the behavior of another entity or system. Although one can code molecules to modify pharmaceutical or chemical systems in a predictable fashion, it is primarily information technology (IT) software that is changing innovation processes. Such software has high impact in several ways:

• Software is usually the key element determining scientific and managerial effectiveness at each stage of the innovation process, from discovery to implementation.

• Software provides the critical mechanism through which managers can lower costs, compress time cycles, decrease risks, and increase the value of innovations by factors of tens to hundreds.

• Software is the heart of the interactive learning and knowledge processes that enable innovations to achieve maximum technical advances internally and highest payoffs in customers' hands.

• Software defines how people interact, the information they use, what they communicate about, where they can be located, and what skills they need. It becomes an integral element of the organization, often determining its very culture and potential directions.

• In many cases the software itself is the major innovative "product" offered to customers. In others it determines the level of "service" customers receive from an innovation and their capacity to create further innovations based on the hooks the software provides.

## THE SOFTWARE REVOLUTION

This revolution demands a basic shift in the way managers approach innovation, from the strategic to detailed operational levels. Some portions of the innovation process may still require traditional physical manipulation, but leading companies have already shifted many steps to software. The payoffs are impressive.

### Dominating All Aspects of Innovation

Well-designed software can compress and facilitate all aspects of the innovation cycle. Through properly developed software, managers can change their entire innovation process, thoroughly integrating, completely eliminating, or merging many formerly discrete innovation steps. Simultaneously, they can dramatically lower innovation costs, decrease risks, shorten design and introduction cycle times, and increase the value of their innovations to customers.

*In Basic Research.* Most literature searches, database inquiries, exchanges with other researchers, experimental designs, experimental modeling, analyses of correlation and variance, hypothesis testing, modeling of complex phenomena, peer review of experimental results, first publication of results, enhancements to existing databases, and so on are performed through software. Software search tools to a large extent determine what data researchers see and what questions they ask. In many frontier fields—like astronomy, semiconductors, and microbiology—researchers may be able to observe, measure, or precisely envision phenomena only through electronic measures or electronic modeling (software). For example, atomic force microscopes can follow protein molecule interactions in real time.[1] In other major examples:

• In 1991, a group at IBM's Watson Research Center completed calculations from a full year's continuous run on its high-powered GF 11 computer. Based on known physical evidence, the group had established the masses of seven basic particles, including hadrons, important in quark research. By 1995, two further years of calculations had established both the mass and the decay rate of an elusive subfamily of hadrons, called glueballs, which had gone unrecognized in preceding laboratory experiments. These massive computations had both discovered a new particle and provided an important confirmation of quantum chromodynamics, the theory governing the behavior of quarks.[2]

• The Human Genome Project could not have proceeded without software to keep track of the 3 billion sequenced bases the human genome involves. Not only does the basic polymer chain reaction (PCR) technique for identifying sequences depend on software, they must be located relative to 30,000 markers that provide the reference points (sequence tag points) on the genetic map. A team spent a year automating a "Genomtron" that can do 150,000 PCR assays per run and a system for tracking, cataloging, and integrating the data produced. Now, identified genetic clones can be stored in the database rather than in a freezer, making them available to anyone on the worldwide Human Genome Project through (http://www-genome.wi.mit.edu).[3]

***Applied Research: Customer Interaction.*** Most basic research activities are common to applied research as well. However, in applied research, practical data about market, economic, or performance phenomena also become important. Most major innovations are preceded by a defined need. In many fields, data about the marketplace, user patterns, environmental trends, or specific constraints to application come directly from software that monitors these external forces. Examples include market shifts sensed through electronic point of sale (EPOS) data, epidemiological measurements of medical problems or outcomes, satellite scanning of environmental changes, and real-time performance data about financial transactions, communications systems' performance, or promotional programs' effectiveness. Properly designed software (like that of Trilogy's Conquer and Selling Chain) is the key to interlinking customer based, downstream, or use data with the other knowledge bases (basic research, developmental group, and external-technical sources) needed for effective applied research.[4] (Chapter 9 details many such techniques.)

***Development.*** Virtually all design of complex physical systems, subsystems, components, and parts is now first accomplished in software. Most things—from buildings to ships, aircraft, automobiles, circuits, bridges, machines, molecules, textiles, advertising, and weapons systems—are designed this way. Specialists and systems analysts try to build into the model all known scientific-technical relationships, physical dimensioning, system constraints, flow rates, and dynamic response patterns understood from earlier technical work, experiments, tests, or operations. For example:

• Nonlinear engineering models can analyze pipeline stresses in complex manufacturing or fluid distribution systems. The analyses specify needed materials, dimensions, and connection points. Fed by data from scientific models and pipe manufacturers' specifications, resulting designs enjoy higher reliability, lower costs, and much shorter times for implementation.[5]

In development, software is the primary means of capturing the experience curve of the enterprise concerning its technologies and their relationships to operations. For example, CAE-CAD-CAM systems interconnect whatever knowledge exists about the underlying physical science systems themselves and their manipulability in manufacturing. Without building physical models, other software systems can test CAD representations of generated designs against anticipated variations in use or operating environments. In many cases, the least expensive and most effective test information comes from simulations of use designed into software models. This is especially true for new service products, extreme environment, submicroscopic, complex dynamic flow, or extremely dangerous situations. But computer prototypes have substituted for physical models in virtually all complex design realms.

*Manufacturing Engineering.* For complicated process designs, software provides the same kinds of data-gathering, analytical, and test capabilities for processes as those just described for physical product design. For process design, software allows inexpensive experimentation, yield prediction, workstation design, process layout, alternative testing, three-dimensional analysis, network manipulation, quality control, and interface timing capabilities that would otherwise be impossible. Software is especially helpful in allowing workers, technologists, customers, and managers to visualize solutions and work together on complex systems. Further, knowledge-based systems now allow manufacturing planning and process control to extend in depth to processes on supplier premises. It permits coordination of design, sourcing, manufacturing monitoring, logistics, and inventory control needed to find and develop innovative solutions worldwide.[6] Already a heavy user of large mainframes for this purpose, Ford is testing new UNIX-based client-server software that it estimates will cut $2 billion in annual costs and time to market by one-third in 1999.[7]

*Interactive Customer Design.* Software models and shared screens allow multidisciplinary (marketing-manufacturing-development) teams to interact directly with customers, capturing their responses through video, audio, and physical sensing systems. Virtually no service system can be adequately designed without active customer engagement in the process, beginning at the idea state and continuing throughout the full implementation cycle. For physical products, interactive software in many cases allows the customer to participate directly in the design process by joining in co-design, "beta site" (first real application) testing, and even interactive implementation activities. For example, customers now participate directly in the design of new or customized fabrics, furnishings, entertainment services, auto and aircraft parts, health monitoring systems, homes and commercial buildings, packaging, insurance, and legal or accounting products.[8] Software allows much earlier, more rapid, frequent, interactive, accurate, and thorough customer participation on a wider scale than ever before. Increasingly, such customer participation is a crucial element in both lowering introduction risks and enhancing the customer value of designs. Software allows innovators to leverage their own capabilities enormously by tapping into the ideas of the great talent pools provided by their customers and the advances created by the interactions of each supplier and that supplier's other customers.

*Post-Introduction Monitoring.* After the product is introduced, software can monitor its effectiveness in use (aircraft), oversee its proper maintenance (elevators), and even add value by introducing new knowledge-based features directly into the customer's system (computers, financial services, or accounting systems). Manufacturers have introduced sensing and maintenance software into a variety of products from health care devices to office machines and home appliances. These devices often anticipate, and even automatically correct, potentially dangerous or disruptive failures. Service companies—like telecommunications, retail, airline, banking, hospital, or wholesaling firms—use in-line sensing (1) to ensure intended response times, signal levels, accuracy of information, and performance reliability, and (2) to search out their customers' utilization patterns in order to improve products further. For example:

• Many retail enterprises, including Wal-Mart, the Limited, and McDonalds, use selected outlets as live feedback, experimental test centers to try out and monitor new product presentations, menus, layouts, or services to guide their product introduction and phase-out strategies on a continuing basis. Health care enterprises (like NovaCare) and consortia are now introducing wide-scale postservice monitoring of patients to understand better the "outcomes" of their various procedures, prescriptions, and preventive (versus corrective) care programs. Eventually data from these systems will provide a more solid basis for physicians to assess the true cost and impact of various alternative treatments.

• Kao Corporation, Japan's largest consumer products company, has developed its ECHO system to capture and analyze consumers' responses quickly and in refined detail. Kao's operators handle over 50,000 calls a year. ECHO enables them to input customers' questions and complaints in terms of key words and even sentences. Operators can use ECHO to find instant answers (often in pictorial form) for people experiencing emergencies with Kao products. Behind 8,000 key words ECHO stores over 350,000 customer questions that Kao employees worldwide can tap into for analysis or recall.

***Diffusion.*** After a company has successfully tested a new product or service in the marketplace, software helps implement introductions across wider geographic areas with higher accuracy, consistency, and performance reliability. This practice is especially widespread in service enterprises such as fast foods, financial services, and maintenance; but it is equally essential in transferring product design or manufacturing know-how from one location to another. Through software, firms like Sun Microsystems, Asea-Brown-Boveri, Intel, Ford, and Boeing ensure that their most advanced know-how and practices are instantly available across their entire enterprises and supplier-distributor value chains.

***New Value-Added Systems.*** Software is often the strategic element in unlocking higher value-added opportunities and indeed in restructuring entire companies and industries.[9] For example: In the late 1980s, Intel was concerned about the commoditization of ICs (integrated circuits). Intel's chips were being copied, and its patents were running out. In early 1991, CEO Andy Grove asked executives to create the basis for a new personal computer with much higher performance, lower costs, and video communications capabilities. This effort required contributions from many other companies, including entertainment, telecommunications, software, and systems groups. The core of the challenge was in software. Grove commissioned a team to learn about all aspects of personal computing, including software, that Intel had not earlier considered its charter. Ultimately these initiatives became a comprehensive strategy to move Intel from a narrow role as a semiconductor supplier to that of a system supplier. These efforts grew into the Intel Architecture Labs, anticipating new uses and applications for personal computers, entertainment, and computing. Through its software interconnections and alliances, Intel has become a center for changing the entire value-added concept of its industry.[10]

## Software: The Critical Ingredient

Software is now a critical ingredient at all levels of the innovation-diffusion process and is especially important for the organizational learning that innovation requires. Software can capture and integrate the best of both internal and external knowledge bases into the design fundamentals and processes innovators use. And it can help less skilled and experienced people perform at a higher level by incorporating critical knowledge elements into the data resources and equipment they use. More important, software can preserve institutional knowledge when human intellectual resources move on. As aerospace, defense, and advanced energy enterprises are sadly learning, the cost of replacing such knowledge can be overwhelming. Essentially all of the immense knowledge built up in the Saturn 5 program was thrown away in NASA cutbacks. Boeing had tried to capture as much data about earlier space lab and space station programs as possible in its Technical and Management Information System (TMIS) system. When key people left the space lab programs during cutbacks, TMIS was the main hope of preserving the expensive knowledge that had been built up in earlier programs. Then NASA and the Congress cut the funds for TMIS. If the United States returns to manned deep space experimentation, the cost will be horrendous.

Software's enormous capabilities have led to huge new markets that could not exist without its extensive support. (See Table 2.1.) But to be effective, both the enterprise's human systems and its software systems must be coordinated to reflect the best current know-how and work practices. For example, in a camera company, the young CAD-CAM group and the more experienced design and engineering groups had little contact with each other and no real understanding of each other's knowledge bases or computer capabilities. Consequently, the CAD-CAM software did not capture and share the depth of the soft experience insights that design and engineering groups had to offer. As the processes of each group became more and more incompatible, product introduction costs and times soared.

**TABLE 2.1**

**Scalar Estimates of Markets and Industries
Largely Facilitated by Software**

| Industry Type[a] | | Year | Source |
|---|---|---|---|
| *Sales Volume or Revenues,*[b] *($ billions)* | | | |
| Computer and software services | 156.5 | 1995 | *ITI 1996 Databook* |
| Fast food restaurants | 100.2 | 1996 | *Frozen Food Digest,* February 1996 |
| Wholesale clubs | 39.5 | 1996 | *Market Share Reporter,* 1997 |
| Discount merchandise retailers | 161.2 | 1996 | *Market Share Reporter,* 1997 |
| Computerized reservation services | 4.9 | 1995 | *AMR Annual Report 1995* |
| Public information resources | 16.0 | 1995 | *Information Week,* August 26, 1991 |
| Cellular telephones | 19 | 1995 | *Consumer Electronics,* Electronic Market Data Book, 1996 |
| Satellite services | 5.5 | 1996 | http://www.ita.doc.gov/ industry/tai/telecom/ satellite.txt, April 1997 |
| *Assets Managed ($ billions)* | | | |
| Custodial accounts | 14,340 | 1996 | *Global Investor,* May 1996 |
| Swaps and derivatives | 13,900 | 1995 | *Institutional Investor,* Jan. 1996 |
| Mutual funds | 2,820 | 1995 | *Mutual Fund Fact Book,* 1996 *Invest. and Co. Institute,* 1996 |
| Securitized home mortgages | 1,895 | 1996 | *Federal Reserve Bulletin,* Oct. 1996 |
| Credit card receivables | 387 | 1995 | *Credit Card Management,* Oct. 1995 |
| Asset-backed securities | 140 | 1996 | *Business Week,* Sept. 2, 1996 |
| *Transaction Volume*[b] | | | |
| CHIPS (Worldwide)[c] | $310 trillion | 1995 | SWIFT,[d] Nov. 1, 1995 |
| FedWire | $222 trillion | 1995 | *Institutional Investor,* Nov. 1995 |
| Foreign exchange turnover | $320 trillion | 1995 | *BIS Report,* April 1995 |
| U.S. Treasury bond market | $65 trillion | 1996 | *Federal Reserve Bulletin,* Oct. 1996 |
| U.S. credit card charge volume | $746 billion | 1995 | *Forbes,* July 1, 1996 |

[a]United States only unless otherwise indicated.
[b]All figures are best approximations only.
[c]Clearing House Interbank Payment System.
[d]Society for Worldwide Interbank Financial Telecommunications.

# SOFTWARE IN FAST CYCLE INNOVATION

There are many aspects to improving the cycle time of innovation.[11] None is more crucial—and has received less attention—than software. When software is used properly, cycle time costs and risks can often be reduced by 90% or more.[12] Software can entirely eliminate many of the traditional steps in the innovation process, combine others into a simultaneous mode, increase the value of inputs and outputs at each level, and provide the disciplined framework for the interactions that multidisciplinary teams generally find critical in complex innovations. In a well-known example:

• Boeing went from software straight into production on its multibillion dollar 777 aircraft project, cutting out many sequential steps formerly used in the design cycle. It installed 1,700 workstations to link 2,800 engineering locations worldwide. Using rules developed from earlier scientific models, wind tunnel tests, field experience, and supplier or customer models supporting their systems, Boeing's 250 multifunctional design-build teams could pretest and optimize both the structural aspects and consumer convenience requirements for each major component in the aircraft's 4-million-part configuration. In earlier years, designs would have been sequentially converted into detailed blueprints and specifications for tool and die makers, machine manufacturers, in-house manufacturing operations, component and subsystem producers, and so on. Instead, Boeing's three-dimensional CAD-CAM software provided each of its fabricators with the capacity to produce its tools, parts, or subassemblies directly. All of the specifications for interacting suppliers could be coordinated directly from digital electronic instructions to ensure precise fits, assembly tolerances, surfaces, machine compatibilities, and so on. Instead of the many "build and bust" tests that were necessary to handle the complex interactions of so many system elements in the past, models pretested such relationships and made "first-off" component and system testing much more reliable. There was a 60 to 90% reduction in prototype errors and rework costs.[13]

When physical tests were needed, the software cut or formed many test models directly. This process avoided most of the delays formerly caused by a subsystem's having to wait for its predecessor or adjacent systems to be tested first. Various simulations' predictive capabilities also helped identify potential trouble spots when subsystem and component suppliers tested their products against dimensional and dynamic performance specs. Using 1.8 trillion bytes of data at the design, prototyping, and manufacturing levels, software systems allowed many groups to operate in parallel, thus decreasing design cycle times and increasing reliability on parts, while enhancing interface coordination.[14] The real test was that the software produced a better-quality, more customer- and crew-friendly aircraft at much lower cost.

## Software for Design and Evaluation

In automobile design and other product industries, desktop solid-modeling software, rapid prototyping tools, and virtual reality environments are used every day to design and evaluate components. Processes that took months only five years ago now take only a few hours or days. The software creates both video- and stereographic models from which toolmakers can evaluate how production will be accomplished. Once approved, designs can go directly from software through CAM systems to models in resin or full-scale production prototypes for physical evaluation.[15] In chemical industries:

• Biotechnology companies generally attempt to design and assess new molecules as much as possible in software before building actual chemical structures. Using biochemical rules about how different structures will combine, researchers can pretest the configurations most likely to be effective for a new biotech entity. They can assess which receptors are most likely to respond in a certain fashion, how they might relocate or reshape a molecule's receptor or bonding structures, and what transport mechanisms can best deliver "bonding" or "killer" agents. By capturing all of the known laboratory data about biochemical processes and the physical characteristics of each agent involved, such modeling decreases errors and makes experimenters define parameters more precisely.[16] When they do physical experiments, researchers can often observe actual interaction processes using electron or scanning tunneling microscopes, which extend observations orders of magnitude beyond ordinary optical limits. Such equipment is itself largely software—electronic sensing and amplification—driven.

• In continuous flow processes, almost all design is done through fluid mechanics simulations, which—based on prior experimentation and measurements—predict relevant flows, phase changes, and interaction rates throughout the system. Advanced software systems like Aavid Thermal Technologies' Fluent (described in detail later in this chapter) allow process designers to design complex multiphase flow systems and then monitor their performance with high accuracy. In microchips, virtually all the circuit design, layer deposition, masking, and etching are done through software. In all cases the result is shorter design times, more efficient processes, and a quality of output that could not be achieved without substantial software support.

• In highway design, Superpave software, developed by the Strategic Highway Research Program, provides a design and analysis system, performance-based binder specifications, and a supporting test system to decrease costs and ensure quality in the $12 billion asphalt pavement industry. Superpave analyzes and specifies based on the unique local materials, temperature ranges, and pavement structures encountered.[17]

## Enhanced Results

People like to emphasize that software cannot do anything that humans could not do themselves, if time constraints were set aside. In fact, many design calculations or operations are so complex that they would take many years or human lifetimes—if they could be done at all—without computer capabilities; hence they become essentially impossible. Without software, innovators often could neither adequately measure nor interrelate large-scale experiments, the physical reactions within a system, or interactions between the system and external environments. Examples range from gene sequencing to life and weather system models,[18] IC circuit connections, atomic orbit calculations, and space flight trajectories.

Process times, although important, may not always be the crucial element. To improve quality, aesthetic effects, and customization possibilities, 70% of the world's automotive design studios now use software to develop, view, and evaluate free-form surface models in an ergonomic environment prior to engineering or actual production.[19] In many cases of complex design, it would be impossible for the required number of individuals to work effectively together on a personal basis to achieve the desired result. Without a computer system, innovators often would have to rely much more on hunches and limited experiments. They could not interrelate the details of scientific measurements, physical interactions within a system, and producer-consumer processes in a way that could be interpreted, manipulated, or reduced to practice within any realistic time frames and with needed precision.[20] Human inaccuracies would quickly throw off calculations, leave out critical variables, cause inaccurate experiments, and lead to wrong results.

## Software as Inventor

Software enables much more sophisticated innovations than humans can achieve unaided. Totally new creations and industries have resulted. For example:

• The digital technologies introduced by George Lucas and Silicon Graphics have changed the movie, television, games, and advertising businesses as radically as did the talkies or technicolor in movies. Directors and producers are freed from any constraints of concrete reality. From only 10% of movies in 1994, over half used digital effects in 1995, and in 1996 they became commonplace. Because of these and digital sound capabilities, entire new modes of entertainment and commercial possibilities are rapidly emerging for the home, communications, entertainment, and computer markets.[21] By the early 1990s software had already enabled other huge new industries worth many $100 billions in sales, assets, and profits. (See Table 2.1.)

In many cases, software itself becomes the discoverer or inventor. Software designed as a learning system frequently generates answers beyond the imaginations of its creators. It may identify and verify totally new patterns and problem solutions. It can even be preprogrammed to search for, capture, and flag the fortuitous incidents or anomalies that are often the essence of discovery. Properly designed software systems can actually create new hypotheses, test the hypotheses for critical characteristics, analyze potential system responses to exogenous variables, and predict counterintuitive outcomes from complex interactions. Software can learn from both positive and negative experiments and capture these experience effects in data files. For example:

• By integrating databases about the genetic structures of various organisms, the Human Genome Program's computer analyses led to the hypothesis that there are 256 genes—together performing about a dozen cellular functions—that contribute a minimum gene set for a modern cell.[22] At the National Institutes of Health, computers process electron micrographs of the three-dimensional structures of viruses, calculating accessible surface areas for possible interaction points and predicting probable output conformations and their utility.[23]

• The Cochrane Collaboration is a massive effort to collect and systematically review the entire published and unpublished literature on the roughly 1 million randomized control trials of medical treatments that have been conducted over the past fifty years or so. Because they are so difficult to access, most of those experiments' results have been ignored or otherwise lost to practitioners. The Collaboration will collect, catalogue, and update these reviews to synthesize the latest state of knowledge about every available therapy or intervention and give its implications for practice and research. In the past, when such clinical data were systematically collected and analyzed, interesting new patterns were discovered that changed many practices like mammography, fetal monitoring, mastectomies, and prostatectomies.[24]

In large-scale systems, "genetic" and related learning algorithms and software can often identify patterns, optimize research protocols, and define potential solutions by trial and error much more efficiently than can direct physical experimentation or a preplanned sequence of hypothesis tests. Such programs can economically attack problems that were of unthinkable complexity a decade ago. In business applications, self-learning programs can identify developing problems or opportunities in the competitive environment, suggest the most likely causes and alternative solutions available, eliminate those of least promise, and pretest or implement promising new options—as they commonly do in telecommunications, switching, power distribution, vehicle routing, and ad campaign targeting and design.

## Leveraging Value Creation

A major contribution of well-designed software is that it allows the original innovator to tap into the creative potential of all the firm's customers and suppliers. Since more than 50% of all innovation occurs at these interfaces, this creates a substantial leveraging of the company's own capabilities.[25] By designing "hooks" to allow customers to modify the product for their own use, the software can help generate further options and valuable uses that the original innovator could not possibly anticipate. For example, on a grand scale:

• AT&T could never have forecast the full range of uses to which its institutional and home customers would ultimately apply the flexible software capabilities designed into cellular or digital telephone systems. Similarly, none of the personal computer's innovators could possibly have foreseen the enormous variety of uses to which such computers would be put. By introducing flexible software interfaces that allowed users to program for their own special needs, microcomputers entered and created a variety of unexpected marketplaces and generated many unanticipated options for new hardware and software. Only after Apple

and Microsoft put a simplified icon-graphics product into customers'
hands did the hardware's value become evident. Early buyers quickly
used the new software "hooks" to create greater value for themselves
and their customers, who then modified the results to add still more
value for other customers. Even now, no one can calculate the total
value produced, but it is clearly thousands of times the value captured
by Microsoft or Apple.

• On a simpler scale, new test equipment software allows customers
to create custom instruments for their specialized uses by writing software that guides the instruments in testing and measuring to their specific functional and dimensional needs. Called "virtual instruments," it
is possible to change the instruments' operations to make different measurements for each sequential product in a "job shop" or "electronic
commerce" fashion.[26] Through software, Andersen Windows has
moved from being a mass producer of predesigned windows to a custom producer of 188,000 different windows, largely designed by customers. In the early 1990s Andersen helped its customers install
Macintosh- and Oracle-based systems whose software lets the retail
outlet (and its architect or home customers) change features until they
find the window they want, checks the design for structural soundness,
and prices it instantly. Once ordered, the software tracks the items
through production and shipment, eliminating the huge number of errors Andersen once experienced.[27]

Because of the low-cost experimentation that software permits
and the dominating importance of the value in use it creates for customers, increasing the efficiency of the program steps in software-
based innovation is nowhere near as important as the potential value
creation the software can create through the functionalities it generates for customers and the multipliers of additional benefits further
customers obtain from it. Too much attention is often placed on decreasing the cost of design steps and shortening internal process
times in the innovation cycle rather than focusing on the critical internal learning and value creation processes that software facilitates.[28] Both are essential for effective innovation in today's
hypercompetitive world.[29]

## IDENTIFYING OPPORTUNITIES INTERACTIVELY

When managers do think about software for innovation purposes, they
tend to concentrate on CAD-CAM, e-mail, process monitoring, or

imaging software. However, external database, strategic monitoring, market modeling, or customer interaction software may be equally important. Software can identify subtle supplier, user, or environmental trends as potential problems or market opportunities long before personal observation might do so. Common examples are the variance analysis trading programs used in investing, the EPOS systems of retailing and fast foods, the customer monitoring programs of credit card and airline companies, and the early warning systems contained in strategic intelligence, environmental monitoring, and weather models. Given adequate models of external environments, experimenters can—by monitoring experimental stores, focus panels, or sales counters—test the impact of different design combinations and permutations in a variety of use or niche market situations to assess which design has the greatest potential value in any single use and across the system. Such software helps define what flexibilities are feasible and optimum to satisfy desired niches and future growth patterns. And it can avoid overselling of new ideas by technical staffs or their undervaluing by old-line managers.

## An Interactive Sales Tool

Software representations of an innovation can also become a sales tool, allowing individuals or customers to visualize a product or concept more easily, experiment with different features, and customize the product for their special needs. Software for this purpose is advancing rapidly. By pressing buttons in a distributor's office or on their home telephone or PC, customers can preview possible features, see physical relationships, and actively design their own products. Software-supported interactive design is becoming common both before and after a product's initial introduction in many fields—for example, the textile, architectural, automobile, plumbing, services, financial, medical devices, boot and shoe, computer accessory, and IC markets. Unfortunately, few companies have effectively integrated their market intelligence and product design systems. This area will provide some of the most rewarding challenges and opportunities for innovation in many firms. By directly connecting users through software to their design processes, companies can virtually eliminate time delays, error costs, and product introduction risks in innovation. More important, by providing customers with more sophisticated visualization, animation, and options, they can substantially increase the psychological or "wow factor" impact of the product when introduced to the marketplace.[30]

## User-Based Innovation and Virtual Shopping

The Internet and the World Wide Web have become prototypes for this new mode of user-based innovation. All innovation on the Internet is in software. Innovators reduce their concepts to practice in software form and present them electronically to customers on the Internet or Web. Customers can utilize the innovation in its offered form, modify it for their particular uses, or ask the selling company to make the necessary modifications and transmit the results directly to them by the Internet or other means. Institutions or individuals seeking new solutions can use the Internet as a "virtual shop" for potential answers, pretest those answers on their own systems, and purchase if desired. Conversely, they can post their needs onto the network to attract potential solutions. A manufacturer can solicit design proposals for new components, product features, or systems anywhere in the world. Or a farmer in the Philippines can query a worldwide network of agricultural and livestock knowledge to find out how best to eliminate an obnoxious weed or insect pest.

## Worldwide Virtual Innovation

New methods for introducing product concepts, transacting, and paying over the system are constantly appearing. As these infrastructures come into place, they are changing the entire nature of innovation worldwide. Anyone with access to the Internet and Web can present innovations instantly to a worldwide marketplace, obtain interactive market responses, and readapt the innovation for specific user purposes. All innovators in the world thus become potential competitors, and all customers and suppliers become potential sources of leverage for internal innovation. Chapters 4 through 9 illustrate how various companies implement these capabilities.

Further, sophisticated users can scan the Web and use advanced visually oriented programs like Visual Basic or Power Object to modify the Web's offerings for their own or their customers' use. With high-level languages, PC users can create electronic products or programs that the computer priesthoods of the past would have found intransigent, if not impossible. They can immediately test their solutions in terms of their specific needs. In essence, the innovation process has been inverted: the customer has become the innovator, and all intervening steps in the innovation process have disappeared.

Few would deny that software is *a* key component in the innovation

**FIGURE 2.1**

**Investment of Venture Capital in Software and Information Services Companies ($ millions)**

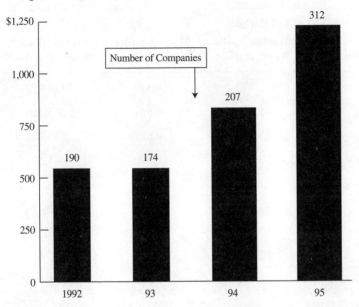

Source: "The Software Industry Survey," *Economist*, May 25, 1996, p. 515. Reproduced by special permission.

*Both numbers and value of venture capital investments in software ventures are growing rapidly.*

process. We argue that because of its dominance in all the above processes, software (1) is becoming *the* critical component in the innovation process, (2) enables innovations that would otherwise not be possible, and (3) is often itself the central element of discovery and innovation. In the past, software has generally been regarded as an adjunct to research, development, engineering, and product and process design. The management of software has now become the crucial element in innovation management. And venture capitalists' investments in software are growing apace; many of the most profitable recent initial public offerings have been software companies. (See Figure 2.1 and Tables 2.2. and 2.3.)

## MANAGING SOFTWARE INNOVATION PROCESSES

Executives can best manage software-based, interactive innovation inside their companies *not* by hiring more programmers but by better

**TABLE 2. 2**

**Technology Initial Public Offerings, 1980–1996 (first quarter), by Business Sector ($ millions)**

| Business Sector | Lifetime Market Value Appreciation | Market Value at IPO | Market Value, March 26, 1996 |
|---|---|---|---|
| 1. Software | $151,423 | $28,379 | $179,802 |
| 2. Networking | 58,908 | 6,341 | 65,250 |
| 3. Services | 35,569 | 8,661 | 45,061 |
| 4. Semiconductors | 32,004 | 11,300 | 43,304 |
| 5. Telecom equipment | 17,732 | 6,910 | 24,642 |
| 6. PCs | 15,362 | 3,062 | 18,424 |
| 7. CAD/CAM | 12,824 | 3,382 | 16,207 |
| 8. Workstations | 12,257 | 1,254 | 13,511 |
| 9. Telecommunications | 4,707 | 1,189 | 5,896 |
| 10. Semiconductor capital equipment | 4,380 | 3,249 | 7,629 |
| 11. Contract manufacturing | 3,032 | 400 | 3,432 |
| 12. Test equipment | 3,029 | 1,661 | 4,690 |
| 13. Internet software | 2,476 | 1,691 | 4,167 |
| 14. Data networking | 2,424 | 1,457 | 3,881 |
| 15. Voice processing | 2,241 | 1,090 | 3,331 |
| 16. Connectors | 892 | 698 | 1,590 |
| 17. Health care software | 811 | 620 | 1,431 |

Source: Compiled from data in Morgan Stanley, *Technology IPO Yearbook*, 2d ed. (Spring 1996).

Reproduced by special permission.

*The market gains of software IPOs have exceeded all other technology IPOs in the last sixteen years.*

**TABLE 2.3**
**Biggest Software Successes, 1980–1996 (first quarter)**

| Issuer | Offer Date | Lifetime Return by % Change in Stock Price | Compound Annual % Change in Stock Price | Market Value Appreciation | Market Value at IPO | Market Value 3/26/96 | Business Description |
|---|---|---|---|---|---|---|---|
| | | | | ($ millions) | | | |
| 1. Computer Associates | 12/91 | 11,878 | 40 | $16,745 | $ 40 | $16,785 | Software |
| 2. Microsoft | 03/86 | 8,709 | 56 | 65,036 | 519 | 65,555 | Software |
| 3. *Novell* | 02/85 | 8,060 | 49 | 4,653 | 24 | 4,677 | Networking |
| 4. Oracle Systems | 03/86 | 7,580 | 54 | 21,231 | 188 | 21,419 | Software |
| 5. Cisco Systems | 02/90 | 7,533 | 103 | 24,905 | 226 | 25,131 | Networking |
| 6. Paychex | 08/83 | 3,827 | 34 | 2,535 | 61 | 2,596 | Services |
| 7. America Online | 03/92 | 3,648 | 146 | 5,445 | 62 | 5,507 | Online service network |
| 8. Parametric Technology | 12/89 | 3,425 | 76 | 4,596 | 90 | 4,686 | CAD/CAM |
| 9. Informix | 09/86 | 2,980 | 43 | 3,992 | 52 | 4,044 | Software |
| 10. Ascend Communications | 05/94 | 2,946 | 519 | 5,582 | 146 | 4,727 | Networking |
| 11. Solectron | 11/89 | 2,800 | 70 | 2,149 | 33 | 2,183 | Contract manufacturing |
| 12. *Telltabs* | 06/80 | 2,255 | 24 | 4,191 | 124 | 4,315 | Telecommunications |
| 13. 3Com | 03/84 | 2,145 | 31 | 6,768 | 80 | 6,848 | Networking |
| 14. Adobe Systems | 08/86 | 1,987 | 39 | 2,294 | 52 | 2,346 | Software |
| 15. Maxim Integrated Products | 02/88 | 1,985 | 47 | 2,127 | 60 | 2,187 | Semiconductors |
| 16. Autodesk | 06/85 | 1,953 | 33 | 1,706 | 69 | 1,774 | CAD/CAM |
| 17. First Financial Management | 03/83 | 1,985 | 26 | 6,134 | 50 | 6,184 | Services |
| 18. Adaptec | 06/86 | 1,953 | 36 | 2,535 | 64 | 2,600 | Peripherals |

Source: *Securities Data Corp.*, Morgan Stanley, 1996. Reproduced by special permission.
Note: Includes all technology IPOs greater than $10 million, except for those in italics, through March 1996.

*The market value increases of software successes have dominated those of other technology stocks in the past sixteen years.*

managing innovation processes through software and by learning to develop and manage software itself more effectively.

## Three Critical Systems

Software systems like PERT (program evaluation and review technique) and CPM (critical path method) were among the early techniques used to plan and monitor hardware innovation processes. Such software is not the proper focus for managing innovation today. Rarely do PERT and CPM implementations exploit the capabilities that open software systems, self-learning programs, and other interactive software processes now offer. To develop these high-leverage interactive and learning capabilities, while supporting the depth of detailed expertise that each important subsystem demands, current software structures generally revolve around three relatively independent, but interacting, modules connected by compatible languages and interface rules. (See Figure 2.2.)

**FIGURE 2.2**
**Three Major Subsystems**

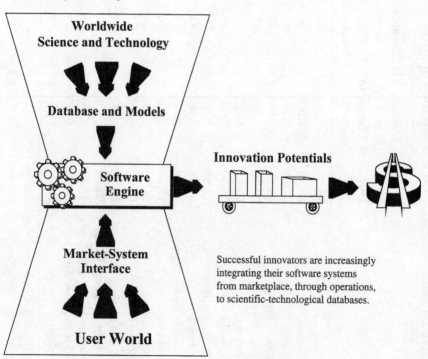

Successful innovators are increasingly integrating their software systems from marketplace, through operations, to scientific-technological databases.

1. The upstream database and model access system, linked to external scientific, economic, professional, or technical sources.
2. The central software (process) engine, focused on internal operating parameters.
3. The market and user interface system, linked to downstream market and environmental sources.

The *database and model access system* embodies both the current raw data and the state-of-the-art external models a manager needs to manipulate data effectively. A properly implemented system is constantly updated to include the latest references, user practices, experiments, transactions, operating data, and models. Structuring the database for constant refreshment and maintaining an open and precise classification system to access its information are among the most difficult of all software system problems. Yet they are keys to continual innovation.

New experimental data and tested models provide constant clues as to needed or possible changes in the rate processes or interaction weightings that can improve a technical system's performance. New conceptual models from research worldwide may redefine both new data needs and the relevancy of old solutions. Clearly those who continue to use old paradigms after they are subverted get wrong answers, as do those who use last year's professional and technical information or solutions for today's problems. Since even the most precise models and operating systems are only as useful as their databases, many successful firms—like Merrill Lynch, Intel, Boeing, and American Airlines—treat their databases as their most valuable assets. Unfortunately, most do not interlink them effectively to other critical modules for innovation purposes.

*Software (process) engines*—which contain the enterprise's primary processing, manipulation, and operating systems logic—tend to receive much more attention. This has traditionally been the glamorous portion of software development, where new or unique algorithms can create fame for their programmers. This is where proprietary intellectual property seems to be created, rather than in improving the flexibility and quality of the data inputs or the manipulability of outputs. Engine design is extremely important to innovation in terms of allowing flexible experiments, increasing operating efficiencies, and ensuring output quality. Nevertheless, many of the highest innovation payoffs recently have come from expanded database availability and easier-to-use software interfaces—such as those first provided by Mac-OS or Windows and later by Mosaic, Oracle, Java, or HTML*—rather than through in-creased sophistication in manipulating the data. For efficiency, how-ever, most of these innovations were accompanied by a new engine, just as next-generation speeds and power demands will probably require new engine architectures, like massively parallel processors.

*Interfaces* are crucial in making critical systems work together and in enabling various users to access important databases for their special purposes. Compatible, and preferably seamless, interfaces are critical to leveraging innovation internally and with external customers and sup-pliers. Software like HTTP/HTML and SQL has been a major step in this regard.† Navigator, Yahoo, and other search and agent software systems have made the Internet and Web much more accessible. But their originators say that intranets within companies will ultimately be their largest users. The best interfaces are as unobtrusive as possible. They are usually a result of interactive development with users through-out all phases of both the design and implementation processes.[31] Well-designed interfaces also incorporate future "hooks" that allow external customers and internal users to create or explore many unexpected in-novative possibilities over time. Conversely, interfaces that convert in-ternal systems into support tools readily accessing details about changing customer interactions and rapidly advancing scientific-techni-cal environments make these systems into invaluable cornerstones for fast-flexible innovation.

## Interacting Subsystems, Not Megasystems

The highest potentials for value-added innovation lie in direct and inte-grated connection among user interfaces, self-learning operations en-gines, and thoroughly compatible external and internal databases. However, few companies have successfully achieved this continuity. More have done so in services than in manufacturing. What can be learned from the experiences of those who have been successful?

First, end-to-end integration through a single megasystem is ex-tremely difficult to accomplish.[32] Those who have been most successful at integration have usually concentrated individually on the three critical subsystems (of databases, engines, and market connections) and used carefully predefined interface standards to link them effectively. This enables each subsystem to contribute as quickly as possible, allows in-

---

*HTML: Hypertext Markup Language.

†HTTP: Hypertext Transfer Protocol; SQL: Structured Query Language.

cremental implementation and interactive learning, and avoids the long and costly development times for which megasystems are so notorious.

Second, the most successful integrators have developed system software that, like the World Wide Web, insulates users from having to understand the complex rules and sophisticated methodologies governing the system's internal operations. Through user-friendly prompts and menus, these intranets enable connecting parties to query and customize the system's central knowledge for their own purposes. They thus encourage maximum innovation around each user's specialized needs. Rather than hoarding or master-controlling all information, effective architectures help decentralized users and customers sort data easily and capture much of each innovation's value for themselves. Properly programmed, the systems can learn from their decentralized users' experiences and make this learning available instantly to others on the network. Financial service systems provide a classic example that is being widely emulated in other service systems like fast foods, retailing, and airlines.

• A brokerage or insurance company's central engine manipulates all transactions data from the marketplace, embodies the most updated financial methodologies and tax, accounting, or regulatory rules for doing business, and provides the quick access and profuse data that decentralized agents or brokers need to adapt the firm's services for specific customers. At headquarters, cadres of mathematically sophisticated analysts both constantly upgrade the system's capabilities and design new products for all the parties it serves. Centralized software commands much of the firm's own internal investment portfolio, based on preprogrammed rules and changing regulations, tax structures, and economic or market trends.

As the center creates new products in response to these changes, they are instantly diffused to broker's or agent's offices for adaptation to individual customer needs. Other software monitors individual customers' transactions and past investment patterns. It helps brokers detect significant changes and signals local brokers when to adjust their clients' portfolios. It warns customers if unusual patterns indicate possible fraud or misuse of their assets and provides up-to-date account data on demand. For effectiveness, the central system's interfaces must match those of both upstream information providers (like government or market data sources) and downstream users (agents or customers) and provide the simplest and most transparent interconnections possible.

Similarly, the system architectures of leading product companies (like Ford, Hewlett-Packard, Nike, Sun, and Boeing) allow researchers, designers, manufacturing engineers, and marketers to call in virtually unlimited modules of capability from databases, on-line operations, or contracted sources anywhere in the world. These companies' capacity to find solutions, mix-and-match options, and test outcomes is paced primarily by their internal system's modeling software and their capabilities to provide interfaces to upstream and downstream knowledge bases. Their systems allow them to tap into worldwide sources of innovation and to connect these in new ways to their customers. Their suppliers can inform them precisely about new options, process capabilities, or problem solutions through software. In conjunction with on-line customer systems, advanced companies and their suppliers can design and pretest a wide variety of innovations in electronics. These include soft-goods designs (interactively on electronic pallets with buyer-customers), aircraft performance or customer comfort designs (through mathematical or graphics simulations), architectural designs (in three-dimensional software models customers can "walk through"), alternate designs for shoreline control strategies (through large interactive models with the actual stakeholders participating), or advanced molecular designs (in simulated life systems or flow process environments).

## INTEGRATING INNOVATION SUBSYSTEMS

Many companies have partially integrated their software systems, from their marketplaces through their production processes. Such systems now allow electric power systems to respond instantaneously to changing demand loads. Oil companies routinely plan their drilling, shipping, pipeline, and refining activities through such models. An entire shipping fleet (like Exxon's) can be redirected within a few minutes in response to changing market price, supply, refining, shipping, tax, or tariff situations. Within a few days' time, automobile companies can reassign an entire model's sourcing based on changes in exchange rates or other critical market characteristics. Few companies, however, have interlinked their marketing and operations systems with their scientific databases and design processes. Such integration can substantially increase the responsiveness, degree of advance, and customer impact of innovations. It can also significantly lower innovation risks, investments, and cycle times. For example:

• Fluent, Inc., a division of Aavid Thermal Technologies, develops computational fluid dynamics software to analyze fluid flow phenomena in industrial processes. Based on equations describing the physical effects of fluid flows under various circumstances, Fluent's software models can handle the entire innovation process from geometry definition to computation, design evaluation, and process control. The model for each specific application is constantly updated to reflect both new research and experimental findings, as well as real-world effects in actual customer use situations. Fluent's software "learns" from these inputs and captures the latest findings in its analyses and design recommendations.

Design and selection of proper mixing equipment are critical in the scale-up of chemical processes. Fluent gathers information on the performance of various mixing devices from tests performed by mixing equipment manufacturers, such as Lightnin and Chemineer, and models the performance characteristics of these devices in its software. Process engineers at companies like Dow and Du Pont then use these computer models to simulate the performance of the mixing devices for the specific fluids, flow conditions, and constraints of their processes. They can test a variety of mixing configurations in software, allowing process engineers to select the best design reliably and inexpensively, thereby bypassing a number of costly scale-up tests. Extensions of Fluent's capabilities can enable an automobile company to pretest the aerodynamic characteristics of various car designs in software, aircraft companies to pretest wing or fuselage designs, or chemical producers to pretest various multiphase flow designs for processes without building costly prototypes and facilities.

## Virtual Skunk Works and Storerooms

Such software systems not only decrease the time and personnel costs of development, they create a virtual skunk works that substantially lowers the investments needed for laboratory tests, pilot plants, and scale-up and increases the knowledge output of the innovation process. Under old mechanical or chemical engineering design paradigms, interaction parameters were poorly understood and very complex. Hence companies had to proceed through a complicated series of ever larger physical test, pilot, scale-up, and plant shakedown trials that were very costly in terms of both time and dollars. Although such empiricism might eventually be successful in practice, the company never knew *why* key interactions worked. By combining process science, physical constraints, and user environments in a single electronic model, experimenters can obtain process insights they never had before. Most important, they can visualize and understand *why* things do (or do not) work. The model provides a reliable discipline for recalibrating key people's intuitions, and its visual and printed outputs help users adopt the innovation faster and with better results.

Going beyond such internal virtual skunk works, designers can also use software representations about the best available *external* suppliers' capabilities to determine an optimum means of manufacture. By constantly surveying external best practices, they can determine the implicit costs of producing internally versus outsourcing. Their models can extend into "virtual storerooms," which optimize specification, sourcing, and logistics for future parts as models and features change.

By tapping into the best worldwide scientific and consumer knowledge bases, these sytems substantially leverage the company's other investments in its development team's skills and specialized facilities. The simulations and their updated databases become major contributors to the company's learning capabilities. They continually capture, codify, and make available all accessible internal and external knowledge about a problem. The software's capabilities are important assets in attracting key technical people and enabling them to attack challenges at the frontiers of their fields. Properly designed software systems allow smaller, more flexible teams to perform at greater levels of sophistication than larger teams can without them. (See Chapters 8 and 9.) Innovation costs decrease, and output values increase exponentially.

Software, however, can also impose its own limitations on innovation. Unless one is cautious, the structure of the software will limit the databases investigated, options considered, manipulations available, and user data evaluated. Managers must keep all three critical systems (database, engine, and market) as updated, open, and flexible as possible. Any modularity (except in the ultimate modularity of a single datum) will introduce some constraints. The capacity of an enterprise to move from one technology's S curve (or technical performance limits) to another's may well depend on whether it has developed adequate transitional software to consider the next S curve's characteristics and needs in its analyses. This often depends on the software's capacity to handle sufficiently refined details about customers, internal systems, and external technical data.

## The Smallest Replicable Units

To avoid such limitations and to maintain needed flexibilities, successful innovation and software managers find it useful to break units of activity and information down to the minimum replicable level of detail for the tasks or data to be analyzed. In earlier years, the smallest replicable measuring unit for organizations and data might have been an individual part, subassembly, office, supplier, or customer class. As volumes

## OBJECT ORIENTATION

In object-oriented programs, each real-world thing or concept is represented by a software object. Each object contains both a method and a variable. The method is a sequence of computer instructions that allows the object to carry out selected actions. Variables are named locations where data are stored. Variables are the same as in other computer languages except that they bear references to other objects, in addition to their own raw data. The methods and variables in an object define the object's class. On the object are references to other "partner objects." These are essentially hooks, which allow one object to combine with others, under rules the objects themselves determine. They define a capacity to interface rather than predetermining, controlling, and limiting the sequences through which any specific interactions may occur.

increased and computer capabilities became greater, it often became feasible for the corporation to manage and measure critical performance variables at much more detailed feature, activity, customer characteristic, or technical levels.

In some service industries—like banking, publishing, communications, or entertainment—it soon became possible to disaggregate the critical units of service activity into digitized sequences, electronic packets, data blocks, or bytes of information that could be endlessly combined or manipulated for new effects or to satisfy individual customer and operating needs. In manufacturing, the capacity to measure and control to ever more refined levels led to the era of mass customization.[33] In all industries, seeking out such micro-units enables the highest possible degree of segmentation, strategic fine-tuning, value-added definition, and cost control to help connect and target new innovations in the marketplace. Interestingly, the larger the organization is, the more refined can these replicability units be, and the greater their leverage is for creating value-added.

Important to the success of American Airlines' SABRE system, Motorola's pagers, AT&T's cellular phones, the Human Genome Project, and the Internet have been their early definition and breakdown of data into the smallest repeatable units and the creation of database rules and interfaces that allowed endless variations of user combinations, types of experimentation, and production options. As object-oriented software (see box) becomes more widely available, the capture and use of such detailed information is becoming easier, as are the corresponding opportunities for innovating in software. Object orientation promises to

accelerate and facilitate for companies the kinds of end-to-end compatibility that the Internet now provides in the public access realm.

## User Becomes Innovator

The Internet's TCP/IP* communications standards have made it possible for tens of millions of computers and their users to "talk" together
and to innovate together. Using similar software, the number of people
connected through intranets within companies is now growing even
more rapidly than the Internet. Web-compatible software languages
(like Mosaic, Java, and HTML) that run well on many different PC architectures now provide a huge virtual disk drive of sources and uses for
innovation. A *Business Week* article forecast, "These will cause a basic
shift in the software business no less seismic than the fall of the Berlin
Wall. . . . [They] will enable the [constant] deconstruction and recon-
struction of new economic models for the software industry."[34] They
provide a potent new model for interactive worldwide innovation, based
on the combinative powers of the Internet's millions of access points.

Using minimum replicable unit concepts, various network softwares
(like Navigator, Java, and Yahoo) have become the mediating structures
through which *users* can innovate their own solutions from the wide variety of alternatives available. More powerful yet may be the instant diffusion they allow for known technologies once posted on the Internet or
the Web. Java creates a 64-kilobyte software virtual computer, which
can be placed inside most interconnecting devices, including telephones, and can make almost any personal computer into a multimedia
machine. This should expand both innovation and diffusion possibilities
for a variety of new concepts, especially if Java is effectively included in
Microsoft's Windows. If such capabilities become widely used, they will
achieve the ultimate in decreasing innovation cycles, costs, risks, and
diffusion times. The customer will become the innovator. Under these
circumstances, adoption and adaptation times and risks for producers
drop to zero. The software "applets" (small computation algorithms) of
a Java-like system may become the minimum replicable elements of effective distributed computing, while the network becomes both the
computer itself and an instantaneous distribution system.

New business methodologies, like giving away platform software
and charging use fees for applet or add-on software or databases, seem
likely to revolutionize many businesses in the software, distribution,

---

*TCP/IP: Transmission Control Protocol/Internet Protocol.

publication, education, banking, communications, entertainment, and professional services fields. The lines between application, content, and support services are quickly disappearing in many markets. The sheer variety of object-oriented, network-capable systems (like Visual Basic, OLE, Colabra, Taligent, and Java) seems likely to accelerate interactive innovation opportunities in most fields.

Virtually any product—from insurance policies to yachts—can already be interactively custom-designed to meet the specific and varying needs of niched markets or individuals throughout the world. Software has thus become the critical element in continual innovation for most enterprises today. For example:

• In manufacturing, clothing designers no longer need to design their line in advance on a make-or-break basis. Instead, they can offer a series of suggested samples that salespeople show to potential buyers physically and electronically. Then, working with the buyer on an electronic pallet, the salesperson and the buyer jointly sketch out precisely what modifications the buyer wants. The pallet can be connected directly to the design unit at the clothing manufacturer's plant, where professionals interact electronically with the retail buyer to detail and price the buyer's exact desires.

## SUMMARY

Software has become the key element in the innovation process for most companies. It is critical to effectiveness at all levels of that process: basic research, applied research, needs sensing and definition, product design, introduction to operations, market introduction, feedback, redesign, dissemination, and diffusion of successes. Software offers infinite opportunities to shorten, merge, or eliminate entire steps in the innovation process, compressing time cycles and lowering risks by orders of magnitude. Even more important, it allows interaction with customers and users in ways that substantially enhance the innovation's value in use. Software has converted the process of innovation into a continuous worldwide, competitive endeavor ever more connected directly to customer needs. Increasingly the customer is becoming a participating innovator. Through software, each business is becoming a connector and converter of worldwide knowledge sources to serve the needs of specific customer groups. Later chapters show how companies can develop strategies, organizations, and entirely new modes of interaction to exploit these revolutionary potentials.

# 3

# Managing Software-Based Innovation

To take proper advantage of the revolutionary opportunities soft-ware-based innovation offers, many companies will have to improve their own internal software management capabilities dramatically. The alternative may be oblivion. Five issues are critical to this process:

1. Designing the software infrastructure as a learning system integrated, to the extent possible, from the marketplace, through operations, to upstream scientific and technological data sources and models.

2. Focusing the system not just on decreasing internal innovation costs, but on capturing, exploiting, and leveraging user information to maximize value-in-use for customers and to support their flexible remodification of innovated products or services with customers further downstream.

3. Recognizing the software system as an integral component of the organization that largely determines the language, modes, and possibilities of human interactions, and hence much of the institution's culture.

4. Utilizing the full capabilities of software as a self-learning system to define new innovative opportunities to interlink remote sources of knowledge in new ways, and to create catalytic growth effects by providing hooks onto which others can attach multiple new innovative capabilities.

5. Establishing a systematic approach to software development appropriate to the company's specific strategy and management style.

No company needs to develop all its own software, but it must know how to manage software systems and software development itself. The software industry has become one of the world's largest ($200 billion) and rapidly growing (13% per year) industries, employing millions of programmers worldwide (see Figure 3.1). Companies can tap into this rich resource for many aspects of their software activities, but they must never lose strategic control over this vital source of innovation and competitive edge.

Software-centered design enables huge leverages in the marketplace, and it changes the very thought processes of innovation. It avoids the trap of thinking that physical materials somehow have a special intrinsic value to customers. Instead, it focuses design on customer or use

**FIGURE 3.1**
**Employment in Software Programming (thousands)**

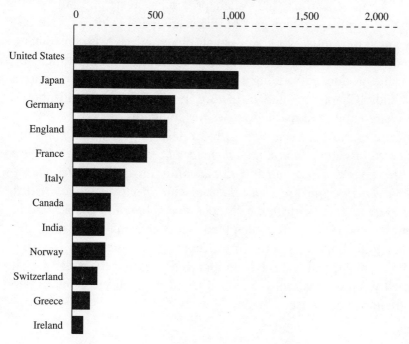

Source: "The Software Industry Survey," *Economist*, May 25, 1996, p. 514. Reproduced by special permission.

*U.S. employment in software exceeds that of other countries by a substantial margin, although per capita employment is much closer in advanced countries.*

features and flexibilities, making outputs more effective and easier to implement. As an end product or a component in a product or system, software itself has no intrinsic value or permanence. Its value lies solely in customers' perceptions of its value in the particular uses to which they apply it. Virtually all the value capture occurs on user premises and accrues to users, not the producers of the software. This effect is multiplied as customers consciously modify and use the software—or software hooks on the product—to serve their own customers. Sensible software design exploits the innovations its customers will later make.

For example, Microsoft's Windows first creates value for its buyers. Then these buyers use the software output to create value for other customers, who may then use those results to add value for still other customers. The total value produced is thousands of times that captured by Microsoft. And most of the true innovation occurs in how Microsoft's customers use the software to serve their own and their customers' needs. The same is true of the value created by smart machines or macrosystems, like SABRE, Economost, CHIPS, UNIX, Excel, Turbotax, HTML, Navigator, and Java. The profits capturable by their innovators pale beside the user value such programs create for others. To develop and capture a major part of this value, competent software designers know they must work actively and interactively with customers, their end users, and their internal process managers—both as the software (or the product embedding it) is being developed and after it enters users' hands. Chapters 5 and 6 develop in detail many organizational and software-supported methodologies for doing this.

*Because of the low costs that software permits and the dominating importance of its value in use, the efficiency of program steps in software is nowhere near as important in value creation as are the functionality benefits it generates for users and the ease and effectiveness with which customers can use the software.* This customer value ratio is obscured in other innovation paradigms, which focus on decreasing the costs of design steps and shortening internal process times, rather than focusing on the internal learning and customer interaction processes, which seem costly, time-consuming and inefficient in themselves but create much greater value in use.

## THE INTERNET MODEL OF INNOVATION

Value in use is brought to its peak in Internet innovation. Under the traditional or physics-based model of innovation, a system once developed comes under the effects of positive entropy: the output or asset value of the physical system generally begins to deteriorate immediately upon introduction or use. By contrast, if learning feedback loops are built into them, software systems tend to undergo auto catalysis, "negative entropy," or positive gain as people link into the system, find entirely new potentials the designers did not anticipate, and enrich the software itself. Netscape conservatively estimates that on average each of its customers realizes twenty times more value from use of its software than Netscape's profits on the sale. The ratio is probably much higher.

## An Innovation Explosion

Like physical products, customers often use the software (and its hooks) in totally unexpected ways. The result is an absolute explosion of possibilities. Only twenty different software features can be arranged to interact or be sequenced in no fewer than $10^{18}$ different ways.[1] Anyone who ignores these potentials is foolish in the extreme. The classic example is the Internet, which expanded radically beyond its initial concept of providing efficient computer sharing between national laboratories into a whole virtual world of products, knowledge exchanges, and communications for its users. By 1999 Internet software sales in a variety of modes are estimated to be over $8 billion, but their total economic impact will be many times this high (see Figure 3.2).[2] Few of these potentials could be foreseen by the Net's founders.

Two key elements in maximizing benefits from software innovation systems are designing hooks onto which others can later connect their particular adaptations, innovations, or unanticipated demands, and providing means by which the system can upgrade itself from feedback concerning uses and innovations occurring at the nodes.

## Exploiting Auto-catalysis

Not surprisingly, the Internet has used these concepts well, as have other successful large-scale systems like COSMOS II, Landsat, Navstar, Economost, SWIFT, MCI, and AT&T, which transformed their industries. The power of these concepts in terms of economic impact is overwhelming. If one multiplies the gain of a software innovation by the exponential impact of the 30 million people now, and billions ultimately, who might use the innovation in their computer systems through the Internet, the potentials become unimaginable. The World Wide Web, through its graphics application capabilities, is daily stirring up imaginative possibilities for a plethora of totally new markets, products, ser-

**FIGURE 3.2**
**Worldwide Internet Software Revenue ($ billions)**

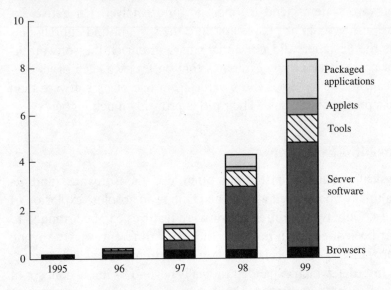

Source: For 1996–1999 "The Software Industry Survey," *Economist*, May 25, 1996, p. 517. Reproduced by special permission.

*Projected worldwide revenue from Internet software will double annually.*

vices, arts, and information potentials. And these will multiply and achieve huge geographical leverages as they diffuse throughout the world. Fully exploiting the auto-catalytic aspects of software innovations rests on three principles.

1. ***Diffusion.*** Software has the capacity to capture and diffuse any state of the art almost instantly and at low cost. No longer does one have to wait on the sequential processes of writing, publication, reproduction, introduction, and distribution to deliver a knowledge innovation to many remote points. In well-designed systems, once an innovation is available at any knowledge center on the system, it becomes available in detail (minus proprietary or security considerations) to all on the system. For example, when experts at the center of a financial house analyze a series of stock trends or investment opportunities, all brokerage nodes can use their results immediately. And the central system instantly commands all accounting and contact personnel's computers on how to comply with new regulations, avoid calculation errors, and control anticipated risks.

For large technical systems, software can instantly update the computers of all team and support participants with the most current design decisions, models in use, purchasing, operations, maintenance data, and so on. For example:

> • Silicon Graphics now has intranet connections for all of its more than 10,000 employees. Different departments have their own Web pages, which others can access through Silicon Junction software. There are now 200,000 Web pages located on 2,400 servers. The company reports "improved timeliness, accuracy, productivity, and strengthened teamwork" as major gains. In addition to facilitating design coordination, purchase order and sales order interaction costs have dropped by 50% each while accuracy and service levels have gone up. Internal designers can find information and self-coordinate on a scale never before possible.
>
> • Litton-PRC's Integrated Tactical Warning/Attack Systems Support (ISISS) program provides sustaining engineering support, modifications, and upgrades for the U.S. space and defense warning systems. Other PRC systems provide similar sustaining support for Jet Propulsion Laboratory's deep space systems, as well as full CADD,* documentation, fabrication, implementation, test, and quality assurance support for the space vehicles themselves.

2. *Open systems.* Maximizing innovation impact in software systems requires as open a system as possible, both to capture innovation at the nodes and to disseminate knowledge to all centers. Total transparency may not be feasible because of the need to protect confidential information or intellectual property at the center; however, as much openness as possible at interfaces will amplify effects. If the system can also capture the learning and use characteristics of those at the user nodes, it can build these into the options available elsewhere on the system. DARPANET was essentially set up as a system where all could share in this fashion and not duplicate efforts. UNIX went one step beyond, creating an open environment community where each person could rely heavily on others to contribute their tools and learning so all could do their jobs better. Openness dominates such systems except for elements that must purposely be kept opaque in order to ensure standard interfaces, availability of basic processing capabilities, and protection against compromises of proprietary or privacy codes or disruptions of the entire system. When used properly, productivity in research soars:

---

*Computer Assisted Design and Development.

• By interconnecting the more than 100 biological databases available on the World Wide Web, essentially complete cellular data are becoming available about specific biological entities like *E. coli* bacteria and *Haemophilus influenza.* By comparing such data with those of other organisms like yeast, worms, or flies, "the underlying determinants of living systems are becoming available at a truly astounding rate." By interconnecting such data, software is creating "the threshold of a new era in biological sciences."[3]

3. *Destruction of hierarchies.* With properly developed software, the need for traditional hierarchy disappears; and with reasonable management support, the often-sought-after goals of flat or fast-response network organizations can generally emerge. The software itself embodies many of the rules-disseminating and consistency-generating roles of hierarchies but without the bureaucracies that hierarchies usually entail. Yet it simultaneously multiplies innovation impacts by diffusing the firm's experience curve quickly throughout the entire enterprise, by providing positive hooks onto which customers can add value in their use domains, and by connecting internal innovators to worldwide sources of new knowledge from external specialists, suppliers, and research centers. (Chapters 4 through 9 describe how advanced firms are redesigning themselves around such systems.) The same principles applied to the national endeavor can engender a huge software-based auto-catalytic innovation system creating massive economic growth multipliers. (Chapters 11 through 13 show how.)

## HOW SOFTWARE INNOVATION ORGANIZATIONS HAVE CHANGED

The key to obtaining these gains lies in effectively connecting external user interfaces, internal self-learning innovation engines, and upstream technology and raw databases on an interactive basis. Why has it taken so long to merge these essential systems? Early software designs often involved use of complex machine languages and mathematical algorithms to perform specific functions. A priesthood of mathematicians emerged who alone understood the formulaic software needed for most systems and applications. They engaged in little direct interaction with non-expert users, who could understand neither the underlying formulas nor the 1s and 0s of binary language. As users in large companies and customer institutions became more sophisticated and higher-level languages became more common, users could participate more in software design. However, advanced software development stayed in specialists' hands within both hardware-producing and user enterprises. And most of the world (both within and outside their own organizations) tended to regard these programmers with awe and suspicion.

## From Priesthoods to Users

Then a transition occurred, led by time-sharing and menu-driven applications software. More innovation occurred at the users' keyboards. A few advanced algorithm (generally mathematician) creators like Seymore Cray still dominated the design of the highest powered computers' software and the more complex open system software of telephone, broadcast, and interactive communications networks, while specialist programmers developed most customized software and virtually all workbench and PC-level operating software. But most innovators on today's huge installed base of more than 50 million PCs are not programmers in any specialist sense. They customize prepackaged programs for their own use; and when they do write software, they use higher-level languages that vary from Word or Excel to Power Object. On networks, prepackaged software like Navigator and other browsers performs much of the finding and data-organizing steps of early innovation, while other advanced programs like Java and HTML allow user-innovators to access and combine inputs from other sources in endless variations for their own particular purposes.

The Internet and World Wide Web have become a software framework for innovating new services through combining various elements (in the form of software) sourced from many different nodes on the networks. Essentially all innovation on the Net now occurs at the participating nodes, with no governing hierarchy or organization giving orders to anyone. The ultimate in decentralized innovation has emerged. Users—not producer organizations or the central system—are the real innovators on the Web, Net, and intranets, and they capture virtually all the innovations' value for themselves.

Many companies' software units have paralleled this development sequence. Most successful innovative companies now provide infrastructures or system intranets that (like the Internet) embody the rules and sophisticated methodologies for their own use. These systems enable many remote organizational nodes to customize the firm's central knowledge capabilities and innovate for their own specialized (internal user or external) customer needs. Although directly connecting user interfaces, engines, and databases could substantially increase the rapidity

of advance and customer impacts of innovations, few enterprises have
fully developed and exploited their systems' integrated possibilities. They
have tended to suboptimize, directly interconnecting only one or two of
the three key systems. Winners in the future will integrate all three.

## Self-Learning Software Systems

In many cases, individual software systems can now learn from their
own algorithms and reprogram themselves to find new optimums for
their subsystems. Using built-in decision criteria, they constantly update themselves based on inputs from exogenous environments. The
National Institutes of Health, MIT, National Weather Service, and
NASA are developing large-scale self-learning systems for their areas of
special interest.[4] In industry, some companies, like the oil majors or retailers, have already integrated their market and operations modules for
interactive learning. Others have integrated their technology databases
and design systems. Self-learning software may teach a subsystem to
take actions directly, as learning-based chess, logistics, and stock trading programs do. Or they may signal humans (or other software systems) that new forms of analysis or action are needed. Some specific
examples will make the point:

• At Citibank genetic algorithms evolve models that can predict currency trends under various past market conditions. Neural networks
then discern which past market fits closest to current trends, and makes
forecasts accordingly. Since 1992 Citibank has earned 25% annual
profits on automated currency trading—much more than its human
traders. Deere and Co. supplements its production scheduling programs with genetic algorithms to reschedule operations when machines
go down. The genetic algorithms can learn from similar past situations
what related scheduling problems were associated with those events,
and can evolve optimized new schedules for the specific circumstance.
MCC combines neural nets and fuzzy logic to decipher reams of data
from chemical plant operations, leading to insights that manufacturing
people did not have in the past. These are tested in a simulation that
generates rules for optimizing the real plant. Users, including Eastman
Kodak, claim large savings.[5]

• Computer models recently revealed that, counterintuitively, approximately 25% of the nitrogen in the Chesapeake Bay comes from air pollution from as far west as Ohio. Conventional wisdom has been that
nitrogen oxide falls out from air fairly quickly. But once sufficient data

were available, the bay's actual nitrogen pollution levels could not be explained in terms of local conditions. Only when two separate sets of data were combined in a self-learning system did analysts discover totally new relationships that defined the problem quite differently, and suggested needed new policy solutions. The Environmental Protection Agency's National Environmental Supercomputing Center combined a digitally fed model of air flows across the country with another model that examined waterborne and earth-source pollution intrusions into the bay. Because of extensive historical data and substantial testing, each of the programs had been found reliable in its field. Both could be updated from direct data or through a relatively few on-site samples to establish local conditions. Such techniques now allow generation, updating, and testing of hypotheses about many complex phenomena, like ozone depletion, disease causes, radioactive contamination, and weather activity. But the models require constant updating of their inputs and testing with real-world experiments to verify their conclusions.

Simulations have long been used to generate and test new scenarios for strategic planning. Self-learning software has proved invaluable in optimizing many flow process, micromanufacturing (semiconductor), health monitoring, and logistics system designs. It is widely used in retailing, financial, communications, and utility service monitoring systems and provides some of the most important problem and opportunity identification capabilities for innovation in these fields. In both manufacturing and services, the ability to collect and analyze large systems' data at the micro level, through self-learning software, has become a key contributor to both innovation and fast-response customer services. Software in these fields has changed the opportunity search process in a fundamental fashion, allowing identification, tracking, and experimenting with small trends or anomalies that would otherwise be overlooked. American Express's Genesis, McKesson's Economost, American Airlines' SABRE, Kao's ECHO, and Trilogy's Conquer (all described elsewhere in this book) are only a few of many interesting approaches.

## FROM SELF-LEARNING TO OBJECT ORIENTATION

The most powerful new software systems for both self-learning and option generation are evolutionary and object-oriented systems. John von Neumann, Benoit Mandelbrot, Stuart Kauffman, and others early noted that the binary system had an analog in evolutionary systems. If one fed

into the computer a non-linear formula in which the value of the unknown, once computed, became an input value for the next iteration,
programs could both learn from themselves and become self-organizing
systems.[6] Given a simple set of rules to guide them, many tended to stabilize by finding a higher level of order and complexity that satisfied
preprogrammed "criterion functions," defining and prioritizing desired
outcome relationships.

Using object orientation, such evolutionary programs can go
even further. Object-oriented systems can emulate a series of self-
identified, precoded entities in large-scale economic, physical science, or life systems. Like atoms or cells in real-life systems these
"objects" are not directed by a higher-order program (or criterion
function), but only by their own individually encoded rules. They
constantly recombine or repel according to these rules until they
self-distruct, stabilize, or emerge into a pattern that is an entirely
new higher-order system—as astronomic gas clouds form into stars,
planetary systems, and galaxies. In the object-oriented version of
this process, each element, or object, acts like a "Velcro ball" with
precoded hooks that allow other balls to freely attach or interface
with it. As these balls combine, they can create entirely new assem-
blies, which may ultimately emerge as new higher-order subsystems
or systems with their own distinctive input and output characteristics; in other words, the software can innovate potential new subsystem and system solutions.

Object orientation has a strong applicability to large-scale service or
disaggregated product organizations where sub-elements of the system
can be discretely described but interactions cannot. Its concepts are
uniquely powerful in converting Internet-like infrastructures into cus-
tomer-producer interfaces capable of generating great innovation and
value. Given combinatory rules and operant criterion functions, objects
can randomly or systematically find each other and combine to create
innovative new solutions. Objects can provide, in easily manipulable
form, the minimum replicable units of data that are the essence of creating mass customization economies and flexibilities. Along with massive
parallel processing, they offer a new and powerful basis for managing
and innovating in such systems.

## Service Sector Applications

An especially broad area of application for object orientation is in service sector systems, which often require considerably less complicated

model manipulation within their engines than do science or production programs. Service manipulations tend to center on relatively simple processing (disaggregating, aggregating, mixing, and matching) of data from a wide variety of input variables existing in small discrete pockets of the database and relating these to a number of different customers' individual needs. For example:

• Retailing involves identifying and handling details about many thousands of products and even larger numbers of customers, but relatively simple stocking, accounting, and billing routines for handling operations. The real complexity is in tracking thousands of objects and their characteristics from suppliers through retail shelves and into customers' hands. Similarly, bank transactions involve handling many thousands of accounts, each with perhaps hundreds of transactions per day, related to many more thousands of transaction partners. Yet transactions within each account are usually relatively simple (addition, subtraction, and interest calculation) manipulations. The same is true for airline reservation, brokerage, home entertainment, communications, monetary exchange, and credit card activities. The bulk of such operations is in handling relatively simple calculations that relate highly disaggregated databases to many remote customer interfaces (with unique geographical, demographic, and use patterns).

Although there may be some very complex calculations at a service enterprise's center—such as air route optimization and aircraft deployment programs in airlines or the sophisticated economic models of financial houses—these depend on the databases and definable objects that make up the main transaction stream of the enterprise. The bulk of activity in many well-run service companies (like AT&T, Wal-Mart, or Federal Express) occurs inside such systems. If data are broken down into sufficient detail and their operating engines permit, companies can simultaneously optimize flexibility at the customer contact point and maximize operating efficiencies that flow from repeatability, experience curve effects, and integrated cost and quality control. Most accomplish this by (1) seeking the smallest replicable core unit of task or information that is useful across the enterprise, (2) developing micromeasures to manage processes and functions at this level, (3) mixing these microunits in a variety of combinations to match localized or individualized customers' needs, and (4) recapturing customer use and operating data patterns that allow the systems to learn from their own results, with or without parallel processing.

## Managing at the Minimum Replicable Unit Level

Managing and measuring critical performance variables at the smallest repeatable—individual customer, departmental, sales counter, activity, or stock-keeping unit—levels has become relatively common in services. So precise are many large enterprises' and nationwide chains' systems (e.g., MCI, American Express, Mrs. Fields, General Mills Restaurants Group) that their headquarters can tell within minutes, or even seconds, when something goes wrong in the system—at a client contact point or in a decentralized operating unit—and often precisely what the problem is. The concept is now so far advanced that some industries—like transportation, banking, communications, structural design, and medical research—can disaggregate the critical units of service production to the level of data blocks, packets, or "bytes" of information. These, and details about customer use, become the "objects" of object-oriented systems.

Broadcast, power, utility, banking, and communications transmission networks, which must analyze and correct problems within split seconds, have long had on-line electronic monitoring and control systems operating at such detailed levels. Often these systems automatically correct identified problems without human intervention. Electronic systems monitor signal strength and quality continuously, and they automatically switch to alternate routings or equipment if telephone, electric power, or nuclear plant measurements move outside preset boundaries. In many cases, however, human intervention is necessary. For example, CNN has found that a broadcast pause of more than ten seconds is a complete disaster, causing massive audience tune-outs. Hence, much of its organizational innovation has gone into preventing or handling such catastrophes quickly once the electronic system identifies them and before the customer ever knows there is an issue.

Strategic use of minimum replicable unit concepts began in the services (telecommunications, retailing, and transportation) industries. They boomed when the airlines in the mid-1960s found they could not realize the benefits of their new wide-bodied aircraft investments without learning to manage customer relationships at the micro level. Once identified and structured in detail, their micro-units of data about customers and operations became the source of many innovations that proved critical to competitiveness: routing, targeted pricing, seating, baggage handling, special services, frequent flyer incentives, minute-by-minute scheduling, massive operations coordination, and interconnected reservations and billing payment systems. Many experts credit the SABRE system, which captures detailed customer and flight data on this basis, with moving American Airlines from being one of the weakest airlines in the early 1970s to its later preeminence, while other previously prominent airlines (notably TWA, Pan Am, Braniff, and Eastern) fell into oblivion during deregulation.

## Creating Added Value

Mass production benefits from standardization are not the real purpose of focusing on the smallest replicable unit of operations. Much more interesting are the strategic and innovation opportunities such systems reveal and help implement. The larger the organization, the more refined these replicability units may practically be—and the higher their leverage for creating value-added gains for customers. Information systems (including both access and manipulation capabilities) represent one of the few areas where true economies of scale still apply. Greater volume allows a larger company to (1) collect more detail about its individual operating and market segments, (2) efficiently analyze these data at more disaggregated levels, (3) experiment with these detailed segmentations in ways smaller concerns cannot, and (4) target operating programs and innovation to individuals and groups in a more customized fashion. Increased granularity can allow more potentially economic variations and higher payoffs for large companies than small. In two major examples:

• American Express is the only independent credit card company with a large travel service. By capturing in the most disaggregated possible form (essentially data bytes) the details of transactions that its 25 million traveler, shopper, retailer, lodging, and transportation customers put through its credit card and travel systems, it can mix and match the patterns and capabilities that each group seeks or has available to add value for each segment in ways most of its competitors cannot. It can identify lifestyle changes (like marriage or moving) or match forthcoming travel plans with its customers' specific buying habits to notify them of special promotions, product offerings, or services that American Express's retailers are presenting in their local or planned travel areas. It can also offer its 2 million retailer and transportation customers more demographic or comparative analyses of customer buying patterns, shifting travel patterns, or needs for individualized wheelchair, pickup, or other convenience services. Until Visa and Mastercard became even larger, no one could match the value-added that American Express could provide its individual consumers and commercial customer groups.

• General Mills Restaurants Group's sophisticated use of technology has been its key to innovating both a friendlier, more responsive atmosphere and lower competitive prices in its unique dinner house chains: Red Lobster, Olive Garden and Bennigan's. At the strategic level, it taps into the most extensive disaggregated databases in its industry and uses conceptual mapping technologies to define precise unserved needs in the restaurant market. Using these inputs, a creative internal and external team of restaurateurs, chefs, and culinary institutes arrives at a few concept designs for test. Using other models derived from its databases, the group can pretest and project the nationwide impact of selected concepts and even define the specific neighborhoods most likely to support that concept. Other technologies combine to designate optimum restaurant sitings and create the architectural designs likely to be most successful at each.

On an operations level, by mixing and matching in great detail the continuously collected performance data from its own operations and laboratory analyses, GMR can specify or select the best individual pieces and combinations of kitchen equipment to use at each location. It can optimize each facility's layout to minimize personnel, walking distances, cleanup times, breakdowns, and operations or overhead costs. Once a restaurant is functioning, GMR has an integrated electronic point-of-sale and operations management system directly connected to headquarters computers for monitoring and analyzing daily operations and customer trends. An inventory, sales tracking, personnel, and logistics forecasting program automatically adjusts plans, measures performance, and controls staffing levels and products for holidays, time of day, seasonality, weather, special offers, and promotions. All of these lower innovation investments, cycle times, and risks.

At the logistics level, using one of industry's most sophisticated satellite, earth-sensing, and database sytems, GMR can forecast and track fisheries and other food sources worldwide. It can predict long- and short-term seafood yields, species availability, and prices; and it can plan its menus, promotions, and purchases accordingly. It knows its processing needs in such detail that it teaches suppliers exactly how to size, cut, and pack fish for maximum market value and lowest handling costs to GMR, while achieving minimum waste and shipping costs for the supplier. Its software systems have allowed GMR to innovate in important ways that others could not.

Critical to effective innovation system design are conceptualizing and implementing this smallest replicable unit concept as early as possible in the software design process. Summing disaggregated data later is much easier than moving from a more aggregated system to a greater refinement of detail. Further, highly disaggregated data often capture unexpected experience patterns, suggesting the potentials for innovation that more summary data would obscure. Much of the later power and flexibility of American Airlines', McKesson's, Benneton's, and National Car Rental's systems derived from making this choice correctly. Less successful competitors' systems did not; they usually chose a larger replicability unit in order to save initial installation costs or designed their systems around their existing accounting or organizational structures rather than around the data blocks that were relevant to operations and especially to customers.

Among the classics of such problems are the banks that captured their data around the account numbers of their clients rather than around the details of each transaction, the particular customer's characteristics and use patterns, and the external market events that made different financial products more (or less) attractive in a given situation. Similarly, in environmental research many ecological models focused solely on animal classes, soil compositions, flora classes, climatic factors, or toxicity levels and essentially ignored the crucial interactions among all these subsystems. Until new data definitions (or software that could make the interfaces between these subsystems transparent) appeared, researchers could not ask or assess the most crucial problems in ecological science.

## Object Orientation and Intranets for User-Based Innovation

Object-oriented technologies allow programmers to design systems more economically using minimum replicable level concepts. Individual objects contain both the desired variables broken down to minimum replicable levels and the methods (embedded instructions) allowing that object to carry out actions. System-wide innovation can occur either by using the objects as elements in a designed system or through employing them in genetic, evolutionary, or other self-learning processes. Object orientation allows users at each major node on internal networks to call forth and combine elements from all other nodes easily. They can readily design customized services for local customers, without breaking any of the firm's operating principles, by using objects or software "buttons" that embed these rules. If the right information and incentives exist at the customer contact point, rapid innovation can occur instantaneously with direct customer participation. By incorporating many of the rules, interfaces, and best-practice patterns that bureaucracies formerly enforced, object orientation provides a long step toward the ultimate in decentralizing innovation processes: disaggregation to the individual user level.

Even without object orientation, many companies now use well-developed intranets for internal flexibility and efficiency and to leverage their professional and creative intellect for customers. For example:

• Arthur Andersen Worldwide has more than 82,000 people in some 360 offices in seventy-six countries. Its ANET is a T-1 and frame relay system linking most of these offices by data, voice, and video. ANET captures the history of Andersen's contacts with major clients worldwide and places these in accessible customer reference files. In addition, auditors or other professionals who find unique solutions to problems can introduce them into the system through carefully indexed subject files available to all. Any field professional can query others throughout the system on an electronic bulletin board to seek alternatives or potential solutions to a new problem. The Andersen Notes system provides an interactive environment for contact people to develop solutions jointly. Andersen's increasing size and complexity make it impossible for its professionals to rely on personal knowledge of whom to call for information. Instead, through its software systems, Andersen can instantly assemble needed intellect from all over the world to generate complex professional analyses and innovative solutions. These systems, when combined with highly specialized software in Andersen's various offices, have led various partners to describe the company's distinctive competency as "empowering people to deliver better quality technology-based solutions to clients in a shorter time."

Internally, over 20% of the one thousand largest companies have intranets, and their use is growing faster than the Internet's. Netscape Communications estimates that over 70% of its software goes to the internal networks. And Zona Research estimates that 43% of the $1.1 billion in Web servers goes to this market, moving to an estimated $4 billion before the end of the 1990s. Such networks use many of the same principles and software as the Internet. The only real difference is that intranets are privately owned and are fenced off by firewalls that let them look outward, while others cannot look in.

## Innovation, the Internet, and a New Economics of Computing

Externally, TCP/IP communications standards, HTML, and various Web-compatible software languages, like Java (a 64-kilobyte virtual machine that runs just as well on one PC architecture as another), now provide the basis for interactive innovation using the power of all nodes on the Internet. Entrepreneurs can leverage their innovations enormously through customers who combine them with others available on the Net, creating new products of their own and disseminating these modifications to countless others who may remodify them for their own or further customers' use. As *Business Week* noted, the Web and Mosaic now provide a huge "virtual disk drive" of sources and uses for innovation.[7]

With Java-like software widespread, software companies will not have to create (nor will they benefit from) unique versions of their products for each manufacturer's computer. Each customer will merely download versions and updates of applets containing desired databases and applications from the Net. In their own way, the applets of the Java system become the minimum replicable elements of effective computing, while the network becomes the computer itself. Such software may well restructure the entire telecomputer industry and redefine the nature of intellectual property.[8] New pricing methodologies (e.g., paying single-use fees for applet software or individual databases) seem likely to cause a secondary revolution in distribution and pricing systems for software, publications, and digital entertainment systems, further eroding the lines between "pipelines," applications, and content.

A whole new economics of innovation is likely to emerge. After the initial investment in software development and debugging is completed, marginal costs of software production and sales are essentially zero. And once the software achieves sufficient penetration, an infinite number of modifications can be sold to supplement it. Once they adopt and learn a new system, existing users are reluctant to scrap their time and financial investments in a software platform. The original software innovator can offer ever more functionality to its customers at low cost and high margins, making it even more difficult for competitors to enter, while supplementary innovations cause sales to soar for all products associated with the software. There appear to be no negative economies of scale in software production, so the strong get stronger until a totally new platform is innovated. This "Microsoft or Nintendo effect" may change the very nature of competition—and needed regulation.

• The Doom three-dimensional game, Maxus's Sim, and Netscape demonstrated this effect on the Web. The basic engine for Doom was created in the form of shareware, which was then put on the Internet. Users could download and test a small but enticing version of the game for free. If they wanted to go further with Doom, they had to send in $25 to get more exciting add-ons for different levels of the game. This software allowed them to have a startling first-person view of various adventures transpiring on the screen, and it was easy for players to write their own scenarios for Doom, creating their own functionalities and tailoring games to their own tastes in endless variety. Similarly Maxus's Sim created an engine from which a huge variety of applications resulted. Consultants or clients could create Sim-based models, customized for their own specific end-user purposes. In this form of innovation, system designers no longer have to think of programming for specific end user needs; instead they design the user interface as shareware and leverage their own ideas through the infinite creativity of their customers. Netscape initially offered its browser free to anyone on the Net and encouraged others to distribute it privately. Once the software had high penetration, Netscape began to charge for further installations and related software.

• In a commercial mode, clothing designers, salespeople, buyers, and manufacturers work together to provide precisely the clothing the buyers want. Virtually any product—from pagers (Motorola), to bathroom fixtures (American Standard), to automobiles (Toyota)—can now be interactively custom designed to meet the specific and varying needs of niched markets and individual customers on this basis. Once the product enters the marketplace, customers and various suppliers can monitor sales and quickly ramp up, phase in, or phase out different features, styles, models, colors, or fabrics to satisfy consumers' desires, reversing the usual innovation process. End users now essentially design products and define feature mixes for a variety of producers worldwide, cutting investments, time delays, and risks enormously.

## REDEFINING INTELLECTUAL PROCESSES AND ORGANIZATIONS

Most past management thinking about innovation has assumed a fairly sequential, physically bounded process which resembles a process flowchart or linear-mechanical assembly line. Many executives even try to chart a complete step-by-step process in advance. Their models feature sequential investigation, discovery, invention, reduction to practice, scale-up, introduction, and readjusment processes—all with their "key decision points" and "gates" to the next stage. This view of the world makes managers very comfortable. It all seems so rational and orderly that many enterprises try to control their innovation processes using their charted sequence. Unfortunately, this approach usually turns out to be very costly and time-consuming. Equally unfortunately, innovation rarely happens this way and trying to force it to do so is often counter-productive.

Innovation tends to occur in fitful, chaotic ways, with many random interactions and unexpected, often unpredictable consequences. The highly interactive, circular, self-learning steps of genetic or ecological self-organizing systems or interactive object-oriented programs seem more appropriate models of the way modern innovations occur. Starting with clear success criteria, experimenters continually explore, assemble, and break elements of a system into new units and combinations until they find a combination (in software) that works together, yet optimizes their desired technical and economic success criteria. Once an appropriate interactive organizational concept and software structure are in place, the innovation process can be as decentralized and time-compressed as one desires. Parts of the work can easily proceed in parallel because the software allows independence yet disciplines the interaction rules among component systems. To compress time even more, many innovators operate projects on a parallel basis or on a three-shift, twenty-four-hour day, handing off development (through software) from one design group and geographical time zone to another (Asia, to Europe, to America) at the end of each shift. Once one competitor does this, others must follow or fall ever farther behind.

## Benefits of More Fully Integrated Systems

Software integration across the innovating organization's databases, engines, and user interfaces, can avoid many traditional costs and time delays in product design, physical prototyping, and multiple testing in real-world environments. Such systems not only compress time and lower the direct costs of development, they decrease the standby physical investments needed for test facilities. By tapping into the best worldwide bases of physical data and the broadest possible customer use bases, such systems also leverage the intellectual value of the firm's, suppliers', and customers' development personnel substantially.

Many of the traditional problems of scale-up disappear as the software "learns" and captures data from its own experiments and the actual experiences of customers and other laboratories with similar products and circumstances. Management can predict scaling issues much more accurately than it could afford to if it had to test and retest physical models. Because no model, by definition, can handle all the complexities of reality, some physical modeling is generally essential before final commercial prototyping. Nevertheless, experience shows that software premodeling and testing of prototypes can shorten cycle times, decrease costs, increase the interrelationships tested, and diminish risks taken by orders of magnitude.

## Capturing Experience and Explaining Why

Software management—the capacity to access and effectively manipulate available physical science, operations, and customer use information—becomes at least as important as the organization's own technologists' knowledge about the particular design field. The system's models become learning systems, updating their databases' and engine's capabilities constantly from new knowledge created in the physical science world and modifications introduced by customers' experiences. A much smaller interdisciplinary team using well-designed software can usually obtain higher-value results than a large team utilizing a physical experimental approach. Perhaps the most important point, however, is that such software upgrades the entire learning capability and output of the development process.

Under the old mechanical-chemical engineering design paradigm, large-scale systems' interactions were too complex and interrelated to be well understood. To overcome unknowns required a series of "build 'em and bust 'em" experiments and an expensive shakedown of the plant during scale-up. By combining process science, physical constraints, and consumer environments in an electronic model, experimenters obtain a detailed (and documented) level of process insights they otherwise could not obtain. They understand why things do (or do not) work, thus gaining a reliable basis for recalibrating their intuition. In turn, this knowledge educates experimenters to innovate faster and refines the knowledge originally put into the software. The software also captures the experience curves of external scientific researchers and diffuses the corporation's total knowledge immediately to even its most inexperienced technologists. By combining the knowledge of customers and the knowledge of the science world, properly designed systems create a potential for a large multiple of value—company knowledge × customer knowledge × scientific knowledge—due to increased interactiveness. The old physically bounded paradigm of innovation is massively inefficient.

## MANAGING SOFTWARE DEVELOPMENT

To exploit such opportunities, companies must be able to manage and innovate in software themselves, a need that will undoubtedly grow as complexities grow and cycle times decrease. But as many have learned to their regret, the very bright, independent people engaged in software development make the activity notoriously difficult to manage.[9] The most innovative companies, in products or services, seem to converge on several approaches, each useful for a different strategic purpose and requiring a quite different management style. Nevertheless, there are several characteristics that all these approaches share. They all simultaneously enable both independent and interdependent innovation, and all involve close interactive customer and expert participation. Like most other innovations, all software is first created in the mind of a highly skilled, motivated, and individualistic person (hence, independence). But to be useful, the software (or device it supports) usually must connect to other software (or hardware) systems and meet specific user needs (hence interdependence). Interesting innovation problems are generally so complex that they require high expertise from many "non-programmer" technical people and users for solution.[10] And users may vary from being computer illiterate to very sophisticated.

How do successful companies achieve the needed balance between deep professional knowledge, creative individualism, coordinated integration, and active customer participation? Table 3.1 suggests the wide variety and scale of some major players. (For others like IBM, EDS, PRC, Andersen Consulting, or CSC Index, accurate figures are not available.) Their strategies and styles, like those of in-house software groups, tend to cluster into five categories depending in part on the nature of the application. Distinctly different approaches are used for: (1) small discrete applications, (2) intermediate size operating systems, (3) large integrated systems, (4) support systems designed to requirements, and (5) legacy system improvements or redesign.

## INDIVIDUAL INVENTOR-INNOVATORS (SMALL, DISCRETE APPLICATIONS)

As in the physical sciences, knowledgeable independent inventors and small groups create the largest number of software innovations, particularly at the applications level. In essence, a few highly motivated individuals perceive an opportunity or need, assemble software resources from existing databases and systems, choose an interlinking language and architecture on which to work, and interactively design the program and subsystem steps to satisfy the need as they perceive it. Those who want to sell the software externally first find some real-life application or customer, consciously debug the software for that purpose, then modify

**TABLE 3.1**
**Top Twenty Software Vendors, 1995**

|  | Revenue ($ millions) |
| --- | --- |
| 1. Microsoft | 7,419 |
| 2. Oracle | 3,777 |
| 3. Computer Associates International | 3,196 |
| 4. Novell | 1,986 |
| 5. SALP AG | 1,887 |
| 6. Sybase | 957 |
| 7. Adobe Systems | 762 |
| 8. Informix | 709 |
| 9. American Management Systems | 632 |
| 10. Sterling Software | 610 |
| 11. Compuware | 580 |
| 12. SAS Institute | 562 |
| 13. Software AG | 552 |
| 14. Cadence Design Systems | 548 |
| 15. Autodesk | 544 |
| 16. Sunguard Data Systems | 533 |
| 17. Computervision | 507 |
| 18. HBO & Co. | 496 |
| 19. Intuit | 490 |
| 20. Parametric Technology | 441 |

Source: Broadview Associates, reported in "Survey of the Software Industry,"
*Economist*, May 25, 1996.

Note: Packaged software accounts for over 50 percent of revenue of those listed.

and upgrade it until it works in many users' hands for a variety of different purposes. In 1995 alone, venture capitalists invested more than $1.2 billion in such enterprises.

Many important computer software innovations, from Visicalc to Mosaic and Java, started this way, as have virtually all video game programs and new customized programs to solve individual local enterprise problems. Millions of inventor-innovators use largely blocks-and-arrows diagrams and trial-and-error methods to design new software for themselves, improve smaller software systems, or create special new effects. Like other small company innovators, there is no evidence that the process is either efficient or consistent in form. Problem identification, imagination, expertise, persistence, and careful interactive testing with customers are the most usual determinants of success.[11] The sheer numbers of people trying to solve specific problems means that many small innovations prove useful in the marketplace, although a much greater number undoubtedly die along the way. Many larger companies have learned how to harness the enormous potentials of independent software inventors to leverage their own internal software capabilities. For example:

• MCI, as a corporate strategy, has long encouraged outside inventor-entrepreneurs to come up with new software applications (fitting its system's interfaces) to provide new services over its main communication lines. AT&T–Bell Labs created UNIX to assist computer science research. AT&T later gave UNIX to universities and, eventually, to others, slowly realizing that as individuals created programs to provide local solutions or to interface with others, they would require more communications interconnections. UNIX was consciously designed to encourage individuals to interact broadly and to share their useful solutions with others. The hooks it provided later allowed AT&T to sell vastly more services than it could have possibly formally forecast or innovated internally.

• Similarly, Nintendo Co. Ltd. has provided one of the world's most successful platforms for innovation by independent software producers. Its licensing programs, linked to use of Nintendo's marketing and distribution capabilities, have created more independent millionaires than any other Japanese company. And its success created the huge electronic games industry that now branches into other entertainment fields. Nintendo controls and leverages the crucial linkages between its own systems and the marketplace, while providing enough of an open interface to allow thousands of individuals to develop new game software.

Other companies use similar network interface and distribution controls to encourage yet coordinate both internal and external software innovators. The best have developed specific incentive systems and access rules to stimulate both innovation and lateral diffusion of new solutions throughout the company. Chapters 5 and 6 provide multiple examples.

## Small Interactive Teams (Operating Systems)

In many of the larger applications houses—like Microsoft, Oracle, and Netscape—small, informal, interactive teams are the core of the innovative process. The complexity of these firms' programs is too great for a single individual to develop them alone. In most cases, the target concept is new, discrete, and relatively limited in scope. Relying heavily on individual talents and personal interactions, these firms typically have made little use of computer-aided software engineering (CASE) tools or formalized monitor programs to manage development. They operate in a classic skunk works style, disciplined by the very software they are developing. For example:

• Microsoft tries to develop its applications programs with very small teams. Major programs typically begin with Bill Gates or a few of his "architects" agreeing to the key performance parameters and the broad systems structures needed to ensure interfaces with other Microsoft programs and its desired customer positioning. Overall program goals are broken down into a series of targets for smaller subsystems, each capable of being produced by a two- to five-person team, which then operates quite independently. Interfaces are controlled at several levels: programmatic specifications to make operating systems perform compatibly, application interfaces to interconnect component systems (like memory or file management), and customer interfaces to maintain user compatibility. Other than these, the original target functionalities, and time constraints, there are few rigidities. Detailed targets change constantly as teams find out what they can and cannot accomplish for one purpose and how that affects other subsystems.

Microsoft's key coordinating mechanism is the "build-test-drive." At least every week, but more often two to three times per week, each group compiles its subsystem so the entire program can be run with all new code, functions, and features in place. In the "builds," test suites created by independent test designers and the software itself become the disciplining agents. If teams do not correct errors at this point, interactions between components quickly become so vast that it is impossible to fit all program pieces together, even though each subsystem might work well alone. As soon as possible, the program team proposes a version for a specific (though limited) real-world purpose, gives it to a customer to test in that use, and monitors its actual use in detail. Once it works for that purpose, the program goes to other customers for beta tests and modification in other uses. This approach both decreases developmental risks and takes advantage of customers' suggestions and innovations.[12]

# Monitor Programs (Large Integrated Systems)

Such informal approaches serve particularly well for small freestanding or applications programs, although Microsoft has used them for larger operating systems. In most cases, designers of larger operations or systems software find some form of "monitor program" useful. These monitors establish the frameworks, checkpoints, and coordinating mechanisms to make sure all critical program elements are present, compatible, cross-checked, and properly sequenced. They allow larger enterprises to decentralize the writing of code among different divisions or locations while ensuring that all functions and components work properly together. No element is forgotten or left to chance, and interface standards are clearly enforced. Weapons systems, AT&T, and Arthur Andersen have used this programming method successfully. Many firms have found that such formal monitors both lower the cost and increase the reliability of large-scale systems designs. For example:

• Andersen Consulting usually must provide under contract both a unique solution for each customer's problem and a thoroughly tested, fault-free systems product. For years Andersen has combined a highly decentralized process for writing each section of the code with a rigorous centralized system for program coordination and control. At the center of its process have been two tools, METHOD/1 and DESIGN/1. METHOD/1 is a carefully designed, step-by-step methodology describing a predictable, repeatable process for modularizing and controlling all the steps needed to design any major systems program. METHOD/1 has a variety of "routes" to use in different increments for different environments and project sizes. In a typical example, at the highest level there are roughly ten "phases," each broken into approximately five "segments." Below this are a similar number of "tasks" for each job and several "steps" for each task. METHOD/1 defines the exact elements the programmer needs to go through at that particular stage of the process and coordinates software design activities, estimated times, and costs for each step.

DESIGN/1, an elaborate CASE tool, keeps track of all programming details as they develop and disciplines the programmer to define each element carefully. It governs relationships among all steps in the METHOD/1 flowchart to avoid losing data, entering infinite loops, using illegal data, and so on. In addition to ensuring that each step in the METHOD/1 is carefully executed, it allows customers to enter "pseudo-data" or code so they can periodically test the look and feel of screen displays and to check data entry formats for reasonableness and utility during development. The integrated METHOD/1 and DE-SIGN/1 environment is extremely complex, taking up some 50 megabytes on high-density diskettes. A dedicated team of specialists continually maintains and enhances these programs.[13]

Many organizations have found that such formal monitors lower the cost, increase the reliability, and allow decentralized development of large-scale systems.

## Design to Requirements (Support Systems)

The most common approach to developing internal operating software is neither as informal as Microsoft's nor as formal as Andersen's. It is a combination of the two approaches. The process tends to follow this general sequence:

1. Establish goals and requirements (what functionalities, benefits, and performance standards are sought).
2. Define the scope, boundaries, and exclusions from the system (what the system's limits are).
3. Establish priorities among key elements and performance requirements (what is needed, highly desired, wanted, acceptable in background, or dispensable if necessary).
4. Define interrelationships (what data sets, field sizes, flow volumes, and cross-relationships are essential or desirable).
5. Establish what constraints must be met (in terms of platforms, network typologies, costs, timing, etc.) in designing the system.
6. Break the total problem down into smaller, relatively independent subsystems.
7. For each subsystem, set and monitor specific performance targets, interface standards, and timing-cost limits using agreed-on software test regimes and monitoring programs. Often the design software itself provides the ultimate documentation and discipline for all groups.

Because quite dissimilar skills may be needed for each, different teams typically work on the database system, the engine (or platform) system, and market interface systems. A separate interfunctional group (perhaps under a program manager) usually coordinates activities across divisions or subsystems. Using a combination of software and personalized performance scheduling and evaluation techniques, this group—supplemented by independent test designers—ensures that task functionalities, component and subsystem performance, time frames, and dependencies between tasks, output, quality, and priorities are maintained. If the software under design has to support existing processes, successful cross-functional teams typically reengineer the processes first, then design the software prototypes while interactively engaging users throughout the full design and implementation process. Top-level executives do not need to understand the details of software programming, but they do need to see that all these management processes are in place and operate effectively when their firms design their own software.

## Highly Disciplined Procedures (Integrating and Improving Legacy Systems)

Often major innovations require the large-scale integration and further development of already installed (legacy or specialized "stovepipe") systems to accomplish new or improved functionalities. Standards tend to be absent or inconsistent among the installed systems; information is distributed and networks are disjointed; data may be unsynchronized, inconsistent, and subject to very different security requirements. Typical examples are ecological, battlefield, and law enforcement systems. Innovations involving such integration obviously require a discipline beyond that necessary even to design a large scale system from scratch. A few large companies like PRC, CSC, and EDS specialize in such systems. They tend to develop their own approaches (like PRC's Software Process Improvement Plan, SPIP) to coordinate the multiple levels of problems involved. Working toward the Software Engineering Institute's capability maturity model (CMM) requirements, these companies try to develop reliable, reusable software modules for broadly applicable subsystems, to update these continually through feedback from actual operational use, and to make sure all key personnel have access to the necessary tools and processes through electronically updated reference guides and libraries.

No single description can capture the full complexity of this approach. However, most of the major practitioners have reduced their approaches to hard copy and electronic manuals, which they will share with potential users. A well-developed system is Litton-PRC's approach:

- Litton-PRC, in early 1993, initiated a process (called Phoenix) with its major programs to systematize and improve its already successful approach to designing, integrating, and improving large-scale systems for the federal government. These programs usually involve major legacy systems as well as modern client-server implementations. Designed around a virtual private internet and a Process Asset Library, (PAL), the PRC system handles the integrated needs of program managers (for communications, performance measurement, overall customer coordination, resource utilization capability), task managers (status, action items, metrics, deliverables), intergroup coordination (schedules, tool information, action items, personnel data), training (needs assessment, training materials, records, etc.), program development, life cycle management, metrics, and lessons learned. Except for confidential information (like personnel records) the system is open to all PRC professionals. Each activity has its own server connected to the network.

Since PRC's strategy focuses on delivering reliable, state-of-the-art software, with predictable cost and performance characteristics, it tries to the maximum extent possible to modularize its software subsystems, maintain detailed interface and compatibility controls, and constantly update all its systems based on actual user experience. Through standard browser technology, the PAL provides access to a thousand files, including corporate processes, briefings, document templates, plans, schedule templates, standards, and procedures that ensure coordinating data are available at all locations. PRC is now implementing an "information finds you system," in order to better fulfill the information needs of all personnel.

Supporting this system are a software process improvement plan which details PRC's approach to software improvement and a PAL Document Tree of PRC software documents, manuals, policies, processes, and products. Organizationally, PRC uses the quality improvement approach originally developed by Florida Power and Light Co. Working with customers and other stakeholders, the team develops a "theme statement" of the priority areas needing improvement, along with quality and performance indicators negotiated with the customer to make sure expectations are reasonable and valid. It then decomposes each associated area into a concise problem description and set of targets for improvements based on these goals and the status of systems currently in place. The team analyzes existing problems for root causes, develops and analyzes potential solutions to each problem, predicts obstacles for implementation, and prepares an action plan (process flowchart) for implementation, monitoring, recording results, standardizing, and replicating the improvements.

As PRC builds each phase of a system, customer-developer teams interact on it and get feedback from users. Often over the course of a project, initial priority demands come to appear routine, and unexpected variations or new functionalities emerge as important and valuable to the customer. Thus, one of PRC's program managers' main tasks is to interact constantly with the development team and users to maintain goal alignment and expectations. PRC says its customers are happiest "when they have been part of the solution, have a say in how well we're doing each step, and have been able to utilize incremental builds of functionality released on a frequent basis."[14]

## SUMMARY

Software has become the key element in almost all advanced design and innovation. It is critical to effectiveness at all levels of the innovation process from basic research to post-introduction support of the innovation in the marketplace. It offers infinite opportunities to shorten, merge, or eliminate entire steps in the innovation process, compressing time cycles and lowering risks more than any other contributor to the process can. Even more important, it allows interaction with customers and users in ways that substantially increase the innovations' value in use. The processes of software design provide a powerful new paradigm for innovation, the ultimate forms of which are now appearing in self-learning systems, on interactive intranets within enterprises, and on the Internet and World Wide Web. These are (1) innovations self-designed by users for their own specific purposes, and (2) software-generated innovations from self-learning, evolutionary, and object-oriented software.

Software processes will forever change innovation thinking and practice worldwide. It behooves all managers to reexamine their existing innovation and software management processes in light of these potentials. Using illustrative practices from some of the world's leading software developers, we have tried to provide guidelines for thinking about these issues. Later chapters provide more explicit, top management, middle management, and micro-organization level approaches to implementation.

# PART II

# NEW ORGANIZATION FORMS

# 4

# Beyond Teams:
# Independent Collaboration

M odels that attempt to conceptualize or manage innovation in linear, sequential stages, as if it were a production process, are useful only for less complex, extrapolative, or production-installation types of situations. Teams are helpful when technical complexity is higher but the number of interacting variables is sufficiently limited that a relatively few people can master the totality without horrendous interpersonal costs. In an increasing number of innovations, however, complexity is so high (as in advanced physics, aerospace, communications, or biotechnology projects) that teams, as they are ordinarily defined, cannot cope as well as collaboration among a large number of relatively independent units. For these innovations, and all software or Internet-based innovations, a more appropriate set of process analogs would be fermentation vats, termite nests, stewpots, or self-learning object-oriented software systems. What do these analogs have in common?

- Each process is extremely nonlinear yet leads to a sought-after goal. Each is dominated by independent action, yet success requires interdependence among all elements.
- The totality of ingredient interactions is essentially infinite for each system. There is no total systemic control, but there are certain implicit rules regulating the elements' interactions. Extrinsic forces can change the behavior of the whole system.
- It is statistically and intellectually impossible to predict the precise

output of any of these systems at the point of initiation. The result is, by definition, a surprise—an innovation.

Although at first seemingly anathema to managers, independent collaborations are common in basic research, large-scale system developments, international finance or design projects, multi-sourced component systems, software design, and creative real estate, legal publishing, or entertainment deals. In almost any significant innovation, technologists and innovating enterprises can interconnect (inside or outside the organization) with myriad potential technology solutions, knowledge and materials suppliers, direct and functional competitors, and customers or marketplaces, through a variety of feedback loops affecting possible outcomes in an infinite number of ways.[1] A project's scale, needed degree of specialist knowledge for different subsystems, or potential number of interactions often make a large coordinated team too unwieldy or motivationally unproductive to be effective. Frequently, only highly specialized units, individuals, or small teams can provide the deep expertise and psychological intensity to make subsystem advances. And only well-developed software can enable, coordinate, and interpret the needed levels of complexity and interactiveness effectively.[2]

## THE SOFTWARE BACKBONE OF INDEPENDENT COLLABORATION

Software becomes the backbone and the central element in managing the kind of disaggregated, individualistic, collaborative innovative activity that increasing scientific complexity and corporate hypercompetition are forcing. Many advanced industry and service leaders—including such diverse enterprises as Sun Microsystems, Microsoft, Bechtel, Honda, AMR, Nike, Boeing, NovaCare, Andersen Consulting, Kao, Wal-Mart, and Merrill Lynch—are exploiting this paradigm successfully in parts of their operations. However, in these companies, like most others, there are many different levels of innovative activity going on.[3] Each may need to be managed quite differently.

### Levels of Innovation

The most common innovation levels and their associated organizational and software approaches are:

*Level 1: Simple solutions,* applying well-understood principles to achieve a unique solution for a new problem. Although the solution may be creative—such as the design of a new machine, textile, or building—results are achievable through normal engineering, suggestion, and construction techniques. Such situations commonly call for individual research, team analysis, and invention, coordinated through scheduling, interface rules, and modeling software.

***Level 2: System solutions*** within existing knowledge bounds, but involving systematically changed interactions among many relatively well-understood variables. Such projects commonly call for a cross-functional or TQM* team type of approach, coordinated by schedules and interface rules, plus system software.

***Level 3: Inventive solutions,*** pushing beyond the established scope of existing disciplines, without creating genuine paradigm shifts. As Gore-Tex in fabrics or Java on networks did, they substantially change the capacity of the whole system without requiring major changes in design or use of other subsystems. These solutions commonly utilize networked individuals and teams, disciplined primarily by scientific rules, system requirements, and software tests of options.

***Level 4: Radical inventions*** (like scanning tunneling microscopes, angiogenesis blockers, hybridomas, or PCR technology), occurring outside existing paradigms. These usually involve interactions among multiple technical domains and change virtually all aspects of existing processes' operating functions. Such innovations overturn past paradigms, force reassessment of old rules, and require new behaviors from those associated with many subsystems. They commonly require independent collaboration disciplined by scientific rules, software models, and system constraints.

***Level 5: Totally new phenomena,*** once-in-a-lifetime discoveries (like transistors, lasers, biochips, buckey balls, recombinant DNA, and high-temperature superconductors). Instead of revolutionizing existing industries, these innovations create whole new industries and domains of scientific inquiry. They generate entirely new sets of rules, players, and interconnections among activity nodes. Such phenomena mainly involve independent collaboration, disciplined classification definitions and interface rules, and network and modeling software.

All are significantly enhanced by software support. However, the organizing mode shifts in moving up the scale of advance from levels 1 and

---

*TQM: Total quality management.

2 (involving mainly individuals and teams within enterprises), toward levels 3 through 5, where widespread individual and small group collaboration across multiple organizations or enterprises becomes the rule. Individual leadership, teams, and macro-organizations like those described in Chapter 8 are very useful in levels 1 through 3. For cxample:

• Wal-Mart, under Sam Walton, was a classic of level 1 innovation. Walton created a strong culture for independent collaboration. He noted, "We're constantly doing crazy things to capture the attention of our folks and lead them to think up surprises of their own. We like to see them do wild things in the stores, things that are fun for the customers and fun for our associates. . . . The culture encourages you to think up all sorts of things to break the mold and fight monotony." Walton claimed that over 90% of all Wal-Mart's good ideas came from the grass roots. To stimulate employees, Walton said, "The more you share profits with your associates the more profit will accrue to the company. Why? Because the way management treats the associates is exactly how the associates will then treat customers. . . . The bigger Wal-Mart gets the more important it is that we think small. Because that's exactly how we've become a huge corporation—by not acting like one."[4] Whenever a new idea worked, it was discussed on Friday and Saturday at store managers' meetings and implemented the next Monday. Walton personified the practices of listening to anyone, seeking new ideas on a personal basis anywhere, and implementing them as fast as possible.[5] He speeded the processes of feedback and sharing by implementing perhaps the most advanced electronics (two-way audio, video, and computer) communication and measurement system in the industry, allowing even new associates to manage and innovate in small "stores within the store" at virtually all locations.

• Motorola's use of its "bandit teams" to develop an automated, U.S.-based production operation for its high-volume Bravo pager line was an excellent level 2 project. It was large scale and had a well-focused technical scope. Scott Shamlin, a respected heavyweight in Motorola's Communications Sector, coordinated an appointed team of co-located individuals representing each of the technical functions needed for the project, plus a human resources person, an accounting-finance person, and a Hewlett Packard employee heading the software development for the new facility. The team created a "contract book" containing the blueprint, work plan, and expectations used to obtain project approval by the board. All top team and senior management people signed on to the document, and the group was housed in a separate corner of the manufacturing facility with open access so others could learn from the team's results. Both program coordination and visualization-test software supported the project. Given full independence within the plan, the team finished the project in eighteen months, about half the normal time for large projects managed across functional operations.[6]

## The Dictates of Collaboration

Much has been written about individual and cross-functional team innovation. Increasingly, however, complexity is driving innovation more toward levels 3 through 5. Success at these levels tends to require much more independent collaboration. This is especially true for IT and other extremely advanced technologies. At the top (fifth) level of scientific complexity, sociologist Harriet Zucherman found that Nobel laureates were much more likely to collaborate throughout their careers than a matched sample of less productive peers. And Michael Schrage in his insightful book, *No More Teams,* notes:

> Real value in the arts, commerce, and indeed one's personal and professional life comes largely from the process of collaboration. What's more the quality and quantity of meaningful collaboration often depends on the tools used to create it. . . . Collaboration is a *purposive* relationship. At the very heart of a collaboration is a desire or need to solve a problem, create, or discover something within a set of constraints. . . . Collaboration is a far richer process than teamwork's handing off an idea or blocking and tackling for a new product rollout or attempting a slam dunk marketing maneuver. The issue isn't communication or teamwork, it is the creation of value. . . . Collaboration is the process of *shared creation:* two or more individuals with complementary skills interacting to create a shared understanding that none previously possessed or could have come to on their own.[7]

Both individuals and small groups have long collaborated on innovations.[8] The key new element is the way software changes the very nature of collaboration. Software substitutes for many of the infrastructures formerly imposed by teams. Collaboration is no longer limited by the social rules, dysfunctional political interactions,[9] and space constraints of direct personal contacts. Software establishes new sets of interaction protocols and enables new and much more powerful modes of simultaneous conceptualization, analysis, and synthesis. Software simplifies or eliminates many formerly required interactions (such as calculations, descriptions, tests, or verifications). Through software, individuals (or very small teams) operating independently can cooperate with more parties, more remotely, in more asynchronous time frames, yet more closely and completely than ever before.

When they do so—as they have on biotechnology, construction, microchip, health, ecology, financial services, telecommunications, advanced aerospace, human genome, or frontier astronomy projects—they can achieve astonishing results in much shorter time and with significantly more accurate results. In fact many of the superlative results achieved in these fields since 1994 alone would have been inconceivable within the lifetime of any scientist—and hence impossible for them—without software-supported independent collaboration.

## SOFTWARE DEVELOPMENT AS AN INNOVATION PARADIGM

The processes of designing software provide useful parallels for organizing the psychological, information, and intellectual processes of innovation in an independent-collaborative mode. What are the relevant aspects of this process? How can executives apply similar concepts to improve their innovation processes? Software creation embodies certain critical characteristics that, upon reflection, are the essence of most innovations today.

### A Focus on Intellectual Content

In software, as in most other innovations, intellect and intellect alone creates value. When innovators implement their experiments and designs in software, they tend to focus on the conceptual elements of the process where payoffs are highest. Freed from many of the arduous and repetitive physical handling steps, slow hand-driven mathematics, two-dimensional drawings, bench experiments, batch mixing, mold making, or metal cutting steps that dominated product or process designers in the past, experimenters can analyze many alternatives and combinations they earlier could not. They are not bound by the cost and space constraints that experimentation in physical systems would present. Software creates an immediate "virtual world," where no physical objects need be built; yet they can be conceptually observed, manipulated in detail, and even destroyed without significant cost. With a click of a switch experimenters can bring in any relevant variables, representations, or models needed for measurement, experimentation, or creation of a new synthesis. Often such models embody a degree of rigor and depth of knowledge that most laboratories would find difficult to achieve without huge cost. A much larger variety of concepts can be tested at minimal cost before undertaking the costs and frustrations of physical experiments. For example:

• In their unending search for new drug possibilities, pharmaceutical companies are increasingly using combinatorial chemistry to combine molecular building blocks in new ways. 3D Pharmaceuticals, Inc., now has software that can first make "virtual chemicals" inexpensively for manipulation and observation on a computer screen. Rapidly and at low cost, 3D's software then searches for similar molecules that have actual or simulated biological effects. Laboratory tests of promising candidates then verify or offer new data about relationships between the structures and biological effects.[10]

• For its chemical process designs another of our interviewed companies employs a special group of chemical engineers in a computation center where—using known chemical principles—they implement in software very sophisticated reactions and syntheses that formerly would have required bench experiments. The group then archives its results and, through software, makes them immediately accessible throughout the firm. By using theoretically pure reagents and precise environmental controls, their models eliminate the effects of many exogenous variables that normally would confuse experiments and alter the results obtained. Consequently, experimenters can concentrate on the targeted variables themselves and the new results sought or achieved, and not get bogged down in the numbing drudgery of endless physical experiments. Their software disciplines the research process and helps prevent experimenters from repeatedly going through all the steps and mental processes of "how we've always done it." As a result, technologists concentrate more on totally new (innovative) options. And only the most promising of these go on to expensive physical tests.

## A Learning System

In any complex physical (or software) innovation, learning is essential. It is impossible for the designer to foresee the net result of all possible interactions in such systems. Software provides a way to code and load data and models to reveal many unexpected interrelationships immediately. Recognizing this phenomenon, astute innovators in the past consciously utilized multiple "build-and-bust" physical experiments to identify unforeseeable interactions and fix the errors these experiments revealed. But the physical systems could not learn from such experiences themselves. Correction took human intervention. In software, innovators can include build-and-test cycles in which the software system itself can identify problems or errors, self-correct them according to preset algorithms, eliminate fake (or suboptimizing) paths, and hence learn from its own errors. In software development, one can explicitly allow for the fact of intellectual flaws (bugs) and design into the system itself the capacity to test for, discern, correct, and learn from its own errors. In many fields the system can seek optima among many variables and discard all other options. In the process, software may become the discoverer of new and unexpected relationships. Microbiology, bioinformatics, chemical, ecological, nuclear physics, integrated circuits, large-scale logistics, and financial analysis systems (among others) have benefited from such approaches.[11]

## A Software-Based Discipline and Culture

As a tool, like any other technology, software creates a discipline. In physical process terms, that discipline eliminates errors, allows more use of data, and decreases many costs and risks of innovation. For example:

• With a product database of more than five thousand items, the Clorox Company was having difficulty working around its disconnected packaging graphics, marketing, proofreading, and label product units. Time lost in this business is critical, as is error control, with millions of dollars riding on the successful launch of new products. Clorox used NextStep software to develop a "virtual workgroup" environment that linked all critical internal units (on graphics teams) with outside design, prepress, and printing firms, completely changing the modes of communication, costs, error rates, and cycle times for innovation.[12]

In human process terms, software, particularly groupware or network software, helps people concentrate energy on criterion setting, information exchanges, and results. It captures past experience and provides a precise language and understood rules for interaction, helping people to move quickly into a new situation. It helps dilute the politics, emotionality, and hidden agendas often found in multidisciplinary teams. Inputs must be relevant and accurate. Unlike interactions with other humans, one cannot consciously deceive a software system without immediate consequences. Software creates a common language, interaction mode, and discipline for groups. It enables or limits the kind of results professionals can generate. The software through which people interact is as much a part of the culture as are the social conventions, style, and value systems inculcated in much-discussed "management cultures." At some point, as in the Polaris nuclear submarine and the Apollo space programs, the software becomes the essential discipline of how people interact and solve problems. In many cases it determines whether, when, and where innovation will occur.

Because people must input according to specific rules—and their data are manipulated by the rules in the model—the structure of the software and the mode of its use often determine what options are considered, how products and processes are designed, how they are implemented, and what machines are necessary to produce the innovation. The software determines what problems can be considered and what skills are relevant. Talented people often join a particular enterprise because it has or supports the most advanced experimental software in their fields.[13] The best talent wants to work with the best. The presence of such experts and their software largely determine who will be successful. Thus, the software system an enterprise uses for innovation quickly becomes as important as the people it selects, the incentives it uses, and the psychological environment it creates for innovation.

## DEVELOPING A COMMON BOND

Granted that software and independent collaboration across organizational boundaries are increasingly critical, how do executives within a firm (or those managing innovation alliances) deal with the highly diverse backgrounds, disaggregated organizations, and multiple locations generally found in these new innovation relationships? The process starts by focusing more on the goals that bond collaborators and on talented people's inherent desire to collaborate with others and to create something truly new and of higher value. As much attention is needed to what *connects* the nodes as to what is *in* the nodes. Talented people collaborate because they want to accomplish something special but lack the capacity to deal with all the challenges they face. They also generally want to work with others and to be associated with groups, both because association is more personally satisfying and because they can accomplish more in collaboration than they can alone.[14] Successful executives build on these intrinsic motivations and add extrinsic incentives that encourage participants to push beyond what they could (or would) have done individually and to associate their personal goals with the wider benefits their institutions seek and can provide. A number of rapidly growing innovative enterprises have implemented these concepts in depth—for example:

• Sam Walton of Wal-Mart lived the value system he wanted reflected in Wal-Mart stores. Walton endowed his store managers with an icy attention to the bottom line and a warm respect for Wal-Mart's 400,000 employees and tens of millions of customers. Walton had begun his business career as a retail sales clerk and never forgot how much a personal example and a friendly salesperson can influence a business relationship. To emphasize frugality, he drove around in a red pickup truck, no air-conditioning, seats stained by coffee. Whenever possible, he wore Wal-Mart clothing, made deliveries with a company driver, and dropped in unannounced at his stores. When there, he walked the aisles, listening for complaints and trading kind words in his homespun style. He often began—or ended—his pep rallies at new store openings by jumping on a table and leading Wal-Mart cheers invented and practiced by Wal-Mart store teams. Walton felt employees liked to belong to a company that wanted them to belong to it; cheering for Wal-Mart was just like cheering for themselves. However, he might also immediately issue a new challenge to do even better in the future. Once, he promised the store's "associates" that if they brought in a pretax profit of 8% that year, he would do a hula dance down Wall Street. They did. And he did (in a grass skirt). Walton maintained an open invitation for any associate to contact him personally with a store problem, a comment, or an idea. Any who wrote received a personal reply from Walton, and tested new ideas were rapidly rolled out across the system using Wal-Mart's video-satellite system to capture all possible efficiencies.[15]

• At Boston Chicken, franchiser of Boston Market stores and one of the fastest-growing food franchise firms in history, CEO Scott Beck has actively instigated a culture of aligned purpose and independent collaboration to stimulate change. In a highly personal style he emphasizes several critical strategic elements: "creativity," "what is important to our other partners," and mutual "equity opportunities" between Boston Chicken and its partners. He describes Boston Chicken's three core competencies as:

1. ***Being a good partner*** in relationships with financial sources, employees, distribution partners, and vendors. The most famous of these is Boston Market's "financed area developers" (FAD) franchise system, which creates goal congruence by helping independent and regional franchisees to invest on their own, to expand through intensifying distribution in their areas, and to innovate in new product concepts along with Boston Market. Boston Chicken provides major capital and product

system support. Franchisees who meet targets can receive very high returns, opportunity for liquidity, and further opportunities in a business growing at 40% per year.

2. ***The capacity to change.*** Beck believes in "continual change." In its short five-year history, Boston Chicken has radically changed its basic markets, image, locations, products, and operating structures. It has implemented a rapid-change philosophy that demands that all projects be completed in sixteen weeks.

3. ***Integrated comunications.*** Beck emphasizes communication of "knowledge in execution," of "know-how from execution," of "refined knowledge from improvements" (made centrally and throughout the system), and "distribution of improved knowledge" continually throughout the system. He emphasizes that knowledge is the firm's real asset; physical assets are really liabilities that must be secured and insured, and can be lost. He also regards "knowledge in process" as a liability. It becomes valuable only when exploited. Consequently, the company's goal is to implement three times as fast as its major competitors through better movement of knowledge.

Beck identifies the key elements in implementing Boston Chicken's strategy as "a clear language to describe our processes, proper measurements to stimulate action, common media to connect people, and a clear and common purpose." A strong believer in the latter, Mr. Beck has implemented an unusually complete grouping of personal, family, organization, and corporate mission statements that guide all his organizations and his personal life. Believing that customer satisfaction is based largely on employee satisfaction, Boston Market has an elaborate means of assessing employees' perceptions of their jobs, supervisors, coworkers, and work environments in each of its units. These are fed back almost daily to each outlet.[16]

Team,[17] network,[18] consensus,[19] and alliance[20] models of behavior are widely discussed as replacing older "responsibility and authority" models.[21] Yet there can be very high costs of dysfunctional behavior and control associated with these models.[22] Now it is possible to utilize much more individually oriented action units linked primarily by software. When these collaborations are properly structured, as they are in many entrepreneurial situations (like Boston Market), people's sense of responsibility tends to exceed their delegated authority, and self-motivation and intergroup cooperation toward shared goals become behavioral norms. Both laboratory and empirical evidence suggest that maximizing such independent collaboration strongly stimulates, accelerates, and expands the scope of innovation.[23] Thinking in these terms helps innovation managers be more effective in exploiting the randomness, serendipity, spirals, circles, and patterns of dynamic interaction that characterize most complex invention and innovation processes today.

## Circular Interdependent Organizations

This concept of innovation is better represented by more organic, circular constructs indicating organizational relations with permeable and fluid boundaries. As Figure 4.1 illustrates, many competing independent efforts to solve a problem generally exist at any given moment at different levels of specificity and completeness in various units both within and outside an enterprise. This is especially true in the emerging software, research-based, high-technology, service, or rapid-response industries that provide today's most profitable growth

**FIGURE 4.1**
**Somewhat Orderly Chaos, with Competing Parallel Approaches (Internal and External)**

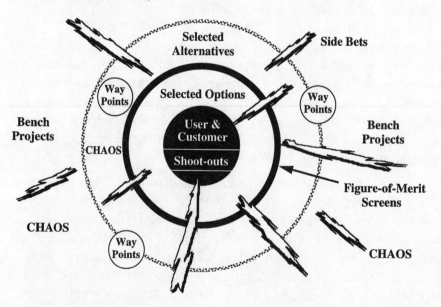

*Independent projects, from both inside and outside the firm, compete to satisfy user needs. They pass through constantly changing way points and screens toward final prototype shoot-outs. Only those that meet figure-of-merit standards become selected options.*

opportunities. Solutions are like independent sperm (projects) projecting themselves toward an egg (market goal) guided largely by their own energy and instincts. In their competitive race, only a few will survive the increasing barriers as they approach the final goal, and only one will achieve the ultimate goal (competitive dominance). Only the strongest, most energetic, and most persistent win. System success depends on making sure the egg (goal) is sufficiently attractive, supporting enough healthy independent challengers (alternatives), and modulating the environment effectively to ensure that a winner emerges in a timely fashion and with enough strength to survive in real-life competition. Later sections and chapters set forth in detail the practical methods successful organizations use to systematically accomplish this.

Many observers, nevertheless, still feel that invention and innovation in large institutions are now so complex that (1) institutional barriers may be insurmountable, (2) highly individualistic innovators are actively discouraged, and (3) only incremental change is possible. Yet customers are demanding revolutionary change. Ford's Team Taurus, Boeing's 777, Motorola's bandit teams, and Sharp's "gold badge groups" (all detailed elsewhere in this chapter) illustrate how some large firms get highly disaggregated groups to cooperate on large-scale innovations. Many of such successes initially use traditional top-down power to get people in functional or product groups to break their old patterns and to refocus on joint goals. Highly visible symbols, like the gold badge at Sharp, are common tools in subverting the traditional hierarchical attachments that impede innovation. Increasingly, however, companies are using circular organizations to emphasize more interactive relationships and to symbolize the death of linear hierarchies.

At Ford, Team Taurus's head, Lew Viraldi, insisted on a circular organization form (see Figure 4.2), indicating that functional groups would no longer be fragmented and that projects would be coordinated simultaneously around and among all groups. Silos of power were no longer tolerable. Each group had to sign off on a project for it to go ahead; all were clearly interdependent. Kao's circular organization diagram (see Figure 4.3)—like those of the "starburst," "spider's web," and numerous alliances described in Chapter 6—are other examples of more circular, interactive structures successfully used to reconceptualize more collaborative relationships in innovative large companies. They encourage people to cross over (former) organizational boundaries and allow people to change career courses without penalties, thus further encouraging flexibility and risk taking.

## FIGURE 4.2
## Ford Team Taurus Organizational Chart

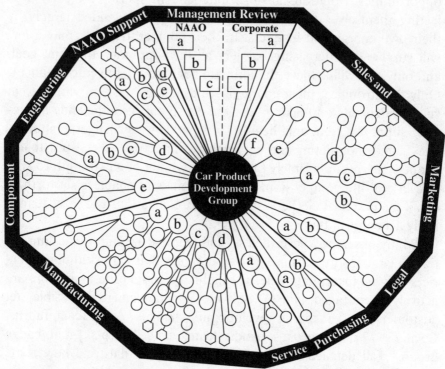

The Car Product Development Group is responsible for overall direction, design, development, control and final approval.

☐ Review committees
*Corporate*
a • Technical Affairs Subcommittee
b • Design Subcommittee
c • Product Planning Subcommittee
*NAAO (North American Automotive Operations)*
a • Taurus Program Control Meeting
b • Taurus Task Force
c • Taurus Sub-system Reviews

◯ Organization/operations
*NAAO Support*
a • Controller-Product Development
b • North American Design
c • Test Operations
d • Product Assurance
e • NAAO Timing
*Component Engineering*
a • Climate Control Division Engineering
b • Plastic/Paint/Vinyl Engineering
c • Electrical/Electronics Division Engineering
d • Body and Chassis Engineering
e • Powertrain Engineering

*Manufacturing*
a • Body and Assembly Operations/
    Engineering Operations
b • Engine Divison
c • Diversified Products Operations
    Components
d • Transmission and Chassis Division
*Service*
a • Ford Parts and Service Division
*Purchasing*
a • Purchasing and Supply Staff
b • NAAO Purchasing
*Legal*
a • Office of General Counsel
b • Environmental and Safety Engineering
*Sales and Marketing*
a • NAAO Operations
b • NAAO Marketing
c • Lincoln-Mercury Divisona
d • Ford Division
e • Marketing Staff
f • Public Affairs
⬡ Dedicated Taurus Personnel

Source: "Team Taurus," *Ward's Auto World* (February 1985).

*Ford's first Team Taurus used a circular organization design to break down old functional barriers and to focus team members on the goals set by the Car Product Development Group at the center. All activities in the design chain, from research to post-sales services and environmental engineering, participated simultaneously.*

## Independent Collaboration

With proper support, independent collaboration can exceed the bounds of even these less constraining organizations. Many scientific, data monitoring, individual entrepreneurial, market interactive, and software projects proceed this way. When visions, strategies, market goals, and figures of merit are clear, individuals and very small groups can operate quite independently within companies—as they have in Cetus, Gore Associates, Boston Market, 3M, Fidelity Investments, Microsoft, and Rubbermaid—yet maintain the discipline and complex information interchanges that highly diverse specialists require to make rapid major technical advances. For example:

• The development of the Nobel Prize–winning polymerase chain reaction (PCR) followed this mode. David Gelfand, Kary Mullis, Henry Erlich, Tom White, and other key players representing different disciplines came to Cetus largely because of its unstructured collaborative style. Understanding of the individual component concepts for PCR had been developed in many different labs. However, it was during a drive in the Sierra foothills that Kary Mullis visualized the integrating concept for PCR as he was trying to solve another problem for Cetus: how to amplify the sensitivity of procedures for identifying a single nucleotide at a single position in a DNA molecule. He had been working with both polymerase experts and computer programs in the laboratory. The similarities between computer "do" loops and chemical reactions led to his crucial insight that polymerase could operate repeatedly on a split strand of DNA to replicate its bases in large quantities and in desired sequences. Working at first almost entirely alone, he found his ideas rejected by the organization. Slowly, however, people like Fred Faloona, Henry Erlich, Tom White, and Steven Scharf volunteered to help with different aspects of the problem. Only after management's skepticism dwindled before ever better demonstrated results from the collaboration did Cetus finally assign the experimental genius Randall Saiki to improve the process sufficiently for external publication.[24]

How does one manage these kinds of fluid, disaggregated nonstructures for innovation? Most effective management of independent-collaborative systems devolves around stimulating aligned purpose, superabundant information, and rich and profuse networks of relationships.[25]

## ALIGNED PURPOSE

Long ago Robert K. Merton stated, "Scientists operating in their own self-interest collectively reinforce the public good."[26] Amitai Etzioni noted that in the technology world the primary task of a manager is "to set up a system or an environment whereby the goals of the individual are congruent with the goals of the organization." The benefits of obtaining goal congruence on large-scale activities—through bottom up or Theory Y styles—have also been widely recognized.[27] In later research Margaret Wheatley and Myron Kellner-Rogers suggest that most talented people desire to be creative, desire to affiliate, and desire to contribute.[28] At Cetus, David Gelfand reflected this view: "The two most important things are: [first] are you going to be able to do what's important for you to do? That requires a commonality of interest between your scientific goals and corporate goals. And second, who are you doing it with? Because 90% of what you do is collaborative."[29]

Much of the work in applied psychology and some strong supporting management and philosophical traditions—centered on Douglas McGregor, Rensis Likert, and Chris Argyris[30] in management and Martin Heidegger in philosophy—have been concerned with people's efforts to balance their personal desires and needs for autonomy against their drives for affiliation.[31] As the Internet is proving dramatically, through voluntary independent collaboration, software allows the conflicting forces of individuality and organizational-market discipline to coalign efforts quite constructively across broad geographic and intellectual landscapes. Active alignment of purpose can go much further in individual enterprises. When properly developed, it can lead to much more creative, higher-order, and greater-value outcomes both within the organization and among the enterprise and its external partners and stakeholders.

The first step in the process of achieving this is generating an exciting unifying vision, as will be detailed in Chapter 6. As Peter Senge points out, this is neither a solo nor a static process.[32] An effective vision is the embodiment and representation of many participants' individual visions. Actively helping individuals create this linkage betweeen their "work life" and longer-term "life work" is a crucial step in generating an environment where innovation and high productivity flourish together.[33] Management cannot control this process or direct it in detail, but it can actively energize and support many linkages between individual purpose (intrinsic motivation) and institutional purpose (extrinsic motivation). Cetus provided one case in point. Two further examples suggest other successful approaches:

• W. L. Gore & Associates—maker of Gore-Tex, vascular grafts, sealants, filtration, defense, and aerospace materials—seeks aligned purpose in all its activities. To encourage personal identity with the firm and collaboration with others, all personnel are simply called "Associates." Before anyone new is hired, an existing Associate must agree to be the new employee's sponsor. The sponsor takes a personal interest in the new person's contributions, problems, and goals and acts as a coach and advocate. New people rotate through multiple areas before settling on a task of their choice. Within Gore's four principles of Fairness, Freedom, Commitment, and "Waterline" (if something may sink the ship, fix it quickly and right), they set their own goals with their sponsor. There are no assigned managers or titles—only "leaders" informally accepted in a coordinative role because of their particular capabilities.

People set their own goals as "commitments." CEO Bob Gore says, "We want people to come here because of the opportunities for growth and the unique work environment." But the performance of each Associate is periodically reviewed against his or her commitments by a compensation team at the facility with the individual sponsor acting as advocate. The sponsor checks with customers and other Associates familiar with the individual's work to learn about contributions made, leadership abilities, and willingness to help others. This subjective evaluation is combined with an economic value added (EVA) calculation to determine profit sharing, which is a large part of total compensation.[34]

• At ICI (Imperial Chemicals Industries) Polyester, despite the company's long history of past innovations, Global CEO Jim Alles and his leadership group became convinced that its employees' innovativeness was in danger of becoming limited by two factors: a pervading sense of disconnection between their life goals and working goals and an organizational set of attitudes representing a "we-they" culture that kept individuals and groups from working together effectively. He assembled seventy-five people from top marketing, technical, and leadership positions worldwide to develop an initiative to improve innovativeness. The core of this initiative was to begin discussing the goals that were meaningful to these individuals in their own lives and to take a fresh look at their organizations' work in terms of those goals. Alles's directive for the project became to "create an environment where people will work at what they are best at doing and what they like doing best." This discussion led to three important steps: (1) active management of the disconnecting "we-they attitudes," starting in the meeting itself, (2) the establishment of a long-term process to connect life-work and work-life at all levels, including qualitative ways to establish progress, and (3) a monitored commitment by all the executives to fully involve themselves in each step they asked employees to undertake.[35]

## SUPERABUNDANT INFORMATION

Superabundant information is also a common characteristic of very innovative organizations. First, the organization develops some selected knowledge sets to best-in-world depth and can deploy these for user needs at will. Second, people have access to all the information *they* need when *they* think they need it, without information control by a central authority. Third, their software and support systems consciously amplify the value of their information. How do companies do this?

• Sun Microsystems, following its corporate slogan, "The network is the computer," in late 1995 converted its one mainframe into just one of 250 servers feeding over 22,000 workstations on its Sun Network. Its own SunDans software enables fast transfer of any process or application to any other station on the net. Another program, Sun Paperless Reporter, automatically distributes data in easy-to-use formats across the system, and a special server connects Sun to its top customers directly on the Web. Its data-sharing software eliminates the need for complex "middleware" between each program at the decentralized nodes. Sun "broadcasts" each key operations transaction over the network; each operation receives only the data it needs, translated automatically for its programs. Although the system, once installed, almost tripled inventory turn rates and halved cycle times from component purchases to revenue collection, Sun's controller noted that the biggest gains were in the personal efficiency of employees.[36]

### Sorting and Visualizing Data

*Data* are superabundant in most organizations if sufficient software access is available. The most innovative enterprises go much further: they convert their data into *information* by facilitating cross-assembly and transform the data into *usable knowledge* through visualization, diffusion, and education processes. Both increasingly mean the skilled implementation of agent or intermediary software to find, distill, and display data in the most useful fashion. In the best cases, the software causes information "to find its user" in a timely fashion when the need develops, as it does in emergency and early warning systems. Firefly and

Wisewire are interesting examples of such software. Since many of the best models for interpreting data are developed externally and the models themselves determine relevancies and weightings of particular data, such models need to be accessible in the database itself. The structure and accessibility of information bases become critical and integral components of the organization itself (see Figure 4.4). How independent and interactive people can be depends on the structure of the information they have available.

Visual software models and interactive simulations are particularly powerful tools for extending independent collaboration. It has long been a common practice in design to produce a physical model to familiarize users or executives with a new concept. Now visual software models, at very low cost, can substantially increase the diversity, intensity, and accuracy of information and enable people from very different backgrounds and locales to comment on and share directly in constructing an idea.[37] The "virtual reality" representation of the idea quickly becomes the "real reality" for participants, just as a photograph through repeated use can often redefine the reality of an event in people's minds. People can interact more easily, precisely, and productively around a visible object or simulation, develop and deal with their possible concerns, internalize the concept for their own purposes, and help modify it more rapidly and practically than they can through conversation or direct manipulation of data.[38]

Combining objects or pictures with other symbol-based (mathematical or verbal) information intensifies and shortens learning cycles enormously. Use of visual software changes the entire collaboration experience. Interactions are no longer filtered through different perceptions. Any idea can be tested immediately, directly, and rigorously. Agent software can bring considerations to bear that participants otherwise would not contemplate. Virtual laboratories can extend personal contacts and make equipment equally available to all, thus decreasing turf battles and misunderstandings. Interaction with images and data through simulations—as in virtual experimental, operations, emergency, product use, construction, or competitive environments—can integrate users into the design team more directly and intensively than any formal organizational diagram ever could.

## The Virtual Organization Becomes the Real Organization

Superabundant information forces a phase change in the way people interact. They cannot cope with great complexity by working in traditional ways. Participants quickly find that disjointed or sequential oral conversations are inefficient. They may first try to cope by co-locating or using e-mail to improve the frequency and effectiveness of exchanges. However, if the problem is sufficiently complex, their interaction soon calls for a wider group of colleagues and an agreed-on model to define terms, rate processes, and interaction consequences. As Karl Weick said in discussing organizational participation, "How can I know what I think until I can visualize what I say?"[39]

They soon realize the software allows advances beyond their imaginations. It can seek and identify patterns and anomalies they cannot see. Genetic, object-oriented, or self-learning programs can create unforeseeable new options. The software can capture and remember all dimensions of an experiment. It extends resources. It lets more people contribute and take more risks. Intelligent software agents become inexpensive additional participants in the innovation process. Internally and externally, as software models' protocols define reality and relevancy more precisely, they help eliminate much of the power-playing, duplicitous, delaying, political behavior that makes teams ineffective.[40] Software changes the very nature of the organization and becomes an integral part of it.

## Asynchronous Organizations

One of the most important (and little recognized) changes is that the organization becomes asynchronous. People can think, experiment, and contribute when they are most able. Insights come in random spurts, not at the time meetings are called. Some people work best late at night, others in early morning. During an innovation cycle, one often needs to pause, tune out the world, or work with manic intensity when the rest of the "team" is not ready to do so. Software allows a kind of personalized time disconnection that teams or traditional organizations would find intolerable.[41]

Asynchronous thought is especially important when seeking outsiders' contributions. As the model design is agreed on, modified, and experimented with, it needs constant external verification. Suppliers, workers, other professionals, users, and external customers usually cannot co-locate or synchronize their schedules to suit the innovator's. But through software they cannot just be consulted, they can participate directly by utilizing models, simulations, shared screens, and interactive queries. As individuals, these outside groups' personnel become true collaborators in the innovation. For example:

• NASA has developed a Web-based collaborative aeronautical design system, called Darwin, that lets its Ames Research Center, other NASA facilities, and industry partners come together in a virtual workspace using NASA's secure nationwide Aeronet. Boeing or Rockwell engineers can use Darwin data from a wind tunnel test at NASA in real time. Video links to the test and direct linkages to NASA's supercomputers, to those of the contractors, and to their respective databases let the parties compare their individual simulations to actual test data while the test is going on. Each party's databases are protected through encrypted protocols, allowing them to work more readily with raw data while choosing their own methods of analysis and display. HTTP and Java application interfaces allow all parties maximum flexibility and access. Experts estimate the system will allow much greater options testing and depth of analysis, while cutting test-design stages for advanced aircraft by 80 to 90%.[42]

• Xerox PARC has developed a software tool, Colab, supporting meeting interactions around the concept of WYSIWIS (What You See Is What I See). Each participant's computer is linked to a shared screen that replaces the traditional whiteboard and its constraints. It can be split into multiple windows and can manipulate data directly from each individual's computer. The system augments verbal communication, allowing people to co-create ideas and concepts instantaneously. Two related software tools are Cognoter for brainstorming and organizing ideas and Agnoter to help participants develop and evaluate proposals. Used either in "same room" or remote meetings, the systems support independent collaboration.

The virtual organization becomes a real independent-collaborative organization spanning different enterprises, time zones, and institutional groups. Beyond mere technical suggestions, collaboration provides major benefits in terms of psychological support, error reduction, greater customer satisfaction, reduced cycle times, and lowered risks for the innovation. As technologies become ever more complex, there is a much greater need to ensure maximum interactive user testing during design and to continue the process after the product is introduced.

• A number of studies have demonstrated, through a plethora of tragic factual histories, how technological failures result from incompatibilities between the way things are designed and the way they are used. From the *Soyuz* and *Challenger* tragedies, to the Airbus 320 Paris Air Show crash, the *Torrey Canyon* wreck, Bhopal, and deadly X-ray accidents, studies show how systems fail without adequate continuing inter- active participation between real users and designers.[43] Software mod- eling and simulations will never prevent all such errors, but they greatly extend the capacity to visualize, test for, and prevent tragic accidents and misuses.

One of the most serious threats that open information systems face at present is that a disgruntled employee may provide key strategic or personal information to competitors or inappropriate parties. To pre- vent this, most companies have software barriers limiting access to in- formation about proprietary technology, detailed financial information, and employees' personal data. A second serious threat is that totally open information can expose early underground or skunk works inves- tigations to undesired scrutiny or opposition before they have time to develop the data needed to successfully argue for these new options. Both can be offset by developing proper encryption, a strong identifying culture, and feelings of mutual interdependence among associates. But, like all other human organization approaches, independent collabora- tion has some inherent drawbacks.

## RICH AND PROFUSE NETWORKS OF RELATIONSHIPS

Software enables two other conditions found in highly innovative orga- nizations: high interconnectivity among individuals, even at remote lo- cations, and permeable boundaries across all systems and work groups. These conditions require a fundamental reevaluation of the very defini- tion of what innovation teams are and how they can be managed for maximum effectiveness. First, a true team is a unit with a shared social identity, performing and being evaluated as a single actor toward a spe- cific goal. However, for many innovations, knowledge, not necessarily people or culture, is what needs to cross organizational boundaries. Often software can facilitate needed knowledge transfers with no orga- nizational change. In those circumstances creating productive knowl- edge interactions among individuals, not figuring out how to cluster or acculturate people on teams, should be management's focal point.

Second, despite the constant emphasis on creating a common cul- ture for a team, the innovative productivity of a collaboration comes from the *differences* of the individuals intersecting with each other, not their sameness. The visionary Steve Jobs at Apple needed the technical brilliance of Steve Wozniak. At Intel quiet visionary chemist Gordon Moore, enthusiastic physicist Bob Noyce, and operations powerhouse

Andy Grove were all required for success. At Lotus, visionary and externally oriented Mitch Kapor needed the technically experienced Jonathan Sachs. And so on. Like most other fruitful collaborators, they all battled ferociously over ideas while maintaining personal respect. Such confrontations are often needed to stimulate and clarify thinking. Successful managers of collaboration try to engender goal congruence at a broad level, while encouraging people with very different backgrounds to confront each other constructively (within nonpersonalizing rules of engagement) at the argumentation level.

For complex innovations, a collaboration at some point must include individual members deeply competent in each knowledge or activity set needed for solution. Often, however, no one knows precisely what skills will ultimately be needed or for how long. Usually to maintain and deepen needed levels of competency, individuals must work relatively consistently and closely with peer experts in the same disciplines, sharing a common language and worldview. However, on innovation projects, these knowledge-based specialists must work with people equally expert in other disciplines. Traditionally, this has meant co-locating to enrich the information exchange. But as very creative deals in the financial world and complex research collaborations in biotechnology have proved, there is no inherent reason people cannot do this mostly from their own home bases or workstations if they are properly connected to others. The only commonality a virtual collaboration shares may be the temporary purpose or problem it is addressing.

## Tacit Versus Specialist Knowledge

Specialist knowledge is relatively easily transferred and shared through software. The most difficult aspects of managing independent collaboration are developing, capturing, maintaining, and diffusing the organization's "tacit knowledge."[44] The organization's culture, its invaluable knowledge about how people in the organization react to each other and how to get things done effectively, and the nuances of how its customers and suppliers really operate. This transfer almost always requires close personal interactions and purposeful mixing of people.

In collaborative innovation, the greatest technical expert (knowledge specialist) may not be as valuable as a very good specialist who is interested in a broad range of different phenomena and is able to relate to other people. Increasingly, human resources people are trying to find and nurture people with T-shaped skills: those deeply knowledgeable in a few disciplines (the vertical part of the T), and with broad interests and psychological capabilities that allow them to connect with other specialties (the horizontal part of the T). A key element in managing independent collaboration is nurturing both aspects of the T. The two branches unfortunately have conflicting organizational imperatives. Deep knowledge requires concentration on specialized topics within peer groups. Connectedness requires wide-ranging interests and a profuse network of interactions with others. This takes time, conscious interacting with different people and skills, and a culture that rewards lateral participation.

Companies have taken many different approaches to building and maintaining this knowledge coordination—for example:

• Arthur Andersen creates technical expertise, a strong bonding culture, and a lifetime network of contacts by putting all professionals through an identical rigorous training program at one of its three training centers worldwide. This has been a major component in Andersen's goal of having "one firm, one voice" worldwide. The program has created a common culture, experience, and language that let "Andersens" immediately work together on projects anywhere in the world. Microsoft's exceptionally intensive selection process,[45] small team mentoring, consciously maintained "high-pressure-but-relaxed" campus atmosphere, and "software-disciplined design" processes handle the problem differently. Sharp Electronics uses a combination of enforced rotation, structured meetings at three different organizational levels, and a powerful central human relations group to identify, develop, and deploy people as needed across the organization. The human relations group ensures that both Sharp's normal development teams and its "gold badge" task forces have the required mix of specialist, team, and functional skills to provide the tacit knowledge they need for success.

## A Three-Level Approach

Given such support, small and medium-sized enterprises can easily work in very flat organizational structures where (1) external and specialist knowledge is captured and held in open software systems, so constructed that the knowledge base becomes a key element in the organization itself; (2) deep knowledge "specialist groups" (associated by discipline, customer, geography, or process) constantly develop and enrich the firm's central and shared knowledge base; and (3) specialists independently collaborate on innovation projects that concentrate, extend, and adapt their joint knowledge for specific innovation or user purposes. (Figure 4.4 diagrams these relationships.) Very large multi-output enter-

**FIGURE 4.3**
**Kao Organization**

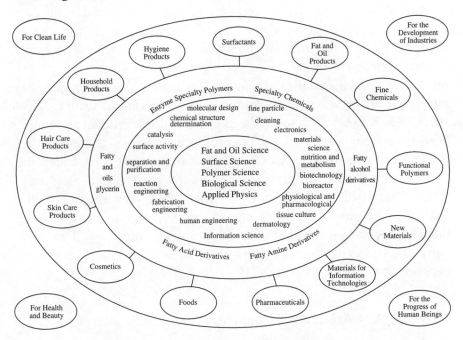

Source: Reproduced by special permission from I. Nonaka and H. Takeuchi, *The Knowledge Creating Company* (New York: Oxford University Press, 1995), p. 176.

*Kao has created a circular organization with permeable organizational barriers to carry its innovations from its five technical core competencies to multiple markets.*

prises may have to break their total activities down to divisional scales for such practices to work, although Kao and Sharp claim success at larger scales. How do these organizations operate in practice?

• Kao, Japan's leading household and chemical products producer, has eighteen product divisions whose primary structures have been traditional hierarchical or matrix organizations. (See Figure 4.3.) Kao's top management felt it had to carefully nurture the deep specialist knowledge in these divisions, yet achieve much more direct interaction across divisions to increase creativity. But it knew divisional personnel could not interact effectively and equally if they had different amounts of information. Thus, "information sharing" became a basic tenet of the Kao organization. To maximize sharing, it initiated certain explicit policies and practices: "free access" to all information (except confidential personnel records), meetings literally "open to anyone," "open floor allocation of space" (to ensure that executives get out of their offices and discuss decisions openly), and "fluid personnel exchange" (moving people wherever and whenever they are needed).

Kao applies project teams for many purposes, not just technical innovation. It captures and recontextualizes knowledge around five critical scientific competencies: fat and oil science, surface science, polymer science, biological science, and applied physics. These are related through a circular organization concept, which encourages synergistic interaction of these scientific competencies in a ring of technological specialties. Kao can thus move flexibly into multiple product areas supporting its four strongly held philosophical missions (stated on the perimeter of Figure 4.3). CEO Yoshio Maruta, sometimes called the "philosopher executive," constantly and actively reinforces these missions in terms of three deeply held basic values—contribution to the consumer, absolute equality of humans, and search for truth and the unity of wisdom—that unify his highly diverse enterprise. The company's ECHO system (see Chapter 9) for monitoring customer desires supports these concepts in detail.[46]

## Why Use Any Arbitrary Structure?

Executives often ask, "How should we organize our innovative activities? By product? By customer? By geography? Or by function?" The more appropriate question is, "Why use any arbitrary structure at all?" As Chapters 6 and 8 demonstrate, specific strategies may call for their own unique organizations to increase focus on particular aspects of the strategy. However, for many situations, the ultimate innovative organization is a free-floating pool of talent that can move onto any project at any time, based on market-like interactions.[47] Consultants, financial services, entertainment, advanced research, emergency support, and medical groups do this all the time. In these situations, depending on the need, payoff, and urgency, a project head—limited by personal time and budgets—bargains with people to join the project and help solve a specific problem. When they finish their activity, participants return to their specialist groups.[48] Higher-level managers see that there are sufficient incentives for individuals to lead successful projects, to seek out projects that use their skills, to maximize customer value-added, and to perform as team members.

Participants are usually selected by project leaders or peers. But top-level coordinators (the ring in Figure 4.4) ensure that the team contains not just the highly specialized functional capabilities needed but also representatives of the total system who are intimately connected to other groups

**FIGURE 4.4**
**Three-Level Independent Collaboration Structure**

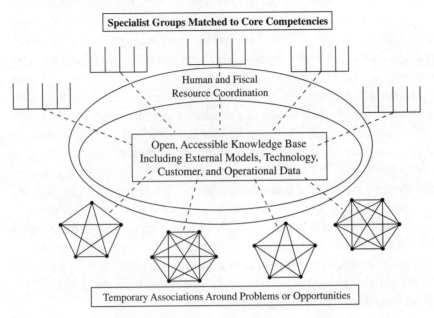

*In independent collaborations, three-level organizations are common, with the knowledge base and access system being an integral part of the organization connecting specialist groups, teams, and individual participants.*

across the organization. This enables the team to function in a much more supportive total system context, rather than being treated like an "antigen" inside the formal corporate "body." Because of their connections, these well-received "ambassadors" or "gatekeepers" are often responsible for bringing a high percentage of innovation insights to the team.[49]

If people or fiscal resources are in short supply, project leaders may go outside or negotiate arrangements with individuals within preset rules for handling cost, overtime, and benefit sharing. To support such flexibility, many groups have adopted software systems like Apple's Spider, Bell Atlantic's Resumex, or Raychem's Insiders to help find people with appropriate skills. In Japan, where personal relationships and context are so important, the human relations staff tends to have among the highest-quality people in the concern. In many companies they carefully track each individual's progress and recommend people for projects, providing a valuable repository and exchange of organizational or "tacit" knowledge.[50] Most U.S. firms try to combine a strong software system with a top-level executive "tie breaker" for serious conflicts.

## Psychological and Work Interconnections

Independent collaboration demands strong psychological and work connections at three levels: to the individual's own goals in life (for creativity and motivation), to others in the enterprise and other support networks (for collaborative work), and between individuals in the enterprise and the larger society (to produce outputs others value). By not emphasizing (and evaluating) these three interconnections, enterprises throw away a high percentage of the value a person can offer the organization Sumantra Ghoshal and others have chided managements on the fact that they force their employees to leave "half of their capabilities in the parking lot."[51] They point out that the same people managements keep so constricted by rules during the day go home at night and responsibly run charitable organizations, school boards, private businesses, and political campaigns with budgets many times the size of their department's activities. If managements could get these people to perform with only a portion of the effectiveness and passion they display in serving these more public functions, profits would soar. Gore & Associates provides a fascinating example:

• W. L. Gore & Associates has never had any titles, structure, or hierarchy. It limits plant sizes to 200, so that everyone knows everyone else. It operates with what it calls a "lattice" relationship (see Figure 4.5). Everyone is connected by a digital voice mail exchange, GoreCom, "because oral cultures encourage more direct communications." The lattice works strictly around "interpersonal interactions, self commitment to known responsibilities, natural leadership, and group imposed discipline." Any person feels free to self-coordinate with any other. When asked how planning and accountability work, CFO Bob Gore says, "Every which way."

Individuals set their own goals, agree to consensus goals if a team is involved, and self-delegate to multiple "leaders" for many different aspects of their work, from coordinating specialist-knowledge activities, to compensation evaluation, to interdivisional coordination. Individuals can ask for any materials or equipment they need to make experiments; and many dramatic products—from vascular grafts to hollow, insulated Gore-Tex— have come from such informal self-driven innovations. People (called "champions") are responsible for setting and fulfilling their own new product sales goals; "there is no command structure or chain involved." Using its approach to "unstructure" and "unmanagement," the company, which admires Du Pont, proudly notes that its patents and profits per employee are respectively three and two times those of Du Pont.[52]

**FIGURE 4.5**
**W. L. Gore & Associates Lattice "Unorganization"**

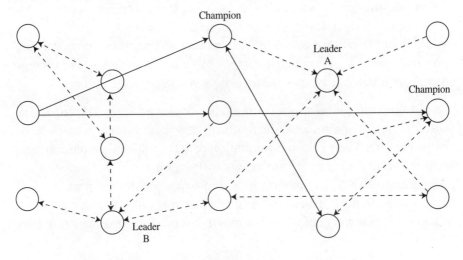

Source: Derived from F. Shipper and G. Manz, "W. L. Gore and Associates, Inc." (case), Arizona State University, Tempe, AZ , 1996.

*All circles are Associates. Anyone may work with anyone else. Associates agree to leaders, who coordinate specific aspects of their work. Champions take over all responsibility for certain goals, but all persons are responsible for their share of the goal. There are no titles or hierarchies. All parties are connected by the GoreCom communication system.*

## Strong Incentives Needed

To support this orientation in an integrated fashion, the most successful innovative enterprises we observed provide evaluations at four levels: for individual performance (by peers), customer performance (by customers), collaborative performance (by other group members and customers), and enterprise performance (by value-added measures). When the enterprise develops the kind of "jointly aligned purpose" suggested above, these four measures converge to a large extent.

One of the biggest problems in achieving independent collaboration is making sure all participants receive appropriate rewards. When small companies or researchers collaborate, the rewards of profits, publication, and individual growth are enough. When larger companies ask people to do this internally, cooperating individuals and groups must foresee benefits that exceed personal threats. When a company can create small businesses or discrete ventures within its structure, individuals and groups can easily join in, and the corporation can essentially create shares in the entity as investment bankers and mutual funds often do.

3M, Hewlett-Packard, and Raychem, by keeping producing units as small as possible and regarding them as "new businesses," have created incentive surrogates for such shares. Chapter 8 suggests options for other larger, longer-term, or more complex situations.

Unless the culture or incentives are very strong, those with existing power positions can subvert progress by refusing to undertake change or to provide needed expertise for a new venture—for example:

- Despite high-level support for a color copier at Xerox starting in the late 1970s, the main forces in the firm were committed to black-and-white copiers. Their role and reputation rested on speed, resolution, and cost reduction. Color was not only a distraction to them; it was an absolute threat. Even the laboratories and experimental support services were dominated by "black-and-whiters." As a result, the color proposal always "almost worked"—until a major Japanese competitor took over the market.

## CHAOS AND SELF-ORGANIZING SYSTEMS

With proper software and incentive support, highly disaggregated individual units or collaborations—utilizing aligned purpose, rich and profuse networks, and superabundant information—can become self-organizing systems ideal for innovation in a highly chaotic environment.[53] As Roger Lewin says, "During times of complex change [like today's], systems near the edge of chaos have a greater chance of survival than more stable systems."[54] Chaos is actually the basic mode of interaction, underlying almost all natural, technological, and economic phenomena. In fact, according to Robert Wesson, "Chaos may be called the uncertainty principle of the macro-world, a broad tendency toward irregularity and unpredictability within regularity and determinism."[55] Matching this chaos, Margaret Wheatley notes: "Innovation is fostered by [disorderly] information gathered from new connections; from insights gained from journeys into other disciplines or places; from active collegial networks and fluid, open boundaries. Innovation arises from ongoing circles of exchange, where information is not just accumulated and stored, but created. Knowledge is generated anew from connections that weren't there before."[56]

Complexity theory says it is predictable that, given time, such systems will cause some new, but unpredictable, order to emerge out of the chaos. The problem in managing independent, interactive innovation systems is to be able to outwait these "unpredictable predictability" realities and to provide appropriate guidance to mitigate the personal distress and minimize the psychological delays accompanying change. Nobel Prize winners have pointed out several critical characteristics of these systems. First, such emergent systems have the peculiarity that "the characteristics of the whole cannot (not even in theory) be deduced from the most complete knowledge of the components."[57] Hence they cannot be directed in detail. Second, "the initial disorder introduced by a change does not lead to the destruction of a natural system. Instead it leads to a new form better suited to the current environment."[58] This explains why, if entropy is the rule, life still flourishes. Independent organisms rapidly adapt to a higher level of complexity. So too will properly supported independent organizations, not overly controlled to meet the needs of the past. But on the way there may be death and anguish among the old components.

## Systemic Order Despite Process Chaos

However chaotic a system may appear if examined microscopically— for example, an atom's nuclear particles, the whirling interior of a tornado, or the chaotic interaction of cells in a living organism—at a higher level it will appear more patterned. Given certain information determining their interactions, the parts become self-organizing and the results more coherent. This information consists of the interaction rules nature imposes on the components: the power of attraction and repulsion forces in the nucleus, the effects of heat differentials and absorption rates in the tornado, the receptor and combinatory rules of cells. Until humans understood these rules, they considered all these systems as merely random acts of the gods; now they can conceptualize and deal with them. Similarly, information and cultural rules in organizations lead to dynamic stability (though not equilibrium) at the systems level. Given a few accepted rules and goals, intelligent organizations—in a manner similar to natural organisms—tend to self-mobilize to eliminate perceived threats or to exploit opportunities.[59] This self-organizing trait is the principle underlying society's faith in the efficiency of marketplaces and the efficacy of freedom in democracy. Yet managers often dismiss such self-mobilizing tendencies, fearing their organizations will be less efficient if not thoroughly "controlled," a process that destroys much value-creating innovation.

People and organizations can grow only through change; hence, seeking control through permanent structure leads to suicide. For healthy growth, change must be an expectation everywhere in the organization. Resistance to change will always exist, reflecting people's need to protect a sense of dignity, pride, and identity (as defined in their past accomplishments). It is not a fundamental tendency toward inertia.[60] But in dynamic systems, minor initial innovations (like chaos theory perturbations) can amplify into enormous changes.[61] In self-mobilizing systems, as in anthills, small-scale inputs (like food signals) amplified positively through feedback can have large favorable effects (whether in exploiting opportunities or countering perceived threats).[62] Too much emphasis on consensus can easily dampen differences, enthusiasms, options perceived, and the strength of potential changes. Consequently there is a need to maintain points of productive tension between the dominant culture and those who create perturbations in it. Given the proper extrinsic incentives (of both benefits and threats), healthy disaggregated organizations can quickly self-rebalance in response to outside changes.[63] Organizational survival as well as growth is best nurtured through tolerating disequilibrium, not enforcing equilibrium. Disorder is the price of progress in a dynamic world.

## Avoiding Suboptimization and Half-Measures

Underlying the faith that organizations will self-mobilize to seek a higher-level stability is the fact that—given a choice of whether their organization will win or lose—few people will choose losing. The problems are really how (a) to avoid their suboptimizing—identifying success at very small (departmental or local) levels rather than at the enterprise level—and (b) to energize everyone for high enough accomplishment. Aligned purpose helps with this. But for maximum effectiveness, it must be reinforced with both identity-creating information about how each unit is contributing to enterprise goals and incentives that support this identity.[64] Multiple performance measures, intimately linked to the enterprise's vision, style, and strategy, are crucial supports for this process.[65] All people (including blue-collar shop workers) within companies—like Chaparral, Intel, Ford, Gore, Lincoln Electric, SAS, Matsushita, Wal-Mart, and most new enterprises—seem willing to contribute more positively when they see this identity clearly.[66] Robert Haas, CEO of Levi Strauss & Co., calls these "conceptual controls." He notes, "It is the ideas of a business that are controlling, not some manager with authority."[67] Gore's lattice unstructure is the ultimate embodiment of this concept.

However, having only a few independent units or teams operating independently, within a larger organizational context that is still bureaucratic, generally creates significant problems. Other groups look at the teams as disorganized, elitist, or specially favored, and team members often cannot break clear of the surrounding organizations' constraining ethos. Margaret Wheatley describes a common result of such half measures:

> I received a call from a client who was deep into a project and very frustrated. His organization had collected data, defined five key problem areas, and created task forces to solve each [as they had in the past]. Yet the managers were having problems coordinating the task forces. The longer the task forces studied the issues, the more they saw the problems as interrelated. Threads of interconnection were everywhere, yet the groups were still acting autonomously from one another. The result was fatigue and impatience. People simply wanted to get on with implementing. Anything would be a relief after so many deadening meetings and detailed plans.[68]

The entire culture, or at least the major divisions involved, must see themselves as integral participants in a change, and the total organization as committed to innovation and progress. This universal attitude toward change is critical and must be engendered from the top. But in business organizations innovators need to be clearly focused on customer needs and feel a compelling urgency to succeed, to win. How to accomplish this pragmatically is the subject of Chapters 5 through 9.

## SUMMARY

Although independent collaboration has long existed, software vastly extends capabilities for individual and group interactions both within the enterprise and in its external environments. In most cases, independent collaboration involves individuals or small units working interactively toward a common goal, with software as a supporting agent. Software allows individuals, their customers, and their organizations to define more precisely the ways in which their activities interlink. It provides the disciplines and processes that formal authority and bureaucracy used to supply, but without their deadening costs. It enables much greater linkages and leverages than individuals could achieve in other ways.

Managing more independent collaboration inside the enterprise and with external partners, through software, has become the key to much fast-cycle, high-impact innovation. Using other well-developed concepts of collaboration, software enables performance to go well beyond the limits traditionally imposed by team management. These concepts focus closely on integrating the intrinsic motivations of people with the overarching purposes of the organization, providing an infrastructure of superabundant information, and consciously developing richer and more profuse networks of relationships than teams allow. Using new circular organization forms—with information-intense specialized core competencies at their center and more circular permeable unit structures to utilize the knowledge—managers can better exploit the random, swirling, nonlinear, exponential learning processes that characterize most complex innovations. This chapter tries to provide some useful insights from what research and practical observation tell us about managing these processes, given the increasing complexity of both innovation and customer use—and the vastly enhanced capabilities of software to deal with this environment.

Advanced software supports human self-learning on a scale never before possible. In organizations without the interconnections allowed by software, individuals can neither extend their ideas to as wide a population nor can they obtain the sophisticated interconnection of ideas that permits others to multiply the value of these ideas in their marketplaces. As important, through electronic simulations and visualization processes, they can communicate, share, and innovate new concepts more rapidly, richly, and precisely. As following chapters will show, software can expand this process enormously by being programmed to learn—and even invent—by itself. In its ultimate forms—networks and object orientation—software can permit individuals to offer ideas to the world (whether invented by themselves or the software) and let those ideas seek their own interconnections with as many other potential users and ideas as is possible. On networks, electronic ideas or "objects" become "Velcro balls" of concepts with hooks to which either other Velcro balls of ideas or user concepts can connect. This leads to the concepts of auto-catalysis and negative entropy for the astonishing, rapid corporate and economic growth we analyze in later chapters.

# 5

# Motivating Creativity Toward Markets

Continual, self-generated innovation requires more than providing information, creating connections, and developing a strong congruence between individuals' goals and those of the enterprise. There need to be accepted methodologies and a genuine passion for creating something new and valuable for users. It is useless to debate whether innovation should be technology driven or demand driven. The answer is, of course, both—and opportunistically. Both really depend on the same forces of creative intellect, passion, and perseverance. Continually innovative enterprises consciously create a climate and mechanisms to motivate innovation toward market needs through independent collaboration as well as the more structured approaches cited in Chapter 8. The key elements supporting high levels of innovativeness directed toward markets include:

- Helping potential innovators systematically expand their repertoire of available techniques and options for innovation.
- Consciously structuring interactions and participation with users to yield maximum serendipity and motivation for both parties to solve problems and introduce solutions.
- Systematically attacking "white spaces" to find totally new solutions.
- Managing the full range of processes needed to create and implement continual change.
- Creating a total organizational philosophy and talent base that sup-

ports rapid, disaggregated, autonomous innovation, driven, not from the center, but by committed decentralized entrepreneurs.

## KEY ELEMENTS FOR HIGH INNOVATIVENESS

All true innovations begin as the first interconnection of two or more previously disassociated ideas in a new context, usually to satisfy a need or solve a problem.[1] In some cases inventor-entrepreneurs can make such interconnections analytically, if they consciously scan and interrelate a wide enough range of alternatives. More often, the first insight is more fortuitous or intuitive, and initial solutions may rely heavily on a "culch bag" approach. Successful sailors, adventurers, or fishermen over the years often develop such culch bags—or piles—of interesting tools, parts, scraps, and pieces that may be useful in an emergency or to solve the myriad problems they may encounter when all alone.

### The Culch Bag Approach

Systematic observations, inventors' seminars, and formal studies of the invention process have demonstrated that inventors tend to share a similar characteristic: they are pack rats. They savor and save clever things (devices, instruments, ideas, clippings, observations, notes) they may someday apply to solving a problem or assemble with something else in a new way to create a new effect. When either occurs, there is an invention—a new construct that changes the past stasis. Similarly, the great creative minds of science, art, or technology—like Newton's, Michelangelo's, DaVinci's, Darwin's, Dali's, Edison's, Kettering's, and Feynman's—have tended to contain a vast hodgepodge of collected but as yet unrelated references, experiences, experimental constructs, and observations about the world. When confronted by a new problem or new data, any truly creative inventor's mind scans its culch bag of possibilities, often subconsciously, to come up with a novel interconnection. Great inventors tend to be more driven and to have a wider range of culch than others. There have been many attempts to stimulate and simulate their ideation processes. In an interesting current example:

• Ideation International Inc. and Invention Machine Corp. have created software to assist in this process. Based on algorithms about the invention process and a problem-solving method called TRIZ, developed by noted scholar Genrich Altshuller—and using a database from some

40,000 actual inventions and patents—the software provides a "think-ing partner" for would-be inventors.[2] Users state a feature of a product or process they would like to improve. Invention Machine's software module, Principle, then presents a broad range of relevant principles and alternative attack approaches people have found useful for that class of problem. A second module, called Effects, analytically sets forth all the potential effects that different geometrical and physical combina-tions might yield. A third module, Predictions, lets users input the sys-tem's performance features or actions they would like to improve, coupled with the objects involved with each action. Ideation's Innova-tion Workbench includes the ability to add a company's own specialized scientific database. The software generates possible solutions to prob-lems posed. Repeated for different elements of a system, the software provides a "virtual culch bag" and initial test ground for millions of con-ceptual possibilities from which inventors can select the most pertinent to test in their particular system.[3]

## Differentness, Not Sameness

In today's complex scientific and technology worlds, each specialist may have a huge repertoire of concepts in a single field. However, to make a real advance, individuals may have to combine their special culch (say, of timing concepts) with another's storage culch, another's liquid crys-tals, another's electrostatics, and so on. In essence, each has an inven-tory of "solutions in waiting" to be assembled with those of other specialists when properly stimulated and interconnected. A key factor in stimulating innovation is to support contacts between people with widely different backgrounds. Differentness, not sameness, is the touchstone of discovery. Sometimes individuals randomly interact to create something new that has use implications, as Herb Boyer and Stanley Cohen's interaction at a Hawaiian scientific meeting did in making recombinant DNA a reality, or as Kary Mullis's informal inter-actions with computer and molecular specialists did for PCR. More often the stimulus is a newly perceived problem or opportunity that old or highly fragmented solutions have yet to satisfy—as was Ted Hoff's interconnection of the various component technological (CPU, ROM, and RAM) systems to produce the first microprocessor or Nathan Mill-stein's integrating the disparate concepts of cell fusion, cancer cell im-mortality, and specialized cells' bonding to specific receptors when he created hybridomas. Most require widespread interactions and inde-pendent collaboration to succeed. In the best history of the Nobel

Prize–winning innovation, monoclonal antibodies, Cambrosio and Keating note:

> Contrary to what some sociologists of science argue, a common culture is not a prerequisite for the emergence of a scientific network. . . . Detailed accounts of laboratory work and of scientific controversies bring into focus the local, contingent nature of scientific knowledge and practice. . . . [In developing hybridomas] The presence of an expanding network was not only a precondition for the circulation of cells and reagents, it was also, and more importantly, crucial to the constitution and maintenance of the properties attributed to those cells and reagents, such as purity and (exquisite) specificity. . . . What one did could not be accounted for independently of a context, which, in fact, became the content. The different contexts, in other words, gave rise to differing interpretations. . . . Not only were [various research] operations predicated upon the use of conflicting interpretive frameworks . . . but in the end those frameworks became increasingly blurred; monoclonal antibodies were at once [both] natural substances *and* artificial tools, able to carry out human intentions at the microscopic level.[4]

Advanced scientific discovery generally becomes a collaborative network process in which different cultures and conceptualizations give rise to totally new insights that would not occur without wide diversity and interaction. Complexity is often sufficiently great that the lines of discovery and invention become so blurred that it is impossible to determine patentability or scientific precedence. The individual motivations and interactions of scientists become the organization itself (if any organization can be said to exist in such competitive collaborations). And advance proceeds with exponential rapidity, bounded only by the intellect and interactions of the scientists and the rules of science.

## Solutions and Uses in Waiting

Software-based independent collaboration increases the probability and creative scope of either type of culch bag intersection. One can scan many more possible solution sources through network search software or attract a wider variety of potential solutions by posing the problem, or pieces of it, on the network. Both expand the ideation base. Working on a common model in a virtual laboratory or passing experimental work sequentially from one laboratory to another in a continual 24-hour-a-day work cycle can achieve similar, but often more focused, effects. In these situations, the network can not only provide many of the interaction features conferences and seminars used to, it can radically increase the frequency and range of such contacts.

Creative interconnection of possible solutions in waiting is relatively easy with "intra" or "inter" nets. But patent and laboratory files are full of inventive interconnections that never saw the light of use—like the hat-tipping machine for gentlemen whose arms are occupied. Successful innovators also either have or connect into a culch bag of "users and problems in waiting." They have clients, employers, friends, users, or institutions they know well enough to understand or find "use relevancies." Computer development has been rampant with examples of this phenomenon.

• John von Neumann was in the midst of the need the hydrogen bomb project had for super-fast calculation. This need led the great mathematician to seek ways to break the constraints that mechanical calculators—and the fixed relays, crossbars, and logic circuits of railroads and telephony—had always posed for fast, flexible calculation. His flash of genius was to recognize that binary electronic interconnections could be made to depend on the state of other switches and relays at the time, and thus could be stored in and directed by the machine itself. His mathematical mind saw that, given the essential unity between data and instructions, a properly designed electronic network could become a self-modifying logic machine to solve not just a few, but many classes of problems. Von Neumann's computer conception intersected electronics' speed, mathematical logic, and a new concept of use.

• Later, a group of programmers and engineers—intensely frustrated by too many "users in waiting" for mainframe computers and familiar with the general classes of "problems in waiting" for the computer—conceptualized time sharing. Their critical insight was to associate the users' needs with the technological difference in speed between the computer's calculation rate (milliseconds) and the users' capacity to communicate with it (roughly 10 bits per second). The difference became a window of time when further users could interact directly with the machine. Later "shrink-wrap software" creators recognized a further problem in waiting—that most users did not want to program at all and resented the loss of control and delays that centralized programming priesthoods caused. These innovators created an interface that eliminated all user waiting, could manipulate users' input directly and instantaneously, and brought the computer much closer to the customer's personalized control. The Internet's innovations went even further: interconnecting multiple users, problems, and solutions in waiting simultaneously. Now Internet appliances, search engines, and parallel processing promise to eliminate even more of these "solution and use" mismatches.

## Structuring User Interactions and Participation

Such innovations have provided many useful technological infrastructures for widespread independent collaboration. But simply allowing inventors-innovators to contact each other (and customers) may not be sufficient in itself to create meaningful innovation. The structure, commitment, and analytical content of that interaction are most important. Several classics suggest how major companies have structured independent collaboration to overcome this problem.

• Hewlett-Packard, in its instrument division, long used what it called the "next-bench technique." Because its test equipment had to perform in conjunction with the world's most advanced laboratory experimentation and measurement systems, its designers worked at the "next bench" to the most advanced laboratory experimenters in the field. If they could solve the problem for those experimenters, similar equipment could be modified for use by interacting with other potential advanced customers, decreasing introduction risks, and possibly leading to a test equipment line that dominated those applications before competitors responded. Both HP technologists and users gained valuable insights from the interactive design and tests the process elicited. HP kept its Instrument Division segments very small so the benefits of innovation to both the individual and collaborating units were clear to all.

For problem finding, HP now uses scanning units—partnerships of two to four people equally balanced between marketing and technical experts—to go out together and visit current customers, former customers, and non-customers in their own environments. Supporting each unit's visit is an enormous amount of background research from other HP groups. From this research and their visits, the units create a "map" of innovation targets that attempts to match customer opportunity areas with internal technical capability areas.[5] Once a project begins, HP screens opportunities repeatedly against ten factors the company has found crucial to product success: understanding of user needs, alignment with HP and divisional strategy, careful competitive analysis and product positioning, technical risk assessment, clear priority among criteria, regulatory compliance, distribution channel issues, continuing commitment to the market, endorsement by upper management, and total organizational support. HP has found that if two or more of these factors are overlooked, the project is likely to fail. Almost all successful projects score positively on all counts.[6]

• Markem Machine Company is the world's largest manufacturer of specialized product marking machines. Its CEO selected a group of individual mavericks and design wizards and instructed them to figure out how to "design Markem out of its existing marketplaces." Gathering data from their own customers, production units, and supplier groups, these individuals worked together to set specifications and establish conceptual designs for multiple products that could make Markem obsolete in its own marketplaces. The company then implemented these before competitors could do so. Other companies have used a "red team–blue team" approach, having two or more groups compete with designs to "put the company out of business."

• Early in its design cycle, Ford's Team Taurus exploded the new Taurus-Sable design into 400 subsystems. For each subsystem, a team visited all qualified suppliers to set best-in-class specifications for that subsystem, based on the best interactive performance that materials and technologies would allow within the three-year design time horizon. It then posed these as challenges for internal inventors to exceed in order to avoid the activity's being outsourced.[7] Further, recognizing that customers associated overall value with relatively small but clever design features they could see, Team Taurus also asked everyone to propose "tremendous trifles" that could intrigue and please the customer at little added cost to Ford. The results both delighted customers and instilled a personal identity with the car for their proposers. The combination created a level of innovation not seen for decades at Ford.

## Caring Why

The motivation of innovators in making contacts may be more important than the mechanism of contact. If the innovator does not respect the customer's people and viewpoint—and really care about their concerns—nothing significant will happen. Merely asking customers what they "think their needs will be" usually just develops wish lists. However, if the questions are phrased differently—"What problems do you have? What issues concern you most?"—they connect better with both innovators and customers. Other questions address issues customers can talk about accurately:[8] "What can't you explain about the way your process or product is working?" "Where do existing products or processes fail to meet expectations?" "What currently limits performance?" "What new performance limits do you foresee?" "What performance measures would cause you to change your practice or replace the current product?" "What support services would significantly improve performance?" "What can't you do that you would like the product to do?" One key in these exchanges is to listen for anomalies: quirks in performance or interactions with other systems, things the technology innovator did not know about actual product performance or thought were already solved.[9] Some of these can come from interviews; others stem from analyzing failure rates, discussing specific problems with users, and tracking actual use in the marketplace. Interestingly, field service people are rarely good at seeing new possibilities. Their future and culture are generally too involved in making the existing solutions work.

However, the main problem in generating needs information is not ideation; innovation managers repeatedly say they are bombarded by too many good ideas, both from within and externally. The problems are to focus ideation more on specifics with competitive impact (i.e., figures of merit) and to motivate innovators toward ends that both technicians and customers really care about and are willing to pursue through to success. Studies at Texas Instruments, 3M, and Hewlett-Packard have reported that virtually all successful projects had self-selected (not appointed) champions heading them. Innovation often requires an emotional shift strong enough to move people from old ideas and comfortable solutions to initially painful, but more beneficial ones. For example, Gillette reports that initially each new razor type loses money, engendering a strong reaction against it. But new razors—those introduced in the last three years—soon dominate the company's profits.

Mere connection may lead to problem solving. Innovation requires prolonged (interpersonal or screen-to-screen) interaction between innovators and users on problems both parties care about. The close interaction and intensity needed for mutual involvement have led companies to develop "virtual collaboration spaces" where people (including users) can see and manipulate electronic images of physical innovation, see and converse with each other during their interactions, and share equipment and measurements electronically. Diversity of viewpoints is essential. Those who actually solve a problem frequently are not those experts one would have expected to do so. As Richard Feynman so well demonstrated, critical insight often comes from someone's associating the problem with a different analog or seeing the data or anomaly for the first time.[10] There are solid reasons why customers make such a high percentage of innovations. They care that the problem gets solved, and they have a different frame of reference from the internal innovator. Conversely, technical experts have a conceptual framework that lets them see anomalies and analogies the customer cannot. Bringing these parties' different perspectives together properly offers rich innovation opportunities for both.

## SYSTEMATICALLY ATTACKING WHITE SPACES

To extend the search process and find truly out-of-the-ordinary solutions, many companies use a "white space" technique to identify where totally new or unexploited opportunities may lie. One white space technique we have used often and successfully with both large and small companies follows:

• Company participants are first asked to identify the most important and interesting trends and environmental factors affecting their firm's future performance and to come as close as they can to identifying specific data points defining current and past performance on these trends. This may take some separate research. Participants then connect the data points and establish trend slopes, carefully utilizing exponential growth assumptions wherever underlying data suggest this is appropriate. The process is repeated for critical performance factors affecting the company's customers and suppliers. The next instruction is to "lay these trends on top of each other, three to seven years ahead," and to ask what opportunities these intersections suggest. Two significant trends intersecting usually define a major new profit opportunity. Where four or more intersect, a whole new business or industry is likely to appear. For each opportunity, executives define figure of merit specifications and timing targets for the intersection, set priorities for urgency and importance, and put processes in place to encourage champions to find solutions.

Hewlett-Packard has expanded on its scanning unit techniques to get more white space concepts in a variety of ways.

• Its Medical Division sends each new engineer to a physiology course, then a two-week internship at Boston University Medical School, where they visit University Hospital and follow residents and doctors on their rounds, to obtain a macro view of the customer's environment. Relying on these and visits with other knowledgeable customers, HP has put together an internal "Hospital of the Future" video, envisioning how technology would improve patient care, lower costs, and handle other customer concerns better in the early 2000s. Scenarios were based on interviews involving many leading-edge hospitals about how specific clinical cases were handled now and combining their knowledge of what technologies could be anticipated five to ten years from now. Multiple scenarios were used to build up a holistic vision of how all HP's technologies could fit together to support patients, clinical staff, and hospitals better in the future.

In seeking such new opportunity sets, software's interactiveness, visualization capabilities, and language and conceptual disciplines enable a specificity and rate of exchange between producers, suppliers, different technical experts, and users that would otherwise be impossible. For example, high-resolution video simulations or virtual reality models can be used to visualize and modify hospital-of-the-future concepts. The value of such software capabilities grows greater as the innovation progresses toward the more costly stages of implementation. All parties can scan and test more options, bring more data to bear, visualize and evaluate options more completely, and discern anomalies and interrelationships among component systems and potential use patterns more effectively. Emergent models using genetic or object-oriented simulations can help identify trends and forecast new configurations, opportunities, or problems at higher levels of use or complexity than individuals can directly foresee—and thus break bottlenecks before they occur.

## Hierarchy-Free Rosetta Stones

Software networks are the rosetta stones allowing independent collaboration to find new effects and uses. They are hierarchy-free, instantaneous organizations. They bypass all those who expect solely to approve, disapprove, or pass on information. In rapidly changing environments, they allow specialists to interconnect as needed to identify new needs, solve complex problems, or create new results. Yet they allow the experts to physically remain in a peer environment that constantly deepens their specialties. Tushman and Anderson suggest that network organizations—because of their multiple contact points with other organizations, their capacities to sense and solve problems quickly, and their ability to assemble resources rapidly to "raid back" if a competitor moves ahead—have become the essence of competitiveness in many fields.[11] These include advanced research, semiconductors, publishing, financial trading, computers, real estate, entertainment, investment banking, test equipment, fashion products, consulting, small consumer products, design engineering, and advertising among others.

The PCR provides a classic example of how such independent collaborations rapidly multiply innovations to find and fill white spaces in an emerging high technology field. Rabinow notes for PCR:

> Within a very short time span some curious and wonderful reversals, and orthogonal movements, began happening: the concept itself became an experimental system; the experimental system became a technique; the techniques became concepts. These rapidly developing variations and mutually referential changes were integrated into a research milieu, first at Cetus, then very soon at many other places. . . . Thousands of scientists and technicians around the globe began using PCR, multiplying the modifications and feedback.[12]

## Swimming in the User's Environment

At the technological level, there are a number of ways to develop new problem insights. Most involve inserting a properly balanced innovation team into the customers' environment of use "to swim in the specific problems and data of interest to customers." Inventions often occur in this process as new minds perceive a problem for the first time, or as more concrete data and a more specific sense of context give people new perspectives. Innovations are pulled through by market demands, thus decreasing the resistances that occur if champions try to push through new concepts. There is no single best way to structure these innovative interactions.[13] As Chapter 8 notes, differently sized, oriented, and styled structures may perform better in different strategic circumstances. However, some examples will suggest how various open interface units have operated successfully to find and exploit customer needs.

The "lead user method" (developed by Eric Von Hippel) structures this kind of interaction for high impact. Searchers first identify the trends and characteristics on which specific users lead in selected marketplaces. Second, they develop indicators specifying those lead users who could expect and obtain a relatively high benefit from a solution. Third, they may co-locate a sample of these users—individually or in groups—to engage in group problem-solving sessions. Fourth, developed concepts from these sessions are tested with a wider sample of those who will be typical future users in that market. Teams co-locate depending on whose information is "stickiest"—that is, hardest to understand or transfer. If both need and producer information are sticky, the teams iterate from site to site for better understanding. The process is based on the fact that each party needs to actively experience the subtleties—or the unstated "tacit knowledge" of the other party—to avoid misunderstandings.[14]

An extension of this is the concept of "empathic design" developed by Dorothy Leonard-Barton, used primarily for adapting known technologies to users' needs. After standard market research and interviews have provided all the information they can, technologists accompanied by someone knowledgeable in the marketplace observe various users' practices in detail, and identify elements of design that would make the product more empathetic in that and similar uses. The technique is used to intensify and extend the innovation into new use areas through modification.[15] Using this technique, HP Medical Products observers found and solved problems that doctors and nurses neither articulated nor perceived. Thermos, Inc. videotaped hundreds of hours of people at home barbecuing to develop unique features for its successful new grill.

When truly motivated innovation suppliers interact with strongly motivated leading user-innovators, a kind of feeding frenzy of "what might be" often results. As each group builds on the others' visions, collaborative ideation reaches new heights and may be difficult to shut off. The "figure of merit" disciplines (set forth in Chapter 7) become very helpful in refining needs.

• Club Med provides an unusual internal application of opportunity generation. Club Med's staff members live and play in its villages along with customers-vacationers. The link between the two is purposely structured on the belief that the staff gains empathy with customer issues by actively sharing experiences with them. Club Med long utilized only an informal oral culture and apprentice system to capture the nuances of need on a personal basis. Although it now uses some written reports to transfer knowledge, the essence of its approach is personal observation while maintaining geographical and ethnic diversity; each culture observes operations and customer needs on a personal basis to bring out different insights. Successful extensions of Club Med's service offerings to conferences and cruises have all been customer initiated and pretested.[16]

• "Concept Engineering" is a more formal customer-centered process of data collection, reflection, and clarification designed to help companies develop product concepts that will meet or exceed customers' expectations. It was jointly developed between 1990 and 1992 by Shoji

Shiba and Gary Burchill at MIT and several members of the Center for Quality Management (Bolt Beranek and Newman, Gen-Rad, Analog Devices, Bose, Polaroid, and others). There are five stages to the process: understanding the customers' environment, converting this understanding into requirements, operationalizing requirements (developing metrics for how well solutions meet needs), concept generation, and concept selection.[17] A project team from development, manufacturing, and marketing usually spends several months identifying a matrix of target customers (from lead users to laggards) and developing an interview questionnaire. Representatives from marketing and technical groups pair off for interviews, with one person being the interviewer and the other the "scribe."

Participants are specially trained so they can better probe and listen, rather than direct the interview. They use a special KJ methodology (based on the "affinity diagram" developed by Kawakito Jiro, a Japanese anthropologist) to distill images and requirements in the customer environment. His principles focus on:

1. Not having a preconceived hypothesis and looking at the situation from many angles (a 360° perspective).
2. Using an interview guide loosely and following the path the customer creates.
3. Utilizing encountered problems or opportunities (chances) to jointly learn more with the customer during the interview.
4. Using intuition (it is the tool for discovery; logic is the tool for proof).
5. Seeking qualitative information (diversity of insight, intensity of cases, and personal experiences are more important than frequency).

Later analytical steps use more formal techniques to quantify the intensity and frequency of perceived needs. The technique is especially useful in high-investment, high-technology, multi-user settings, where it has identified both industry-wide and specific user requirements.

Through such processes, leaders of successful, continually innovative companies create a heightened focus and sense of opportunism, urgency, common purpose, and strategic targeting to stimulate their individual innovators, diverse specialist organizations, and collaborating units toward useful results.[18] Unfortunately, even with the best formal systems in place, successful innovations rarely leap responsively, full blown from the brow of an inventive genius or a group. They usually require much dogged development, amplification, modification, psychological leadership, support, and trial and error to become effective.

## A PROCESS FOCUS FOR COLLABORATIVE CHANGE AND INNOVATION

Any innovation involves a change process. It threatens the status quo of the company's existing products and resources, the way the company and its units relate to markets, its organizational structures, and in many cases its whole strategic posture. Because innovative changes are highly sensitive to context, and management establishes much of this context, researchers have found relatively consistent prerequisites for change in continually innovative organizations:

- Change generally has top management support.
- Successful change is built on the unique strengths and values of the organization.
- The specifics of change are not imposed from the top.
- Change tends to be holistic because changing one part of a culture requires other changes to achieve efficient consistency among all parts.
- Successful change tends to be planned but nimble.
- The plan itself tends to be incremental, continually reviewed, and modified.
- Changes occur not just at the surface but into the very guts of the organization.
- Change tends to be approached from a multiple stakeholder viewpoint, with the primary impetus usually coming from external environments.
- In successful enterprises, change becomes an accepted, ongoing process.

In his excellent work, O'Toole summarizes as follows: "[In these firms] nothing stands still. [They] think approximate and continuous, not exact and complete. . . . They recognize that all change is personal; every innovation in products, machine processes, or plant layouts causes disruption for some parties, power gains for others, and losses for many. . . . This is as true of customer organizations as it is internal ones."[19]

### Emerging Organizations and Results

Each innovation subsystem tends to move at its own rate, and each organization tends to mutate actively to support or resist change to reflect its own self-interests.[20] Hence overall change tends to flow incrementally, with each part moving in its own rhythm.[21] This emergent process is the inverse of the "rational analytical" or "formal" strategic planning process (of analyzing environments, analyzing strengths, weaknesses, opportunities, and threats, defining alternatives, choosing among them, and then implementing). Henry Mintzberg discusses the increasing irrelevancy of such highly structured formal processes in his articles on the demise of strategic planning.[22] What has emerged in truly innovative organizations is a highly creative focus on strategic vision, developing flexible competencies, intensive interactions with customers about needs, starting many new initiatives, rapidly adapting to tumultuous change, feeding successes as they grow, terminating failures quickly, constantly redeploying resources into new patterns as partial successes emerge, and developing and motivating people to actively support the vision and continuous change.

## A Managed, Not Haphazard, System

The overall process is experimental, nonlinear, organic, evolutionary, and purposeful. Within successful companies, it is far from haphazard. Continual innovation occurs largely because a few key executives develop a broad vision for their organizations, inculcate a sense of aligned purpose among their people toward this vision, and consciously manage their enterprise's value systems and atmospheres to support it. From top management to bench levels in our samples' most innovative companies, executives seem to focus relentlessly and opportunistically on seeking and solving customers' emerging problems. Early signals for major strategic innovations rarely arrive with complete clarity or full-blown solutions in hand. Many innovators say their first perceptions usually occur as "something you feel uneasy about," "inconsistencies," or "anomalies" between some aspect of performance and some general perception of what the market or future environment is likely to call for.

To make sure their organizations respond rapidly to these early signals and to avoid internal information screens, effective innovation managers consciously develop multiple, credible internal and external sources to provide continual, jarring, and objective views to their people about the company and its surrounding environments. Some consciously develop a sense of "competitive paranoia": that disaster can come from many directions because the goal is so important that it will attract strong competition. At first, they seem consciously to generate and consider a wide array of alternative approaches without getting irrevocably wedded to any. They accept that they do not know what the right solution is or what will actually work in the final situation. In large enterprises, they actively encourage those with concerns about new issues to experiment with new ways of working. As early ideas crystallize, they may consciously allow alternatives to go underground until they are proved enough to counter entrenched positions. Since innovations threaten existing power centers that might kill important changes aborning, guiding executives often keep alternatives fluid until they have sufficient information to argue persuasively against preconceived ideas or past practices.

## Partial, Tentative, and Experimental Processes

At this stage, processes are likely to involve many individuals' studying, challenging, questioning, listening, and talking to creative people outside ordinary decision channels. Managers generate many options but try to avoid irreversible commitments. Top executives may sense the general directions they want to emerge, but purposely offer only broad visionary statements and endorse a few key figures of merit as guides, preferring to let others shape specific solutions and become committed to them. Early solutions tend to be partial, tentative, and experimental. As experiments succeed, their successes are amplified in new legends and with greater resource support. Errors are killed as quietly as possible unless they can contribute to "what-not-to-do" legends. Successful units get to expand their tasks and budgets. Healthy components in the organization's ongoing posture are carefully supported, while shifting momentum at the margin toward attractive new possibilities. By now, the heads of successful experimenting groups have become champions—not just buying into the idea but actively looking at the project as a ticket to success. The project is not planned, then implemented; it may well be half implemented before it is formally announced.

Only as the projects become large enough to require substantial capital may explicit formal planning techniques be necessary. Obviously, before major plant, distribution, marketing, regulatory clearance, or equipment expenditures occur, there must be formal analyses of their payoffs, using the best techniques available. Up to this point, projects may be kept small, ad hoc, and not integrated into a formal program or strategy. At some point, however, executives may want to extend support by selectively exposing the project through wider team membership, committee discussions, task forces, or retreats. In addition to facilitating smoother implementation, many companies report that such interactive consensus building substantially improves the quality, timing, and consistency of implementation decisions. As important as getting the concepts right is the positive and innovative assistance participants will give in working out solutions when things go wrong, as they always do in any major innovative change. Successful transitions focus more on people and the processes of change than on formal structures of organization or control systems.

## Intervention Points

Because of the complexity of interactions, most managers say that they can intervene most successfully at five points: establishing the vision and culture, endorsing winning strategic targets, guiding people selection, formulating and implementing incentive programs, and managing the atmosphere of innovation. Chapter 6 covers the first four in detail. The fifth requires further amplification. Executives have to balance the forces of independence and collaboration carefully. Various projects will require different balances of each. It is important that incentives and rewards match the needed balance on each project. (See Chapter 8.) When high degrees of collaboration are essential, great differentiation between individual rewards is unwise. When great independence is needed, the opposite view would apply. A single system applied across all projects is unwise, unless all projects are rather similar.

In a knowledge-generating organization, a primary criterion for success (and hence rewards) should be the quality of the knowledge created. Unfortunately, most performance measures tend to be transactional: how many projects, interchanges, papers, patents, and so forth individuals or teams produced. A conscious effort is needed to reward the quality of each person's performance in all relevant spheres, as Sony did with the presentation of its Crystal Awards for outstanding technical achievement, its awards to innovators of a percentage of first-year sales for new products, and its sharing of high-profile public awards to give bench-level participants high prestige. For these evaluations, there is no substitute for a series of close-at-hand observations by knowledgeable, professional peers and managers.[23]

## CHANGING THE TOTAL ORGANIZATIONAL PHILOSOPHY

No chapter or list of concepts can capture the full complexity of managing independent collaborations. But Kevin Kelly's (slightly paraphrased) definition of the characteristics and rules for managing productive self-organizing systems is interesting as a guideline:[24]

- ***Distribute energy and initiative.*** Recognize that the culture of the organization, the behavior of a market, life within a biological body, or energy in an anthill all derive from a multitude of smaller parts.
- ***Control at lower or outermost points.*** Since everything is connected to everything else in a distributed network, control must rest at multiple locations, not just the top, with each agent relatively free to act within its own context.
- ***Cultivate increasing returns.*** Whenever a concept or skill is successful, strengthen it by creating positive feedback.
- ***Grow by chunking.*** The only way to make complex systems work is to base them on autonomous interacting modules.
- ***Maximize the fringes.*** Unified entities are vulnerable during rapid change. Dynamic health depends on diversity at remote borders, where a healthy fringe speeds adaptation, increases resilience, and generates high levels of innovation.
- ***Honor errors.*** Advancement demands going outside conventional methods, which necessitates errors; evolution is systematic learning from both successes and errors.
- ***Pursue no single optimum; have multiple goals.*** Simple systems may be efficient in the short run but are vulnerable in the long run. Complex adaptive ones may be inefficient in the short run but efficient in the long run.
- ***Seek persistent disequilibrium.*** Equilibrium is death; life involves persistent disequilibrium.
- ***Allow change to change itself.*** Nothing is fixed in the evolving universe; change changes the relevant rules for itself over time.

To these we would add *maximize information availability and use.* Hypercompetition demands that decisions both be made faster *and* with more information. Already demand is up so much (three times) for IT-competent people that IT-trained male college graduates command a 40% premium wage, and IT-trained females gain a 50% premium over their peers. Those with entrepreneurial attitudes and proved team skills are even more sought after by business schools and employers. To support these professionals, the need for technicians is growing at 16 to 20% per year, with ubiquitous "fix-its" being in even higher demand for skunk works teams, while demand for blue-collar production workers continues to drop. The job market is rewarding the full range of innovative intellect—know what, know how, know why, and care why—with high premiums representing its value. Software is at the heart of independent collaborative endeavors. But it needs to be supported by people who can use it well in a collaborative mode.

Some interesting rules are emerging for recruiting, developing, and managing innovative enterprises in the future. Most current data and studies say that successful innovation managers in this independent collaborative world will be:

- **Winners,** driven to be Number 1, but understanding that winning takes a collaborative effort. In today's winner-take-all markets, Number 1 frequently makes multiples (four to ten) times the return of others.[25] In high technology, second-best performance gets blown out, while the best sees more advanced problems, attracts the best people, can learn faster than competitors, and makes even higher returns later.

- **More specialized than ever,** but with a mind-set and capacity to link to others. T-shaped skills are essential to have the depth to make advances and the scope to genuinely relate to customers and the other specialists needed to make a significant advance.

- **Network persuaders,** who do not rely heavily on delegated authority. On networks, executives must persevere by persuasion, logic, their capacity to assemble relevant information, and the power of their models and data.

- **Excited by novelty,** ambiguity, learning, and solutions. While tolerating the great disorderliness of multiple competing idea sets, they must convey the challenge and excitement that truly novel solutions create versus the sense of mediocrity that copying brings. Innovative managers like to experiment, nurture ideas, and expect to succeed.

- **Process oriented,** who care about people and are not order givers. Primarily managing culture and information, they excite others, introduce sizzle into concepts, and understand entertainment value in work and products.

- **Software familiar, contract managers, and deal makers.** They understand how to manage software development and use, interconnect people and organizations, and make cooperation beneficial to all parties. They are the gatekeepers, connecting the unit to others. Though not programmers, they must understand what software can do realistically and keep up to date on its potentials.

- **International in outlook.** Increasingly, finding solutions and leveraging innovation's full potentials will require a truly international viewpoint and comfort in working in that world.

There is little question that these more disaggregated modes of software-enabled innovation will require major changes throughout most organizations. Those who want to win will not delay in beginning these changes.

## SUMMARY

One of the most important aspects of innovation management is actively motivating people to solve *user* problems with *new* solutions. A starting point is to consciously extend people's culch bags of possible solutions by encouraging wider personal and software networking with a more diverse range of users and other technical experts. But successful innovative collaboration requires more than mere contact; it demands deep understanding of the unique performance parameters and qualitative context of the problem itself. It requires a genuine will to seek new solutions that may be harder to find and to implement than accepting the costs of present inadequacies. Successful solutions must not only satisfy the WIIFM (what's in it for me) question for customers; problem solvers must become engaged enough, and feel rewarded enough, to put in the enormous effort innovations usually involve.

All of these factors suggest an innovation system where technologists actively live in the customer's environment, engage with many outside sources of ideas, and interact with both customers and other experts as tightly as possible around simulations, models, or prototypes that help discipline their thinking as well as visualize each element of their interaction as specifically as possible. This chapter sets forth a number of organizational and software methodologies that support innovation at the customer interface and stimulate the identification of new innovation potentials in the white spaces between existing demands and potential future demands. Market connectedness is perhaps the most important single dimension in business innovation. But continual innovation will occur at this interface only if the full panoply of management structures and attitudes (described in Parts II through IV of this book) is in place to support it.

# PART III

# TOP MANAGEMENT'S ROLE

# 6

# Vision, Leadership, and Strategic Focus

The most critical single role in stimulating innovation is top management leadership. Only top managers can establish the palpable visions, focused strategies, and challenging, rewarding support environments that most encourage innovation. To provide these, the CEO does not have to be a technologist. Many companies—from Genentech and Merck, to AT&T, Wal-Mart, NovaCare, and Pilkington Bros.—have thrived innovatively under nontechnical managers. However, in all of our sample's most innovative companies, top managers clearly expect, appreciate, and actively support innovation. They personally stimulate and champion:

- A truly exciting corporate vision built around challenging strategic goals.
- A genuine technology strategy that defines how and where the firm will be preeminent.
- A balanced portfolio of programs clearly structured to achieve these goals and to provide the time horizons to meet them.
- A few selected core competencies that give the company best-in-world capabilities and provide unique value for customers.
- A set of figure-of-merit performance targets that crisply define what winning competitively means in each critical arena.
- Highly disaggregated, self-directed, nonbureaucratic organizational structures that both leverage interactive innovation and maintain strategic focus.

- High-profile risk taking and entrepreneurial incentives to reward those who take on the struggles and ambiguity of innovation.

This and the next chapter develop these concepts in sequence.

## INNOVATION ALONG MULTIPLE DIMENSIONS

Top managers tend to make truly innovative organizations inventive along many different dimensions simultaneously: for example, in technology, human relations, finance, marketing, management processes, organizational forms, and incentive systems.[1] In fact, innovation in one area often would be ineffective without innovativeness in the others. Most innovation exemplars in both manufacturing and services—like Intel, Wal-Mart, Sun Microsystems, Hewlett-Packard, Silicon Graphics, Sony, MCI, Astra-Hässle, Federal Express, Disney, W.L. Gore, Genentech, Polaroid, Kyocera, and Microsoft—have been creative in both technology and other support areas. For example:

- Intel, in its early years under Robert Noyce and Gordon Moore, created a variety of new concepts to support its hardware innovation approaches. These included forming part-time councils to handle the firm's staff activities, the "McIntel" approach to expanding capacity by cloning successful smaller production lines in discrete units rather than creating ever bigger production units, and the use of conscious "vertical mixing" to ensure a variety of different ages, experience sets, and skills on design teams.

- Polaroid, under Edwin Land, pioneered in the use of small, ad hoc, skunk works organizations; no-dividend policies to maintain cash and increase shareholder gains; and strategic outsourcing of all its electronics, camera production, and film substrate activities to lower its investments and leverage its internal intellectual capabilities.

- Merck, under CFO Judy Lewent's guidance, innovated new financing techniques to support its large ($350 million per project), long-term (ten- to fifteen-year), high-risk (three successes in ten) project development activities. Using the kind of options analysis common in stock evaluations, Merck evaluates risks and payoffs in broader terms that consider the loss of options forgone and the value of knowledge built up on a project that might not use it directly. Lewent notes: "Our success or failure won't result from the quality of our scientists alone; it will also come from the quality of our thinking about where to invest."[3]

- Kyocera, a world leader in ceramics innovation and selected electronics fields, has invented unique organizational forms, accountability measures, motivational programs, and corporate giving strategies to support its technological innovation. Chairman Kazuo Inamori calls this approach his "amoeba management practice." Kyocera organizes into the smallest possible units (amoebas) for profit-and-loss responsibility. Although Kyocera is a $10 billion company, each amoeba contains only two or three people. The approach emphasizes teamwork, entrepreneurial spirit, and fast adaptability. Each amoeba is responsible for clearly specified tasks, implementation of its own initiatives, and profitability of its task. Kyocera uses three metrics for each amoeba: (1) productivity = outputs produced ÷ hours worked by the amoeba, (2) value added = amoeba income − amoeba expenses, (3) hourly efficiency = amoeba value added ÷ amoeba hours worked.[4]

## CONTINUAL, PULSING, AND ORGANIC INNOVATION

In such organizations, innovation is continual, not necessarily continuous.[5] Continual innovation deals with the full life cycle of innovation and implies that there will be a relatively steady flow of innovations into the business over time. But there will also be a constant pulsing within various groups or market sectors among discovery, reduction to practice, initial commercial success, diffusion, maturity, and phasing out. Even the most innovative groups are rarely continuously innovative. They periodically end projects, refresh psychologically, help exploit the last innovation, or pause to develop or assemble new skills before moving on to the next problem. To maximize corporate benefits, innovative teams must help renew and diffuse knowledge as well as create it. Top executives must expect and deal constructively with this pulsing behavior.

Continual innovation requires consciously managing multiple projects at different phases in their full life cycle within a bubbling context of strong external forces that constantly demand strategic and tactical attention. These include (among others) changes in: competitive environments, supplier capabilities, technological possibilities, customer desires, demographic structures, resource availability, institutional threats, and totally new system possibilities. Each force and project pulses with its own unique rhythms and complexities. Even attempting to think linearly about the interaction of all these dynamics is a misconception.

One needs to visualize processes more in terms of biological or cellular analogies. In such systems, all units individually absorb new nutrients from a generalized environment and interactively fuse them into an organically growing structure. The complex interactions between science, technology, markets and changing resource options force a process of continual adaptation, accommodation, fusion, discarding, and building. For success, all elements of the organization must join in this pulsing continuum. How can top managers best guide and focus this labyrinthine endeavor?

## INNOVATION, PROFITS, AND HUMAN VALUES

The most innovative companies rarely espouse profits alone. They are innovative, humane, profitable, and dynamic at the same time. They make all change—whether near term, intermediate term, or long term; whether productivity generating, product supporting, organization or image enhancing, or new product creating—seem exciting, challenging, and honorable. While targeting profits carefully, they also project other strong overarching values, such as pushing the technological envelope, leadership and risk taking, impeccable integrity in all scientific or business dealings, continual growth and personal challenge for employees, and creating unique value for customers and stability for their communities.[6] These overarching purposes help integrate the more specific, and sometimes competing, goals of different divisions.

### Multiple Companies Within the Company

Because it is difficult for people to focus simultaneously on too many goals, many larger firms create "multiple companies within the company," and often multiple cultures within their overall culture. For example:

• Miscrosoft notes that "there is no single Microsoft culture. You might find twenty or thirty different cultures as you move from one project area to another." Nevertheless, there is a strong commonality of purpose and atmosphere across Microsoft: to be preeminent in desktop software. To achieve its goals, Microsoft has cash cow divisions innovating almost exclusively on current processes or products (like Word or Excel), while other groups innovate new products for the short and intermediate term (Windows extensions). Others focus on large, emerging areas (Internet software), and still others concentrate on next-generation concepts (Nathan Myhrvolds's Advanced Technology Group). There are even groups within the enterprise consciously trying to replace successful divisions in their existing marketplaces. ("If we don't replace ourselves, outsiders will.")[7]

## Lateral Diffusion and Learning

One of the true complexities of top management is understanding, balancing, guiding, and leading all these various cultures, with their different organizational forms and constantly changing environments.[8] Many talented organizations, like Thinking Machines, fail because they focus only on the "creative" culture of the enterprise. Creativity and innovation are not enough.[9] In robust firms, exploitation and diffusion of knowledge and capability enjoy at least equal emphasis. Lateral diffusion and learning—across all lines—are as important as longitudinal diffusion toward the marketplace. Managements that stimulate both innovation in the organization's individual cells and its lateral exploitation throughout the firm achieve much higher and more stable payoffs than those that merely exploit innovations in their original contexts. Chevron provides an excellent example.

• Chevron, with $32 billion in volume, operates in over one hundred countries. In its high-volume, narrow-margin businesses, a small margin shift translates into hundreds of millions in profits, but individual divisions were not sharing solutions they already had. In 1992 Chevron created a group (now numbering twenty-five) of very experienced "process masters" who seek out innovations in the divisions and help managers in other divisions to understand and implement them. It also established a best-practices discovery team to help link groups within the company dedicated to better practices in everything from safety to cost cutting. Housed within the corporate quality group, the team developed a "best-practices resource map" of both official and informal groups willing to share their knowledge on specialized subjects across the company and helped connect these groups through e-mail and conference mechanisms. Although neither group has line authority to implement changes, Chevron can cite examples of significant savings achieved.[10]

Diffusion is frequently the key to creating huge intellectual and financial multipliers from innovation. Yet surprisingly few companies target diffusion and learning as a portion of their innovation strategies. Two examples will suggest how lateral and longitudinal diffusion together lead to huge payoffs and why technical and nontechnical innovations so often go hand in hand.

• When Bankers Trust (BT) automated its back offices to handle highly sophisticated trusts, it began a long, profitable diffusion process. At the outset, BT could not foresee the wide range of products that would flow across that system and the impacts the system would have on other elements of the organization. First, because it was able to handle more complex trusts more efficiently, BT could make more profits. Trust Division profits soared. With its improved information base, BT could offer a variety of new trust instruments worldwide. It withdrew from many less profitable commercial and retail banking activities and focused its efforts on new trust-related opportunities, becoming a pioneer in the derivatives field for risk hedging or asset leveraging. As these endeavors flowed together, in related organizational innovations BT simplified its organization, shifted more toward a partnership form, and in key areas moved away from its past hierarchical command-and-control structures.[11] BT's profits grew six times between 1985 and 1994 while its staffing dropped by two-thirds.

• As Honda Motor Company developed its extraordinary depth in small engine design, not only was it able to achieve a competitive edge in motorcycles, it could use its engine innovations to move into small automobiles, pumps, generators, outboards, lawnmowers, snowblowers, and other areas. Each application in turn required more sophisticated engine technologies and thus fed back higher value into the engine design process itself. To support its product innovations, Honda created novel ways of financing and distributing its products and a unique "paperweight" organization form with a strong horizontal orientation in engineering and development. The novelty of its new products in conjunction with its management innovations allowed Honda to change the competitive structure of several industries (like motorcycles) in which it participated.[12]

## A PALPABLE VISION

How do top managers create cohesion among all these diverse elements in large organizations? One most visible, high-payoff practice stood out in all of the most innovative companies we studied. The top management team conveyed, exemplified, and constantly reinforced a clear, palpable, and exciting vision for all critical stakeholders.[13] One can literally feel the vision everywhere in the enterprise. Because the "V word" has been so overworked in the fad-of-the-month literature, we will emphasize only its practical, high-payoff features and highlight some critical, yet often missing, elements. Scientists, technologists, employees, customers, investors, outside support communities, and suppliers will all work harder and contribute more if they enthusiastically support the company's goals and clearly see bright futures for themselves in the company's success. What is essential in a vision to make this happen?

## A Glittering Sense of Purpose

First, there must be a *glittering* sense of where the enterprise is going in the long run—a desired future state. The vision must appeal to each critical stakeholder in a clear fashion.[14] Most mission statements markedly fail to do this. Second, in a few sentences—*not* pages—the vision should capture:

- Who are we? What do we intend to be? What do we stand for?
- What do we do for the world? What makes us attractive to each important stakeholder? Why should they support us? What is our long-term unalterable focus, intended area of preeminence? Answers must maintain consistency, engender necessary time horizons, avoid panics and oscillations, yet be broad enough to accommodate many different potential solutions.
- What makes us exciting? What makes this enterprise different? What is it best at? How does it provide unique value to customers and the community? This is perhaps the most critical element in the vision.
- How will we provide challenge to our people? How will we extend and grow? What are our key technologies? Intellectual skills? Concepts of customer service? This element should contain a few overarching goals with long-term dimensions. Often specific numbers are not essential. People can agree on challenging abstractions like being "the world's leading innovator in ———— markets, or ———— technologies" without numerical details.[15]
- How will we define success? How will we measure it? A few measurables inculcate belief and confidence for employees, create credibility in the outside world, avoid frustration, and provide meaningful benchmarks for more detailed performance targets.

## Pragmatism, Not Bland Abstractions

Well-thought-out visions are not bland abstractions. They convey the practical essence of the enterprise.[16] For example, at Genentech, Herb Boyer and Robert Swanson included this vision statement in their first prospectus:

> Genentech will be the first company to reduce to practice this remarkable

new [recombinant DNA] technology. It is Genentech's goal to select products that are in great demand and to specifically engineer microorganisms to produce those products. We plan to build a major profitable corporation by manufacturing and marketing needed products that benefit mankind. . . . We intend to be a portion of the scientific community with responsibilities both to our own scientists and science at large. Genentech is not to be just an innovative research and development organization that coordinates major research projects, it will be a fully integrated business organization. . . . The future uses of genetic engineering are far-reaching and many. With Genentech's technology, microorganisms can produce protein to meet world food needs or produce antibodies to fight viral infections. Any product produced by a living organism is eventually within the company's reach.[17]

More important than the vision's written statement is whether it becomes a palpable, living component of action within the organization. At companies like Intel, Genentech, Bell Laboratories, Microsoft, Sony, Federal Express, Club Med, and Frito-Lay one hears the vision repeated in almost the same words and phrases from the CEO to the bench levels of the organization—for example:

• At Intel bench researchers used the exact same phrases as chairman Gordon Moore: "We intend to be the leading innovator in the semiconductor field. We intend to be the revolutionaries changing the way products are made and management performs its tasks."
• At Bell Laboratories, the congruence with which bench researchers and top managers expressed their goals was uncanny. The result was a level of trust, alignment, and willingness to allow the independent action that made its component units into world innovation leaders.
• Microsoft's clearly understood vision has been, "To be the leading provider of software for personal computers." This short but clear message was long Bill Gates's guiding vision for Microsoft's success, but will require revision as the technology moves into more network-like phases.

Too often vision statements sound like motherhood (or is it fatherhood?). But successful innovating companies have found clear values and visions to be practical keys to higher profitability. They are not frail abstractions but rocklike foundations. Strongly held and inculcated values tend to generate at a minimum the powerful, pragmatic benefits outlined in Table 6.1. These are practical results meaningful to even the most hard-nosed executives. And they create even greater benefits for owners. In an excellent study, John Kotter and James Heskett demon-

**TABLE 6. 1**
**Pragmatic Impacts**

*Clear exciting visions and values management help:*

• Attract good people (create trust)

• Allow delegation (self-coordination)

• Promote motivation (productivity)

• Engender teamwork (fewer controls)

• Stimulate creativity (long time horizons)

• Create identity (high morale)

• Encourage flexibility (mutual support)

• Enable use of intuition (opportunism)

• Minimize personal squabbles (protect secrets)

strate conclusively the significant positive impact that corporate culture has on competitive performance. They found that firms with cultures strongly emphasizing clear visions for all the key constituencies (customers, shareholders, and employees) and reinforcing them at all managerial levels outperformed firms by huge margins that did not do so. "Over an eleven year period, the former increased revenues by an average of 682% versus 166% for the latter, expanded their workforces by 282% versus 36%, grew their stock prices by 901%, versus 74%, and improved their net incomes by 756%, versus 1%."[18]

## Dream Spinners and Legends

Visionary innovation leaders are really dream spinners. They create images of the future that attract people to work together and with energy. They honor critical elements in past cultural patterns but are willing to throw off the limitations of the past. Their visions provide continuity over time and a basis for people to see their own roles as growing in the future. Despite their own (often profound) human flaws, dream spinners' organizations tend to cherish them. People lower in the organization connect their own dreams to those of the dream spinner. The ultimate anchoring of a vision occurs when it enables people to identify their work-life with their life-work.[19] How does this happen?

Excitement is the soul, and reinforcement the heart of vision. Top managements in innovative companies are excited by their vision. They teach the vision constantly, stating portions of it, reiterating it in communications, keeping it stable over a long period of time, and, most important, living it themselves.[20] They help create legends about the company that are central to this process.[21] Powerful innovation leaders personify and project powerful innovation stories, in both their past history and current behavior.[22] And they constantly refresh and reinforce these in speeches and publications. The firm's legends become amplifications of its visions, repeated by people at the bench level as characterizing behavior in the company.

These legends tell multiple stories about leadership, processes, and values. They are not just interesting tales. Each one provides hooks as to what can be learned from the particular event—whether it was a success or failure experience. In innovative firms, failure stories can be very constructive; they define certain types of failure as acceptable and honorable if one learns from the event. A company's legends become teaching parables about what leadership means and provide guidelines about what to do when in doubt. For example:

• At 3M, the overhead projector program had been officially killed, but people kept working on it underground. When the program finally received go-ahead funding, there was suddenly a hiring freeze in the company. The team could not get enough engineering time to obtain design drawings internally. In this case, a purchasing agent solved the problem by helping the team contract externally for the drawings. This behavior became a portion of a teaching parable in 3M, suggesting that in even more routinized areas, people can seize the reins and contribute enormously to innovation.[23]

## The Essence of Leadership

Constructive visions rarely just happen in large organizations. Leaders help create a new reality.[24] Actions are elaborated, elevated, and honored through legends. People in the legends exemplify desired behaviors, receive genuine recognition, and are long remembered. 3M, for example, embraces "conscious storytelling." It once hired a cultural anthropologist to go over potential myth-creating stories, point them up, and teach managers how to present them in a positive fashion.[25] In continually innovative cultures, the dominating legends deal with successful, creative, and growth-generating behaviors. Non-innovative cultures' stories, by contrast, tend to reflect and reinforce a mood of discouragement, as they did in General Motors, W. R. Grace, and U.S. Sprint in the early 1990s. They often relate blocking or political behavior, who was at fault, fragmentation versus cohesion, in-groups versus out-groups, and how things went wrong rather than how people reached positive outcomes. They often emphasize financial or quantitative outcomes rather than qualitative dimensions like sense of purpose, obstacles overcome, contributions to the community, or personal fulfillment. Without conscious leadership, such stories can easily proliferate. The way events are portrayed can change their impact enormously. For example:

• Avery Dennison produced a thirty-page booklet about the founding of the company, but it contained no exciting portrayals about the innovative actions and adventures of Sam Avery, who had created the company. Although videotapes of the founder were core references and there was significant evidence of innovation in these, the book's authors had not personalized or emphasized such elements, "because they did not look at such stories as a portion of their mission."

The essence of leadership is the ability to see and make vivid to others the positive connections between external events and their lives.[26] Leaders enable people to imagine and create their own positive futures inside the enterprise and on behalf of a larger societal purpose. A skilled manager's single highest-leverage tool is inculcating and embedding stimulating visions. Yet juggling the roles of dream spinner and business realist is a difficult task for many executives. In the early stages of innovation, the balance must favor the dream-spinner role; later, when continuation gets expensive, hard-nosed analysis becomes more important. In the flow-process or mass-marketing industries, the need for this transition is especially clear. It has not been unusual for each succeeding stage of innovation—lab discovery, scale-up testing, prototype manufacture and test marketing trials, and first mass commercialization—to require ten or more times the asset commitment than the preceding stage. On such long-term projects, the dream spinner often works best in concert with a trusted implementer who can help others "plan through to success." Both talents are important, but a clear vision helps both.

Effective visions call forth energy, creativity, and productivity well beyond what people themselves thought was possible. Vision is the true engine of the passion, inventiveness, and persistence that drive highly innovative organizations. Visionary leaders understand and act out the adage: "Once you get the vision properly in place, the whole enterprise turns out right."[27] A recent survey by Mercer Management Consulting notes that the least profitable companies are those that delegate least well. Delegation and innovation depend largely on the sense of shared direction and trust that clear visions create.[28]

# FROM VISION TO STRATEGY

To guide innovation most effectively, most enterprises need three more levels of specificity beyond a well-understood vision: (1) defining a true technological strategy, (2) converting this into a conscious portfolio of commitments, and (3) developing "figures of merit" that clearly define the physical-performance and economic characteristics needed to "win" in competition.

## A True Technology Strategy

Most companies unfortunately do not have a genuine technology strategy. A well-formulated strategy marshals and allocates an organization's resources into a *unique, viable, and winning posture* based on its relative internal competencies and shortcomings, anticipated changes in the environment, and contingent moves by intelligent opponents. The strategy defines how the enterprise will be *superior* to its opponents and how it will deploy resources for that purpose. The strategy itself integrates the organization's major *goals, policies,* and action *programs* into a cohesive whole. Successful strategies support *multiple goals,* not a single simplistic concept like maximizing profit. Goals that are comprehensive, stimulating, and compatible are integral to an effective vision. If achieved, they will also optimize long-term profitability.[29]

*Goals* (or objectives) state what the enterprise is to achieve and when results must be accomplished, but they do not state how the results are to be achieved. All enterprises have multiple goals existing in a complex hierarchy—from overall enterprise objectives, which establish the nature of the enterprise and the directions in which it should move, to a series of less permanent goals that define targets for each organizational unit, its subunits, and finally all major program activities within each subunit. Among them, only major goals—those that affect the entity's overall direction and viability—are strategic goals. Microsoft's goal to be preeminent in PC software is strategic; its goal of maintaining a single campus for all its programming activities is not. A key element in setting strategic goals is defining precisely how the firm *will be better* than its existing or potential future competitors, how it can "win," where it will be best-in-world at satisfying its customers along some

**FIGURE 6.1**
**Structure of Strategy**

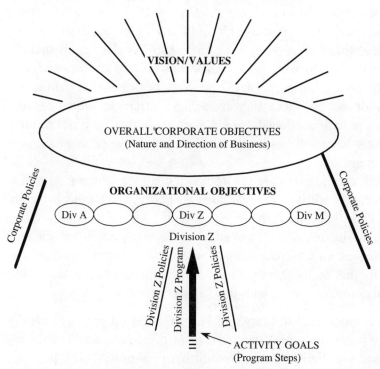

Relationship of Goals, Policies, and Programs

*A true strategy integrates the enterprise's major goals, policies, and programs into a unique and consistent pattern that supports its long-term vision and objectives.*

critical dimensions. This is the function of defining a firm's core competencies and the figures of merit for strategic innovation programs.

*Policies* set the limits, boundaries, or rules within which these goals will be achieved. All policies can be stated as negatives: what will *not* be done. Like goals, policies occur in a hierarchy from corporate, to product, divisional, program, or micro-organizational levels. Only a few— those that establish the overall direction or viability of the activity—are strategic. Microsoft's policy not to develop scientific software is strategic; its policies about time clocks are not.

*Programs*—the sequence of steps to achieve goals within policy constraints—also exist in a hierarchy. Similarly, programs that determine the organization's overall directions and viability are strategic. Others are not. Figure 6.1 sets forth the relationship among these three elements of strategy.

Unfortunately, most companies do not have a true strategy—structured and prioritized goals, policies, and programs—for either technology or innovation. In our recent studies of IT use in large service companies, many firms claimed to have IT strategies, but closer inquiry made it clear that only a few (10 to 15%) had (1) clear goals that defined what it took to win; (2) policies that defined the firm's focus, uniqueness, or preeminence; or (3) program priorities that defined the sequences of actions necessary to achieve strategic preeminence.[30] Companies or nations, divisions or departments that have not thought through these key relationships are unlikely to achieve or maintain their strategic intent.

But such formal plans are far from sufficient for success. Any well-designed strategy will also have *planned flexibility* as one of its key components. This is particularly true for technological and innovation strategies that, by definition, must adapt to the many unknown scientific or technological capabilities, demand changes, or complex social and power shifts that so frequently upset implementation of any rigid plan. Successful companies cope with this in a variety of ways.

• Some companies, like Sony and Honda, build up pretested idea or technology pools they can draw from to respond to changes. IBM has done the same to be responsive to antitrust pressures; AT&T has used technology pools as bargaining chips in responding to different rate-setting bodies or its regulators. Other enterprises, like the auto and computer companies, develop outsourcing networks of specialist suppliers that can provide options and surge capabilities on call. Still others—like Rubbermaid, Kyocera, Hewlett-Packard, 3M, consulting, and financial houses—rely on fast-moving ad hoc team structures to adapt solutions from their core competencies to meet individual customers' needs.

Increasingly, software is providing many needed flexibilities. At low cost, database software can tap into the most current databases and external models that outside scientific and technical groups may offer to assist in research or design revisions. CAD-CAE-CAM and flexible manufacturing systems (FMS) offer fast design-to-manufacturing response capabilities. Customer interface software is used to pick up market changes quickly and transmit these to the firm's integrating software engines, where technologists match up potential technical solutions and market needs in the fashion Chapters 2 and 5 describe.

These four elements—goals, policies, programs, and planned flexibility—are the essentials of a true technological-innovation strategy. In a properly formulated strategy, the linkage among strategic organizational structures, innovation, and profitability is clear and compelling. In our studies, we have observed at least twenty-two distinctive innovation strategies, each requiring different organizational structures and support. The most effective and provocative follow:

- Core competency strategies
- Network-innovation strategies
- Starburst strategies
- Basic research strategies
- State-of-the-art development strategies
- Multiple small product line strategies
- Incremental innovation strategies
- Market-dominant strategies
- Large-scale systems strategies
- Customizing or problem solution strategies
- Risk-your-company strategies

Each strategy requires a unique alignment of resources, organizational forms, and measurement-incentive structures for success. Often multiple strategies exist in individual divisions of the same company. Because of the great difference among each of the twenty-two strategies, a search for a single always-useful innovation approach is simplistic. Copying even the most successful companies' strategy (like 3M's or HP's) will lead to failure unless the copier's circumstances and strategy are identical. In the next section, we illustrate precisely how some of the most successful innovative companies have uniquely aligned their mid-level organizations around their particular strategies and competencies to match the external environment's needs for flexibility and responsiveness. Two summary examples will illustrate the critical top management points here.

• A relatively small ($50 million in sales) company's management wished "to grow in a series of protected small niches in the chemical specialties industry." The company's top management focused its organizations and commitments on "new small-scale chemical solutions to problems of non-chemical OEM producers." To carry out its concept, the management group established its own R&D programs as extensions of its customers' (dominantly mechanical or electronic) research activities. It developed very close relationships with its customers' technical groups through intensive on-customer-premise marketing and technical service activities. It did no basic research but developed a few applied areas like sealants, insulators, lubricants, and surface interactions to world-class levels. It organized its production-technical activities around small pilot-scale production capabilities, fast-response development teams, and marketing-led program teams that (with customer personnel assisting) developed proprietary solutions adapted to specific customer needs.

It eliminated from consideration high-volume chemicals that would fit better and be more profitable in other companies and chemicals that did not require depth in its sophisticated operations or small-scale production technologies. It protected its market positions through both a very aggressive patent program and a careful pricing strategy, which demanded very high initial margins on new technical solutions. But it rapidly dropped prices to delay competitive entries as the technology became more widely understood. The company generally sold off products or lines when they became large enough for bigger companies with full-scale plants and mass distribution to enter the market. Its corporate strategy had to override division heads' requests for investments targeted at higher-volume (and sometimes seemingly more profitable) chemicals that would have moved the company from its true expertise.

• A large aerospace company's top management, after several abortive tries at developing leading-edge technology, realized that the company's true expertise lay in "arriving late and overwhelming" opponents with its huge development and production capabilities. Consequently, the company designed its research program primarily to listen for developing new technologies, to be able to force cross-licensing if necessary, and to be able to move rapidly with coalition partners once markets became clear. Management slowly built up substantial resource reserves and access in several areas. It established very advanced modeling and test facilities in critical areas (like advanced materials and fluid flows), excess capacity in various prototyping shops and specialized advanced engineering groups, world-class flexible assembly and manufacturing centers for advanced materials components, and flexible access to large-scale borrowing from local banks or insurance companies.

All of these allowed the company to move quickly and massively when it chose. The company cut back on many small-scale new-product endeavors it had been spawning. As interesting large markets emerged, the company targeted them as a "strong second," using the massive personnel and capital capabilities it had put in place. Corporate headquarters provided the incremental investments needed for new knowledge areas and surge facilities. The corporate strategy demanded that for several years individual divisions override their high margin–high return financial ranking systems for projects and use criteria that gave priority to very large-scale markets in which others took on the initial development risk, while they undertook only the more predictable risks of quality manufacture and service support. The company became one of the two dominating forces in its fields.

## A Portfolio of Commitments

A vital step in implementing a corporate innovation strategy is to consciously design a risk, timing, and payoff portfolio. An effective portfolio (a) converts the company's vision into a limited number of divisional and cross-divisional thrusts, and (b) clearly defines the timing and priority areas for the firm's resource deployment.[31] To ensure that the firm's broad conceptions of purpose (strategic goals) are met, top managers need to distill out a few—more than two, fewer than ten—principal thrusts that are the essence of the firm's overall strategic posture. An enterprise usually cannot maintain a focus on more than five or six critical thrusts. Some of these may logically be a mission of only one division or unit. Often, however, several divisions will have to commit portions of their total resources in concert to implement a major corporate thrust effectively. The corporate strategy, as expressed in these principal thrusts, must override all other allocation or structural priorities within individual divisions or units,[32] as it did in the two examples cited.

Conceptually, one can envision these principal corporate thrusts (comprising the major elements of the strategy) as a matrix of coordinating plans laid across the functional or operating units that must carry them out. (See Figure 6.2.) Within its own plans and budgets, each division must provide sufficient support for each corporate strategic thrust and make sure that thrust is effectively implemented. This is the essence of mission planning. As anyone knows who has tried it, this is a most difficult task in both an intellectual and political sense. But its payoffs are high.

## FIGURES OF MERIT: OVERALL FINANCIAL TARGETS

The process is eased if each principal thrust is assigned a fiscal cutoff point, hurdle rate, or imputed cost of capital appropriate to that particular strategic mission. Overall these should be "figures of merit," defining what it takes to "win" competitively in financial terms. They must override the normal internal program evaluation criteria of each cooperating group. Otherwise resources will flow disproportionately to those

**FIGURE 6.2**
**Portfolio of Thrusts**

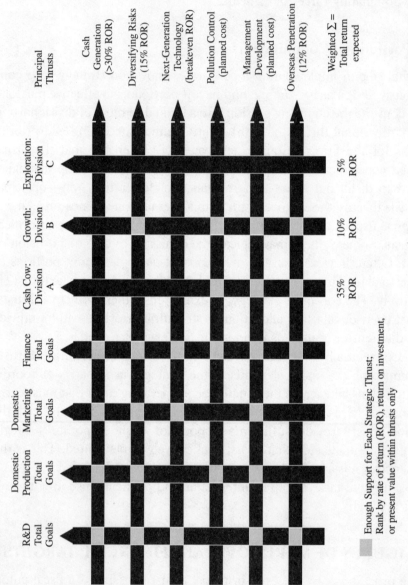

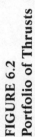 Enough Support for Each Strategic Thrust;
Rank by rate of return (ROR), return on investment,
or present value within thrusts only

*Average expected current RORs should reflect each division's or program's strategic role and need not be the same. The overall portfolio must meet all financial and qualitative goals.*

activities most financially attractive in the short run and starve other elements of the strategy. As in the diagrammed example, programs supporting cash cow activities might have to exceed a relatively high *current* internal rate of return (ROR) of 30%; new products diversifying corporate risks might need only a 15% current ROR; next-generation technology investments could be acceptable down to breakeven RORs in their inception stages; depollution technologies might not have measurably positive financial returns at all; and managerial development might have to be budgeted as a planned cost, with no attempt to measure current financial benefits.

## Overriding Pure Financial Rankings

To maintain the corporate strategy, each division may have to override the purely financial rankings of its internal projects to make sure that the division dedicates enough resources to each horizontal (corporate) thrust to ensure that it fulfills its defined role in that corporate strategy. These points are represented by the cross-hatched areas in Figure 6.2. Entire books have been written on program evaluation, and we shall not duplicate or challenge them here. But a few key points need emphasis. If a division merely ranks and supports projects in terms of their present value (PV) or rate of return, two disasters occur. First, such allocations will undercut the strategy of the entire company. Second, they will force the company to overinvest in short-term, sure-payoff projects and subvert longer-term, less quantifiable projects of greater importance.[33] For example:

• In the late 1980s the R&D division of IBM had hundreds of ideas for improved printers, each with a high potential payoff. But it made no sense to invest in them when IBM was getting out of the printer business. Conversely, it would have been disastrous for IBM's R&D or PC divisions *not* to invest in software projects for handling non-roman alphabets—which might not have had immediate payoffs—at the time that IBM's strategy was further penetration of Asian markets.

• It would have been disastrous for Volvo's brake division to emphasize high-payoff process automation projects—and to underinvest in lower-payoff product quality and quality-of-worklife programs—at a time when the corporation was emphasizing safety and job continuity as critical to its market positioning and labor relations strategies.

Clearly high-level strategies must override individual project rankings. Thus, one cannot directly compare the marginal ROR of a project supporting one strategic thrust, such as cost reduction, against that of a project supporting another major thrust, such as worker stability or overseas penetration. One must compare each mission's (or thrust's) goals against competitive missions' goals first, and then make sure each strategic thrust has enough support behind it to be successful.[34] Within each thrust, one should, of course, rank various projects as to how well they support that mission's particular goals. But for Volvo's strategic "safety" positioning in the marketplace to be sacrificed so its brake division can make 0.5% more current ROR through cost cutting is irrational. Yet such financial rankings of divisional projects are constantly defended as the ultimate in hard-nosed managerial logic. Nonsense.

## Alternative Costs, Not Just Incremental Gains

Another common irrationality is to measure only the direct incremental yields from a project against its own incremental investment costs or against similar direct returns from other projects. Such analyses ignore alternative costs—the losses that will occur if the enterprise does not invest in the project.[35] The potential gain from the project is the sum of losses it avoids and the direct incremental gains it obtains. A former head of Ford's Development group noted that failure to think in these terms in the 1970s was one of the main causes of the U.S. auto industry's decline. By not investing in small cars, not only did U.S. companies lose the incremental profits they would have made on those cars, they lost all the experience curve and customer loyalty benefits they would have gained by production, while their Japanese competitors realized those gains.[36] When they finally decided to produce small cars, U.S. companies for years lost actual cash as they played catch-up on the alternative costs their analyses had ignored. Similarly, ancillary benefits (portfolio or technological multipliers) to other units should be considered. Often budgetary practices force the proposing unit to show only benefits or costs accruing to itself. Severe suboptimizations occur when cross-unit analysis is not required, as in the portfolio examples explained above. The basic payoff matrix for an innovation project should at least look like Figure 6.3.

A number of sophisticated analytical techniques, especially those (like Merck's) evaluating the future options permitted or lost by early R&D expenditures, can add further important dimensions to such analyses.[37] But managers should not be mesmerized by the seeming precision that more elaborate models accord to forecasts—especially for totally new concepts and very long-term impacts—whose error range is often greater than their ordinal value.

**FIGURE 6.3**
## Alternative Cost Analysis: Direct and Indirect Payoffs

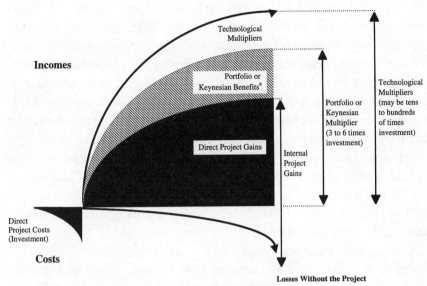

[a]Keynesian multipliers apply to government project investments. See Chapters 11 through 13.

*Project returns should be compared against the alternative costs (losses) associated with no action. Appropriate multipliers, beyond direct project returns, should be added for benefits to other divisions (or for public benefits on government projects).*

## The Aggregate of Thrusts Must Equal Strategic Intent

In the aggregate, regardless of which specific mathematical evaluation approach is chosen, each division's portfolio of projects must meet its overall strategic goals (both quantitative and qualitative), and its total returns must exceed those specified for its role in the corporation's overall strategy. The sum of all corporate thrusts must, of course, aggregate to fulfill its strategic intent[38] and to meet *all* the corporation's financial and nonfinancial strategic goals. Most successful innovative companies use some variation of the portfolio approach to ensure that they maintain a desired balance between short-term, intermediate-term, long-term, and next-generation technology development, as well as other corporate goals. Once communicated properly and supported by performance figures of merit (as developed in Chapter 7), this framework supports maximum decentralization of the innovation endeavor, within a defined overall strategy.

Not forcing each division or corporate thrust to meet identical payoff criteria is entirely rational in economic terms. Few large investors buy only one class of high-yield or growth stocks. Instead, they typically honor a full range of timing and risk preferences by investing in a mix of some high-dividend, cash cow stocks; some currently low-yield, high-growth stocks; some steadily growing nondividend stocks; some insurance policies; a few small high-risk ventures; some companies with products or managements they admire; perhaps a real estate development that may lose money but make their community more pleasant or secure; and some low-yield stocks that eventually may create very stable businesses in whole new growth areas. Venture capitalists achieve the same purposes by purposely dividing their portfolios among seed-capital ventures, emerging companies, leveraged buyouts, alliances, joint risk taking with other venture capitalists in complex deals, and so on. They do not use the same current return criteria for each of these segments of their portfolio. Nevertheless, the total portfolio must match or exceed their expected returns.

A continually innovative company can most rationally deploy its resources in a similar fashion, ensuring both current profits and longer-term innovation simultaneously, by developing a conscious portfolio of goals, risks, time horizons, and returns among the technological endeavors in its various divisions. Time horizons are an important element in the portfolio. For example:

• Microsoft deploys relatively small support units behind its well-established, very profitable operations and applications software units handling MS-DOS, Excel, or Word. The low maintenance cost and high continuing sales of these products have long made them into natural current cash cows for resources Microsoft could deploy into other areas. Earlier deployment of this sort included large near-growth endeavors like Windows, which took years of investment and absorbed several hundred million dollars, before Windows 3 and Windows 95 exploded in the marketplace. Simultaneously, intermediate-growth projects like Windows NT had longer time horizons and lower current return expectations. Meanwhile Microsoft also developed a number of smaller, still longer-term probes (like Visual Basic, OLE, and Explorer) for the network marketplace. At the same time, Bill Gates diverted large sums from current profits to invest in Nathan Myhrvold's Advanced Technology Group, which investigated next-generation options for future software, like Blackbird. These may soon become Microsoft's greatest near-growth ventures.

Like any other management technique, however, the portfolio approach can be pushed too far. For example:

• Texas Instruments perhaps overformalized the portfolio approach as a complete system in its famous OST (objectives, strategies, and tactics) system. OST provided a basis for the formal planning, review, and monitoring of projects within single divisions and across multiple divisions. At the corporate level, a stated set of corporate objectives set forth the company's broad economic purposes, the reasons for the company's existence, and its responsibilities to various stakeholders. For each major objective in this set, there were one to several complete strategies cutting across the various groups, divisions, and product centers of the company. Each strategy had designated milestones for accomplishment, and a series of tactical action programs (TAPs) specifying the essential steps necessary to accomplish these milestones. Specific managers headed each objective, strategy, and TAP. They might simultaneously head a complete operating unit, but they would have a separate budget for their strategic programs, distinct from their operating budgets.

Unfortunately, such systems are so appealing at the rational level that they become rigid and constraining straitjackets to control research, development, and innovative activities through detailed budget-like mechanisms. When formal portfolio mechanisms are pushed too far—as they were at various times in such otherwise highly innovative companies as Polaroid, GE, Hewlett-Packard, and 3M as well as Texas Instruments—they can be disastrous. These companies all had to back away from overly formalized systems of this sort after new top managements and their controllership groups sought to "tighten things up" or to "manage programs more professionally" in mechanistic ways. Such formal structures are very helpful in facilitating the communications and resource deployments that support innovation. Properly used, they provide a crucial strategic framework that allows highly decentralized, interactive, relatively small units to self-guide their activities effectively toward the company's strategic intent. Pushed one step too far, they can destroy the essential chaos and personal commitment needed for innovation itself.

## SUMMARY

The most crucial element in stimulating innovation is top management's outlook. In the most innovative companies, top managers clearly expect, appreciate, and actively support innovation. They project and personify clear, exciting visions that embrace the aspirations of their employees, customers, and other major stakeholders. They support these constantly in their own lives, in their speeches, and by repeating legends that add substance and reality to the vision. Such visions are not the pap of most mission statements but stirring, practical dreams through which people can connect their work-life to their life-work. They are further supported by clear, distinct strategies that define where and how the enterprise will be unique and preeminent in its fields and by a pattern of programs and investments to ensure that needed current cash flows, near-growth demands, and future growth needs are met in a winning fashion. A carefully designed portfolio of strategic programs clearly overrides any mechanistic use of accounting or present value tools that would undercut the strategy itself.

This three-level structure—vision, strategy, portfolio—provides the critical top management framework to allow small, disaggregated units to proceed with the independence necessary to stimulate creativity, interactiveness, and commitment, yet with the focus necessary to achieve efficiency, strategic timing, and performance goals. They are the core elements of good leadership, attracting good people, engendering high motivation and morale, creating pride and identity, allowing delegation, and promoting teamwork, opportunism, and value creation. But they must be anchored in further specifics to become operational. This is the subject of the next chapter.

# 7

# Creating "Best-in-World" Capabilities

Vision, clear strategy, and balanced deployment of resources provide essential frameworks for high innovation, but they are not sufficient in themselves. Top managements in successful innovating enterprises go much further: they ensure their firms will win in competition. They see that their strategies embody:

- Figure-of-merit targets that, if hit, ensure competitive success.
- In-depth development of a few core competencies that give the company best-in-world capabilities in a few key areas critical to customers.
- More intellectual resources focused on these key areas than anyone else in the world.
- Maximum leveraging of the enterprise's resources through alliances with and strategic outsourcing to best-in-world outside parties.
- An incentive structure that clearly supports innovation and the strategic deployments that ensure these best-in-world capabilities.

## FIGURES OF MERIT

Each of the most innovative companies we studied had developed an interesting mechanism that was critical in focusing the innovation process—and simultaneously supported the interactive chaos that inno-

187

vation programs generally require. This device is the "figure of merit."[1] Figures of merit define the performance-economic characteristics that *if hit, win.* Far from being straitjackets, figures of merit stimulate creativity, innovation, and commercial success by defining in challenging terms the technical-economic characteristics essential for success. They are essential in anchoring corporate visions and strategies. Chapter 6 described how portfolio analyses set hurdle rates and investment patterns to ensure that the company meets all its strategic goals. Performance figures of merit carry this process to the next level of ensuring "winning" performance.

## Not Just Benchmarking

Figures of merit go well beyond current benchmarking techniques. They do not just match the performance characteristics that others will have available in the marketplace. They demand performance exceeding competitors' capabilities by a margin that will ensure that the innovator has sustainable commercial success. In the industries we studied, successful innovation managers had an uncanny—sometimes intuitive— ability to set these targets meaningfully. Those who solely benchmarked current practice slowly fell behind their competitors; those who matched future performance maintained share; those who hit figures of merit won. How do figures of merit look in practice? A few examples will make the point.

• At Motorola, Robert Galvin set a "Six Sigma" quality target which created a whole new wave of innovation. A Six Sigma quality target means that the probability of an error is only 1.74 in a billion. Intuitively, Galvin and others realized that in Motorola's strategy of preeminence in mobile wireless communications, the capacity to handle transmissions accurately at gigabyte rates would be crucial to future quality. If fiber optics could successfully handle $10^{10}$ bits of information per second, wireless transmissions would have to do the same. In order to avoid losing extremely valuable information (for example in the global financial marketplace), it was essential that error rates be kept compatible with these transmission frequencies. The Six Sigma goal released a whole new level of energy and creativity concerning quality. Previous practices could not possibly reach this goal. Consequently, teams had to reassess their whole approach to design, manufacturing, and postmanufacturing reliability and quality control to meet this goal. Later, under George Fisher, Motorola set a "10X" goal for its innovation programs: the target was to shrink the time each element took in the innovation cycle to one-tenth its former time. Once again, rather than extrapolative thinking, 10X called for totally new approaches to problems, stimulating much greater innovation at all levels of the company to improve its market performance.

• At Hewlett-Packard, Bill Hewlett was known for his capacity to set effective figures of merit. He would visit the bench of his most talented new engineering employees and ask what they were working on. He would then ask them what the targets were for their projects. After commenting on how delighted HP was to have them aboard and how important the project was, Hewlett would go away, leaving the new employee feeling important and appreciated. A few days later, Hewlett would reappear and say that he was very excited about the project, but the target was wrong. Based on his knowledge of the field, he would then set a much higher target (perhaps a 50% improvement in performance versus the 10% targeted). The new employee would be startled by this target, but—not knowing that "it couldn't be done"—would totally rethink all the basic underlying technical and performance relationships, often significantly improving his or her own contributions and the performance of HP products in that field.

• At Intel, Gordon Moore's concept that the number of semiconductors per chip doubled every year created a continuous challenge. No one thought that component density could continue to grow annually at a rate of $2^n$ for long. Nevertheless, with this as a challenge, Intel could screen out projects that did not meet the criterion and urge its engineers to much higher performance levels than they had dreamed possible. So powerful was the paradigm that it has driven the industry for at least twenty years and seems valid for the next few years.

• At Sony Corporation, CEO Masaru Ibuka repeatedly set figures of merit for performance and price that drove his company's marvelous innovative machine. In the 1950s he set the seemingly impossible standard of a "pocketable transistor radio," which seemed beyond belief at the time. This goal led Sony to push beyond the size limits of the first Texas Instruments-Regency transistor radio toward a truly pocketable device. Both market researchers and technicians were skeptical. Nevertheless, given this challenge, they succeeded and established Sony's position in the marketplace as the most innovative producer of miniaturized electromechanical systems in the industry. Later, Mr. Ibuka insisted on the "superior technology" and "unique product of our own" targets that triggered Sony's hugely successful single-gun, three-cathode Trinitron tube development.

Ibuka set the succession of targets for videotape recorder (VTR) prototypes that enabled Sony to quickly move beyond Ampex's early dominance of that market. For broadcast recorders, Mr. Ibuka set a target of commercial broadcast quality at a price of 20 million yen, at that time about one-fifth the price of the Ampex machine. Later he set the target of a commercial color video recorder to sell for 2 million yen which became the U-matic system and, when upgraded, was the commercial standard for years. Later he set a target for a home color VTR at 200,000 yen ($550). Nobutoshi Kihara, who headed this project, later noted, "I was not sure we could meet this challenge." Nevertheless, with this as a target, Sony introduced the first truly successful home VTR, the Betamax. In each case, Mr. Ibuka had set a combination of specific technical and economic targets that were sufficiently challenging to force a rethinking of all basic innovation parameters.

## Establishing Figures of Merit

A portion of establishing such figures of merit is clearly analytical. A portion is intuitive. When properly established, such targets can change an entire industry. For example:

• Nucor and Chaparral both started with an analysis by some young mavericks in the steel industry who believed they could change the entire performance characteristics of the field. They analyzed the U.S. versus Japanese steel industries and realized that a U.S. company could have lower energy costs, lower transportation to market, lower transportation costs for raw materials, lower overhead, faster cycle times to market, and at least equal producing technology to the then-dominant Japanese producers. They targeted and carefully benchmarked best potential U.S. performance (versus Japan and Korea) for each of these factors and selected optimized locations that lowered costs as much as possible relative to their targeted user segments. Once all of these controllable costs had been optimized, they set a target for labor cost per ton that would be acceptable to American workers yet ensure that "if hit, we would win." In Chapparel's case, this was established as "the trans-Pacific cost per ton of shipping steel." If Chapparel could hit all of the other benchmarks, the Japanese and Koreans would have to produce at "a negative labor cost" to participate in the U.S. marketplace.

The labor force was willing to accept this objective target, help design the plants, take on new responsibilities for quality, and decrease labor content per ton while sharing in the benefits below the figure of merit of "less-than-trans-Pacific transportation cost per ton of steel." For its part, management decreased overhead by creating very flat, no staff, organizational structures in a bare-bones setting. The upshot was the creation of the minimill industry in the United States.

## Analytical Methods for Setting Figures of Merit

A variety of analytical techniques exist to establish figures of merit. A few follow:

**Theoretical Limits Analysis.** One of the most interesting is to examine each performance parameter underlying a product's positioning in a marketplace. Technologists and analysts then ask what this product would look like if they pushed each of these performance characteristics to its technical theoretical limits, that is, the ultimate limits—like the speed of light or absolute zero—science or the technology itself sets for that technology's performance characteristics. Analysts first plot the current state of the art for each key parameter, then analyze and plot rates of advance in each technical characteristic and for technologies that might potentially substitute for these characteristics. This can be done using well-known Fisher-Pry or other technological forecasting techniques.[2] The Fisher-Pry model says that once a technology takes off, progress will follow roughly a Gaussian (cumulative normal distribution) curve until performance approaches the technology's theoretical limit as an asymptote. As long as there is demand, successive technologies will improve performance exponentially in a series of "envelope curves" until performance approaches scientific limits.[3]

Analytical teams can easily plot these three critical performance characteristics. In conjunction with marketing groups, they can then ask, "What would the product look like if we reached these theoretical asymptotes?" Often, as it did in Mr. Ibuka's analysis of the radio or electronic still-imaging markets, this question will suggest totally different product or componentry targets than have ever existed before. Next, the team can analyze the intersections of the important underlying technological trends at different points in time and ask what the characteristics of the product might look like at each of those intersections when achieved. The upshot is a set of intermediate designs for products that provide startlingly different challenges for the technical and innovation groups. Managements have used this technique repeatedly to revise a firm's position in its marketplace and define entirely new technological concepts for products and services.

***Aggressor Company Technique.*** In the aggressor company technique, management asks a team of original thinkers, mavericks, or rising technical stars to "design us out of our existing markets." The team begins with complete knowledge of the firm's current technical-economic performance capabilities. Management then empowers the team to seek out (internally or externally) any approaches that would substantially make the company's existing line obsolete. The team must both analyze the performance characteristics needed and design a program that combines various best-in-world potentials to "blow the company out of its existing markets."

In the process the team has to define how rapidly this competitive position might be achieved. It must determine the products' specific technical-economic performance characteristics, when they could be achieved, and the investment base it would take to create such preeminence (1) from start-up, (2) from a component supplier's position, or (3) from a "most capable competitor's" position. The results are frequently startling enough to completely retarget major R&D and new product programs. They often lead to programs for outsourcing, partnering, or forming strategic alliances with critical technology suppliers whose best-in-world capabilities the firm cannot hope to match or exceed. The technique is also very useful in assessing the real vulnerabilities and potentials of each company's existing products in their marketplaces and in setting innovation targets to avoid these.

## Winning with Figures of Merit

The power of thinking in terms of figures of merit is very great. Yet in recent interviews with large services companies about how they set targets for information technology development, we found limited explicit use of figures of merit. Strikingly, however, service companies that had explicitly used the technique had achieved a continuing competitive edge from their information technologies. State Street Boston, American Express, Bankers Trust, BancOne, Federal Express, Vanguard Investments, and MCI have used this technique to advantage in various aspects of their operations. Microsoft uses "if hit, win" techniques in setting the targets for its major programs. Bell Laboratories' Systems Engineering Group long used similar techniques to set the "black box performance criteria"* for future systems at AT&T. Although the less progressive service users of IT did not use figure-of-merit analyses, their successful technology providers often did use them to design and update their products.

Figures of merit, along with a strong vision, clear strategic concept, and portfolio targets, are essential in creating focus for innovation activities, without constraining the approaches to problem solutions participants can undertake. Once these structures are in place, it is much easier to disaggregate, delegate, stimulate, and coordinate the kinds of small, interactive, empowered, ad hoc units that generally prove effective in innovation. The next several chapters explore specifically how managements can establish, nurture, coordinate, and lead these disaggregated units inside and outside the enterprise for maximum effectiveness.

## CORE COMPETENCY STRATEGIES

A powerful strategic starting point is to build a selected set of core intellectual competencies—important to customers—in such depth that the company can stay on the leading edge of its fields, provide unique value to customers, and be flexible to meet the changing demands of the market and competition.[4] The essence of all strategy is to be able to focus more capability on a concentrated area than any other competitor can, yet maintain the needed flexibilities to meet unexpected environmental changes or competitive assaults. For a long time this meant concentrating more power on a product area than anyone else.[5] But in the past decade, new technologies have created both the capability and the necessity for more refined strategies focusing on underlying intellectual- or service-based capabilities. Such "core competency strategies" uniquely allow companies to be simultaneously most efficient and most flexible in their marketplaces.

### The Value Chain: A Series of Intellectually Based Activities

These strategies came about because a company's value chain[†]—when closely analyzed—turns out to be mainly a series of intellectually based service activities.[6] This is true for both manufacturing and service com-

---

*AT&T-Bell Labs' Systems Engineering group analyzed system demands 25 years ahead and set targets for each major component or subsystem in terms of the inputs, outputs, costs, and required performance for each of these "black boxes," without defining how this performance could be met.
†An enterprise's value chain consists of the sequences of tasks (usually grouped in activity clusters) through which it creates value for its customers.

panies. Because new technologies allow services to be so easily produced anywhere in the world and transported across corporate and geographical lines without tariffs, it is possible (1) to disaggregate the total organization substantially, (2) to outsource many activities at which the firm is not outstandingly competent, and (3) to concentrate the company's own resources on those few activities where it can achieve best-in-world capabilities. If the company is not best in world at an activity (including all transaction costs) and it produces that activity in-house, it gives up competitive edge. Modern technologies allow producers to outsource and coordinate many activities that used to be considered integral to the enterprise. Since virtually all activities are clusters of services and can be produced (and often shipped cost free) anywhere in the world, this has led to substantial use of "core-competency-with-outsourcing" strategies. These are especially powerful in leveraging innovation.

Figure 7.1 sets forth the value chain for a typical manufacturing company. Note two points. First, virtually all activities in the value chain (and at the staff level) are services that can just as easily be produced elsewhere. Second, almost no integrated manufacturer can be more effective than the world's best specialized external providers at producing all elements in its value (or staff support) chain. Determining where to focus one's resources internally and what can be better outsourced are the essentials of core competency strategies. Both are also critical in leveraging the firm's intellectual and innovation resources to the maximum. No individual firm can out-innovate all its suppliers or lateral competitors in all the areas of expertise relevant to its goals. But it can do so in those few areas where it can develop best-in-world competencies. Elsewhere, tapping into best-in-world external sources may be the only way to maintain leadership.

## Defining Core Competencies

How does an organization develop a core competency strategy along these lines? Unfortunately the literature, with a few exceptions, has not been very helpful.[7] "Core" competencies have been defined tautologically as "critical," "central," or "important."[8] This is hardly enlightening. To develop a core competency strategy, a company needs to select those few (two or three) activities most important to customers where it has or can achieve best-in-world capabilities. These are its core competencies, where it can create unique value for customers. Combining these is where it can make highest potential profits. Those other activities

**FIGURE 7.1**
**Value Chain for a Typical Manufacturer**

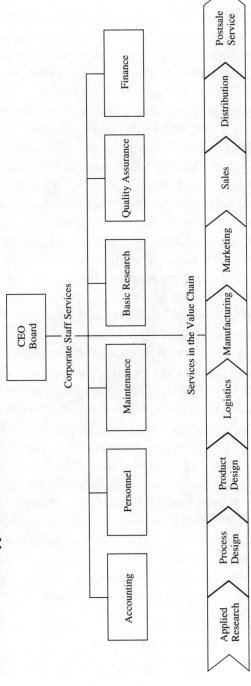

*Service activities dominate the value chain and staff activities of most manufacturers, as well as service enterprises.*

(groups of tasks) where it is not best-in-world are not its core competencies; they are someone else's core competencies. Some of these may be essential activities, which customers insist on the company's providing. However, *if the company is not best in world at the activity, it is giving up competitive edge to the extent that it does not either improve the activity up to world standards or outsource it to others that can perform it better.*

Each company is in competition laterally with the best-in-world providers of each activity in its value chain. The only way it can achieve strategic preeminence is to (a) focus its resources on those few activities where it can (or must be able to) provide unique value for customers and (b) selectively outsource and coordinate the other elements of the value chain from best-in-world (internal or external) suppliers in a way that creates a unique value package for its customers. Superior skills or systems in its selected areas of excellence—and the capacity to target and coordinate these for specific customers' use—allow it to serve customers better. These intellectually based skills and systems are the true foundations for higher rates of return.

Examples of innovation-based core competency strategies might include: Merck, which focuses on basic research in certain therapeutic and chemical classes and superior marketing capabilities; Amgen and Genentech, which concentrate on being the best applied researchers in certain realms of biotechnology; Sony, which emphasizes superior product development and marketing in the consumer mechanical-electronics field; Matsushita, which centers on superior process technology and distribution capabilities for mass-produced products; Nike, whose core competencies are superior marketing-distribution capabilities and product design in the athletic footwear field; State Street Boston, which concentrates on low-cost flexible handling of custodial accounts; and Honda, with best-in-world small engine design and superb creative marketing-distribution capabilities.[9] Each has a core competency strategy for innovation that ensures the enterprise can focus more intellectual power on its selected set of competitive skills than anyone else in the world. This concentration is the foundation of competitive advantage.

## Characteristics of Core Competencies

Careful study of both successful and unsuccessful corporate examples shows that most effective core competency strategies focus on:

*A Few Critical Activities.* Successful companies target two or three—not one and not more than five—activities in the value chain most critical to the firm's future success. These are typically not the traditional functions, like production, engineering, finance, or sales, around which organizations were formed in the past. Instead they usually involve multifunctional activities like product design, logistics, technology development, or customer service—which cut across these traditional organizational structures. Defining competencies in this cross-functional manner also helps to avoid some of the turf arguments and power-building maneuvers that frequently occur as each functional or product group tries to seek center stage as the core competency of the company.

***Skill or Knowledge Sets, Not Products.*** Executives need to look beyond the company's products to the intellectual competencies, databases, systems, and skills that actually create a maintainable competitive edge. These are the true sources of strategic superiority and continual innovation. Products can be too easily reverse-engineered, duplicated, or replaced by substitutes. In most cases, the core competencies that provide a competitive edge rest on knowledge-based skills, information bases, or management practices developed in depth over many years. 3M, for example, concentrates on four critical technologies in great depth and supports these with an innovative system adapted to its particular small-discrete-product-line strategy that is without peer in its field.

***Elements Important to Customers in the Long Run.*** At least one of the firm's core competencies should relate directly to understanding and serving its customers (the right half of the value chain in Figure 7.1). High-tech companies with the world's best state-of-the-art technology (like Cray Research) often run into trouble when they ignore this caveat. On the other hand, Merck matches its superb basic research with an ethical drug marketing know-how that is equally outstanding. The examples of Sony, Honda, Matsushita, State Street Boston, and Nike all have customer contact as well as technical core competencies. By aggressively analyzing its customers' value chains, a company can often identify where it can specialize and provide an activity for a variety of customers at lower cost or more effectively than the customers themselves.

In effect, such companies recognize that their customers have the same motivation to outsource as they do and can leverage their own core competencies by becoming outsource partners to their customers. Such analyses have created whole new industries—like the specialized mortgage broker, syndication, secondary market, transaction processing, escrow, title, and insurance businesses that have now taken over

**FIGURE 7.2**
**The Disaggregated Mortgage Industry**

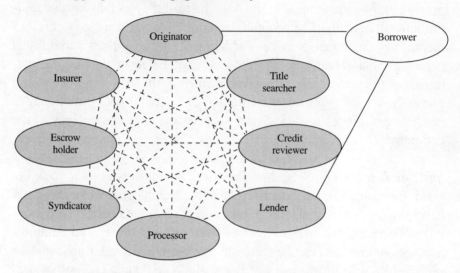

*Industries and segments of industries are disaggregating toward firms specializing in specific activities in the value chain.*

these risks and functions for banks and have disaggregated the entire mortgage industry. (See Figure 7.2.) Similarly, biotechnology has disaggregated into microbiological research, cell line, small-scale process, clinical clearance, regulatory clearance, mass production, mass distribution, postsale monitoring, and other specialist firms, which combine and recombine into new alliances for each new biotech product introduced. (See Figure 7.3.) Almost all major new enterprises in the telecommunications, ASICs,* financial services, health care, and other fields are following similar formats. Such industries—and most companies within all industries—must now be responsive to the competition and opportunities offered by such horizontal disaggregation.

***Where the Company Can Leverage Its Unique Intellect in the Value Chain.*** Effective strategies seek out places where there are market imperfections or knowledge gaps that the company is uniquely qualified to fulfill. These offer many companies truly unusual profit opportunities. These are frequently points where innovation can be highly leveraged; they are opportunities waiting for solutions. For exam-

---

*Application Specific Integrated Circuits.

**FIGURE 7.3**

**The Biotechnology Industry: Specialized Companies and Coalitions**

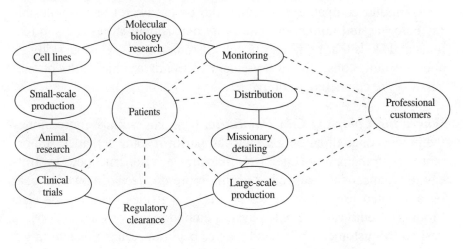

*Many high-tech industries are innovating through coalitions of enterprises that specialize in specific aspects of the innovation chain.*

ple, in industries noted for their mass production and commodity characteristics, Raychem and Intel have long concentrated not on volume production of standardized products but on in-depth knowledge of certain materials and processes, highly specialized automated design and test-feedback systems for development, and carefully targeted advanced knowledge-based products with proprietary protection. This focus enables them to counter and leap beyond the experience curve advantages of their larger competitors. Similarly, Morgan Stanley (through its TAPS* system) and Bear Stearns (through its integrated bond trading technologies) have developed in-depth knowledge bases providing unique intellectually derived competitive advantages in their commodity marketplaces.[10]

*Flexible Long-Term Skill Platforms.* Too many companies try to focus on those areas where they currently excel—usually on some product-oriented skills. The real challenge is to build a dominating skill set in areas that the customer will continue to value in the future. Motorola is doing this with its "superior quality, portable communications" focus. Toys "R" Us has done this with its best-in-world information and distribution systems for toys; and State Street Boston by developing advance

---

*Trades and Processing System.

information systems to manage large custodial accounts. Problems occur when managers choose to concentrate too narrowly on products (as computer companies sometimes did on hardware) or too inflexibly (as FotoMat and numerous center-city department stores did) on formats and skills that no longer match customer needs. Flexible skill sets and constant, conscious reassessment of trends are hallmarks of successful core competency companies.

***Where the Company Can Dominate.*** Companies make more money than their competitors only if they can perform some activities, important to customers, more effectively than anyone else. True focus in strategy today means the capacity to bring more *intellectual* power to bear on a selected use sector or set of service activities than anyone else. Products themselves are only physical embodiments of a set of services desired by customers. When companies begin to realize this and target their investments and strategic thinking on service skills and embodied services—rather than products—they become much more flexible, future oriented, innovation targeted, and customer focused.

## Now and in the Future

Strategic focus once meant owning and managing all the elements in the value chain supporting a specific product in a selected market position. Not now. Some outside supplier—by specializing on the specific skills and technologies underlying a single element in the value chain—can often become more proficient at that activity than can virtually any integrated company spreading its efforts over the whole value chain. In essence, each company is in competition with all the potential suppliers of each activity set in its value chain. It must constantly benchmark its selected core competencies against all lateral potential suppliers of that activity, and continue to build its selected core capabilities until it is demonstrably best in world. However, it must look beyond where it currently *is* best in world, to areas where it *can be* best in world, and where it *must be* best in world because customers will demand that capability. This is the basis of virtually all successful knowledge-based, technological, innovation, or diffusion strategies in services or manufacturing today. And it provides the essential leverage for the increasingly disaggregated, highly flexible innovation organizations that are becoming predominant in all industries.

All this changes the basic nature of strategic analysis from an industry analysis[11] or product perspective to a horizontal analysis of capabilities across all potential providers of that activity regardless of what industry the provider might have been considered to occupy in the past. Today AT&T, Motorola, Microsoft, Sun Microsystems, Arthur Andersen, American Airlines, Fidelity Investments, American Express, Federal Express, Citicorp, Netscape, and IBM are all in competition with each other. And Intel, Silicon Graphics, Johnson and Johnson, Merck, Exxon, Ford, GE, GM, and other manufacturing firms are in competition with the best-in-world service providers for each element in their value chains as well. (See Figure 7.4.)

## Preeminence: The Key Strategic Barrier

In its selected core competencies, each company must ensure that it maintains absolute preeminence relative to some customer set. It may also need to surround these core competencies with defensive positions, both upstream and downstream. In doing this, it may have to perform some activities where it is not best in world, just to keep existing or potential competitors from learning, taking over, eroding, or bypassing elements of its special competencies. In fact, managers should consciously develop their core competencies as a strategic block between suppliers and the marketplace—and avoid like the plague outsourcing such strategic activities or giving suppliers access to the knowledge bases or skills critical to their core competencies.[12] Honda, for example, does all its small engine R&D in-house and makes all the critical parts for its small motor design core competency in closely controlled facilities in Japan. It will consider outsourcing any other noncritical elements for its products, but builds a careful strategic block around this most essential element for all its businesses.

Of paramount importance is the fact that as a company's intellectual preeminence in its field grows, its knowledge-based core competencies become ever harder to overtake. Knowledge bases tend to grow exponentially in value with investment and experience.[13] Intellectual leadership tends to attract the most talented people, who then can work on and solve the most interesting problems. The combination in turn creates higher returns and attracts the next round of outstanding talent. In addition to the examples already cited, companies as diverse as Bechtel, AT&T–Bell Labs, TRW, Microsoft, Boeing, McKinsey, 3M, Arthur Andersen, HP, SCI, Nike, Mayo Clinic, UPS and Wal-Mart have found these kinds of strategies—with their associated innovation capabilities—the key to continuing dominance in their marketplaces.

**FIGURE 7.4**
**Lateral Competition**

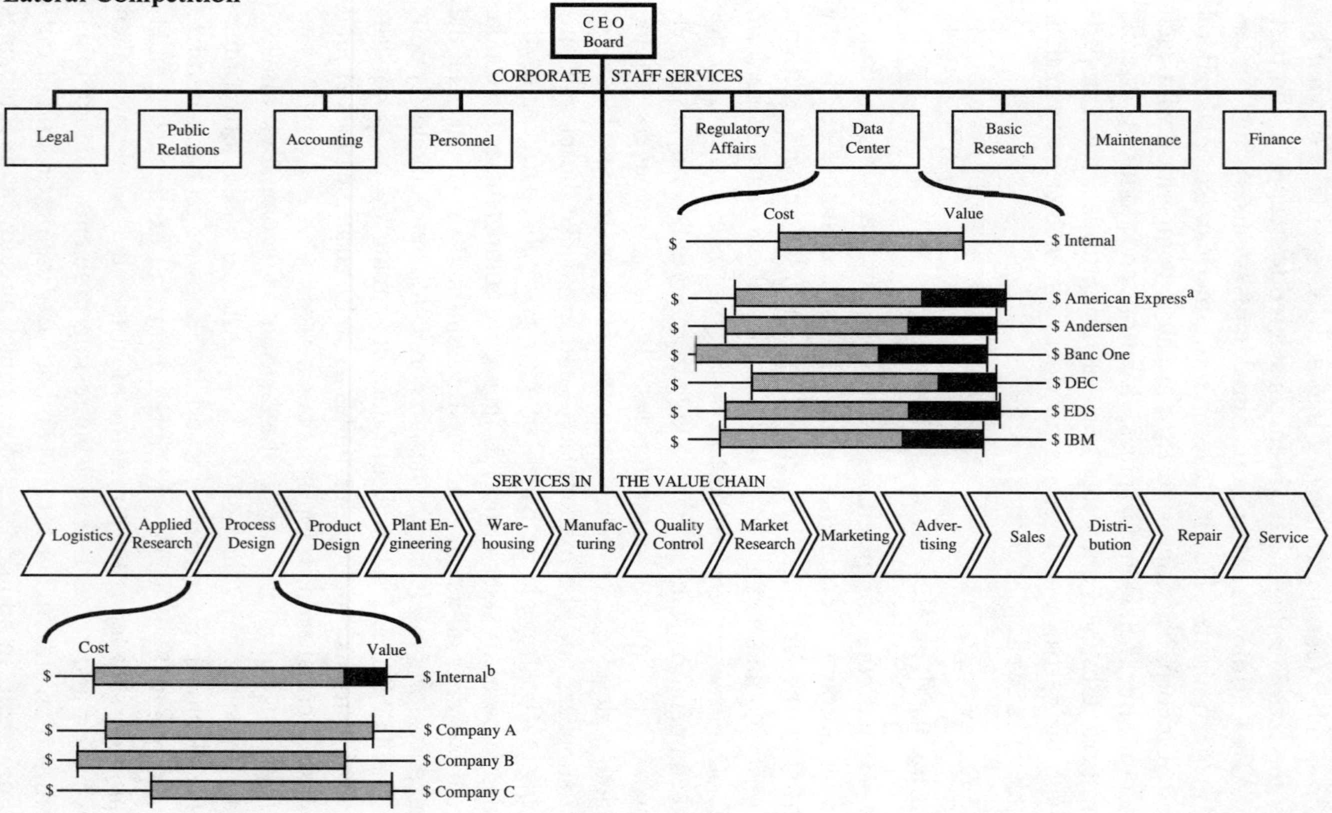


[a]Shaded areas represent potential gains from outsourcing: cost reduction and increase in output value. All values are for demonstration only.
[b]Shaded areas represent potential gains from insourcing: cost reduction and increase in value.

*Enterprises should compare their internal costs and value-added against best-in-world providers of that activity. If the company cannot match these providers' capabilities, it should consider outsourcing.*

ED:> Adjustment
to be made to all
this figure to fit or
page, Please adv

# LEVERAGING INNOVATION THROUGH OUTSOURCING

Core competency-with-outsourcing strategies have led to the much-touted concepts of the "intelligent enterprise," the "virtual corporation," the "horizontal company," and similar shorthand terms for disaggregated, intellectually based, software-coordinated enterprises. This same set of forces has led to the vastly expanded use of strategic alliances, industry partnering, and strategic outsourcing that today is restructuring virtually every industry. A critical top management issue is how to manage and leverage innovation using the opportunities that these complex organizational relationships offer internally and externally.

Although there are many emerging and successful high-tech companies that could provide examples, two examples developed in somewhat greater detail may make the point more adequately. These suggest that innovative companies using core-competency-with-outsourcing strategies and highly disaggregated organizational forms can leverage their own internal capabilities by factors of hundreds or more.

• The first well-documented U.S. example of this strategy was Apple Computer. Knowing it could not be best in world at making chips, boxes, monitors, cables, keyboards, and the other components for its explosively successful Apple II, Apple Computer Company in its early years outsourced 70% of its manufacturing costs and components.[14] Instead of building internal bureaucracies where it had no unique skills, Apple outsourced critical items like physical design (to Frogdesign), printers (to Tokyo Electric), and even marketing (to Regis McKenna, which achieved a $100 million image for Apple when it only had a few employees and about $1 million to spend for the purpose). Apple focused its internal resources on its own Apple DOS and later Mac OS (operating systems) and the supporting interface software to give Apple's products their unique "look and feel" for users. Its open architecture policy in its early years stimulated independent software groups to write the much-needed applications software that gave Apple II's customers uniquely high functionality.[15]

Apple thus avoided unnecessary investments, benefited from its vendors' R&D and technical expertise, kept itself flexible to adopt new technologies as they became available, and leveraged its very limited capital resources by a huge margin. Operating with an extremely flat organization, Apple for years enjoyed three times its competitors' capital turnover and the highest market value versus fixed asset ratio among major computer producers.[16] It lost this position only when it allowed

Microsoft to usurp its core competency in user-friendly software between the customer and the screen. Microsoft did this by developing comparably user-friendly software that could serve a variety of hosts and new functions.

• Nike, the largest supplier of athletic shoes in the world, outsources essentially all of its shoe production and manufactures only key components of its Nike Air system. Athletic footwear is very technology and fashion intensive, requiring continual innovation and high flexibility at both the production and marketing levels. Nike creates maximum value by concentrating on preproduction (research and development) and postproduction (marketing, distribution and sales) activities linked together by perhaps the best marketing information system in the industry. It uses a carefully developed on-site "expatriate" program within suppliers' plants and an extensive software infrastructure to coordinate its foreign-based suppliers.[17] By codesigning new products with these key suppliers and outsourcing the critical advertising portion of its marketing program to Weiden and Kennedy—whose creative advertising helped drive Nike to the top of the product recognition scale for minimum expenditures—Nike maximized capital returns and minimized its risks. It also maximized its flexibility and leveraged its innovation potentials substantially, growing at a compounded rate of 20% in sales and 31% in ROE on its limited investment base through most of the past decade.

Core-competency-with-outsourcing strategies make special sense in rapidly changing marketplaces and technological situations. They decrease risks, shorten cycle times, lower investments, flatten and lean organizations, and make their sponsors more responsive to customer needs. They leverage intellect and innovation to the maximum extent through software coordination with customers, partners, and vendors.

## Strategic Outsourcing: Handling Vulnerability

If supplier markets were totally reliable and efficient, all rational companies would outsource everything except those special activities where they could achieve unique competitive advantage—their core competencies. Unfortunately, most supplier markets are imperfect and do entail some risks. Strategic outsourcing mitigates these risks, while providing added support for the central strategies of the firm. To develop a true outsourcing strategy, managers must focus on several key strategic questions as they consider different activities for outsourcing.

**FIGURE 7.5**

**Competitive Edge versus Strategic Risk**

| | | Low | Moderate | High |
|---|---|---|---|---|
| Potential for competitive edge | **High** | | | **Strategically control (produce internally)** |
| | **Moderate** | | **Moderate control needed (special venture or contract arrangements)** | |
| | **Low** | **Low control needed (buy off the shelf)** | | |

**Strategic Risk of Outsourcing**

*By ranking activities according to their potentials for competitive edge and possible risk, enterprises can determine in a strategic fashion which they should keep inside or can outsource safely.*

First, what is the company's potential for obtaining competitive advantage in this activity? Second, what is the potential for failure in the supplier marketplace (that is, to what risks would the company be vulnerable if it purchased externally)? These two factors can be arrayed in a simple matrix (see Figure 7.5). Third, what can be done to alleviate any necessary vulnerability?

The two extremes are relatively straightforward to handle. When the potentials for both market failure and competitive edge are high, the company needs a high degree of control. It usually should manage the activity internally or control its sourcing through joint ownership arrangements. The opposite case occurs (as in office cleaning) where little competitive edge is usually possible and there is an active and deep market of supplier firms. The company can buy these items off the shelf. In between there is a continuous range of exposures requiring different degrees of control and strategic flexibility. At each intervening point, the question is not just whether to make or buy, but how to implement a desired balance between independence and incentives for the supplier ver-

**FIGURE 7.6**
**Options for Flexibility**

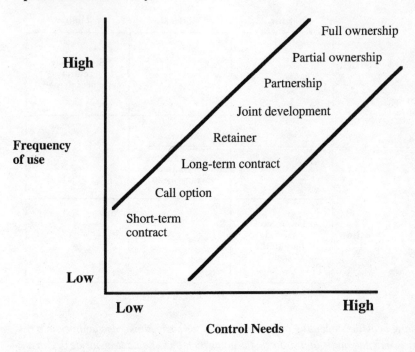

*A variety of options exist for outsourcing, depending on the frequency with which the enterprise uses this activity and its needs for strategic control.*

sus control and security for the buyer. Figure 7.6 illustrates a range of possible options, depending on frequency of use.

Many companies unfortunately assume that, because they have performed an activity internally in the past or it "seems integral" to their business, the activity should be insourced. However, on closer investigation and with careful benchmarking, the buyer's capabilities may turn out to be significantly below those of best-in-world suppliers' potentials, especially in technology-intensive areas.

• Ford Motor Company in its original Taurus-Sable project found that many of its internal groups' innovation, quality practices, and costs were nowhere near those of external suppliers when it began its famous best-in-class-in-the-world benchmarking studies on 400 subassemblies for the new Taurus-Sable line. By carefully surveying and developing external sources, Ford substantially decreased its risks, lowered its investments, shortened its cycle times, and tapped into a stream of continuing innovativeness it could not have duplicated internally. To support this increased outsourcing, Ford restructured its purchasing offices, purchasing practices, monitoring software, and design practices in significant ways.[18] This radical reconceptualizing of Ford's (formerly sequential) innovation process into a "simultaneous design" process with worldwide outsourcing projected Ford into the number one profitability position among automobile companies in the world. Unfortunately, Ford's redesign of some later cars ignored many of these experiences.

## Internal and External Transaction Costs

In all calculations for outsourcing strategies, analysts must include both internal transaction costs and those associated with external sourcing.[19] If the company is to produce the item or service internally over the long term, it must be prepared to back up its decision with continuing R&D, personnel development, and infrastructure investments that at least match those of the best-in-world external supplier. Otherwise, it will lose competitive edge over time. Managers often tend to overlook such "internal transaction costs," as well as the losses from laggard innovation and nonresponsiveness from internal groups that know they have a guaranteed market. They also ignore the headquarters and support costs of constantly managing insourced activities. Two of the great gains of outsourcing are the decrease in executive time used in managing peripheral activities and the benefits of focusing top management's time more on the core of the business. On the other hand, analysts and top managers also frequently ignore the discontinuation costs of shutting down an operation to outsource it. Various studies have shown these internal transaction costs can be extremely important when they are thoroughly analyzed.[20]

Several questions should pervade the strategic outsourcing decision. They should be approached in the approximate sequence below:

1. Can we produce the good or service most effectively internally on a long-term basis? Are we willing to make the backup investments necessary to be best in world in this activity? Is the activity critical to defending our core competency? If not,
2. Can we license technology or buy know-how that will let us be best in world on a continuing basis? If not,
3. Can we buy the item as an off-the-shelf product or service from a best-in-world supplier? Is this a viable long-term option as volume and complexity grow? If not,
4. Can we establish a joint development project with a knowledgeable

supplier that gives us the desired capability to be best in world at this activity? If not,

5. Can we enter into a long-term development or purchase agreement that gives us a secure source of supply and a proprietary interest in knowledge or other property of vital interest to us and the supplier? If not,

6. Can we acquire and manage a best-in-world supplier to advantage? If not, can we set up a joint venture or partnership that avoids the shortcomings we see in each of the above? If so,

7. Can we establish controls and incentives that reduce total transaction costs below those of discontinuation or producing internally?

Within this framework, companies are outsourcing much more of what used to be considered integral elements of their value chains or essential staff activities.[21] Because of greater complexity, higher specialization, and new technological capabilities, outside suppliers can now perform many such activities at lower cost and with higher value-added than can a fully integrated company whose core competency is not that activity. In some cases, new production technologies have moved economies of scale toward the supplier level. In others, service technologies have lowered transaction costs substantially, making it possible to specify, transport, store, and coordinate inputs from external sources so inexpensively that the balance of benefits has shifted from insourcing to outsourcing.[22] In certain specialized niches, outside specialists have grown to a sufficient size and sophistication that they have developed such economies of scale, scope, and knowledge intensity that smaller or more integrated producers cannot effectively compete with them. To the extent that knowledge about a specific activity is more important than knowledge about the end product itself, specialized suppliers can often innovate and produce higher value-added at lower cost than almost any integrated producer.

## Innovation Leverage, Not Short-Term Cost Reduction

Too often companies look at outsourcing as just a means to lower short-term direct costs. Through strategic outsourcing, however, companies can also lower their long-term capital commitments significantly, as Apple, Nike, and MCI have done.

From an innovation viewpoint, strategic outsourcing can also provide the buyer with much greater flexibility, especially when acquiring rapidly developing new technologies, support services for fashion goods, or the myriad components for complex customized systems. It decreases cycle times for the buyer, which can have multiple best-in-class suppliers working simultaneously on individual components of its system. Each such supplier can have greater depth in personnel and knowledge about its particular specialty and support more specialized facilities to produce higher quality than the coordinating company might possibly achieve alone. In addition, strategic outsourcing spreads the company's risks for component and technology developments among a number of suppliers. The buying company does not have to undertake the full failure risks of all component R&D programs or invest in and constantly update production capabilities for each component system. Further, the buyer is not limited to its own innovative capabilities; it can tap into a full stream of creative new product and process ideas and quality improvement potentials it could not possibly generate itself. Because increased affluence forces much greater attention to new product ideas, quality details, and customization, the buying company can exploit the greater responsiveness of many specialized smaller suppliers.

For these reasons outsourcing has become an important strategy for leveraging internal technical capabilities and tapping into the rapid response and innovative capabilities of smaller enterprises.

• At MCI, Richard Liebhaber, chief strategy and technology officer, said: "MCI constantly seeks to grow by finding and developing associations with small companies having interesting services they can hang on to the MCI network. Although we employ only about 1,000 professional technical personnel internally, 19,000 such personnel work directly for us through contracts. . . . Now we do about 60% of our software development internally, but we manage [in detail] the other 40% in contractors' hands. We do all the specification, process rating, operational procedures, and system testing inside our company. We design the overall system. We control the process. Then we let others do what they can do best."[23]

• Chrysler has worked hard to develop constructive innovative relationships with its 60,000 suppliers. Since it lacks the purchasing clout of its other Big Three or large Japanese competitors, Chrysler seeks its competitive edge by being easier to work with. Through its Score program, Chrysler tries to work with—instead of squeezing—its suppliers to make innovation as mutually profitable as possible. The target is for each supplier to create innovations that lower costs or increase value by at least 5% of its billings to Chrysler each year. It reports that the program has led to $2.5 billion in savings so far. By innovating in its supply chain, Chrysler has cut its supplier base by 36% and generated a stream of over 16,000 innovations, now rolling in at over 100 per week.[24]

Contrary to concerns about losing essential skills, many companies have found that they actually improve their knowledge bases through strategic outsourcing, as Chrysler and Ford did when they moved from 50% to 70% insourcing to 66% to 70% (respectively) outsourcing. If outsourcing is done under a license from the buyer, the buyer or co-venturer can insist on receiving knowledge access to all supplementary inventions of the seller—as Pilkington Bros, PLC, did with float glass—to give it even higher knowledge capabilities and technological access in the future. By constantly surveying and analyzing potential suppliers, top managements can place pressures on their internal supply groups to be competitive with the best external benchmark companies. They find they can question subordinates with a much higher knowledge base than ever before, and the threat of outsourcing helps keep internal groups innovative and competitive. By actively networking with the best outside suppliers and experts, top-level personnel obtain more stimulation and insights than any insider group could possibly offer—unless, of course, that group is really a core competency of the organization.

## Faster, Better Innovation

Much of the disaggregation and downsizing of organizations today comes from outsourcing formerly integral corporate activities that have grown ineffective. One result is the type of network companies and industries noted above. Another is a new form of faster, more effective innovation.

• To leverage their research capabilities, companies like Du Pont are outsourcing much of their precompetitive research. In fields where they have used the technique, they claim that some 90% of their really new ideas come from these sources at only 30% of their internal research cost. Eaton codevelops new gears for its mechanical products with Illinois Institute of Technology, claiming an ROR of 90% on this activity. By outsourcing to downstream bottlers and distribution centers, Snapple claimed to have shortened its product introduction times by 75% and cut costs, with less risk, by 90%. Upjohn outsources most of its cell line research and clinical trials. And so on.

Using core-competency-with-outsourcing strategies, each company concentrates its investments on what it does best in the innovation cycle. Using these skills and proprietary protection wherever possible, it develops a strategic block between its suppliers and the marketplace. The company substantially leverages both its capital and its intellectual resources by outsourcing to specially talented suppliers. All of the specialized innovation forms developed in the next chapter are variants of a core competency strategy developed internally. Each focuses the organization's resources on those particular skills, knowledge bases, and structures that create unique value for customers and then targets these competencies toward specific customer needs. All connect their internal competencies directly to customers, interact with customers in the innovation cycle, and develop a continuing competitive advantage in some crucial intellectually based capabilities—like databases, software systems, customer information systems, or motivation and reward systems.

Until a core competency is captured in the organization's systems, it is not a maintainable competitive edge. In most cases, this involves embedding a portion of the system in software and another portion in sophisticated management practices, or "thoughtware." Once both occur, the company's intellectual assets become genuine intellectual capital and can be leveraged substantially through strategic outsourcing of other elements of the value chain. The combination yields lower costs and risks while increasing the value of results for both the company and its customers.

## Maximizing Efficiency, Flexibility, and Stability Simultaneously

There is another extremely important feature of core competency strategies for innovative companies. Once the company's core competencies are clearly identified and in place—if these are basic skills important to customers—a wide variety of innovative new products or services can be rolled out based on these same competencies. Such strategies realize a strategist's dream. They obtain maximum efficiency through focus, maximum flexibility as markets change, and maximum stability through participating in multiple independent marketplaces. Companies like Sony, 3M, HP, Frito-Lay, Pepsico, Moulènex, Matsushita, American Express, and Procter & Gamble offer excellent illustrations. These companies concentrate their resources on selected internal skills where they have a competitive edge, thus obtaining maximum efficiency from internal investments. However, unlike product-focused strategies, they can leverage their skills or technologies across multiple markets and thus become independent of the vagaries of a single industry's cyclical characteristics. With core competency strategies, systemic risk does not increase with focus as it does in companies linked to narrower product-based or market strategies. Nor do the financial markets consider these companies conglomerates, although they may participate in as many as 50,000 different product segments.

Analysts recognize the increased payoffs possible through core competency strategies. Many studies verify that profitability, rates of return, and Q ratios (market value/net fixed assets) increase most rapidly for companies that focus on a core competency that is purely intellectual yet serves multiple markets (as Morgan Stanley, Microsoft, Oracle, and Netscape do). Within the same industries, enterprises with core competency and outsourcing strategies tend to outperform vertically integrated companies by a significant margin. Consequently, financial markets reward these strategies highly. Strategic focus now lies not so much in narrowing or limiting the firm's product line and product market scope as in (1) focusing strategy around a uniquely developed set of core intellectual and service capabilities important to customers and (2) outsourcing and coordinating less essential activities with best-in-world suppliers (in terms of value versus cost).

## PERFORMANCE MEASUREMENT AND RECOGNITION SYSTEMS

The firm's recognition and reward system is a final critical element in creating the framework that highly innovative organizations utilize to perform most independently and effectively. The motivation system must operate both systemically (across all relevant activities) and systematically (with continuing consistency and rigor) to achieve best outcomes. Corporate and individual units' performance measurements and rewards must support the firm's unique strategies and missions, its desired core intellectual competencies, and the performance figures of merit it seeks. Otherwise intended performance goals will not be achieved. Nor will people be motivated to undertake the uncomfortable learning, waiting, risk taking, and ambiguity that innovation involves.

### Rewarding Innovative Behavior

Perhaps the most basic finding of all psychology is that behavior which is reinforced will be repeated or amplified. This is the core element of effective motivation systems. Yet too often corporate incentive systems reward safe, bureaucratic behavior rather than the risk-taking, individualistic behavior characteristic of innovators. In stimulating entrepreneurial or innovative behavior, research demonstrates that intrinsic (personal psychological) motivations are generally more effective than extrinsic (monetary or hierarchical) motivations.[25] Substantial research also suggests that innovators respond most to a mix of financial and nonfinancial incentives and that most talented people, to feel ful-filled, need a concrete sense of adventure, appreciation for their hard work, and recognition for successes achieved.[26] As Bob Noyce once said, "We are seeking high achievers. And high achievers love to be measured because otherwise they can't prove to themselves that they are achieving. Measuring them says you care about them."[27] Although indi-viduals vary significantly, innovators generally respond most to (1) challenges, (2) personal recognition, (3) freedom of activity, and (4) fi-nancial rewards, roughly in that order. But the measures must fit the strategy.

• MBNA, the Delaware-based credit card company, has innovated a special niche in this commodity industry by emphasizing fast service to its upscale affinity-group customers. MBNA continuously measures its performance on fifteen metrics, most relating to speed and quality. It has a "no more than two-ring" policy and measures on-line each group's performance against this and its twenty-one-second transfer-and-pickup standard. Special credit service requests by platinum card members must be answered within fifteen minutes even though they in-volve multiple departments. Results against these standards are pub-lished daily on sixty scoreboards around the company. Every day that MBNA's 98.5% standard for service responses is met, money goes into a bonus pool for all nonofficers. The system drives all innovation at MBNA. Since 1991 its stock has gone up 602%.[28]

## High-Profile Rewards

Both meaningful financial awards and clear personal recognition are es-sentials in any well-administered corporate incentive program. Yet we are constantly amazed at how few companies make millionaires of the innovators who create $100 million businesses for them and how many offer only token in-house newspaper snippets or small ($1 to $50) awards for patents as recognition for large technological contributions. The most common reason for such practices is that "large individual awards or high-profile personal recognition would be disruptive." Not surprisingly, such companies stay bureaucratic. One of the keys to in-novation is the selection, development, and rewarding of people whose values and behavior support the intended directions of innovation.[29] This is a major reason that small companies so often out-innovate larger enterprises. Small companies seek and reward the kind of offbeat, fa-natic, risk-taking behavior that large firms do not. The most innovative large companies we studied, from Microsoft and Sony, to Intel and 3M, had also found ways to do this.

• Sony provides incentives at several levels. It has long given a prestigious "crystal award" for outstanding technological or scientific achievement, regardless of whether it resulted in commercial applications. It also rewards innovative teams with a "small but significant" percentage of first-year sales on new products they conceive. Microsoft's and Nintendo's incentives have made more innovation millionaires (and in Microsoft's case, billionaires) than any other companies in their home countries. Financial and investment houses and retailers routinely let their innovative executives share directly in the profits they produce from innovation. 3M often lets innovators head the units they created; at the time of our investigations, all but one of its corporate vice presidents had been an innovation champion. Genentech and Intel experimented with various forms of "shadow stock" and limited partnerships (based on actual commercial performance) to reward their innovative teams.

The following chapter will show how performance measurements and incentives can best be fitted to specific technology strategies. The top manager's job is to see that such incentives exist throughout the company, are matched explicitly to the company's strategies and time horizons, and are implemented fairly but with a high enough profile to elicit the kind of innovative behavior the company needs. Too often companies allow the bureaucracy to capture its incentive systems and, in the name of "fairness to all," to dilute incentives to the point where they are meaningless. In our national study of IT productivity, less than 5% of the companies sampled had changed their incentive systems to match their newly installed technological capabilities and modified organizations.[30] The results were predictable.

## SUMMARY

The process of managing innovation is one of creating the excitement and focus that drive innovation, while supporting the decentralization and chaos that are essential elements of most innovation. Top management is the critical element in bringing cohesion to these two seemingly conflicting forces. The first important top management actions in this process are (1) creating a clear, exciting, challenging vision that all elements of the organization understand and embrace, (2) defining a unique technological strategy that enables competitive preeminence, and (3) establishing a conscious portfolio of innovation thrusts that balances the company's long-term, short-term, geographical, defensive, and growth needs in a way that defines all divisions' and players' roles clearly in this strategy.

For these to be effective, top managers must see that their internal programs genuinely create best-in-world or winning capabilities in critical strategic areas. This requires (1) creating figure-of-merit goals in each important area and defining "winning" competitively in such clear terms that decentralized units can use them to self-guide their activities, (2) developing a few core intellectual competencies to best-in-world levels and focusing more intellectual resources on these than anyone else in the world, (3) leveraging these competencies further through carefully structured strategic outsourcing to lower the company's investments and risks, while increasing its flexibility, innovation potentials, and value-added for customers, and (4) establishing performance measurement and reward systems that support company strategies and encourage all decentralized units to innovate meaningfully and profitably for customers. Many pragmatic methodologies for implementing the latter are explored in the next chapter.

# PART IV

# MIDDLE MANAGEMENT ISSUES

# 8

# Matching Strategies, Structures, and Incentives

Perhaps the most difficult role in innovation is that of middle managers. They are the key implementers of strategy, and implementation is always harder than conceptualization or formulation. Middle managers often find themselves in conflict with both top managers and technological innovators as they try to maintain the strategic focus and fulfill the operational performance goals top managers demand, overcome the inevitable operational resisters to change, and live with the chaos that effective innovation always involves. In addition to providing motivating visions, challenging strategic goals, and figure-of-merit targets for their operations, they must:

- Implement a clear strategic, market-oriented focus across all technology and operating units.
- Ruthlessly flatten internal organizations and encourage aggressive, decentralized, multiple-competing innovation units to collaborate laterally across the organization.
- Empower and reward innovators, champions, risk takers, and change agents, while honoring those who crunch out profits.
- Appropriately match incentives to each unit's unique strategies and time horizons.
- Provide long-term leadership, enthusiasm, and sustained commitment while living in the chaos of innovation.

# FOCUS AND CHAOS

Most major technological innovations do not occur in the linear mode that more formal planning mechanisms might suggest. They emerge from a relatively chaotic sequence of events typically involving an early vision; numerous fits, starts, and lapses in progress; random interactions with outside parties; frequent intuitive insights and personal risk taking; and even some lucky breaks, which ultimately lead to success.[1] While in retrospect a technology may seem to progress (worldwide) doggedly up a Gaussian curve toward its ultimate theoretical limits,[2] detailed observers see a series of "relatively small steps marked by frequent unanticipated obstacles and by constant random breakthroughs interacting across laboratories and borders."[3] Initial discoveries tend to be highly individualistic and serendipitous, advances chaotic and interactive, and specific outcomes unpredictable and chancy until the very last moment. Even the highly planned first communications satellite blew up when it was deployed.[4]

If formal planning were all that was required for innovation, many more companies would be successful at it. Most fail because they can neither tolerate nor manage innovation's bubbling, probabilistic, intuitive processes—which are more akin to a disorderly fermentation vat than a sequential production line.[5] Divisions seeking strategic advantage through significant technological innovation need to recognize the turbulent, long-term realities of how this process operates, and design specific organizational and management practices to motivate and guide it properly. Our multiple-year studies show how some of the world's most innovative large companies both tolerate—indeed stimulate— such chaos *and* maintain the strong strategic focus and practical controls so essential to efficient operations.

# MANAGING CHAOS

Technical people generally know about the chaos of innovation; managers frequently need reminding of this fact. Perhaps the most difficult issue middle managers face is maintaining the innovation team members' enthusiasm and top management's support throughout the long time horizons and utter chaos that accompany major innovations. In the past, most radical innovations—like jet aircraft engines, computers, float glass, videotape recorders, recombinant DNA products, fiber optics, xerography, nuclear power, space flight—if commercially successful at all, took seven to twenty-five years from first discovery to net positive cash flows.[6] Two major innovations will make the point:

• In the late 1930s Russell Marker was working on steroids called sapogenins, which make a soaplike foam in water. In the process he found a technique that would degrade one of these, diosgenin, into the female sex hormone progesterone. Marker found that diosgenin was abundant in certain Mexican yams. By processing about ten tons of these in rented and borrowed laboratory space, he extracted some four pounds of diosgenin for experiments that led in 1944 to a tiny company, Syntex, producing steroids for the laboratory market. But it was not until 1957 that Searle started marketing a derivative, norethynodril, as a menstrual regulator—with a specific warning against "possible contraceptive activity." In 1962, over twenty-three years after Marker's early research, Syntex obtained Food and Drug Administration (FDA) approval for its oral contraceptive.[7]

• The unraveling of DNA's structure first followed a convoluted and somewhat disjointed route through various nations' biology, organic chemistry, x-ray crystallography, and mathematics laboratories until James Watson and Francis Crick's Nobel Prize-winning conception of DNA as a spiral staircase of matched base pairs.[8] Years of painstaking and highly individualistic research on gene structures and enzymes followed in hundreds of laboratories around the world. These generated alternating periods of optimism and discouragement, but few salable results. All at once, in 1972, the possibility of practical recombinant DNA suddenly emerged when two outstanding scientists, Herbert Boyer and Stanley Cohen, randomly interacted over sandwiches at a Hawaiian meeting. This discussion ultimately led to the first true biotechnology company, Genentech. But even now, almost four decades after Watson and Crick's insights and two decades after Boyer and Cohen's first experiments, only a few of recombinant DNA's commercial applications are making money; most are still moving in fits of insight and frustration toward the market. And most of recombinant DNA's major early expected uses (like self-fertilizing plants, interferon, or commercial waste decomposition) are still far from payoff.

Although many cycle times are shortening, radical innovations (like high-powered lasers, fiber optics, stealth aircraft, fusion power, tissue plasminogen activator (TPA), electric automobiles, and heart transplants) still take over a decade to implement successfully. One of the darlings of today's stock market shows how long time horizons still are in basic fields:

• In 1967 Judah Folkman began research on angiogenesis. Within a few years, he realized that the growth of cancerous tumors depended on the formation of thousands of tiny blood vessels that feed them nutrients. But not until the early 1980s did he pinpoint the molecule that induced this state, called angiogenesis. A decade later, one of Folkman's doctoral students interested in ophthalmology, while looking for an angiogenesis blocker to prevent blindness, found the first counteragent. When he merged databases on drugs that interfered with bleeding (menstruation) in women and caused birth defects (fetuses require angiogenesis in their early development), the computer found only six candidates, including thalidomide. Inadvertently, the computer had discovered why thalidomide caused deformities. Further research in 1996 by Folkman found angiostatin, an even more potent inhibitor that could suppress the growth of tumors in mice by 95% to 100%. EntreMed moved to commercialize the drug, and the race for tumor blockers was on—after twenty-nine years of serious technical work.[9]

Platform-level innovations (like Microsoft's Windows, McKesson's Economost, and Sony's CCD optical converters for camcorders) take three to seven years to implement. If 30% net present value returns are required, many such innovations become anathema to large public companies, which gauge their (and their divisions') success in terms of quarterly profitability; to intermediate managers, who are often rotated in two-year patterns; and to public laboratories, dependent on annual or biennial political elections for their support.[10] However, an increasing number of innovations occur in very short—weeks to months—cycles. Middle managers have to operate in multiple time frames to maintain both their daily operations efficiencies and longer-term innovation strategies.

## SOMEWHAT ORDERLY TUMULT

The innovative environment is always dynamic, opportunistic, and unpredictable, calling for highly flexible, responsive, decentralized organizational structures in most cases. Yet problems tend to be very knowledge intensive and complex, calling for high specialization and hence centralization of skills. Since adhocracies are the only organizational form that can deliver both great flexibility and high specialization simultaneously, they are most extensively used for innovation.[11] Recognizing the limits of formal plans, procedures, and control systems, the most effective innovative middle managers (like their top management compatriots) guide their ad hoc units primarily by establishing the frameworks—described in Chapter 6—that motivate, challenge, and focus team activity. Yet they leave these units maximum freedom in choosing their technical approaches and in interacting with internal and external knowledge sources.

## "Builds" and "Way Points"

Some middle and top managements attempt to guide progress in much more detail, insisting that projects surpass a sequence of hurdles or milestones as they move along a preordained path to commercialization. These techniques implicitly assume linearity and predictability in development. As software increasingly allows more interactive, organic forms of innovation, this milestone approach becomes less and less appropriate. Detailed project targets now tend to change continuously as software-based experimentation proves them feasible or infeasible and as more readily available market information discerns changing customer preferences. Increasingly, instead of rigid timing and progress milestones, successful firms use periodic software "system builds" and electronic "screen tests" to check on progress.

Under these circumstances, criteria and timing laid down in early program plans tend to be viewed more as way points in sailing than as milestones in hiking. Way points acknowledge that many things affect an optimum future course and are changing simultaneously (like the winds, currents, surface, and competitive conditions in sailing). Many successful middle managers use interactively shared "software skunk works" and market-directed way points (jointly developed with customers) to guide their innovation units. The latter determine and seek more specific technical goals in any way they choose—within the program's agreed-on overall targets, limits, and figures of merit. Design and monitoring software makes sure that program performance goals, priorities, costs, dimensions, fits, and tolerances stay coordinated among units working in parallel.

The resulting process is one of somewhat orderly tumult. Early bench-scale projects may pursue many options with little integration into a total program. At first, using multiple software models and databases, innovators may create a wide variety of partially tested options and amplify the knowledge surrounding key variables. Only after key variables are understood and demonstrated in laboratory or software models may more precise planning be at all meaningful. Even then, many factors remain unknown, and internal competition can usefully continue toward various possible solutions. However, as teams pass agreed-on way points, only those options that still have the vigor to meet the program's redefined targets may continue. Managers may even consciously place several small-scale side bets to test other options in case something unanticipated goes wrong. In a surprising number of cases, these alternatives prove successful when the initially planned approaches later fail.

As the program approaches ultimate exploitation, resistance and costs escalate, and uncertainty for the surviving options decreases. (See Figure 8.1.) This is where formal economic evaluation, planning, and progress monitoring techniques pay high dividends. Only projects meeting figure-of-merit standards go on. By then interactive, software-based, incremental experimentation has built a broad information base, numerous options, more knowledge about customers and greater certainty of outcomes, higher commitment levels on scientific-technical teams, enhanced comfort levels for management, and heightened political support for the innovation to compete and succeed against alternatives (like acquisitions or marketing programs) that seem more familiar, and hence less risky, to higher management. While allowing more productive interactive tumult during all stages of innovation, properly designed software disciplines the entire process, captures more critical information, and provides a monitoring system that makes sure that all critical variables are considered and tested. But at some point, a decision to move ahead with larger investments and volume production becomes necessary, and organizations and analyses must focus more sharply on cost efficiency. Again, well-designed software is critical for this transition.

## Strategically Oriented Adhocracies

It is a genuine mistake to try to get rid of the chaos in earlier stages of innovation. Instead, managers need to establish organizations that are effective in this kind of climate and manage in the chaos, not attempt to deny or change the essential nature of the process. To quote Henry Mintzberg: "To innovate means to break away from established patterns. Thus the innovative organization cannot rely on any form of standardization for coordination. It must avoid all the trappings of bureaucratic structure: sharp divisions of labor, extensive unit differentiation, highly formalized behavior, or an undue emphasis on planning and control systems. Above all, it must remain flexible."[12]

In effective innovative adhocracies, the lines between administrative and operating activities, organizational groups, managers and workers, and different disciplines tend to blur or disappear. Self-directed, cross-

# FIGURE 8.1
## Chaos and the Product Development Program (PDP) Concept

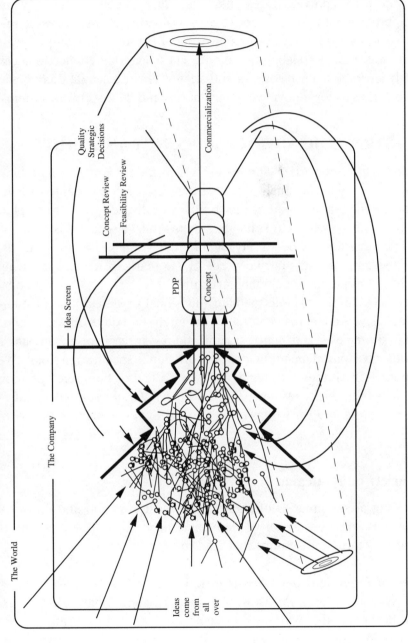

Source: Polaroid Invention and Innovation Research Project. Reproduced by special permission: K. A. Zien and S. Buckler, "From Experience: Dreams to Market: Crafting a Culture of Innovation," *Journal of Product Innovation Management*, July 1997.

*Innovative projects tend to start in chaos but need to be systematically focused as they approach commercialization.*

functional teams are common for problems of moderate to high complexity. Independent collaboration is common on innovations of the greatest complexity. The customer, the task, the technology, and the software system provide the essential disciplines of control. When teams are appropriate, the most productive typically operate as open systems, with strong liaisons with outsiders who can help solve difficult problems in an independent collaborative mode. These external connections can greatly leverage team resources and should be an essential component in most designs for innovative organizations and their software systems.

## STRATEGIC ADHOCRACIES, NOT ANARCHIES

In successful enterprises, innovation organizations are not anarchies. They are unique and finely tuned structures carefully adapted to the particular innovation strategy the company or division wants to emphasize. All management and software systems must support this strategy. We encountered a wide variety of different strategies in our studies, each focusing around specific needs of the marketplace and involving relatively unique organizational structures. Most of the organizational differences lie in how intermediate (divisional or departmental) management levels relate to each other. One might find quite different innovation strategies—and hence organizations—in each of a company's various divisions depending on that division's specific missions. We cannot detail all these strategies here, but a few of the more common will show their distinctiveness. *It is dead wrong for one company or division to imitate another's innovation structures unless their strategies are the same. Structures must support strategy, or neither will be effective.*

### A Variety of Strategies

Following are summaries of some of the most common and powerful technology strategies we encountered and the widely different organizational structures and systems that tend to support them.

***Inverted Organizational Strategies.*** These can be the most empowering of all innovation forms. Rubbermaid, Kyocera, Sharp Electronics, SAS, Bechtel, and NovaCare, as well as merchant banks, priority medical and defense research programs, and consulting and law firms, have used them to great advantage. They are most useful when an individual or small team is the primary locus of knowledge, must customize that knowledge for a particular customer set or problem, can work relatively

**FIGURE 8.2**
**The Inverted Organization**

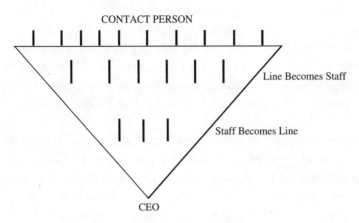

When the enterprise's dominating intellect is in the brains of its contact people, when they can operate independently of each other, and when they also make the adaptations to consumers' needs, the organization can be inverted.

independently, but must call on the full power of the firm to be effective. In these organizations, the contact person or team "gives orders" to the rest of the organization relative to their program, and the organization "must respond." (See Figure 8.2.) The normal "line" hierarchy becomes a "support" structure not intervening except in emergencies—as might the environmental officer if an expensive legal case seemed probable. The function of line managers becomes bottleneck breaking, developing special studies, arranging for resources, and providing service economies of scale; in other words, the former line hierarchy becomes a staff support system.

Inverted organizations work well (1) when innovating, customizing, or servicing for the customer at the point of contact is the firm's most important activity, (2) when the company's personnel at the point of contact have more information about the customer's problem and more knowledge about how to solve it than anyone else, and (3) when each of these contact people or groups can act relatively independently of the others. Nevertheless, because they present unique problems, inverted organizations should be used sparingly and not as gimmicks to make people "feel empowered." The apparent loss of authority can be very traumatic for former line managers. And contact people, once empowered, may strongly resist any organizational rules or other enterprise-oriented norms. Empowerment without adequate controls can be extremely dangerous, as the collapse of People's Express and Barings Bank so dramatically demonstrates. When critical software and value systems are in place, inverted organizations can be flexible and very powerful. Sharp's "gold badge program," Rubbermaid's tiny three- to five-person product teams,[13] SAS's aircrews,[14] merchant banking's client-partner teams, Honda's process design groups,[15] and Microsoft's three- to five-person software development units are successful variations on this approach, which is quite widely used in professional services situations.

There are several important performance evaluation and incentive issues in inverting an organization. First, those persons or teams at the contact point must evaluate the performance of people in the intermediate-level hierarchy (their bosses in other structures) for compensation and promotion purposes. Otherwise true inversion never occurs. Second, contact people must themselves be evaluated as creative professional entrepreneurs, based on their innovativeness, professional competency, and profit performance. Third, the software must provide contact members with sufficient information about their customers, their costs, and their (expected and actual) performance that (a) they can self-control their own activities and (b) other organizational specialists can see how well they are doing and support their needs. When any of these elements is missing, inverted organizations can quickly turn into dangerously fragmented anarchies or out-of-control risk centers, as parts of the Barings and Daiwa banks did.

***Network Innovation Strategies.*** Some companies or consortia (e.g., McKinsey & Co., biotechnology joint ventures, international investment groups, cancer or AIDs researchers, and most Internet companies) innovate in a true network mode. Most independent collaborations operate largely in this fashion. To differentiate their structures from other network-like organizations (such as matrices), we use the term *spider's webs* to describe this organizational form. (See Figure 8.3). The sources of needed specialized knowledge are in widely dispersed locations, often outside the coordinating enterprise. Yet to create effective solutions, they must interact often and in depth. Customers or users may also be in diverse locations and demand highly localized customization. In innovation, the performing nodes typically collaborate only temporarily to develop a solution for a specific problem or customer set, although some consortia may exist for longer terms. Spider's web formats work extremely well for problem-finding, exploratory, or analytical projects where problems are ill defined and no one person or organization may

**FIGURE 8.3**
**The Spider's Web Organization**

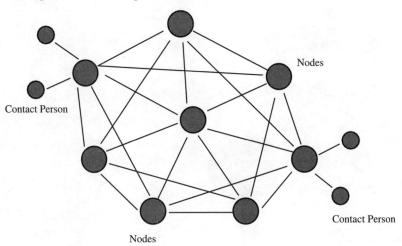

*When the dominating intellect of the enterprise is at the contact nodes, when these nodes must interact for effectiveness, and when they adapt the firm's capabilities for customer needs, a spider's web organization is appropriate. The software and incentive systems must support these relationships.*

know where all the answers reside. On a given project, there may or may not be a single authority center. Often decisions merely occur through consensus or informal processes if the parties agree. However, such consensus processes may be poor for fast decision making. When such needs exist, one of the nodes needs decision authority.

In most networks, information about the market and potential technical solutions comes directly from the contact nodes and is shared instantly by all, usually electronically. Different units in the network typically specialize in different aspects of the process, such as individual scientific or technical disciplines, prototype creation, large-scale production, market testing, marketing, distribution, or specialized support skills. Success depends on all cooperating. Hence, allowing each node in an internal network to be merely a profit center rarely works. Performance measures, incentives, and success measures should focus on the entire network's output.

Such structures lie at the heart of many multicompany alliances and the independent collaboration approach developed in Chapters 4 and 5. Its powerful leverages can extend into the international development realm. The U.S./Israel Binational Industrial Research Foundation has

**FIGURE 8.4**
**The Starburst Organization**

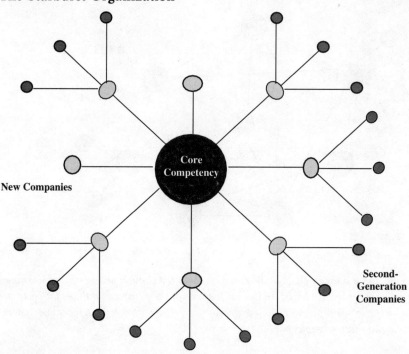

*When the firm has a very complex core competency, serves multiple discrete markets also requiring critical knowledge, and entry to these markets calls for much personal knowledge and entrepreneurial skill, a starburst organization can be very effective.*

been a successful vehicle for bringing together temporary partnerships of U.S. and Israeli companies to work on joint projects that need initial funding support and have high economic development potential for Israel. By sharing expertise, the companies create new ventures that ultimately become freestanding or are bought out by one of the partners. Experiments are underway to extend this approach to other countries.

*Starburst Strategies.* In many cases (publishing companies, software houses, telecommunications companies, movie studios, mutual funds groups, Thermo Electron Co., venture capitalists) innovative companies consciously structure themselves to peel off more permanent but separate units like shooting stars from their core competencies. (See Figure 8.4.) These spin-offs remain partially or wholly owned by the parent, can raise external resources independently if desired, and are controlled largely by market mechanisms. The center retains deep expertise in some common knowledge base (financial market data and managing no-load funds at Vanguard; film selection, capital raising, risk taking, marketing, distribution, and talent assembly skills at Disney). The nodes, which are essentially separate permanent business units, not individuals or temporary clusters, have continuing relationships with their markets and are the locus of important specialized, market, or production knowledge.

These enterprises are not merely conglomerates or holding companies. The center contains a genuine specialized core competency that is constantly refreshed along new dimensions as units spin out. The separate units develop their own core market-oriented competencies and often cast off further starburst units, perhaps financed separately again. They frequently pay a fee to or remunerate the center for its support and provide it with specialized information that refreshes the corporate core competency.[16] The center then uses this knowledge to support other nodes in their designated markets. Starbursts work well when the core embodies an expensive or complex set of competencies and houses a group of knowledgeable risk takers who know they cannot micromanage the diverse entities at their nodes. The starburst's main use is for innovative growth through smaller-scale, discrete, new lines positioned in diverse marketplaces where it is difficult to estimate outcomes without undertaking a specific market test. They operate best where entrepreneurship, not merely flexible response, is critical. Incentives therefore tend to be based on joint ownership or sharing in the node's profitability.

***Large-System Technology Producers.*** These organizations, like AT&T-Bell Labs, Boeing, and the "oil majors," design large-scale systems that may cost billions of dollars and must last reliably for decades. They perform extensive long-term formal marketing and technology forecasts of system needs, define these carefully as performance specifications at both the customer and system interface levels, and allow two or three simultaneous projects on each system to compete for best performance at the prototype level before choosing one for implementation. (See Figure 8.5.) Because of the huge cost and permanency of their systems, they test potential new solutions for substantial periods before making systemwide commitments. They plan for long-term incremental improvements even as a new system is being invented. They usually have strong basic research programs to understand developing scientific and technological possibilities in their fields and to prevent others from shutting them off from a key technology. They have traditionally scaled up their systems incrementally to full-size test runs before releasing a new product or service because their systems are so

## FIGURE 8.5
## Strategic Innovation Structures

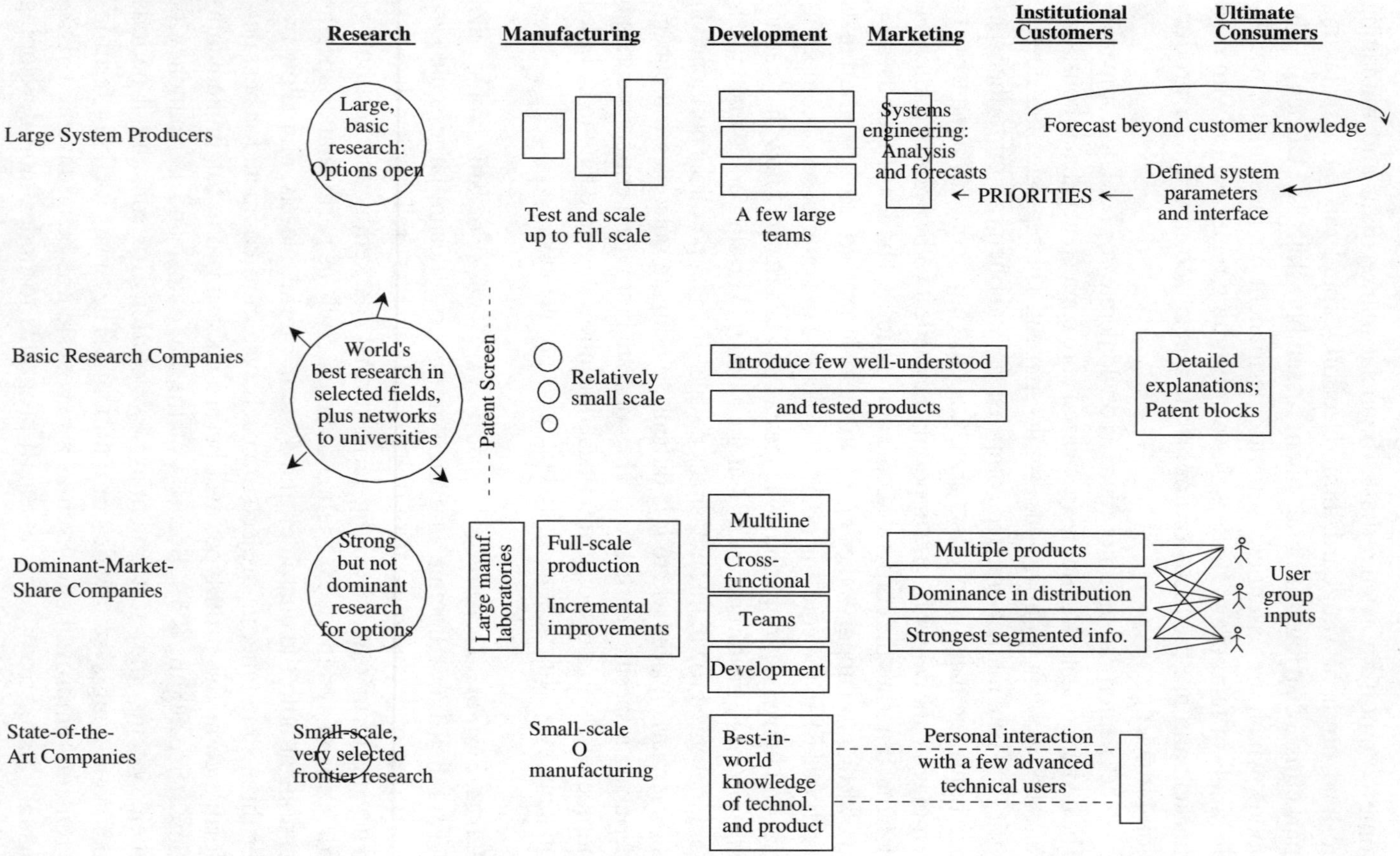

The size, structure, basis of interaction, and management style for innovation groups should be adapted to the specific strategy that gives the firm competitive advantage in that marketplace.

232

costly that they must be right when installed. Often they trade off speed of entry for long-term low cost, performance reliability, or avoidance of major errors at the time the system is installed. Software-based innovation is rapidly compressing many of these design stages.

***Basic Research Companies.*** These companies, like Hoffman-LaRoche and Merck, take their risks at the research stage, supporting large science laboratories with better facilities, higher pay, a wider range of inquiries, and more freedom than is found in most universities. They leverage their internal spending through external research grants, clinical studies, and research consortia in many universities throughout the world. They select product entries carefully. They often are forced to make trade-offs against faster entry of their products in order to ensure greater defensibility in the marketplace or safety and efficacy in use. Before they invest the $20 million to over $300 million commonly needed for drug clearance, they want to be sure they will have a patent-defensible, safe, and effective drug in the marketplace with as much understanding as is possible about the science of its curative capabilities, side effects, and metabolism in the human body. Their organizations are designed to be on the cutting edge of science, but to be very conservative in terms of testing, quality control, and reliability. A few successful drugs build a company. One error could destroy it.

***Dominant Market Share-Oriented Companies.*** These companies, like Matsushita and IBM, often are not the first to introduce radical new technologies. They have traditionally not wanted to disturb their successful product lines any sooner than necessary. They support large, basic research laboratories to keep all technological options open and to obtain early warning signals about new technologies, but they do not rely on these laboratories to drive products to market. As market demands appear, they try to establish very precise price-performance windows and form competitive project teams to come up with the best available state-of-the-market solutions. To decrease market risks, they have their industries' largest distribution networks, which provide them with more detailed market information than their competitors can possibly have. To enter the market with highest potential impact, they utilize full-scale product "shoot-outs" as close to the time of market entry as possible, develop extreme depth in production technologies to keep costs low and quality high from the outset, and try to dominate the distribution of any products they do release. They depend on their market power, incremental product improvements, and phased releases of new products essentially to overwhelm state-of-the-art producers. They often sacrifice market timing to achieve lower long-term costs, greater reliability, and decreased market risks.

***State-of-the-Art Technologies.*** These technologies, like those of Cray Research, Rocketdyne, Genentech, Hughes Electronics, and Kyocera, are often developed in freestanding technical units that are not directly connected to formal marketing groups. Heads of their projects often know more about their technologies than anyone else in the world, including potential customers. So long as demand in the industry to which they sell is driven solely by technical performance criteria, the lab head can essentially define the characteristics of the next generation of products. Timing and technical performance, not subjective taste or product presentation, give their intellectual outputs value. In these cases, pure technology skunk works of small, interdisciplinary technical teams operating alone can exist almost independently of other functions. This is the way many classic inventors have operated in their private laboratories. It can also work effectively in larger enterprises when a strong primary market for sheer technical performance exists.

***Multiple, Discrete, Freestanding Product Lines.*** By contrast, the product lines developed in companies like 3M, Sony, and HP's Instrument Group use a very different approach. They form units that look and act like complete entrepreneurial start-ups. The parent company usually has a strong applied research unit with dominance in specific classes of technology. Each entrepreneurial unit comprises a small team led by a self-nominated champion, usually operating in low-cost facilities. (See Figure 8.6.) Parent companies allow many different proposals to come forward and test them as early as possible in the marketplace. They have control systems to spot significant emerging problems on any single program and to act quickly. They are more willing to take risks at the market level, knowing that market research studies for unique small-scale products can cost more than losses in the marketplace. Such studies will also miss some big winners and are rarely as effective as actively engaging in sale of the product and modifying it interactively with their customers' help.

***Limited Volume or Fashion Companies.*** These companies operate differently again. Single designers or small teams tend to sketch up initial concepts, make small-scale layups, or create electronic models to present to actual buyers and to obtain reactions or actual orders before

# Strategic Innovation Structures (Continued)

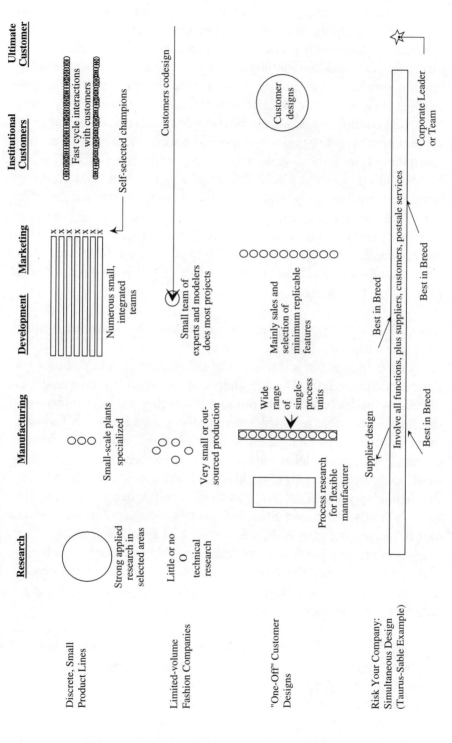

*The size, structure, basis of interaction, and management style for innovation groups should be adapted to the specific strategy that gives the firm competitive advantage in that marketplace.*

235

introducing any products. Based on these reactions, they test other concepts until the subjective tastes of enough buyers and the designer merge. Even then, early production phases may proceed with much further direct feedback among buyers, customers, and designers, modifying the product continuously until it reaches completion. Designer clothing, military weapons, buildings, ships, movies, theatrical productions, and commissioned art are all examples. An intermediate mode involves interactive design and pretest of concept models followed by a commitment to limited-scale production volumes of new lines, as Steuben Glass, Edward Marshall Boehm, and Franklin Mint do. Overpowering capabilities in some scientific arena, artistic endeavor, or physical or service technology and a specialized methodology for interpreting consumer and expert panel responses are usually the keys to success for this strategy. Increasingly interactions are done in electronics; although where subjective touch, taste, or feel is involved, physical models may be essential.

***One-Off Job Shops.*** These are an extreme form of creative strategy. Here the customer provides most of the continuous creativity. But today's job shop is not just a low-tech tail wagged by a large or sophisticated customer lion. The job shop can maximize its own and customers' value by breaking its product-producing potentials down into the smallest possible replicable units, designing its processes for maximum flexibility in handling these units, providing the most user-friendly customer interface to allow customers to create their own designs using these units, and managing a worldwide network to coordinate the selection and fabrication of the best quality-cost components to fit each customer's needs. American Standard fixtures, Motorola pagers, Toyota and Buick self-designs, ASICs, software, and specialized financial services systems provide a few examples of such situations—combining and highly leveraging the specialized intellect of smart buyers, producers, and specialized machines to allow high-value, uniquely customized solutions for customers.

There are myriad other continual innovation strategies. These vary from those of individual inventors, through those of raw materials–dominated enterprises, through process-based strategies, to mission-based strategies like those of the armed services. The point is that each of these represents a very different challenge for leveraging creative intellect to maximize value-added for both the producer and customer. And each requires a unique organizational configuration as well as specifically designed supporting control and incentive systems to make it work properly. To suggest that any one system will fit all strategists' needs is dangerous nonsense.

## INNOVATION INCENTIVE SYSTEMS

In supporting this process, rewards pose a special complexity. Most large concerns do not believe they can offer internal innovators the millions of dollars they might make if they successfully built their own companies. Lack of personal investment by the innovator and concerns about fair play to others are the main reasons cited. Yet the few firms that have made innovative leaders very rich—like Microsoft, Nintendo, and the investment bankers—do not seem to have suffered inordinately. And those who do nothing are protected by the fact that losses caused by potential innovators' leaving (or not performing) do not appear on income statements. Boston, Seattle, Minneapolis, Los Angeles, and San Francisco are ringed by successful companies started by erstwhile champions not appreciated properly by their former employers. It is the familiar case of pay now or pay more later.

The most innovative companies also recognize that innovative champions tend to work for more than just monetary rewards.[17] They try to offer those who champion innovation significant personal recognition, increased independence of action, appropriate power or visibility within their organizations, or that most cherished of technical incentives: the right to a leading role in the next big innovation.[18] Increasingly companies are seeking to supplement such recognition with much larger financial awards to keep their most productive people from jumping outside to competitors or forming new enterprises themselves.

### Different Structures and Incentives

Like the different organizational structures needed to support each different kind of innovation strategy middle managers have to implement, so must incentive structures vary. At the highest level, incentives must support the intended portfolio role of the unit. Cash cow divisions should reward cost-cutting or cash-generating activities, growth divisions compensate more for new product or market innovations, next-generation groups more for option building, defensive groups for contingencies avoided, and so on.

Below this level, innovative teams' structures and goals may differ enormously in complexity and time span. Each division's specific strategy may call for very different planning horizons, team sizes, skill mixes, management styles, innovation approaches, pricing strategies, and hence different support policies, incentives, and reward systems. Many of these are keyed to the normal design cycle and product life cycle of the innovation. By comparing their situations with other industries or operations having generally similar cycles (or having time cycles they are trying to emulate), middle-level managers can gain perspectives on how they can best adapt their existing organizations, leadership styles, support policies, and especially their incentives to fit their particular strategic intent. Too many enterprises try to adopt a new organizational form (especially those intended to shorten cycle times in innovation) without (1) asking whether it is really appropriate to their particular strategy or (2) adjusting all the necessary support structures needed for effectiveness. Not surprisingly, most fail.

As we have illustrated earlier, different time horizons are essential for different projects and in various industries. Pharmaceuticals take five to ten years for clearance, automobiles two to four years to introduce, and consumer products only weeks or months to become obsolete. Within each industry or company, however, there are other important influences. Individual companies because of their strategies may have markedly different time horizons from the industry norm. Further, within an individual company, different divisions (or even departments) may have their own specific strategic and time horizon requirements.

• Within the pharmaceutical industry there are companies with very long time horizons like Merck, Amgen, and Hoffman-LaRoche (whose strategies are based on proprietary basic research), specialty chemical divisions (with three- to four-year horizons), generic producers (that may operate on time horizons of one to two years in most of their activities), and distribution units with horizons of six months to a year. Similarly, within the financial services industries it might take three to seven years to develop a large proprietary information network or two to three years to reshape a distribution network. Once those networks are in place, product innovation might take only a few weeks, product introduction a few days, and most decision cycles minutes or even fractions of seconds.

There may also be quite different time horizons on specific projects within or among divisions. For example, when a consumer (or electronics) home products company designs a new plant, it may have a two- to four-year time horizon for land acquisition, regulatory clearance, plant design, construction, and facilities installation. When it conceptualizes a new platform for a new product series, it may have a one- to three-year time horizon, yet new features may demand only sixty- to ninety-day cycles. Sony provides a specific example. When it lays down a plant for CCDs, it must look ahead three to seven years; basic platforms for its camcorders last two to three years, but totally new camcorders are introduced every ninety days with radical new features. Both its management techniques for the concerned units and its incentives must reflect these realities. Although companies can now compress original innovation time frames enormously, to achieve large-scale production these projects may have to coexist with longer-term plant clearance, construction, product replacement, market positioning, supplier buildup, and customer support programs. The mix will be successful only if the company installs performance measurement and reward systems that support each phase and goal appropriately.

## Time Horizons and Incentives

Some concrete examples will show specifically how different innovation and product life cycles, as well as technical complexity, profoundly affect appropriate team sizes, management styles, and incentives.

*Instantaneous Response to One-Year Cycles.* In this group are fashions, fast foods, toys, shrinkwrap software, theater productions, financial services, and most "features" innovations. Innovations usually involve individual or very small team structures, based on the creativity of a few specialists or artists. Organizations frequently form around a creative genius on the basis of highly personal relationships. In these situations, innovative units may tolerate very ego-centered or authoritarian styles, with few articulated policies or plans of any sort. They focus tightly around the current new concept, customer need, performance target, deal, or product to be provided. High risks are common, and skim pricing tends to dominate. Since teams (or companies) may dissolve once the sale season is gone, short-term profit sharing or cash bonuses are the most appropriate incentives.

*Two- to Four-Year Cycles.* These companies—like auto, large computer, chemicals, and machine tool firms where platform innovation dominates—tend to use somewhat larger teams with more specialists and supporting infrastructures. Since many different skills are necessary for initial success and people must work together for extended periods, more participative styles are common. Teams design platforms flexibly so that new features, parts replacements, maintenance support, and so forth can be supplied at a later date. Although champions provide leadership in platform development, both teamwork and deeply specialized skills are also important. To maintain continuity and later support, these innovations require much more documentation and articulated rules. Planning horizons must extend out three years or more and include much more formal waypoints, progress tracking, and coordination software support. Innovators "design through" or establish hooks on the current generation of products to accommodate future incremental innovations at low cost. Incentives focus on cooperation, creativity, passing waypoints, and meeting figures of merit. Stock options with three-year and longer vesting periods become appropriate rewards.

***Five- to Seven-Year Cycles.*** In this group are major energy development, telecommunications, and construction projects, which tend to involve extensive research cycles, larger support system developments, and long regulatory clearances. Such programs usually require a series of very specialized teams to handle different phases of the project and even more formalized plans or permanent support bureaucracies to maintain continuity and expertise levels. A whole team of champions and a sheltering high-level "protector," as in the original Ford Taurus-Sable or Microsoft Windows projects, may be necessary. Since investments may be large, teams often contain management specialists (as well as technical specialists) assigned to the project for substantial periods. To maintain institutional memory, these programs usually require extremely careful documentation and systematic strategic and performance reviews. Planning horizons extend at least five years, with highlights beyond. Pricing tends to be more strategic depending on the proprietary protection available, the penetration needed to spread innovation costs over more units, or the desirability of sending negative signals to potential competitors. Common stocks with delayed vesting rights are commonly used incentives.

***Ten- to Fifteen-Year Cycles.*** These groups (like those for human genetic studies, deep space probes, environmental systems development, pharmaceuticals, and large telecommunications infrastructures) may require an almost bureaucratic approach. Large phased teams, with a mixture of managers and specialists, are common. Much of the innovation may occur within specialized database development, research, construction, testing, regulatory clearance, and other bureaucracies designed to handle limited, low-risk, highly specialized phases of the problem. Quite formal program planning, system management, and evaluation procedures are essential to maintain focus across multifunctional activities. Joint ventures or cost sharing are often essential to lower risks and decrease front-end investments. Joint ventures share costs and profits on a formula basis. Pricing depends largely on industry practice and the defensive need to ensure recovery of very high investments in development. Internal incentives tend to be salary reviews supplemented by a few "special recognition" awards.

***Fast Development but Long Product Life Cycles.*** These organizations, like branded foods and household product firms, tend to build up strong brand franchises supported by incremental product and process improvements over many years. Innovation groups concentrate on making innumerable small changes, interactively tested directly in the marketplace. Highly specialized groups in research, production, and marketing constantly fine-tune technologies, processes, and market positioning. Often the consumer is not even aware of specific changes. Stable bureaucracies protect deep functional expertise within the company, seconding individual experts to participate temporarily on project-oriented cross-functional teams. Product managers often coordinate activities across functional lines. Excellent software coordination is essential. Since ordinary workers or salespeople may originate many innovations, suggestion plans can pay high dividends. Because of people's continuity in their specialized roles, salary reviews, supplemented by occasional special suggestion or invention awards, provide most of the common incentive structures.

***Long Development but Short Product Life Cycles.*** Venturers generally prefer not to be in these activities. Such enterprises are usually headed by frontier technologists who may have expected their technologies to last longer or to come to fruition sooner. Some involve advanced technologies (like some military, information network, or biotechnologies) that are advancing so fast that, despite long innovation cycles, competing technologies may quickly supplant them in use. Given the high uncertainties and long development cycles on these ventures, innovators tend to be either genuine fanatics on their subjects or high-tech researchers supported by government funding. Organizations, rewards, staffing, pricing, and systems are obviously quite different depending on the funding or innovation source.

***Network Innovation and Hybrid Cycles.*** These are becoming increasingly common. Different players, with quite different internal development times, innovate together internally or respond to demands or inquiries posted on networks, like the Internet. In the external networking mode, numerous companies may post their particular concept on the Net or Web, expecting customers to mix and match their offering with a wide variety of others on the Net to create a new package that meets their own customers' special needs. Once initial interest develops, each individual customer uses the offered products within its own product-development and life cycle strategy. These customer-innovators frequently interact with the original offerer for the detailed amplification or support needed to fulfill their needs. Within the customer entity, the offerer may have to interact with a variety of organizations, each with different time horizons. In these exchanges, the network software defines the nature of most organizational interactions. The software becomes the organization itself and dictates much of the project's culture. Most incentives on external networks are market based. Chapters 4 and 5 deal with this type of innovation in detail.

Each of these situations represents a rather typical class of innovation system. Details will vary a bit with the strategy of each enterprise within each class. Nevertheless, the "product development–product life cycle" framework helps in thinking about managing the widely different organizations and supporting control-reward systems that characterize many types of innovation situations. Middle management systems for successful innovation do not all fit neatly into the small, mobile, ad hoc, networking team models often suggested as a panacea for all firms. Enough do want shorter cycle times to make this a useful target and paradigm for organizational design in many situations. However, thoughtful middle managers may well trade off more rapid time cycles against other elements of cost, risk, or investment.[19] The key is to find incentives that simultaneously support the company's intended strategic focus and stimulate the tumultuous, decentralized, highly personalized, interactive entrepreneurship that characterizes most innovation.

## SUMMARY

Much of the implementation of strategy falls to middle managers who must balance the imperatives of long-term corporate strategy against the practical realities of making current profits, pragmatically dealing with internal resistances to change, and getting different specialist organizations to cooperate toward innovation goals. Like their top management compatriots, they must create appealing visions, challenging goals, a portfolio of investments and programs, and a genuine commitment to achieving the performance figures of merit that define winning in competition. However, for success they must go beyond this. They must also manage the detailed chaos most innovation involves, while maintaining the strategic forces that create cohesion and efficiency.

The two most powerful structural instruments they have for doing this are the choices of the organizational form used to focus action strategically across functional and specialist groups and the incentive systems that make joint actions effective. This chapter presents a variety of practical organizational and incentive structures that companies have found effective for achieving strategic cohesion in specific situations while allowing innovators to operate in the highly disaggregated, relatively small-unit mode that usually most encourages innovativeness. But each is useful only for its purpose. When the aims change, the relevancy of systems changes. There are no universal panaceas. The next chapter deals with the basic management attitudes and practices needed to make these systems effective in virtually all companies.

# 9

# Middle Management:
# The Basics

L ike any other sophisticated activities, these kinds of focused, disaggregated, laterally oriented, innovating groups will work only if managers pay attention to the basics. Middle managers must convert the more ephemeral aspects of the innovation process into concrete reality. The best of these managers:

- Actively seek emerging opportunities, establish very demanding goals, and expect success.
- Encourage differentness, constructive confrontation, high performance, and mutual trust.
- Protect flexibility, time horizons, underground activities, and direct access to information.
- Focus on champions, concepts, competencies, uniqueness, and customer reactions, not specious numbers.
- Encourage multiple self-guided, entrepreneurial units to compete and prove their ideas in objective performance terms.

## CHARACTERISTICS OF EFFECTIVE LEADERS

A true leader *stimulates others to achieve extraordinary results* they would not have conceived or accomplished on their own.[1] Innovation leaders have a unique sense of changing demand structures and how their enterprise can benefit the wider society.[2] They are expectors and appreciators of innovation; they are not CTOs—"chief tormenting officers" looking for impossibly detailed financial justifications of projects. Nor are they mere coordinators, balancing proposals, passing on them, and watching while others act. Instead, they participate, make their expectations for innovation clear, and actively support and reward innovative behavior.

## Demanding Goals, Applauded Success

These leaders expect success, and when it occurs, they actively point the spotlight on others. They share. They applaud, not bow.[3] They give the public accolades to their bench-level contributors and to their innovation champions, as Sony's CEO, Ibuka, did (for the Trinitron tube) when he refused to accept the first product Emmy ever given, unless it was presented to the innovation team, not just himself. When innovators fail, as they often do, middle management leaders see that their organizations do not blame, but learn from the event. The upper and middle management cultures of all the highly innovative companies we observed reflected such norms.[4] They set extremely high standards for innovation, were very comfortable with (or reveled in) change, and established a supportive atmosphere for constant experimentation, risk taking, and implementation of new ideas. They often set seemingly overstressful goals, operating with a sense of competitive paranoia (Intel and Microsoft) or as if they were on a burning raft at sea (as Motorola does).

- At Boston Chicken (now Boston Market), President Bruce Harreld and his top team insisted that the entire organization operate on a sixteen-week innovation cycle. Each innovation has to be designed and implemented so that all components are technically complete and effectively in the market within this short cycle. This goal drives the collection of information, analysis procedures, implementation techniques, and expectations within all operating organizations. In commercial terms, it means that Boston Chicken will always have something so new that competitors cannot emulate it quickly enough to prevent Boston Market from making attractive profits on the innovation.

- One of the largest U.S. printing companies, knowing the impact of electronics on printing, has established a policy that it will allow its technologies to go public six months after it enters a market with a new technological process. This establishes for all employees a clear and urgent need to stay ahead of competitors relative to the next technological step and to exploit innovations rapidly in order to create preemptive positions. Although the pressure for innovation is relentless, everyone in the organization and all its systems are oriented to support this imperative.[5]

• At Sony, Ibuka and Morita repeatedly turned down marketing's demands for copycat products. Instead they insisted, "We must have a product of our own," discarded many new but extrapolative approaches, and patiently held on until a totally novel product was ready. Then they set almost impossible targets for transition into production. Their belief in the technological concept and in their people's capacities to succeed inspired an almost fanatical level of loyalty and commitment.[6]

## Constructive Confrontation and Trust

Good innovation managers recognize that an open style is crucial in getting people to share really new insights and opportunities. Honesty and trust are essential in empowering the small, independent units described in earlier chapters.[7] People will not willingly share with those they distrust, nor will they disclose ideas to others if they feel they will be attacked over as yet untested concepts. Both large and small companies and teams suffer from such disclosure inhibitions.

• In the late Gould Corporation, everyone knew that (despite its protestations to the contrary) top management would use only return on assets employed to evaluate internal proposals. As a result, long-range projects were never honestly proposed. Middle managers would either kill proposals on the way up or would be deceptively optimistic about short-range expectations. In most companies, modest inflation of expectations is common, but in Gould an air of distrust inflated these to major proportions.

Even in organizations that have become rigidified by tradition, increased sharing, stimulated by top management trust, can quickly lead to massive sharing of ideas for innovation, as it did for Richard Teerlink at Harley-Davidson and even in the federal government on Vice President Gore's Reinventing Government team.

To stimulate a trusting environment, many highly innovative companies in the United States, and interestingly in Japan, consciously develop a culture of open confrontation to encourage direct exchange of ideas and to get the most objective possible evaluations of concepts. They generally set up carefully constructed rules for these exchanges to avoid personalizing conflicts over facts or conceptual ideas. And, whenever possible, they establish individual or small group responsibility for results.

• Intel works diligently to create a commonly shared culture. This allows the company to decentralize into relatively small operating units where people often have several bosses, depending on the problems at hand. Within teams and units, all people participate as equals, with new members free to challenge top managers in a style of constructive confrontation. Each member of a team is expected to challenge ideas aggressively, but never to attack an individual's motives for presenting an idea. Employees say, "Things can get very rough in a meeting. You'd be surprised at the things people can say. But if you are seeking a solution, it's okay." CEO Andy Grove himself sets the tone: "When he walks into the room, things can get electric. . . . I've seen him listen to a carefully prepared report for a while and then shatter the room with, 'I've never heard so much bullshit in my life.'"[8] The company has courses on constructive confrontation for all its rising executives and emphasizes the concept in its early training of employees about Intel's culture.

Why is this style so prevalent? Managers need decision systems matched to the velocity and complexity of their fields. Open confrontation avoids the dishonest, time-consuming maneuvering, blocking, backbiting, behind-covering behavior of more bureaucratic and political organizations. And it short-circuits bureaucrats who attempt to set up unnecessary rules or hoard knowledge. Two key components help confrontation processes work more effectively: a high diversity of backgrounds in the group and open access to information for all participants. Wide diversity allows ideas from people with very different skills, perceptions, and mind-sets to interact in new ways.[9] Open access to information discourages people from playing power or sandbagging games by claiming special or secret knowledge. Openness and disciplined sharing are endemic in most innovative smaller companies. Studies by J. Bourgeois and others show that larger high-tech companies with diverse top managements and open confrontational styles outperform others by a substantial margin.[10]

## Flexible Resources to Break Barriers

Effective managers in larger companies also try to maintain flexible resources they can quickly access to break the inevitable barriers and stalemates that occur in innovation.[11] If one group becomes a bottleneck, by its own fault or not, these managers can get critical units through the crisis or move to other options. In less innovative enterprises, R&D is often committed for the entire year in both budgetary and staffing terms. In essence, these firms are saying that no significant innovation or new needs will emerge beyond what people can clearly foresee and schedule a year ahead. When adhered to, such rigidities quickly destroy real innovation—and increase bureaucratic processes, cycle times, and risks. How do companies develop needed flexibilities?

• Many outstanding research and innovation groups have their units operate basically as "coat racks of talent," where people receive extra rewards and challenges if they willingly volunteer or are selected to fill special needs in overcoming crises or bottlenecks during the process of an innovation. Most highly innovative, small software and service companies signal everyone—through their cultural practices, legends, and incentives—that merely working forty-hour weeks and meeting their own unit's plans are not enough. People are expected to work nights and weekends as necessary to break bottlenecks. Larger companies may give managers a small slush fund and time or financial reward flexibilities they can deploy to encourage desired behaviors.

• Honda approached this problem on multiple levels. Its development process centered on its interactive SED (sales, engineering, development) system. Interactions among the different groups on a SED team were based on a principle the company described as mutual aggression. Each group was encouraged to pursue its individual position aggressively until a final decision was reached. Even the newest engineers were to "argue frankly for their positions." Within Research, different subgroups pursued competing solutions until one was selected by the team. Once development began, the SED team established very specific schedules for each project, and no deviations were permitted. People had to work "as hard and long as necessary" to maintain planned progress. For its part, the company provided maximum assistance to analytical and design teams through an elaborate software system that interconnected three Cray 2 computers and one of the most highly developed desktop computer networks in the industry.[12]

If such flexibilities are to be achieved, managers must understand innovation processes well enough not to be panicked by the inevitable chaos, risks, discouragement, and individual project failures that innovation involves.[13] Managers tend to assign higher probabilities of success to things they understand. Great innovation managers like Scott McNealy at Sun, Andy Grove at Intel, Bill Gates at Microsoft, Ralph

Saritch at Orbital Engine, and Akio Morita at Sony provide classic examples. They have marvelously calibrated intuitions and an ebullience that believes "things will work out well if we attack them right." This is especially critical in the earliest stages of innovation. Success is often so distant that managers must be willing to discount what others think are low probabilities of success and see a way to success when critical analysts might not.

## Direct Access to Decision Makers

Since well-calibrated optimism can come only from hands-on experience, an innovative company's upper management team will always include some credible members from past innovation successes. But having only innovators at the top of a company or division can be as dangerous as having none. Most innovative companies have a few innovation champions in their upper echelons and develop clear mechanisms for key bench-level groups to contact the top. They realize that each layer of hierarchy between innovation teams and the top dilutes the accuracy and currency of the information the top team has to evaluate potential innovations. Layers also increase the "yes/no ratio" bias against innovation, because each layer must say yes to go ahead, but only one no can stop the project.

• 3M, where innovation has been considered central to survival, has dealt with this problem by making a no decision riskier than a yes for middle managers. An individual or small team first proposes a new innovative project to the next level up. If the proposal will cost less than some threshold number, these middle managers can say yes without seeking approval from above. If they wish to say no, on the other hand, they must get authorization from the next layer up. 3M also specifically permits 15% of its laboratory budgets to be used for bootleg projects. These projects require no special review or authorization. To maintain such projects' relevance, 3M depends on the technical staff's understanding of the organization's goals and their confidence that successful projects meeting those goals will result in personal rewards.

Many firms start by allowing innovators direct access to the top, but this becomes less practical as the company grows. Consequently many select a conscious mix of projects whose leaders can have access to the top. Some are in the early stages where top level understanding is essential. Others represent a selected few projects in later stages where payoffs and risks are much larger and more predictable. If the mix is kept dynamic, such interactions provide useful learning experiences for both top managers and bench-level innovators—and a useful focus for the overall program.

• Sharp Electronics of Japan has an interesting technique for doing this. The top management selects a few "gold badge" or urgent projects, which it deems critical to the company's future. The heads of such major projects are given a special gold badge, which allows them an unlimited budget and the right to go anywhere in the company to select human resources, acquire needed equipment, or demand priority handling for their project. The whole organization understands that the gold badge holder represents and has direct access to the president on these projects, and that members on a task force wearing gold badges are to receive maximum support. The project runs for only a specified time and to meet specific targets. Once these are met, the gold badge leader and all team members return to their regular organizations.

## Protected Time Horizons and Underground Activities

All the most innovative enterprises in our sample had found ways to protect intermediate managers from the restrictive biases of short time horizons. In some cases, both investors and the entire management team accept that the very nature of the product or its industry demands a longer-term view.[14] Pharmaceutical firms, public utilities, forest product companies, aircraft manufacturers, and many others must live with very long time horizons imposed by their environments. When asked how they maintained these time horizons, executives in these industries looked perplexed. They usually answered, "That is what this industry requires." Multiproduct companies or divisions with only individual subunits competing in such industries must adjust their internal management systems to permit their units to operate on sufficient time horizons; otherwise the divisions will fail. (This is a major function of the portfolio planning system described in Chapter 6.)

However, long time horizons alone do not ensure innovativeness. Some long-term companies are innovative; others are merely bureaucratic. The key element is vision. A nontechnical division manager who is a visionary can often sell the rationality of longer time horizons for specific projects better than technologists can, as Alastair Pilkington did for float glass, Wilson Nolen did for McKesson's Economost, and Vincent Learson did for IBM's virtual memory development. If top managers are negative, middle managers can frequently hide expenditures (especially in multidivisional companies) long enough to bring innovations to reality.

• In Polaroid Corporation in the late 1970s, a group of middle managers became convinced that electronics was the key to the company's future, but they could not convince key top-level people to support the major effort needed. Several of the managers, operating within their own realms, decided to silently build the key components of an R&D infrastructure for electronic imaging. This became invaluable in updating Polaroid's line and generating new products as time went on. But valuable time was lost because the top never officially supported the effort until visible commercializable results began to appear.

A number of the most successful technical directors and innovative middle managers we interviewed commented, in essence, "We know a lot of things are going on in our shop that we do not know about in detail. We actually encourage a bit of underground activity. This allows people to pursue things, within reason, that they are enthusiastic about." Newly formed concepts can rarely compete politically or in information terms against projects that others have been working on for years. Yet it is surprising how often these informally pursued activities lead to valuable commercial results. Some companies, as 3M does, encourage such activity formally by allowing 10 to 15% of a technical person's time to be spent on "projects of their own selection." Although hard to police, this kind of culture stimulates people to look outside the bounds of their routine activities and to contribute new and useful knowledge to justify their flex-time. At 3M the environment encourages people to work around their superiors if necessary to enable the company to grow where its scientists and customers lead. If the individuals' own units do not have the funds, they can seek funds from many other venture sources in the company or from a "Genesis Grant" allocated by fellow scientists.[15]

## TARGETED ADHOCRACY

Our studies show that a number of other more specific interventions, reflecting the normal processes of innovation, are basic to the very decentralized, interactive, persistent, highly self-motivated, yet coordinated behavior that leads to significant innovation.

## Market Orientation and Interactiveness

Almost 70% of all innovation is market driven, and 100% of large successes are market sensitive.[16] Consequently middle management innovation leaders consciously link their visions, plans, and practices tightly to the realities of the marketplace. Each truly innovative company in our studies had developed specific techniques, adapted to its particular style and strategy, to create (1) a strong market orientation at both the top and middle management levels of the company, (2) early customer interactions with internal innovators, and (3) cross-functional tracking mechanisms to ensure that intended project priorities were maintained. Sometimes this was implemented through fairly formal mechanisms.

• Until the AT&T breakup, Bell Laboratories maintained a rigorous Engineering Complaint System through which it collected technical problems and inquiries from its (customer) operating companies. These inquiries had to receive an action response within a month; that is, Bell Labs had to specify how it could solve or would attempt to resolve the customer's problem and notify the operating company in writing of its action.[17] Motorola, established its 10X program to cut the cycle time for innovation by a factor of ten to improve its response to identified customer problems or when introducing new innovations. For example, it reengineered its personal pager operations so that customers could design their own pagers from the most current available combination of features. It flexibly automated its pager production line so that a customer's order would go into production within twenty minutes of receipt of the order itself, for completion within two hours. Its goal was overnight delivery of a custom-designed product.

Many companies have tried to use formal market research to target their innovation activities. Most have found that although such guidance works extremely well for incremental product line extensions or improvements on existing lines, it has severe limitations in guiding early-stage research or innovation. And formal market analyses are frequently quite misleading when applied to radical innovations. Among many classic examples are the following:

• Studies said Intel's microprocessor "would never sell more than 10% of the mini computer market." But within two years, microprocessor-installed power was greater than the combined power of mini- and microcomputers. Sony's marketing researchers initially said its hugely successful transistor radios, mini-television sets, and Walkman concepts "would fail in the marketplace" because the public had always associated small size with low quality.[18] Conversely, many highly touted, superb technical concepts (like hovercraft, bioengineered interferon, Pilkington's 10-11 shatterproof glass, and IBM's Josephson-effect devices) never fulfilled their carefully estimated market potentials. Many of industry's largest failures were actually overplanned and overresearched on paper (like Ford's Edsel, IBM's FS System, and FAA's* supersonic transport) rather than interactively developed with genuine customer feedback.

Frequently neither innovators, market researchers, nor users can quite visualize a totally new product's real potential. Initial market success often depends on highly opportunistic interactions that uncover unspecified or unsuspected needs.

• James Gosling of Sun Microsystems originally wrote Java as part of a failed effort for Sun to pioneer equipment for interactive TV. The Global Positioning System (GPS) was created to locate military forces, not direct autos, emergency units, and farm tractors or locate hijacked or lost trucks and pleasure craft. Recording English-language programs for Japanese schools and songs in Japanese bars provided the first commercial markets for Sony's audiotape recorders. The Hovercraft became profitable only when its original air cushion and amphibian use concepts were abandoned because ferryboat operators insisted that rigid sideskirts and direct power drives be extended into the water.

Innovative companies try to structure interactive user participation as early as possible in the innovation process. They both improve results and lower risks by incorporating some of the users' innovative ideas and by foreseeing what the product's actual use, abuse, and desirability characteristics may be.

• Sam Walton said that 90% of his company's best ideas came from contact personnel's suggestions. Hewlett-Packard, 3M, Microsoft, Sony, Wal-Mart, Rubbermaid, Raychem, and Nintendo—among the most successful and sophisticated diversifying innovators we encountered—generally introduce radical new products through small teams that closely participate with users, learn from them, and rapidly modify designs and entry strategies around this information. In the past, these interactive contacts have been largely on a personal basis. Increasingly, critical information is captured through groupware and intranets, which allow instant and complete documentation of questions, problems, and solutions.

---

*FAA: Federal Aviation Administration.

• To meet its customers' customization needs, Toshiba has created seven software factories. Each develops and produces software for one of seven application areas. Each factory produces a variety of programs for customers using standardized procedures, tools, and components reusable across different customer projects. Interestingly, Toshiba found that innovative successes mainly depended on quality; customers and profits were not much influenced by the impact of "efficiency" improvements in the software development process itself. However, by concentrating on the quality interface, Toshiba was able to increase efficiency, flexibility, and customer value simultaneously.[19]

Chapters 2, 5, and 8 detail how a number of companies implement effective customer-innovator interactions. Electronic networks and virtual workspaces have created entirely new ways in which customers can be active team members in innovation.

## Multiple Approaches

All innovation is probabilistic. No one knows at first whether the desired result can be achieved at all or which of several possible approaches may work best in practice. Generally no one knows precisely when the result will be achieved, what competitors will accomplish in the meantime, or how customers and potential suppliers will react to these competitive offerings. Finally, no one can predict quite how customers will use the innovation when it occurs or which approach will dominate the field as it develops. Initial insights can come from almost anywhere, and the right insight can create a whole new industry or offer dominance to its discoverer for years. Several well-known innovations provide examples:

• A gust of wind, blowing mold on Fleming's cultures, created the antibiotic age. Sir Alastair Pilkington was washing dishes when he got the critical insight that led to float glass. The microcomputer was born because Ted Hoff happened to work on a complex calculator for a Japanese client just when DEC's PDP8 architecture was fresh in his mind. Carl Djerassi's group at Syntex was not looking for an oral contraceptive when it created 19-norprogesterone, the precursor to norethindrone, which became the active ingredient in most early contraceptive pills. DARPA developed the Internet primarily to allow laboratories to share information and to utilize large-scale computers more efficiently.

Lucky "accidents" are involved in almost all major technological advances. A soldering error led to the *n* junction transistor.[20] A researcher looking for a blocker for angiogenesis-induced blindness discovered the most promising potential intervention for preventing, and perhaps curing, cancer currently available. And so on. In fact, Murphy's Law works because scientists work within their paradigms and engineers design for what they can foresee; hence what fails is what theory did not predict or what human error introduced. Even the most sophisticated testing may not define all the interactions of components and subsystems over the complete performance envelope of a complex device's anticipated operations.

• Elaborately designed ring seals failed on the *Challenger* space shuttle, thoroughly tested jet engines failed in an Iranian sandstorm during the U.S. attempt to rescue its Embassy's personnel held as hostages, and patients were horribly burned when a minor software change was made during X-ray tomography treatments.

While software models now enable innovators to manipulate and handle many more such variables, ultimately there must be tests of the full system under multiple actual operating conditions—and provision for feedback and correction of errors and use problems at all stages of innovation.

Recognizing these characteristics of development, most innovative companies in our sample consciously started multiple component and prototype programs in parallel, thinning down the number of alternatives only as probabilities of success approached certainty or cost became prohibitive.

• Sony in its videotape recorder program pursued ten different major options, each with two or three subsystem alternatives. It now creates technological pools of tested subsystem and component options it can introduce quickly in response to new market demands or innovative concepts. Having multiple options available allows it to introduce a new Walkman every two weeks and a new camcorder every ninety days.

Planned redundancy and flexibility clearly can help cope with some of the inherent unpredictability in technical development and early market introduction. Multiple development approaches, especially those that can be implemented and tested in software, also encourage testing of more options interactively with customers. Constructive competition of ideas helps motivate groups, shorten cycle times, and improve the quality and reliability of results.

## Objective Performance Shoot-outs

To maximize the motivational and informational benefits of multiple competing approaches, many companies consciously structure performance "shoot-outs" between the competing approaches of various teams after their projects reach advanced prototype stages. Many shoot-outs can be performed in software. But physical prototype comparisons are needed to test subjective or tactile elements like taste, smell, feel, sound, visual, entertainment, physical access, or ergonomic features. Ultimately, of course, the product or process must be given a physical test under actual use conditions. Because of their expense when used, physical tests should be designed to maximize the level of objective data available for decision purposes by allowing teams to critique each others' approaches, minimize risks by making tests as close as possible to the actual marketplace, and stimulate each multifunctional team's commitment to the point that it is ready to move ahead immediately if its option wins.[21]

Although anathema to many who worry about presumed efficiencies in R&D, multiple approaches, by allowing greater effectiveness in choosing a right solution with commitment behind it, can easily outweigh any duplication costs, especially when early-stage shoot-outs occur in software. Multiple prototyping and performance shoot-outs are likely to be warranted when the market rewards significantly higher performance or when large volumes justify increased technical or cost sophistication. Under these conditions, competing approaches can improve probabilities of success, decrease development times, and decrease costs in both the short and the long run.

Properly rewarding and reintegrating losing teams is perhaps the most difficult and essential skill in managing competing projects. If the total company is expanding rapidly or if a successful project creates a substantial growth opportunity, competing team members can generally find another interesting program or sign on with the winner as it moves toward the marketplace. For the shoot-out system to work continuously, however, executives must create a climate that honors high performance, whether the performer's specific approach wins or loses; reabsorbs people quickly into their technical specialties or onto other projects; and accepts and expects rotation among tasks and groups. W.L. Gore, Sharp, Honda, Merrill Lynch, and the other examples of collaboration cited in Chapters 4 and 5 suggest how this is best implemented.

## Smaller, More Flexible Skunk Works Units

Most successful midlevel innovation managers in our studies tried, whenever possible, to use relatively small units and flat organizations to stimulate commitment, interactiveness, and rapid response to user needs. Most thought the optimum number of key players per team was from three to seven, although it might have to be much larger for highly complex systems requiring a variety of skills. This small size generally seemed to provide a critical mass for accessing needed skill bases, foster maximum communications and flexibility, and allow reasonable latitude for individual creativeness and commitment. Although software facilitates larger team sizes, higher numbers tend to interfere with personal communications.[22]

The first skunk works, named after "Kelly" Johnson's successful group at Lockheed, were merely small teams of engineers, technicians, and designers working together with no intervening organizational barriers. Now companies may put innovative production, marketing, worker, supplier, customer, corporate staff, and postsale service people on the team, as Ford did in designing the original Taurus-Sable. But vastly increased software support is needed to maintain communications and technical cohesion as team sizes expand. Even in the strong planning-oriented cultures of Europe and Japan, the most innovative groups we observed used skunk works to improve their innovation potentials. Few were as thoroughly developed as Ford's original Team Taurus. Nor, interestingly, was Japan's much publicized *ringii* decision-making process evident in their skunk works situations.

• Sony's founder, Ibuka, and his technical successor, Kihara, participated directly with their design groups and made rapid on-the-spot decisions at key junctures, as did successor CEOs Morita and Ohga. Nintendo's CEO, Yamauchi, personally makes the decisions on which games and features are acceptable for his company. Soichiro Honda was known for working with his engineering and design groups and often emphasizing his own views by shouting. Face-to-face discussions among different technical and management levels in these companies are common, with constructive confrontation encouraged at the design level.

Why do such direct interactions work so well? Progress in technology is largely determined by the number of successful experiments made per unit time. The biggest causes of delays in large enterprises are bureaucracies' and hierarchical organizations' effects on decision cycles. Skunk works help flatten organizations, eliminate bureaucratic delays, allow fast and unfettered communication, and permit the quick turnarounds and decisions that multiply experiments and stimulate rapid advance. Groupware, virtual workspace, or modeling software that enables diverse and remotely located team members to interact around a common problem can increase advance rates even more.

## Flat, Externally Leveraged Organizations

To encourage fast, effective decision making, innovative middle managements consciously try to create very flat organizations with as few organizational layers between bench participants and top decision makers as possible. By keeping total division sizes below 400 people, they enforce a maximum of two intervening decision layers to the top. In units much larger than this, people quickly lose touch with the total concept of a product or process, bureaucracies grow, and projects must go through more and more formal screens to survive. The improved communications and discipline that software imposes on design groups enables flat organizations to function more effectively than ever. With proper organizational software, a number of small teams can operate in parallel on a single large, coordinated project, as they did on Boeing's (2800 engineering location) 777 aircraft or Ford's (400 subgroup) first Taurus-Sable project. Before attempting such wide-span projects, middle managers should make sure that appropriate software, culture, performance tracking, and incentive systems are firmly in place.

The most innovative enterprises also consciously tap into multiple external sources of technological capability. No company or research group can spend more than a small portion of the world's (approximately $300 billion) R&D budget. Yet scientific knowledge and technological advances from outside sources (and seemingly unrelated fields) often interact to create totally new concepts or opportunities important to the enterprise. Recognizing this, many concerns have active strategies to develop information for trading with outside research or technology groups, and special teams and software to tap these sources. Often these programs, typically implemented through "gatekeepers" of technical exchange, are responsible for initiating a very high percentage of successful innovations in constantly innovative organizations.[23] In a textile company we examined, one man found and introduced 90% of its major innovations; in a smaller chemical company over 70%; and so on. At a minimum, such strategies ensure that the company stays intimately in touch with its most important technical and user communities.

Increasingly, well-designed software is a key element in monitoring and communicating with these sources. Such leveraging relationships have expanded substantially in recent years, especially in larger companies that participate (as joint venturers, consortium members, limited partners, guarantors of first markets, venture capitalists, or spin-off equity holders) in a variety of projects. Such leveraging relationships now rival the imagination and variety of structures used in entrepreneurial start-ups.[24]

## Champions, Experts, and Rewards

Despite all the other supporting structures a management may put in place, a determined champion must generally inject the enthusiasm and persistence needed to overcome the soul-wrenching disappointments and setbacks most major innovations seem to encounter.[25] In large organizations, the process of innovation is especially uncertain, frustrating, and debilitating. Few people head more than two large projects in a lifetime. Both producing and receiving organizations (production units, customers, or one's own peers) often revise their practices to resist change. Often only a fanatic can survive the strain, and even then some ultimately give up.

• The frustrations of Armstrong (creator of FM), Carothers (synthetic fibers), and Diesel (the diesel engine) led them to commit suicide before their great inventions reached full commercial success. Goddard (champion of rocketry), Whittle (jet aircraft engines), Carlson (Xerox), Sikorsky (helicopters), Ibuka (videotape recorders), Ovshinski (amorphous semiconductors), and Folkman (angiogenesis) are typical of those who poured frustrating decades into their radical innovations before they became commercial successes.

Their fanaticism makes innovator-entrepreneurs underestimate the length of time and obstacles to success. Since time horizons for radical innovations make them essentially irrational from a calculated financial investment (present value) viewpoint, fanatics proceed when others would not. This is why fanatics are at the heart and soul of most small start-up entrepreneurial ventures, substituting sweat capital (or entrepreneurial rent) for actual dollar investments and discounting the long time horizons, low probabilities of success, and unfavorable financial (present value) prospects that make others give up.

Although called champions rather than fanatics, a few determined people have almost always driven any innovation in larger enterprises. Now, a single individual can rarely carry out an entire innovation alone. Innovations are so complex that most internal champions desperately need extensive added technical expertise and business support at crucial times. Some of the most difficult problems middle managers face in large organizations are learning how to tolerate and nurture the kinds of offbeat, driven personalities who become champions, how to utilize them successfully on teams, and how to reward both champions and experts appropriately.

## Professional Venture Teams?

In frustration, many companies have tried to assign identified innovation projects to new venture teams with the needed professional (technical, marketing, and finance) skills to see them through. These teams rarely succeed if the innovation's champion is not a volunteer—and preferably the head of the team. Texas Instruments, for example, made a study of some forty of its own innovations and found no projects that were successful where management had chosen the team head.[26] Developing an innovation seems to be much like raising a human baby. For high probability of success, an innovation needs a parent (a champion) who loves it emotionally and will stay with it when others would give up, another parent (an authority figure with resources) who can support its vicissitudes, and many pediatricians (technical experts) and friends (supporters) who can see it through the special technical and political difficulties that always complicate progress. Unfortunately, in their design of venture teams, many companies turn the task over to just their "pediatrician" technical specialists and overlook the other nurturing sources that innovations need. Effective innovation usually requires a mammoth amount of psychological support, leadership, and personal commitment at intermediate management levels. How to develop the human dynamics, strategic focus, time horizons, communications infrastructures, and incentive support for innovation in the rapidly changing world of business hypercompetition has been the subject of the book to this point. The remainder will address how these forces affect—and can be best managed for—economic growth and other national goals.

## SUMMARY

Middle managers have perhaps the most difficult job in innovation. They must operate at the interface between the broad strategic demands of top management and the highly diverse, conflicting operational forces that determine or restrict innovativeness. They must manage both the chaos that is an essential part of any innovation process and yet maintain the focus essential in effectively fulfilling corporate strategies.

Successful intermediate managers provide clear leadership guidance yet empower the kind of roiling, tumultuous interactiveness that most supports innovation. Like successful top managers, they provide a clear vision, technology strategy, and figure-of-merit targets for their operating units. But they also actively manage the interfaces among competing operational interests.

They deal effectively with the basics of innovation. They specifically recognize the limitations of formal planning for innovation. Instead of rigidities, they create an atmosphere of challenge, expectation, and support. They encourage an open, confrontive style with as much access as possible for innovative entrepreneurs to the tops of their organizations. They emphasize cooperation and trust, flexible resource access, reasonable time horizons, market-oriented interactiveness, small and malleable unit structures, multiple competing teams, and objective performance shoot-outs. They rigorously keep everyone's eyes locked on markets and costs, and they find ways to reward winners and champions. Without such infrastructures, disaggregated units tend to become anarchic, fissiparous, and destructive.

# PART V

# NATIONAL STRATEGY CONSIDERATIONS

# 10

# The Politics of Science:
# The Nature of Scientific Knowledge

M any of the most pressing issues and opportunities in science and technology require government support and participation. Yet—like many other national decisions—needed actions seem to be hung up in endless political bickering, controversy, and bureaucratic infighting. If the scientific endeavor is as objective as it is supposed to be, how can there be such mammoth differences in factual viewpoint as there are among proponents and opponents in the controversies on fusion and fission power, acid deposition and global warming, Gulf War syndrome, animal-to-human transplants, defense capabilities and technologies, the impacts of various drugs, nutritional effects on health, impacts of clear-cutting and monoculture, sustainable levels of fishing and farming, the safety and impacts of biotechnology, and so on?

Protagonists understandably have different risk preferences, degrees of optimism, and relative propensities toward different outcomes. Individual scientists also have an emotional commitment to their past methodologies and conclusions. And estimating future economic and social impacts is tenuous at best. But many controversies occur over "what the scientific facts really are" as policymakers attempt to make informed decisions. Authors of professional journal articles attack each others' positions with haughty disdain. Experts appearing before leg-

We thank Professor James F. Quinn, Division of Environmental Studies, University of California, Davis, for the major contributions he made to the conceptualization and development of this chapter.

islative committees often conflict wildly in their conclusions. And in public decisions, the popular press compounds problems by amplifying these differences and giving disproportionate weight to the opinions of people who may have no objective basis at all for generalized conclusions. It is little wonder that confusion, poor policy, and distrust result. These differences are the source of many of the controversies and much of the disillusionment about science and technology.

## AN OVERLY SIMPLISTIC VIEW

While public discussions will never be free of emotionalism and misinformation, can one not hope for better in controversies about science and technology? Much of the current discussion is frustrating to policymakers and wasteful in the extreme. Large amounts of effort now go into: (1) developing and defending doomsday or utopian scenarios (based on incomplete data) whose primary purpose may be self-aggrandizement or fund raising, (2) casting doubt on others' views to maintain or enhance one's own budget, PR position, or bureaucracy, (3) working on minuscule issues one can "prove" with mathematical precision, while ignoring larger problems where small, incremental changes could make large advances, and (4) finding and publishing elaborately conceived small advances that keep policymakers or executives believing one's organization is still progressing long after other or newer approaches have made its purposes obsolete.

These plagues affect business, government, and educational institutions alike. Many are inherent in the organizational bureaucratization of science and technology. Unfortunately, a large component of the confusion derives from a misunderstanding of what "scientific facts" are and how scientific-technological progress actually occurs. We have suggested how disorderly, discontinuous, and tumultuous technological advance and innovation are. Despite some widely held, but very mechanistic, views about how scientific knowledge develops, it too is subject to a similar amount of chaos and uncertainties about what scientific facts truly are and what their implications may be. And strong political forces can attach their interests to these uncertainties.

In particular, the simplistic view of the scientific process—that scientific knowledge is absolute and comes only from stating, testing, and rejecting hypotheses in controllable experiments—is quite misleading. As history amply demonstrates, scientific knowledge is not created solely by such processes, nor does it progress in an orderly way or remain unchanged over time. A far greater amount of useful, verifiable knowledge comes from a complex of other systematic processes that continually reshape the nature and content of what is currently considered scientific knowledge. Some experiments test only one aspect of that knowledge; others test another. There are few tests of whole bodies of intersecting knowledge. Hence knowledge is always partial and evolving. Much of what is accepted knowledge in one decade is challenged in the next by newer and better instrumentation, more refined insights, or indeed whole new realms of science itself. Many of the conflicts about the viability of certain viewpoints and the validity of "research" versus "practical" knowledge in business, academic, legal, and national policy circles rest on different perceptions about what constitutes scientific knowledge at any given time. This conflict is distorting much of the research endeavor today, causing underinvestment in some areas, overinvestment in others.

## EXPERIMENTAL HYPOTHESIS TESTING

Basic viewpoints about what constitutes scientific knowledge derive from two rather different traditions. One of these is the body of theory concerned with determining how one establishes the validity of knowledge or truth. In 1620, Francis Bacon's *Novum Organum* established this theory's basic premises of proposing alternative explanations and conducting explicit tests to distinguish among them as the direct route to scientific understanding.[1] Newton's *Principia Mathematica* then elaborated this into the classical structure for the hypothesis-proof approach to physical science that most other disciplines wishing to be "scientific" now emulate.[2]

In the modern era, the writings of Karl Popper and his followers have carried this one step further.[3] They emphasize that theories or hypotheses can never be actually proven universally true, since contrary future events might always invalidate them. Hypotheses, however, can be proven incorrect by observations that fail to fit their predictions. They argue that scientific knowledge advances only by rejecting previously tenable propositions about the real world.[4] Their theories have been interpreted into dogma for many fields and academic publications. Although these theories have provided a highly desirable framework for certain disciplines (notably the laboratory sciences), they have seriously impeded progress in others, such as ecology and the behavioral sciences.

Contrary to these rigid views, it is well known that probabilistic predictions cannot be strictly falsified by contrary observations, since observed events could merely represent improbable outcomes of a correctly described process. This is especially true of large-scale, complex technology, or economic systems containing large numbers of interacting forces. For example, many ecological, large network system, or policy situations are unique and defy reasonable experimental replication. Many variables cannot be held constant or be assumed neutral. Variables that are measurable, predictable, and testable may be trivial in impact. On the other hand, single dominating (but totally unpredictable or unknowable) events can render all other system parameters impotent in explaining outcomes (e.g., an atomic bomb is or is not constructed by the Nazis first; volcanic activity chills the earth to deadly levels). While useful for some purposes, formal hypothesis testing is by no means the sole source or validation method for scientific knowledge.

## SCIENCE AS A CONTINUOUS, TUMULTUOUS, CONTINGENT PROCESS

A second approach to understanding knowledge generation and verification, with equally long roots and strong modern advocates, treats scientific knowledge as a learning process. The Greek philosophers as well as Aquinas, Russell, Bronowski, Kaplan, Polanyi, and Kuhn, have been major contributors to this view.[5] They conclude that a variety of different approaches may establish what becomes accepted as truth in specific circumstances. And in many cases this truth is not verifiable through a controlled, replicable experiment.

Kuhn has become the primary recent synthesizer of this more comprehensive viewpoint. He argues that knowledge proceeds through the establishment of new paradigms in eras of scientific revolution. Interspersed are lengthy spans of normal science in which researchers add, brick by brick, to the edifice provided by the paradigm, while simultaneously eroding its specific validity, drop by drop. The original paradigm is eventually overthrown when the weight of post hoc additions and anomalies becomes a burden and some new, simpler, and more satisfying propositions better account for the expanded body of data. In practice, the accepted scientific truths of an era are not immutable but are established by a social process that incorporates certain practical and aesthetic, and even political, judgments about what are allowable deviations from the dominating paradigm and the range of deductive inferences one can legitimately draw from experimental evidence.

In most complex business, national policy, sociological, or ecological situations, the number of potentially interacting variables is so great that all cannot be anticipated in advance, monitored, or often even measured in retrospect. In these circumstances researchers must often live with the problems inherent in a sample of one or the vagaries of the incomplete, biased, and often contradictory data available to a careful observer. Yet there is a constant pressure to deny legitimacy to research that cannot satisfy the hypothesis-falsification mainstays of "the scientific method." This is the core of many contentious arguments between microbiologists and medical doctors, laboratory biologists and ecologists, research psychologists and psychiatrists, and among policy researchers, micro- and macroeconomists, and so forth. And it leads many young researchers to attack infinitesimally meaningless experiments whose results they can "prove" to the satisfaction of hypothesis testers rather than working on problems of greater merit.

## OTHER VALID SCIENTIFIC PROCESSES

In reality, other processes make major contributions in the hard sciences and deserve much more legitimization in other realms, particularly in large-scale systems, business, economics, and policy situations. Knowledge tends to emerge as a series of partial truths that are useful for a period and a purpose.[6] Scientific models may be useful, though not strictly true (the atom as a whirling ball of electrons around a stable nucleus), or true in detail but ignored as not useful for most purposes (the atomic nucleus as a chaotic collection of mesosomes, quarks, etc.). The history of science and technology suggests that at least seven definable activities create valid knowledge. These activities blend with each other, amplify knowledge, and continually redefine new problems and opportunities in a nonlinear, roiling, turbulent interaction that constantly forces and feeds all innovation processes. Understanding the complex and tumultuously nonpredictable interaction of these processes is crucial to understanding innovation itself.

Two well-known series of historical examples from the field and the laboratory sciences—respectively, classical succession biogenetics and identification of the hypothalamic-releasing hormones—will briefly demonstrate how each process contributes to a healthy innovative endeavor.

### Observation, Exploration, and Description (Creating a Database)

Most of our knowledge about the world and perceptions of new needs and concepts come from direct observation. Before phenomena can be explained or dealt with, they must first be perceived or described. In many cases, scientists or innovators do not even know there is a problem (or scientific anomaly) until they simply bump into it. Then, just assembling adequate descriptive data may make a new truth obvious (e.g., huge gas clouds in outer space) or narrow zones of conjecture sufficient to specify particular and perhaps otherwise nonobvious conditions as relevant (floods on Mars). Even without understanding causal mechanisms completely, scientists can often verify the presence or absence of phenomena by systematic observation. Especially in the early stages of knowledge building or innovation this activity can define truth as adequately as any form of experimentation or testing.[7]

• Darwin's systematic observations on the *Beagle Expedition* provided essential knowledge about species throughout the world. Especially important was his identification of fossil barnacles, similar to shore species, high in the Andes. It was probably the use of his powerful and diverse field database—along with his citing of overwhelming observations from animal breeding, data collected for an entirely different purpose—that gave credibility to Darwin's later theories and most distinguished him from earlier proponents of evolution, like Buffon, Erasmus Darwin, and Lamarck.[8]

• The whole search for brain hormones was perhaps launched by Selye's early *observations* that when the body is exposed to stress, it produces a characteristic response, releasing hormones mediated by the pituitary and adrenal glands.[9] Poppa's 1930s *descriptions* of the portal vessels between the hypothalamus and pituitary and other anatomists' observations concerning the lack of nerves to the anterior pituitary suggested to Harris in 1955 that chemicals might trigger the release of pituitary hormones.[10]

## Cataloging and Classification (Developing a Taxonomy)

As managers know in other contexts, communication about complex systems, evaluation of data or results, and generalizations to wider systems are impossible without an adequate nomenclature. While Mendeleyev's grouping of chemical elements into the Periodic Table and Gell-Mann's arrangement of hadrons into "particle octets" led to discovery of critical new physical units, the lack of such taxonomies has confused other fields (including biology and management theory) for years and has led to errors and controversy in other sciences. The skills and procedures of a taxonomist are important and quite different from an explorer's or laboratory experimenter's.

• Darwin's careful structuring of his data on finches, coral reefs, barnacles, orchids, and so forth provided major steps in developing a systematic worldwide biological science and was an important contribution in itself, obtaining recognition for Darwin as an outstanding scientist long before he proposed his integrating evolution theories.[11]

• Roger Guillemin's and Andrew Schally's 1977 Nobel Prize for identification of the chemical-releasing factors affecting the pituitary involved much more careful measurement and classification of the complex chemicals extracted from millions of animal hypothalamus glands. Perhaps the most critical portion of the entire venture were Andrew Schally's, Roger Burgus', Wylie Vale's, and Hisayaki Matsuo's use of carefully constructed keys and essays, developed for other purposes, to achieve unambiguous identification of CRF, TRF, and LRF (hormonal-releasing factors) from a few selected micrograms of extracted hypothalamic material.[12]

## Search for Generalized Patterns (Understanding Subsystem Relationships)

Defining new patterns in data (creative induction) is often a major contribution in itself.[13] Because of expense or complexity, physical scientists, like their colleagues in the policy, social, or natural systems sciences, are often able to study a given system under only a small number of specific conditions from which they must attempt wider, though limited, generalizations. Such insights often involve conjectures from statistical data (like epidemiological studies) or patterned observations from a systematic but nonstatistical sample (like Ignaz Semmelweis's reducing infections in hospital wards).[14] This frequently intuitive process is often most important in hypothesizing potential subsystem laws and opening further major avenues for research or verification.

• Darwin found that recurring structures within animal groups (notably Galapagos finches) suggested a common ancestry, yet at the same time differences (in bill and limb sizes and shapes) apparently resulted from local environmental challenges. These observed patterns led to his later theories of adaptive radiation and speciation. The occurrence of apparently maladaptive features (ornate feathers and gaudy colors in some birds) then led to his theories about possible sexual selection.[15] In both cases, his samples were systematic but clearly not statistically structured for global generalizations.

• In the laboratory sciences, experiments are generally reproducible. Hence, nonstatisticality of samples often does not present significant problems unless experiments are very costly. Nevertheless, knowledge even here typically grows from a series of partial insights, incrementally leading toward fuller understanding of the total system. Guillemin's and Schally's important experiments—placing hypothalamic tissue into test tubes with exhausted ACTH-producing pituitary tissues—offered an important pattern but only partial insight about the interaction between the two organs.[16] They established the fact of some relationship, but not its explicit nature, activating mechanism, or relationship to other brain and glandular activities.

## Proposal of Hypotheses (Suggesting Mechanisms)

This is often called the creative act of science.[17] At its best, this activity creates the revolutionary paradigms that separate the scientific greats from the elegant practitioners. But several caveats appear: (1) in many cases the hypothesis follows the data-gathering step or experiment that led to it; (2) at the time most major new paradigms are proposed, they can rarely be fully tested; (3) those who pose major paradigms are often not the ones who accomplish their definitive tests. Kuhn's data suggest an average of some twenty-five years between the initial statement of a revolutionary paradigm and its first definitive test.

• To provide the causal mechanism behind his patterned observations of adaptive radiation and speciation, Darwin hypothesized the process of natural selection. After 140 years Darwin's proposed explanations are still being modified, and only a handful of examples exist where the linkage from environmental stress to mutation of individual genes is understood in an experimentally verifiable sense. Nevertheless, biological theory was revolutionized in 1859 by *On the Origin of Species*.

• Around 1900, scientists recognized that the pituitary gland is an important source of the hormones that control other glands. For four decades, nerves from the brain were thought to be the triggering mechanism for releasing these hormones. But later research revealed no nerves into the anterior pituitary, the source of the known hormones. In 1944 Harris proposed the concept that the hypothalamus released some chemical factors to the pituitary to trigger the hormones.[18] For at least ten more years, there was great scientific controversy, with many eminent scientists strongly opposing Harris's theory and citing seemingly contrary evidence.[19] The first postulated hormone was not found for another ten years, and the last was not isolated until 1976, thirty-two years after the hypothesis.

## Tests of Hypotheses (Experimenting and Testing)

When feasible, formal hypothesis testing can be an important part of the scientific method, but such testing may not be possible or meaningful in specific situations.[20] The technology to test a hypothesis unambiguously may not exist at the time it is proposed—or perhaps ever. Yet the hypothesis may still be useful in the interim, as Harris's was, or as many of the hypotheses about the universe or health care now are. But even today's testable knowledge may be upset by tomorrow's better measuring or observation techniques, as astronomical, medical, and atomic theories so often have been. A definitive test of a major new paradigm may not be possible within decades of its proposal (if ever), yet partial tests of its applicability and limits (made anywhere and by any discipline) can be important in knowledge building.

• Evolution by natural selection is most difficult to test in natural systems. The fittest survive, by definition. The first real test of selective adaptation in Darwin's wild animal populations did not take place until the El Niño of 1984 caused the death of all smaller-billed Galapagos finches on one island. The formation of new species by the natural accumulation of numerous small genetic changes has rarely been conclusively demonstrated, although it is consistent with most of the available data. However, speciation by mechanisms not anticipated by Darwin (e.g., gross chromosomal rearrangements or changes in chromosome number) is common, particularly in plants. Such observations lend credence to parts of Darwin's paradigm, while simultaneously undercutting its total validity.

• Over eight years, Harris developed a series of elegant tests showing that although the portal vessels to the hypothalamus carry blood to the pituitary, it was something else that made the pituitary become active.[21] Harris's "neural control" concept seemed persuasive to many. However, others attempting to verify his findings failed at first due to inadequate laboratory technique. Until some of the actual hormone-releasing factors were isolated by Schally and Guillemin, there were still believers and nonbelievers.[22] And even some thirty-five years later, some of the hypothesized releasing factors had yet to be identified and their full effects in individual humans known.

## Synthesis (Merging Theories for New Paradigms)

Often insights from previously disparate disciplines or findings combine to formulate new understandings. New assumptions may reorder previously presumed relationships, as did Einstein's recalculation of effects assuming a constant speed of light. Asking the right questions can itself lead to interesting new answers, though answers may be currently untestable. Often a field may learn much more from theoretical syntheses—like particle physics and astronomy—than from ever more elaborate testing of uninteresting or old questions.

• Haldane, Dobzhansky, Mayr, and others in the pre–World War II era merged Darwin's theory with classical genetics to generate the new synthesis.[23] Sir Ronald Fisher and Sewall Wright combined the findings of Mendelian genetics with new mathematical and statistical techniques to analyze population dynamics, thus forging the basis of modern population genetics. More recently, large-scale molecular chemistry, biochemistry, and genetics have merged in innumerable biotechnology investigations. Knowledge available from each preceding system was incomplete without the later syntheses, and the syntheses themselves are still being tested.

• Understanding hypothalamic-releasing factors often required insights from multiple disciplines. An anatomist identified the portal vessels to the anterior pituitary and the lack of nerve cells in it. Physiologists developed the techniques for obtaining experimentally pure hypothalamic materials; microbiologists and microchemists defined the chemical content and amino sequences of the releasing factors; and the physics of mass spectroscopy confirmed their conclusions. Neurologists and endocrinologists applied and extended laboratory findings in human health research. The knowledge of each discipline would have been incomplete without the final synthesis, which led to the new discipline of neuroendocrinology.

## Manipulation for a Purpose (Technological Development and Diffusion)

Technology defines new truths in a manner similar to science. A given set of relationships leads to definable results under specified circumstances. Yet technology does not necessarily determine in detail why a result is achieved, only its fact. Edison's experiments demonstrated results, not causes. Technology thus often precedes science. The steam engine preceded thermodynamics, telescopes preceded astronomical science, and scanning tunneling and electron microscopes have been necessary adjuncts for much microbiological and surface physics theory. Technology allows answers to previously unanswerable scientific questions and defines new ones as relevant, as the Hubble telescope, Pathfinder, and Voyager spacecraft have.

Various studies have shown that much scientific discovery and innovation occurs as users first apply technologies[24] and that an interactive learning relationship between theory builders and systems users often improves the quality of knowledge for both parties.[25] Finally, effective diffusion of knowledge to nonspecialists increases available knowledge by orders of magnitude, creating unforeseen new insights, questions, and options for solving old questions. From an economic viewpoint, making knowledge available for wide (and perhaps unanticipated) uses is often far more important than a few more detailed, elegant, and esoteric articles shared by the elite.

• Myriad purposeful applications of selective breeding in animal husbandry, agriculture, and forestry occurred before either their causal mechanisms or their ecological effects (as in monoculture) were understood. Observations derived from these applications led to new scientific questions and understandings about the effects of nutrition on animal and plant health, the control of diseases and pests, and the potential effects of perturbations on human and ecological systems. Testing of actual causal mechanisms in fields like biological succession, heredity, genetic disease, or cell mutation was impossible until technology permitted experimentation with segmented DNA and gene structures. In terms of future impact, greater geographic diffusion and widespread use of genetic technologies will undoubtedly lead to radical changes in education and understanding for people throughout the world. And these people's use, testing, mistakes, and contributions may turn out to be more important to future knowledge and economic value than any other direct consequences of today's laboratory biology research.

• Once the hypothalamic-releasing factors were identified, further experimentation paused until technology could synthesize sufficient quantities for larger-scale clinical and scientific investigations. As quantities became available, other factors were investigated for their effects in a wide variety of situations: controlling reproduction (LRF), altering sleep patterns (TRF), and suppressing body sugar levels (GIF). These became the first of a broad class of substances still at the core of brain peptide research, where new results are now being announced almost weekly.

## IMPACTS ON SCIENCE AND TECHNOLOGY POLICY

All of these stages of knowledge building are important at both the corporate and national levels. It is a mistake to deride one in favor of another in the overall science and technology (S&T) endeavor and within disciplines. Some of the most productive inquiries are at the interfaces between different activities: among database generation, pattern seeking, and hypothesis testing *or* between technological application and hypothesis generation. Isolating such phases conceptually—and especially organizationally as happens in university science versus engineering, medical school biochemistry versus clinical versus medical system research, or in industry and government basic research versus development organizations—is dangerous and counterproductive. Cross-group mission-oriented planning, programming, and interactions are likely to have higher payoffs.

Perhaps the most destructive features in recent national policy structures, however, have been the cutbacks in funding for much-needed new databases in the economic and ecological arenas and lack of attention to the high paybacks available from better diffusion of S&T knowledge. As Chapters 11 through 13 will show, current economic and technological data are quite inadequate, and indeed are misleading in a knowledge- and services-based economy. The data to make sensible economic-environmental or medical-economic policy are missing, and many data definitions are misleading in the extreme. The results are misguided policy, excessive controversy over what should be factual matters, and wasted national resources on a huge scale.

Effective diffusion of S&T knowledge generally has much higher payoffs than profits from the earlier stages of knowledge generation. Neither should be ignored. But broad understanding of both the principles and the specific applications of physics, mechanics, dynamics, biotechnology, ecology, health care, computers, chemistry, and software by the population lets people apply, use, and innovate new solutions on a scale that dwarfs the profits or benefits to the original innovator. Software networks, popular books, videotapes, TV programs like *Nova* and *Wild Nature,* computer programs, and other skilled explanations of useful science have diffused scientific knowledge to such an extent that many elementary school students have seen, internalized, and can discuss topics college students did not understand a decade or two ago. Because of video games and early introduction to computers, youngsters are more computer literate than many of their elders. Knowledge diffusion has provided them with a powerful platform for further education and relevant new job skills. Yet in recent years there has been a strong political attempt to cut back on federal support for such programs.

At the university level, much research is driven toward trivia by the need to "prove" results in a mathematically rigorous format to be academically acceptable. Research published in books or practitioner journals, however rigorous and useful, is disdained, despite the often higher payoff for the society of such work, if well done. Academic articles, whose readership in many journals averages fewer than ten, are praised, while articles purchased in reprint form and referenced by the thousands in others are disparaged. And no one in academia has quite figured out how to deal with the knowledge diffusion that publication on the Internet allows.

If even these anomalies in the scientific knowledge spectrum were addressed adequately by policy, we would be well ahead. But entrenched ideas and political forces make such progress problematic. The next three chapters will suggest some proved, useful approaches to certain key problems. All successes will rest on a wider understanding of how science and technology actually progress.

## SUMMARY

Scientific-technological knowledge creation involves at least seven important conceptual levels. Although progressing in the general order presented, all seven typically occur simultaneously, tumultuously, and interactively in any healthy area of inquiry. Unfortunately, the most widespread descriptions and popular conceptions of the scientific method focus simplistically and almost exclusively on only two scientific processes: hypothesis generation and testing. However, as much or more valid knowledge is generated through activities other than formal hypothesis testing. Exploration, systematic observation, classification, technology building, and dissemination probably create more of our valid knowledge pool and are far more important in creating competitive advantage, economic value, and social benefit.

A healthy scientific-technological, knowledge-generating system in academia, industry, or at the national level does not necessarily mean more R&D. Instead, it consciously and systematically honors and taps into all stages of knowledge development. It actively recognizes and exploits the highly independent, unpredictable, interactive processes that underlie all major scientific and technological innovation. Unfortunately, this balance is not evident in many areas of scientific endeavor today, especially those having to do with the large-scale systems that will determine the future livability of the planet and the quality of life on it. Scientific observation, database building, refining taxonomies, large systems modeling, and knowledge diffusion are underfunded and underreported, while trivial hypotheses are tested and reported endlessly. Later chapters will suggest some measures to redress the balance.

# 11

# National Technology Competitiveness: Government-Industry Strategies That Work

Despite some undoubted flaws, no system has worked as well to promote innovation and to generate wealth as has the constructive interaction of democratic governments and private producing enterprises, working in a market economy, along with carefully constructed social and economic regulation. Unfettered markets, by contrast, are no panacea—as the inhumane, exploitive, and frequently destructive practices of the industrial revolution and colonialism, the pillaging of nations by dictators and warlords in the pre–World War II era, and the disastrous collapse of the former USSR's economy dramatically prove. For effectiveness, markets require substantial public infrastructures of accountability, education, law, transportation, communications, waste disposal, distribution, national banking, product and worker safety, environmental protection, and public health, among others.

Beyond this, active government intervention and support in other modes actually creates large positive increments of innovation, totally new markets, and other public values. Past successes include:

- Supporting large-scale database, basic research, and development programs—like biotechnology, weather monitoring, and satellite systems—that private companies could not justify.
- Providing education, information, transportation, recreation, health, safety, and communications networks generating public values no private firm could effectively exploit.

- Subsidizing initial product and service developments—like airmail or large dams—requiring more capital, longer time horizons, or greater risks than private firms could absorb.
- Establishing standards, competitive practices, and social safety nets to protect individuals against injury others might inflict when acting in their own self-interest.
- Aggregating fragmented private demands in ways that create whole new domestic industries and international growth opportunities, like pollution control, public health, advanced computer, and air flight control systems.

When governments use these mechanisms properly, history demonstrates that they lead to greater innovation, higher economic growth, increased personal security, greater equity to individuals, larger private market opportunities, and much greater national wealth than would otherwise exist.[1]

## GOVERNMENT-SUPPORTED INNOVATION

It is currently popular to deride the potentials of "industrial policy" for the United States.[2] America basks in a mythology and self-image, perpetuated through continuous repetition, that only private enterprises or rugged individualists can create real economic wealth. Many assert that government cannot create wealth, only distribute it. Although we authors are true devotees of the private enterprise system, we find such assertions to be incompatible with fact.

### Some Industrial Policies Work

Governments actively create positive wealth through a variety of mechanisms. In fact, elements of government policy have been critical in generating or nurturing virtually every major industry in which the United States is world dominant today. The general scale of some key industries and their corresponding government support modes, listed in Table 11.1, indicate the wide range and high impact of these interventions.

These industries, aggregating over $5 trillion in GNP, and many others, would not be operating at today's scale, complexity, or efficiency if they had not enjoyed significant government support. Other government actions help expand total market opportunities by assisting international trade, increasing available technical and consumer information, stabilizing the economy, creating new options through research, buffering externalities that otherwise would destroy individual customers and companies, and maintaining infrastructures of education, transportation, and communications that support a wider, more unified marketplace. All of these actions increase economic efficiency. They also lower the marginal cost of innovation, increase potential market payoffs, and decrease risks for innovators. All assist the development and use of technology.

There are virtually no industries today except perhaps domestic personal services (and even there immigration policies assist) that do not benefit from some form of government support. And as populations grow and the natural systems providing fishing, waste recycling, water, and open space become more limited, countries are likely to find that they need more government intervention—not less—to maintain economic stability, quality of life standards, and human safety. It is fatuous to suggest that governments cannot create desired services and output values beyond those generated by private markets. The question is not whether governments have a role in wealth creation, but where and how they can participate most effectively.[3] These are the essential issues for technology strategy at the national level. Nonintervention itself is a strategy. Any reasonable survey of history will show that, in the technological realm, nonintervention would have led to large losses; while constructive interventions and partnerships with industry have helped grow great industries. What policy lessons do these experiences teach?

## Generic Interventions Support Private Markets

In the 60 to 70% of a modern market economy's transactions, where individuals or private institutions have adequate resources to create effective demand and where there are a sufficient number of competing producers and customers, markets work very well. In these realms, the government's role is primarily that of a facilitator, decreasing transaction costs among parties and handling externalities the parties cannot (or will not voluntarily) cope with. Stimulating technological innovation in these circumstances primarily involves creating a level playing field for fair competition, keeping national overhead costs as low as possible, decreasing the factor costs of production (such as those for capital, communications, or health care), increasing information availability, creating new options through technological research and development, educating workers and executives, and providing fair means for resolving legitimate disputes. Such generic interventions make all markets work more efficiently and decrease the inherent risks of innovation for all players.

**TABLE 11.1**
**Industries Receiving National Support**

| Major Industry Supported | Examples and Modes of Government Support | Scalar Indicators of Current Market Size[a] ($ billions) |
|---|---|---|
| Aerospace | Military and NASA R&D, first purchase of new designs, test facilities, avionics, airflight-control technologies | 125 |
| Airlines | Airmail subsidies, airflight control technologies, military pilot training, international agreements, safety systems, airport construction | 80 |
| Consumer foods | Agriculture research, farm price stabilization, quality certification, standard weights and measures, process regulation and monitoring, fair trade practices | 500 |
| Pharmaceuticals | NIH[b] basic research, vaccine development and distribution, health statistics, patent protection, FDA quality controls, Center for Disease Control | 110 |
| Automobiles | Road construction, safety standards, fits and tolerance standards, antitheft measures | 450 |
| Communications | Standards coordination, eminent domain and access rights, satellite and advanced wireless technology development, monopoly rights for AT&T and early broadcasters, frequency allocation and enforcement, military R&D, advanced semiconductors | 150 |
| Agriculture | Seed and stock development, quality standards, agriculture research and extension services, water resources development, pest control, subsidies, soil management | 90 |
| Software | Basic mathematics research, military R&D, encryption, language standardization, military purchases of systems, intellectual property rights, interface standards | 80 |
| Lumber | Forestry techniques, harvesting on public lands, development of improved species, pest control, watershed regulation, product standards | 15 |
| Computers | Basic research, large-scale development, first purchase, software support, componentry development, mass market development through education | 150 |

282

| Industry | Description | |
|---|---|---|
| Biotechnology | Basic microbiological research, safety standards, human genome research, equipment development, information dissemination | 8 |
| Electric power | Dam development, REA[c] market creation, safety standards, alternative technology development, monopoly grants, eminent domain | 200 |
| Medical care | Hospital construction, medical standards, public health investments, health insurance, health statistics, medical education, insurance support | 1500 |
| Semiconductors | Materials research, first quantity purchase, military research, Sematech, advanced system development, large-scale systems deployments | 90 |
| Energy | Depletion allowances, geographical surveys, antitrust exemptions for oil fields, monopolies for pipelines, international alliances | 500 |
| Banking and financial services | Full disclosure regulation, FDIC[d] account protection, Federal Reserve credit and currency support, consumer banking regulations, international monetary agreements | 300 |
| Construction | Roads, buildings, dams, waterways, bridges, and tunneling purchases | 140 |
| Environmental controls | Market creation for exhaust emissions, scrubbers, waste processing, waste disposal, water resources development, flood controls, national forests | 110 |
| Weapons systems | Research, development, maintenance, and operations purchases | 200 |
| Laboratory equipment | Market creation through research, development, and state-of-the-art design projects | 10 |
| Education | Basic research, technique development, materials dissemination, construction, market creation, financial support of students, communication networks | 420 |

[a]Definitional difficulties make it impossible to determine more precise industry sizes.

[b]National Institutes of Health.

[c]Rural Electrification Administration.

[d]Federal Deposit Insurance Corporation.

Sources: *Standard and Poor's Industry Surveys 1996* (New York, 1996); U.S. Department of Commerce, *Statistical Abstract of the U.S.* (Washington D.C.: Government Printing Office, 1995); and Lotus One Source.

On the other side of the generic equation, positive interventions that increase the rewards to all innovators will clearly change the cost-benefit perceptions of potential innovators and increase total innovation. Most economists agree that numerous incentive changes—such as Japan's (1950s–1970s) low cost of capital policies and John F. Kennedy's (1962) tax cut—had large positive impacts, as did the increased information, Regulation A registration, and lowered brokerage fees the Securities and Exchange Commission's (SEC) policies facilitated in the mid-1970s and 80s.[4] However, even such broad interventions have selective impacts on different sectors. For example, the vacuum tube industry was overturned by semiconductor innovations stimulated in part by (generic) government-sponsored physics research and capital gains tax policies of the era. Similarly, some individual brokers and financial institutions suffered from the lowered registration and transaction fees that financial services deregulation brought.

Any intervention—including nonintervention—creates some winners and losers. Those who would have died without government-sponsored health research, public health regulation, and vaccine development represent positive winners of broad-based interventions. Conversely, the hundreds of thousands whose lives were wrecked or prematurely terminated by nonexistent seat belt and air pollution regulation prior to the 1970s paid a high loser's price—as did unprotected coal miners, textile workers, and consumers of ineffective or unsafe patent medicines in an earlier unregulated era. The function of government is not passive. It is to provide levels of security, fairness, and opportunity that individuals cannot effectively achieve on their own.[5]

## PAST U.S. TECHNOLOGY STRATEGIES

The United States has never had a single, stated, integrating technology strategy, largely because of its checks-and-balances philosophy and the contentiousness a single announced strategy would create. It has, however, rather successfully utilized a series of specific interventions to influence technology development and utilization. Taken together these became the technology strategies of each era. In many respects, the United States preceded all other countries in such practices. Its broad strategies can be divided into roughly four periods, all relatively successful at first and then losing effectiveness as they became bureaucratized, or corrupted, or as conditions changed. (See the box.)

During the 1960s and 1970s a vast majority (90%) of federal S&T funds went first into the Department of Defense (DOD), Department of

# PAST U.S. TECHNOLOGY STRATEGIES

*Phase One (in the 1800s)* involved both generic and industry-specific initiatives. These included (1) massive support of transportation infrastructures (railroads and canals) through land grants and permitting utility companies to have monopoly positions, (2) educational support of public primary and secondary education and stimulation of agricultural and mechanical technologies through the land grant universities, and (3) strong support of the basic mining and metals industries through tax and mining rights concessions. Believing that technology had led to the North's victory in the Civil War, Congress created the National Academy of Sciences in 1867 to provide it with independent scientific advice. Patents and the protection of intellectual rights to stimulate invention were essential features of the U.S. system from the nation's beginning.

*In Phase Two (late 1800s through the 1930s),* government helped develop new transportation and communications infrastructures. Government support of airmail, aircraft development, radio communications, airport construction, and monopolistic route structure grants stimulated the new technologies of the aircraft and airline industries. Road and bridge construction, tax incentives for energy development, oil reserve "proration laws," and standardized fits and tolerances for parts all supported greater development of the automobile industry and its energy and mechanical-products support technologies. Government helped stimulate the steel and shipbuilding industries through its massive construction-infrastructure investments, naval purchases, and merchant shipping support. And its seizures of German chemical company assets in two world wars gave impetus to U.S. dominance in that industry.

Through the 1930s, the federal government helped develop and extend agricultural and electrical technologies through its agricultural extension and Rural Electrification Administration (REA) programs. The Army Corps of Engineers' and Bureau of Reclamation's huge dams and irrigation projects brought needed electric power and water that created new markets throughout vast undeveloped areas of the country and gave the United States world leadership in large construction technologies. Without the electric power of the TVA and Columbia River systems, the massive aluminum buildup for World War II—and the postwar nuclear, aluminum products, and aircraft industries—would have been much delayed. Federal, state, and local governments provided the public health systems that made large cities feasible and created the market for early vaccines, hospital equipment, and pest control systems. Government-granted monopolies helped nourish emerging firms in the telephone, communications, and wireless industries. And the U.S. government developed the Federal Reserve and Savings and Loan banking structures that stabilized banking and encouraged the savings, investment, and fi-

*(continued)*

## PAST U.S. TECHNOLOGY STRATEGIES *(continued)*

nancing for homes and industry that later facilitated post–World War II prosperity. This era substantially created the infrastructures for U.S. industry's midcentury dominance of the mechanical and electrical industries worldwide.

*In Phase Three (post–World War II)*, convinced that science had contributed significantly to victory in the war and offered boundless prospects for economic growth in the postwar era,[6] a formal national science policy hierarchy emerged in Washington to concentrate on increasing the nation's commitment to basic research and public technology development and better coordinating the government's own R&D investments at the national level.[7] The National Defense Education Act (GI Bill) created a larger pool of college-trained people for the United States than any country had ever known. The basic research role fell largely to the National Science Foundation (NSF) for science in general and to the National Institutes of Health (NIH) for the medical and health sciences. Elsewhere each agency also supported basic research related to its mission and allocated internal resources to develop technology programs supporting specific elements of that mission.

*In Phase Four (1970s and 1980s)* new forces combined to create new needs. The energy crises (caused by the oil embargoes of 1973 and 1978) stimulated a flurry of alternative energy technology and user-incentive programs to shift patterns of energy consumption and production. In many areas these efforts converged with policies and programs—exemplified by the Clean Air, Clean Water, and Occupational Health Acts of 1970–1973—aimed at ameliorating or reversing the negative human safety and environmental impacts of modern industrialization. By the late 1970s double-digit inflation, a deteriorating trade balance, and the emergence of Japan as an industrial power led to concerns about "U.S. competitiveness"[8] and "the lack of US innovation." In 1978, the Commerce Department led studies that generated some new broad-based policies for better protecting intellectual assets, lowering capital costs, and allowing joint cooperation among companies to enhance innovativeness.[9]

Because of their huge scale, federal actions began to distort the nation's entire technological posture. They restructured universities' science and engineering toward currently funded programs.[10] They drew talent away from producing industries and into government-dependent laboratories and industries. And they created large national technological bureaucracies (as in the AEC, NASA, DOD, DOE, NIH, and national laboratories) whose economic output was difficult to measure. Some magnificent technical achievements in aerospace and medicine masked the scale of these distortions until measured U.S. productivity began to falter seriously in the late 1970s and 1980s.[11]

Agriculture (DOA), Atomic Energy Commission (AEC), National Aeronautics and Space Agency (NASA), and later to the Department of Energy (DOE) and National Institutes of Health (NIH). Government R&D expenditures exploded during this era. (See Figure 11.1.) Industrial technology was presumed to "fall out" from these efforts, although there were some increased tax incentives to perform private R&D. Griliches and others calculated social returns on government advanced research and technology investments in commercially related areas to be 40% or more compounded.[12] These government-stimulated efforts were so successful that Europe saw an insurmountable technology gap developing in favor of the United States and increased its own S&T allocations in response.[13]

Although conceived as a top-down allocation process—and despite an elaborate science and technology policy apparatus attempting to coordinate S&T resource allocations and policies in the Executive Branch—the overall effect of government actions was very ad hoc.[14] The President or key members of his administration frequently ignored

**FIGURE 11.1**
**Federal Obligations for R&D by Major Agencies**

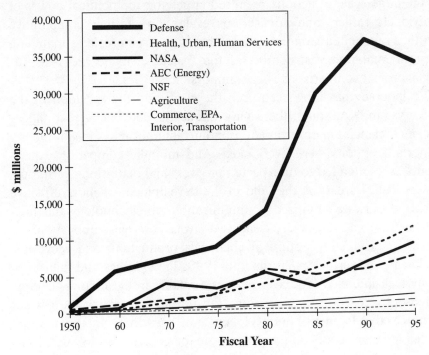

Source: National Science Foundation, *Science and Engineering Indicators—1996.*

*Defense, Atomic Energy, and NASA dominated R&D spending until the mid-1980s, when Health R&D began to emerge.*

or bypassed the S&T policy groups.[15] And individual Congressional committees and their parallel executive agencies often developed powerful symbioses that overrode even the Executive's most careful analyses and diligent coordinative attempts.[16] Rather than representing competing positions, individual agencies' interests often directly supported the power and influence of the Congressional committee members who reviewed their actions. During the 1970s, science and technology became additional weapons to expand each agency's size and scope.[17] Concomitantly, high-profile S&T programs—like space, medicine, military, and energy development—became tools for individual members of Congress to achieve further patronage, prestige, power, and headlines.

In the early 1980s, under pressure from unemployment, dropping corporate profits, trade and fiscal deficits, and diminishing standards of living, Congress and the Executive undertook an uncoordinated hodgepodge of employment policies, trade negotiations, and educational support programs to improve U.S. competitiveness. Without a coherent strategy to guide them, the net effect of all these actions was fragmented and highly questionable. The problem was not so much the adhocracy as the huge scale of actions premised largely on the political power of individuals rather than any serious evaluation of their comparative worth. Fragmented Congressional committee structures and matching departmental power structures of the Executive made cross-institutional project comparisons almost impossible.

Adhocracy has long been both the curse and the salvation of the U.S. system.[18] Although there have unquestionably been great allocation inefficiencies in government programs, pluralism has meant that no important options were overlooked. And multiple competing experiments have often led to unexpected progress and better long-term outcomes in key areas, as they did in the development of more effective network software, digitized communications, biotechnology diagnostics, natural gas resources, clean two-stroke internal combustion engines, by-product recapture in chemicals production, and recyclable packaging. Nevertheless, in the mid-1990s the excesses and failures of many well-intended federal programs (notably in agriculture, energy, defense, space, education, housing, transportation, social welfare, water resource development, and worker and environmental protection) forced a major debate on the proper role for government in S&T. In its zeal to implement corrections, however, this debate has often tended to overlook the major contributions that government S&T support has made to U.S. industrial progress. A fairly robust baby appears about to disappear with the cleansing bath.

## LESSONS FROM THE PAST

What guidelines have America's—and other country's—experiments suggested about effective technology partnerships between business and government?

### Technology's Perceived Role in National Growth

The framers of the Constitution and America's early patent laws specifically supported only invention and discovery as key growth ingredients. In the 1800s, at the state level, publicly financed primary and secondary education built basic skills, while nationally instigated land grant universities provided the huge agricultural and mechanical knowledge underpinnings needed for the industrial revolution in the United States. Not until the post–World War II era did nations attempt conscious policies to generate and nurture scientific knowledge per se as a growth force.[19] Significantly these early attempts were termed "science policies." There were two components to science policy: *policy for science,* which encouraged the healthy growth of the scientific endeavor, and *science in policy,* which attempted to use and allocate science more effectively in support of national goals.[20]

It took two more decades for policymakers to recognize that technology, not science alone, was the driving force behind wealth creation. As the United States had before them, Japan and Israel in the 1960s and 1970s vaulted to economic prominence largely through technological adaptations and heavy investments, but with relatively small scientific endeavors. Despite the pioneering work of Schumpeter,[21] formal economic models during this era had no specific modules dealing with the impact of technological change on growth; technology was treated as a residual contributor after the effects of land, labor, and capital were calculated.[22] Only in the 1970s and 1980s did nations seriously probe behind their investment-driven economic policies to investigate whether technological innovation, entrepreneurship, and diffusion might be the more critical leverage factors in the growth equation. Finally in the early 1990s, services, information, and intellectual development increasingly began to emerge as the crucial dimensions in advanced countries' and corporations' growth.[23] What have theory and practice taught us to date?

## Markets First, But Not Alone

First, when proper infrastructures exist, market mechanisms generally provide the most effective vehicles for maximizing wealth production and technology development in democratic economies. Markets are an extension of democratic choice philosophies into the economic realm. They are essentially large networks linking the most extensive possible relevant resources of intellect (technology and innovation) with any given user group having resources.[24] When properly constructed, markets allow the greatest freedom of choice for customers to optimize personal value and self-expression. They also stimulate active search for novelty and problem solutions by innovators, producers, and users. Innovator-supplier-user interactions tend to leverage the intellectual capabilities of all groups.

For these reasons, any sensible national technology strategy will use private market mechanisms to the maximum extent possible. However, private markets allocate resources very badly when (1) individual buyers and sellers do not internalize all the market's costs, (2) individual buyers cannot aggregate their demands effectively, (3) large-scale institutions have the power to constrain mobility, (4) government is a monopsony buyer, (5) risks are too large for individuals to assume, (6) large intangibles cannot be valued, (7) private exploiters' costs do not increase as resources are depleted, (8) secondary or public benefits substantially outweigh private benefits, or (9) fairness is more important than immediate cost. Unfortunately, these conditions apply in many marketplaces. Chapter 12 explains in detail why and how governments have intervened successfully to offset both particular market inefficiencies and to create major new private market opportunities.[25]

## Use and Diffusion, Not Just R&D

Effective technology strategies encourage both the effective generation and use of technology. Fortunately, markets do both.[26] Use is an important dimension in this equation. Studies show that over half of all innovations occur in the users' hands.[27] Early science policies, focusing on scientific research alone, collapsed in large part because so much of the knowledge they created never made it to application (although they did add substantially to the pool of scientific knowledge). Early technology policies, which followed a command-and-control model designed to allocate resources more rationally within government, were also often less than successful because they substantially ignored the entrepreneurial

and diffusion processes that would have aided utilization of their technologies. Both sets of policies were most successful when creating technologies needed for government itself or when coordinating first proof
of technologies (like biotechnologies) that were too expensive or risky
for the private sector to initiate. As many countries discovered, neither
science nor technology contributes much to economic growth when
they remain in secret government archives, solely within the minds of
elites, or captured as monopolistic secret art inside government or
large-company oligarchies.

However, early Israeli, Japanese, and U.S. technology policies that
stimulated all four phases of the knowledge process—knowledge building, discovery and invention, entrepreneurial innovation, and diffusion—were enormously effective. Until the late 1970s, most other
countries' science and technology policies gave much lesser focus to innovation and diffusion. Yet these generally provide thousands of times
the direct benefit of mere discovery or invention. Automobiles, semiconductors, synthetic fibers, videotapes, hybrid seeds, plastics, computers,
and refrigerators (to suggest only a few technologies), once diffused
into the hands of masses who neither discovered them, built them, nor
understood their science in detail, created huge new production and
support industries, generating entrepreneurial innovation and growth
beyond the wildest dreams of their original creators. Because of the
changed (software-based) nature of innovation processes and the vastly
expanded diffusion capabilities of the information age, the four basic
knowledge processes are even more intimately linked and leverageable
now. They will require much more balanced attention in future national
strategies.

## EXTENDING TIME HORIZONS

One key element in realizing these potentials is creating the institutional
time horizons necessary to achieve them. Many have expressed concerns about both American industry's and its government's short time
horizons and the impacts these have on longer-term investments, particularly on development of new technologies.[28] There is no doubt that
government structures and policies have had extraordinary impact on
private and public time horizons. In some cases impacts have been extremely negative.[29] In others they have been quite positive. Developing
intellectual bases, creating new technologies, and recovering the investments to support them take time. Since these are the primary drivers
behind future economic growth, productivity, and competitiveness, it is

critical to understand how significantly government actions influence innovation time horizons.

## Government, Capital Costs, and Time Horizons

Many sophisticated observers cite capital costs, largely induced by national fiscal and monetary policies, as critical to innovation and productivity. Relative capital costs for nations are very difficult to measure.[30] However, there is strong evidence that for decades higher capital costs forced U.S. companies to use shorter time horizons in their investment decisions than competitors in low-capital-cost countries.[31] During the late 1970s and 1980s, average capital costs in Japan were one-third to one-fifth of those in the United States.[32] Simply expressed, if managers invested $1 million at a capital cost of 5% (Japan's rate in the 1980s), they could rationally wait 14.2 years to get their money back; but they could wait only 5.4 years if capital cost was 15% (the U.S. rate at that time). They can wait only 2.6 years if acceptable internal corporate investment hurdle rates are 30% (as they currently are in many U.S. companies).

For years, Japan's enforced savings policies and its national culture encouraged high savings rates and lower debt costs there. During this period, Japan's closed debt markets provided loans to Japanese companies at rates approximately one-third those in the United States. As electronic integration of world capital markets occurred in the late 1980s, debt costs tended to equilibrate between countries. However, the close relationships between banks and producing companies in Japan encouraged a much higher percentage of debt versus equity capital than that allowable in the United States. Even as equity costs later equilibrated, the greater debt leverage allowed by Japanese practice kept average Japanese corporate capital costs low. In addition to these structural practices during the 1980s, the Japanese government and banks made favorable financings available through special arrangements to targeted industries at a cost of from 0% to 6%. As a consequence of these financial arrangements, many Japanese companies were able to invest in projects that would not have been rational for most U.S. companies.

In the late 1980s, under Japanese tutelage, other Pacific Rim countries began similar low-cost-capital policies to support their companies. For their part, European countries often invested directly in selected industries (like commercial air transport) to make their industries more competitive. By contrast, during the 1970s and 1980s U.S. government practices systematically increased average capital costs for most American companies. The federal government increased its national debt (from $541 billion in 1978 to $4,921 billion in 1995), at times overexpending its revenues by more than the country's entire net capital accumulation in a given year. Government pressures on domestic debt markets raised interest costs for private companies. To cover its deficits, the government had to offer higher yields on its own debt to attract foreign investors. Continuing deficits raised uncertainties about future inflation and led to anticipations of higher future taxes (and consequently lower future investment returns) to pay back the debt. The combination of deficits and negative trade balances raised both present and implicit future capital costs for U.S. companies during the 1970s and 1980s and ultimately led to the collapse of the dollar in the mid-1990s exchange markets.

## Not the Government's Fault Alone

Although capital cost pressures were undoubtedly important factors in the lagging competitiveness of the United States in the 1980s, integration of world capital markets by 1995 had largely equalized capital costs among various competing countries, except for the continuing uncertainty about U.S. dollar exchange rates and the differentials given those industries directly assisted by government.[33] But many U.S. industries now had to make up for underinvestments in the 1980s.

Government policies and higher U.S. capital costs were by no means the sole cause of U.S. competitive problems. Top managers were often inexcusably late in adopting available technologies and quality improvement techniques, dismantling outmoded bureaucracies, and breaking out of oligopolistic management practices. It is notable that within virtually all U.S. industries facing similar external constraints—including those of capital costs, government regulations, and international pressures—some individual U.S. companies performed exceedingly well. For example, in the most besieged industries, Intel and Motorola (in semiconductors), Chaparral and Inland Steel (in ferrous metals), and Newport News (in shipbuilding) did very well despite their industry's performance, which was considerably less effective. Although government policies were important, such major differences in company performance suggest that external causes, such as high capital costs or government inefficiencies, were not alone responsible for U.S. companies' lagging investment, technological development, innovation, and competitiveness during this era.

**FIGURE 11.2**
**Typical Time Horizons by Industry, Mid-to-Late 1980s**

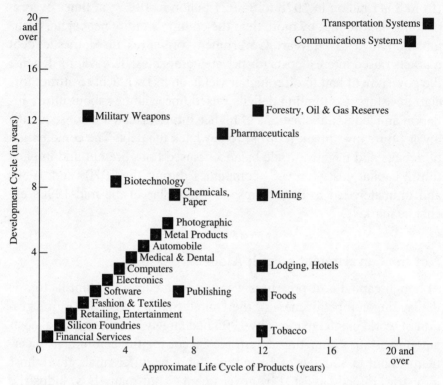

*Approximate mid-1980s time horizons (based on industry interviews) represent an average of the major planning cycles for these industries. Each company and project may vary, as indicated in the text. Some development cycles have dropped radically since 1990.*

## A Strange Anomaly

In fact, government actions may well have been the single greatest offset to shortsighted U.S. management practices in the 1970s and 80s. As we investigated the data in Figure 11.2 of typical time horizons by industry and compared them with further analyses of where the United States has been most and least competitive, we noticed a strange anomaly. The United States was competitive both in the longest-term industries (like energy, lumber, communication systems, biotechnology, aircraft, utilities, transportation, pharmaceuticals, and chemicals) and the very short-term industries (like software, retailing, entertainment, financial services, and publishing). The places where U.S. competitiveness was most severely damaged in the 1980s were in the intermediate-term

**FIGURE 11.3**

**Net Exports as a Fraction of Shipments for Selected Industries, 1979–1988, versus Characteristic Time Horizon (years)**

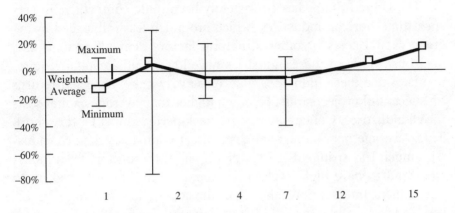

Source: Figure prepared by John Ehlers.

*Net exports in midterm year time horizon (two to seven years) industries were weaker than those in shorter- or longer-term industries in the 1980s.*

(three- to five-year) horizon industries (like steel, automobiles, electronic appliances, and machine tools).

It is extremely difficult to find meaningful objective measures of international competitiveness on an industry-wide basis because the ranges of company performance within each industry are very wide. However, Figure 11.3, which analyzes exports versus time horizons of U.S. industries in the 1980s, in combination with rankings by other knowledgeable competitiveness analysts, seems to confirm this general hypothesis.[34] If the major cause of competitive problems was capital cost, one would expect the long-time-horizon industries to be America's least competitive. Yet they have been among the nation's most competitive. Why has this peculiar pattern developed?

## Government Assistance to Long-Term Industries

Elements of federal policy have overcome or ameliorated major time horizon problems in virtually every industry in which the United States is most competitive today. This is especially true for those industries with very long time horizons. Table 11.1 outlined the specific types of policy support each received. In each case, government actions effectively decreased some critical factor cost: R&D expenses, development risks, first market risks, unfair competitive actions, capital availability, externality costs, demand instabilities, catastrophic risk insurance, and so on.

The United States has consistently been quite competitive in very short-time-horizon industries, which are much less influenced by average capital costs or other structural factors demanding long time horizons. Many of these industries have lower initial capital requirements. Since these industries tend to be very risky, expected returns on successful projects must be much higher than average capital costs for all industries. Concomitantly, payback periods must be very short. Thus, average national capital costs affect companies in such industries much less stringently. In addition, all of these short-term industries tend to have high levels of competition and do not need much government intervention other than those generic regulations necessary to level the playing field. Consequently, the fiscal and monetary policies of the 1970s and 1980s that led to high U.S. capital costs did not tend to affect their innovations as heavily.

The United States has also seemed to do extremely well in two other types of industry. First are those where development cycles are short but life cycles for products and services are much longer (like lodgings and hotels, foods, and tobacco and cigarettes). Success in most of these industries derives from establishing brand names, mass merchandising, and market positioning based on careful segmentation and market analysis. These are realms where the United States enjoys unique advantages from its large integrated markets, open publication policies, large services and data infrastructures, and deep mass-marketing expertise. Even here, however, one can argue that some industries (like cigarettes and tobacco products) have been heavily subsidized. Many foods have enjoyed hidden or direct subsidies. And hotels and lodgings were long favored by tax laws that selectively encouraged real estate investments. At the other extreme are long-development-cycle industries that have relatively short life cycles once their products go into use (like biotechnology to date or some military weapons). Such industries have obviously been heavily influenced by the government's market-creation or long-term research investment policies that have offset critical risks.

## The Strange Anomaly: Two- to Four-Year Industries

Most intriguing is the fact that the industries where the United States became least competitive (automobiles, machine tools, metal products, electronic appliances) were those with development times and life cycles in the two- to four-year range. One explanation may be that these were industries where capital investments were heavy and few direct U.S. government subsidies recently existed (although supports were often present in earlier years). Patent protection has not been as important in these industries as it is in chemicals, pharmaceuticals, or biotechnology. All were industries where (1) mass markets existed for products that could be improved by constant quality changes, (2) markets were price sensitive, (3) plant and equipment investments were relatively high, (4) U.S. investments were relatively antiquated, and (5) labor was an important component of costs. Such industries became natural attack points for countries, like those in East Asia, that had both capital and labor cost advantages.

For years, U.S. companies in these industries had been protected by America's geographical isolation and the difficulties foreigners had in obtaining U.S. distribution or sophisticated information about the U.S. marketplace. As transportation, distribution, and information technologies eliminated these entry barriers, they facilitated much greater foreign competitiveness. Unfortunately, managements in these "smokestack" industries were slow in responding to the changed competitive environment that foreign governments' policies and new technologies had engendered.

## Negative Government Impacts on Time Horizons

The ledger is hardly one-sided. The federal government and its regulatory systems often were major factors in diminishing specific industries' time horizons. The government's continuing deficits have been the single greatest pressure increasing U.S. capital costs. Regulations (such as those supporting the Clean Air and Water Acts, Endangered Species, Toxic Substances, and Occupational Health and Safety Acts) have often been issued at the last minute with less than adequate consideration of cost-benefit implications. When this occurs, U.S. costs and risks increase, and U.S. companies' planning capabilities decline, relative to foreign competitors. The willingness of courts to entertain almost any product liability or environmental claims, and the relative size and randomness of damage awards when they do issue, also raise corporate risks and tend to foreshorten the time within which companies rationally seek to recover their investments. Prolonged court cases, drug clearances, plant sitings, licensing procedures, and other government-required permissions also force companies to seek higher short-term returns in order to offset perceived risks. While the goals

## FIGURE 11.4
## Investment Versus Economic Growth

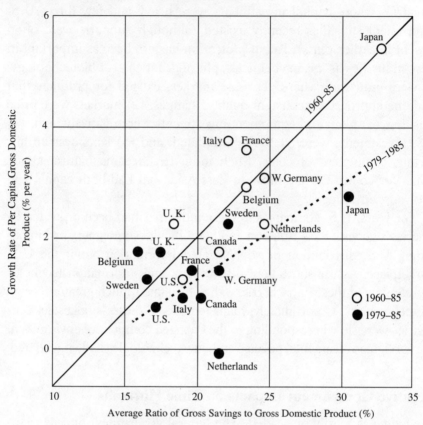

Source: Ralph Landau, "U.S. Economic Growth," *Scientific American* (June 1988): p. 50. Reproduced by special permission.

*Growth per capita correlates strongly with savings rates.*

of such regulation and the protections government interventions provide are often desirable, the way they are implemented and adjudicated often creates needless uncertainties and increases costs and risks for American-based companies relative to others.

Political pressures often inordinately compress time horizons to the two- to four-year frames of election cycles or the one-year frame of government budgetary cycles. This effect has been most apparent in funding for education, construction, aerospace, research, energy, and environmentally based industries. Serious inefficiencies occur because these industries cannot systematically build their technological and institutional resources for the future. The National Academy of Engineering has recommended some relatively straightforward changes in government poli-

**FIGURE 11.5**

**Savings and Investment, 1970–92 Average**

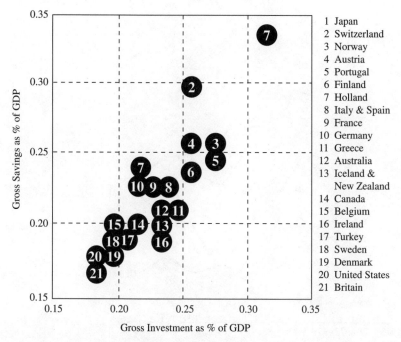

Source: Reproduced by special permission from "Global Capital Flows: Too Little, Not Too Much," *Economist*, June 24, 1995, p. 91

*Savings rates and investment as a percentage of GNP correlate highly. The U.S. and Britain have been at the bottom of both categories.*

cies or procedures to mitigate many of the government's negative impacts on corporate time horizons, and hence innovation, when they do occur.[35] Chapter 13 will suggest further policy remedies. However, as noted earlier, the major responsibility for developing and maintaining company time horizons rests with corporate top managers themselves.

## Impacts on Government Functions

The most tragic impacts of high-deficit, high-money-cost strategies are on a government's own functions, notably on those programs with long delayed impacts, like environmental, educational, and infrastructure building programs. For example, at a 10% interest rate—low for many countries—economic rationality asserts that governments can spend only $73 today to achieve a $1 million gain 100 years from now. If interest rates were 2%, they could afford a $250,000 investment to achieve a

**FIGURE 11.6**

**Household Savings as a Percentage of Disposable Income**

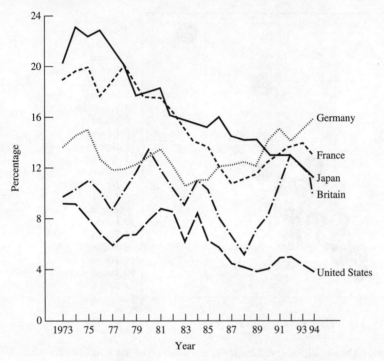

Source: Reproduced by special permission from "Whatever Happened to That Rainy Day?" *Economist*, January 21, 1995, p. 68.

*U.S. personal savings rates are among the world's lowest.*

similar gain. Such capital-cost-induced disincentives are especially important in less developed countries, where inflation, risks, and hence interest rates are higher than in most affluent countries. Further, high inflation rates in those countries put a premium on consuming now versus saving for the future, exactly the opposite of what all economic studies say encourages investment, innovation, economic growth, and wealth generation. (see Figure 11.4.)

Policies that discriminate against savings or encourage current consumption, as U.S. deficit spending and tax policies have, discourage the industrial investment, technological development, and infrastructure creation that are the very touchstones of future wealth. Not only do such policies decrease productivity directly, they increase the burden on the younger population to support the elderly, increase national overheads, and make it more difficult for entrepreneurs to assemble capital for innovations that could break the cycle.[36] In both developed and de-

**FIGURE 11.7**

**Comparative U.S. Ten-Year Bond Interest Rates**

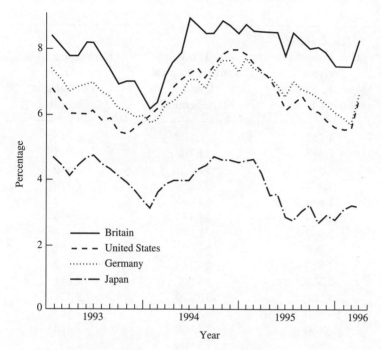

Source: Reproduced by special permission from "Finance and Economics," *Economist*, March 16, 1996, p. 74.

*U.S. ten-year interest rates have been high compared to other major competitor nations.*

veloping countries, macroeconomic stability, low inflation, and savings-inducing policies go hand in hand with increased innovation, economic growth, and environmental protection. They engender confidence about the future, lower capital costs, and make market signals easier for decision makers to interpret. Unfortunately, U.S. fiscal and tax policies have long run counter to these truisms, with the result that the U.S. per household savings rate is less than 5% compared to France's and Japan's 13 to 14% and Germany's and Britain's 10 to 12%. And U.S. ten-year government bond (virtually risk free) interest is twice that of Japan's (see Figures 11.5 through 11.7).

## INCENTIVES WORK

When government does intervene to change incentives in positive directions, it can release large entrepreneurial and innovative re-

**TABLE 11.2**

**U.S. Venture Capital Industry, 1969–1994**

**($ millions)**

| Year | New Capital Committed to Private Venture Capital Firms Only | Total Venture Capital Under Management[a] | Disbursements to Portfolio Companies |
|------|------|------|------|
| 1994 | 3,765 | 34,126 | 2,741 |
| 1993 | 2,545 | 34,760 | 3,071 |
| 1992 | 2,548 | 31,074 | 2,540 |
| 1991 | 1,271 | 32,870 | 1,348 |
| 1990 | 1,847 | 35,950 | 1,922 |
| 1989 | 2,399 | 34,430 | 3,395 |
| 1988 | 2,947 | 31,100 | 3,847 |
| 1987 | 4,200 | 29,000 | 3,977 |
| 1986 | 3,300 | 24,100 | 3,242 |
| 1985 | 2,300 | 19,600 | 2,681 |
| 1984 | 3,200 | 16,300 | 2,771 |
| 1983 | 3,400 | 12,100 | 2,581 |
| 1982 | 1,400 | 7,600 | 1,454 |
| 1981 | 867 | 5,800 | 1,155 |
| 1980 | 661 | 4,500 | 608 |
| 1979 | 170 | 3,800 | 457 |
| 1978 | 216 | 3,500 | 288 |
| 1977 | 15 | 2,500–3,000 | 159 |
| 1976 | 28 | | 107 |
| 1975 | 20 | | 92 |
| 1974 | 25 | | 100 |
| 1973 | 33 | | 201 |
| 1972 | 30 | | 128 |
| 1971 | 91 | | 134 |
| 1970 | 78 | | 83 |
| 1969 | 121 | 2,500–3,000 | 100 |

Source: *Annual Review: Venture Capital of Industry*, published by Venture Economics, Inc., Boston, 1995.

[a]Total venture capital under management remained static from 1969 through 1977 at approximately $2.5 to $3.0 billion, with new funding more or less equal to withdrawals. Placements then exploded as tax laws became more favorable.

sponses. In the 1800s, it opened the West through land grants and monopolies given to railroad and communications companies. Its depletion allowances in the 1920s through 1960s encouraged high (perhaps even excessive) rates of mineral and energy development by U.S. companies.

In more recent years, 1970s tax law provisions that offered tax shelters for real estate ventures shifted entrepreneurial endeavors into that realm on such an unprecedented scale that real estate project investments quickly surpassed those of all industrial companies in the United States. Reversal of these special provisions in the 1984–1986 tax laws (consciously stimulated by policy thinking) immediately drew investments into the industrial sector again. When the government established tax-sheltered Keogh, IRA, and pension fund accounts, it helped generate the $2.6 trillion mutual fund industry and vastly expanded corporate access to investment funds. For a short while, the dramatically lowered marginal tax rates on upper incomes in 1978 and 1986 supported a shift from consumption toward investment, which helped revive the venture capital industry and return key U.S. industries to greater competitiveness during the late 1980s (see Table 11.2). These investments became the basis for one of the longest-term, low-inflation periods of growth in U.S. history. And contrary to much political and press rhetoric, the highest incomes increased the percentage and amounts of taxes they paid, while taxes on lower incomes dropped (see Figure 11.8).

## Not Just Financial Incentives

Successful incentives have not always been financial or tax based. The National Defense Education Act (GI Bill) following World War II encouraged millions of veterans to complete college educations and provided the intellectual infrastructure for the rapid growth of innovative high-technology industries in the 1950s and 1960s. By the late 1960s, college education had become a norm in the United States, with over 40% of all eligible students participating; Europe's universities remained elitist, with only 13% to 16% participating. While America's World War II allies chose to control prices and to continue wartime rationing in the postwar era, the United States after a brief period turned to free market incentives. Despite dire warnings of runaway inflation and shortages that would result, after a few months' hiccup the U.S. economy went into the long low-inflation 1950s boom, while Europe encountered continuing shortages and stagflation. A similar shock strategy in the early 1980s,

**FIGURE 11.8**
**Tax Paid by Different Income Groups, 1990**

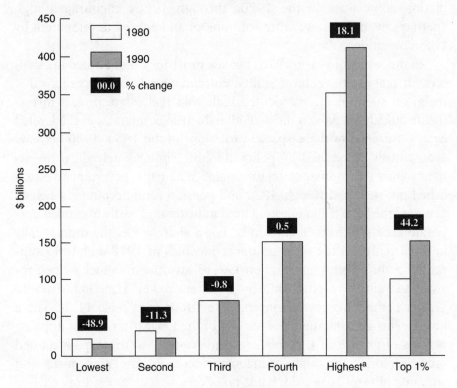

Source: Reproduced by special permission from "Tax-Making, Tax-Breaking," *Economist,* February 4, 1995, p. 27.

Note: Excludes social security taxes and local taxes.

[a]Includes the top 1 percent.

*The actual levels and percentage of taxes paid by higher-income groups in the United States expanded as their marginal tax rates dropped.*

deregulating energy prices after earlier attempts at price fixing in the 1970s, quickly broke the back of an energy crisis inflation in that era.

Similarly, after years of protecting the telecommunications industry, the government and courts opened up U.S. competition in the mid-1980s as new technologies made such competition feasible. Again, this action preceded that of most other OECD countries by a decade,* providing a powerful new infrastructure for U.S. competition in the 1990s. America's generally free trade policies, though often painful to individual companies and industries, ensured that U.S. consumers benefited from

*OECD: Organization for Economic Cooperation and Development.

the global competition that developed in the 1980s, while more protected OECD countries' consumers, notably those in Japan, paid much higher prices for the same goods. Without significant cost during this era, the government-sponsored Baldrige Awards brought a new awareness toward quality. When positive incentives were used, they worked.

## Failures Ignore Incentives

By contrast, the government's greatest policy failures have occurred when the marginal nature of incentives was ignored or when perverse incentives were put in place. The most striking of these have been in the government's handling of incentives in U.S. welfare, alternative energy, health care, western water supply, and agricultural price support programs. Incentive theory suggests that people respond to the differentials between the gains offered by one action versus another, including inaction; rewards should relate to results sought; and free goods are always overexploited. The devastating effects in the welfare, health care, and agricultural arenas are increasingly being recognized here and in Europe, but the same principles apply in myriad other fields.

• In airlines, the courts have kept bankrupt firms in business (no cost, all gain), thus ensuring huge overcapacity and submarginal profits for all players. Deregulation of banks—while insuring their accounts and acting as if banks and S&Ls were too important to their communities to be allowed to go bankrupt—led to outrageous risk taking with depositors' money and great public cost. Government agency personnel's pay depends largely on the number of people they supervise, not on net value-added or agency efficiency; hence bureaucracies grow. For years various government agencies like the National Science Foundation, The National Institutes of Health, and the Department of Agriculture insisted that the technologies created under their grants be available free to all comers, and few private companies were willing to undertake the investments and risks of exploitation. Yet when private patents were finally allowed, innovation and exploitation blossomed.

Negative incentives have clearly impaired innovation. As the U.S. airlines' economics collapsed, their capacities to be lead technology customers for Boeing diminished. Small commercial bank and S&L innovations lagged as these potentially large IT markets faltered. Government agencies' pay policies encouraged underinvestment in IT to an extent that many agencies' systems—notably the Federal Aviation Administration and the Internal Revenue Service—reached critically dangerous levels while their bureaucracies grew unnecessarily. And major cost-reducing innovations did not occur in health care practice until changed policies shifted fee-for-service pricing toward capitation, diagnosis-related group (DRG) pricing, and more open competition.

## Expenditures Create Perpetual Support Polities

The worst misallocations occur when relatively small initial program expenditures or incentives build sufficiently to create strong support polities that continue misallocation pressures for generations. This is especially true when programs begin to support small but powerful interest groups in multiple state, regional, agency, and congressional jurisdictions. Some of these groups become major sources of election funding, actively resisting needed corrections. The B-2 bomber, tobacco support, water resources, Medicare, and superconducting-super-collider programs are classic examples. Often the results are not just wasteful, but outrageous.

• In August 1985, a team of economists supported by Ford Foundation grants reported that in the Bureau of Reclamation's Central Valley project in California, the Westlands Water District consumed about 25% of the water the entire project had for sale. By their calculations, the true cost of the water used by Westlands was $97.00 per acre-foot, although farmers were being charged only $7.50 to $11.80 per acre-foot. Taking the average farm size in the district into account, this translated into a subsidy of around $500,000 per farm, or $217.00 per acre yearly. The average total revenue from an irrigated acre of Westlands was only $290.00. However, the main Westlands crop was cotton, which at the time was in substantial excess supply because of price supports and other subsidies. Overall, the Bureau of Reclamation's project was paying a huge subsidy to a few large California growers to raise crops that were driving cotton farmers in Texas, Louisiana, and Mississippi (who had plenty of free natural water) out of business. Once water sales to farmers began, a strong polity of farmers, farmworkers, farm suppliers, local businesses, federal bureaucracies, farm towns, and county governments lined up to support the misallocation in perpetuity.[37]

## Perverse Subsidies

Many governments perversely support misallocations through subsidies by holding down electricity or gasoline prices and by not enforcing pollution standards on their industries, thus redirecting their limited investment funds into fields that harm their own people.

• By subsidizing the clear-cutting of tropical forests, inefficient milling practices, and the creation of uneconomic ranches and farms, many tropical countries have captured only 10 to 20% of their forests' value and have forgone the unmeasured wealth their animal populations, chemical and pharmaceutical, and future forest yields could have attained. Robert Repetto estimates that only 1% of these forests are being managed for sustainable yields.[38] Germany subsidizes coal mining, thus paying thrice—the real cost of coal, plus the subsidy, plus pollution—for its fuels. Most rich countries subsidize agriculture, encouraging monoculture and greater use of fertilizers and pesticides—and higher environmental costs—than mixed cropping would.

In the United States, the greatest anomalies have tended to occur when regulations or programs in one large department of government were inadequately coordinated with those of another. Some inconsistencies are inherent in the fact that large institutions must serve many conflicting parties and power interests. These are not artifacts of government alone. Large private industries can also cause major misallocations of resources to serve special short-term interests. Tobacco and asbestos companies, for example, continued to make products they knew to be dangerous, and large mining and manufacturing companies for generations created lunar landscapes around their plants, ignoring the health of their communities, the safety of their workers, and potentially crippling future liability claims.

In most national policy areas, positive net incentives—not direct expenditures—allow the highest leverage for government interventions. In fact, a policy will only be successful if incentives are strong enough to change management or consumer behavior in the private sector. Private behavior depends most on perceived net incentives (potential capturable benefits minus personal costs)—the WIIFM (What's In It For Me) calculation. As one contemplates the rapidly moving software, information, and services economy of the future, attempting to direct specific programs centrally will be impossible. Incentives will be the most crucial element guiding directions, and the more market-like they are, the better.

## Eliminating Barriers to Development

The government's capacity to quickly break down institutional barriers to progress will also be vital. In the past the U.S. government has frequently intervened to remove such barriers in priority areas. Several such interventions helped establish U.S. dominance in the critical industries of the World War II and postwar era. For example, working closely with Merck and other pharmaceutical producers, the government set aside innumerable antitrust and regulatory barriers to rush penicillin to the World War II battlefronts and operating rooms of the world. Similarly:

• In the summer of 1941, the Petroleum Administration for War (PAW) was established to coordinate the development of petroleum products (notably 100-octane gasoline) for the World War II effort. The government's main role was to provide "the direction, coordination, red tape slashing, and encouragement to accomplish the impossible."[39] In order that the fullest cooperation of the industry might be possible without conflicting with antitrust laws, PAW obtained Department of Justice approval for joint research and for exchanges between companies and individuals of information concerning processes, products, patents, experimental data, and general knowledge.[40] In four years government-industry cooperation increased 100-octane output a thousandfold. Similar techniques were used to accelerate synthetic rubber production. Within eighteen months the nation moved from no synthetic rubber output to production on the scale needed to serve both the U.S. economy and history's largest war effort.[41] Both industries became postwar giants.

• By breaking down barriers, the government has often readjusted competitive structures to encourage new forms of innovation without "picking winners." In the 1980s, as a result of a Commerce Department task force on innovation, antitrust constraints to cooperation on precompetitive research and joint equipment development were set aside to enable consortia like Sematech and MCC, and the seventeen-year coverage for patents on pharmaceuticals was adjusted to begin (assuming diligent development efforts) at the end of the FDA clearance cycle. The government also eliminated intermodal transportation regulations, which had prevented the introduction of containerization, piggybacking, and single-carrier responsibility for multimodal pickup, trunk, and local delivery services. The Telecommunications Act of 1995 eliminated long-standing barriers to technology diffusion and competition among the broadcasting, telephone, ground telecommunications, satellite, and cable industries.

Each of these interventions rapidly created whole new industry structures and released entrepreneurial energies with huge economic impacts.

## Similar Opportunities Today

Similar opportunities exist in the health care, banking, software, education, and environmental industries today. If it is successful in actions now being initiated, the federal government could lower the cost of health care by at least 50%. Specifically, constructive interventions could:

• *Speed drug clearances.* New drugs that cure diseases, support new procedures, or ease morbidity have been among the few efforts that have genuinely lowered medical costs. Yet drug clearances now commonly cost $200 million to $300 million and take an average of seven to eight years. At an average capital cost (not risk discounted) of 15%, this implies that a $400 to $600 million investment must be covered through product sales. Even if there were no manufacturing costs, firms would have to sell 400 to 600 million pills at $1.00 each to break even. One of the most effective ways to lower drug costs would be to amplify current efforts to speed FDA clearances and thus move forward the time when open competition can lower drug prices.

• *Force standardized billing forms.* Hospitals claim that a substantial portion (15 to 20%) of their administrative costs could be eliminated by standardizing billing and payment practices across all payors.

• *Eliminate excessive malpractice suits.* The combination of defensive medicine and insurance against malpractice has been estimated to cost 30% in many medical specialties and 15 to 20% for well-run hospitals. Many proposals exist for accomplishing this; few have been passed into law.

• *Increase medical outcomes analysis and dissemination.* Because of the difficulties of collecting longitudinal data concerning outcomes, most doctors do not know on a statistically valid basis how effective their procedures are in the long run. Classic studies by epidemiologist John Wennberg indicate that doctors in one geographical area may use certain surgical procedures 10 to 15 times as frequently (without proven medical benefit) as doctors in another area (standardized for demographic differentials).[42] When these variations are fed back to doctors, they tend to voluntarily move their practices closer to the norm, and to support clinical studies to define most effective treatment options.

• *Facilitate the "last thirty days" decision.* Thirty to 50% of an average person's lifetime medical costs occur during the last thirty to

sixty days of life. Methods to allow "painless rights to dying" for patients, while preventing abuses, could save as much as one-half of these
costs.

• ***Encourage managed care and publish benchmark practices.***
Incentives to use outpatient, special therapy facilities, and home
care can release expensive hospital space and lower care costs substantially. Estimates indicate that 10 to 15% of hospital care costs
could be recaptured if these were widely implemented. To decrease
their costs, insurance companies have already moved from being
merely payors to managing the care process through preferred
provider organizations and preventive care on employers' premises
or in health maintenance organizations. More extensive publication
of observed best practices and methods to prevent abuses could help
all parties.

• ***Develop cost-sharing incentives.*** Eliminating the perception that
health care is a free good (through forced cost sharing by most patients,
providing incentives for preventive care, or prioritizing access to expensive curative procedures and facilities) has proved to reduce costs dramatically when effective and medically appropriate guidelines are
developed.

Private market mechanisms have started many of these changes in
the $1.1 trillion health care industry. However, government actions
on these items could achieve further dramatic cost reductions, improve medical care quality, and encourage innovation in many
spheres. Similarly, more market-like, information-sharing, barrier-
breaking, and incentive-based interventions could—without substantial government investments—radically improve output values in
other public service areas like environmental controls, education, and
transportation.

## Current Policy Approaches

The Clinton administration and Congress have recently endorsed many
types of policies that led to economic growth in the past. Among the
most important actions of the past few years are:

• Extending the R&D tax credit (through June 1995, when it lapsed).
• Lowering capital gains taxes on investments in start-up companies.
• Extending patent protection through the General Agreement on
  Tariffs and Trade (GATT).

**TABLE 11.3**
**Highlights of the President's R&D Budget, 1997:**
**Total R&D by Agency (budget authority, $ millions)[a]**

| | FY 1996 (Est.) | FY 1997 Request | FY 1997 Approved | Change, FY 1996–1997 |
|---|---|---|---|---|
| Department of Defense | $35,842 | $35,522 | $37,592 | 4.9% |
| NASA | 9,416 | 9,700 | 9,263 | -1.6 |
| Department of Energy | 6,057 | 6,604 | 6,260 | 3.4 |
| Health and Human Services | 12,077 | 12,620 | 12,998 | 7.6 |
| *National Institutes of Health* | *11,443* | *11,901* | *12,227* | *6.9* |
| National Science Foundation | 2,400 | 2,479 | 2,424 | 1.0 |
| Department of Agriculture | 1,489 | 1,495 | 1,543 | 3.6 |
| Department of Interior | 622 | 580 | 573 | -7.9 |
| Department of Transportation | 602 | 671 | 626 | 4.1 |
| Environmental Protection Agency | 528 | 628 | 593 | 12.3 |
| Department of Commerce | 932 | 1,226 | 1,004 | 7.7 |
| All other | 1,246 | 1,207 | 1,113 | -2.8 |
| **Total R&D** | **71,111** | **72,731** | **73,991** | **4.0** |
| Defense R&D[b] | 38,444 | 36,260 | 40,454 | 5.2 |
| Nondefense R&D | 32,667 | 34,471 | 33,537 | 2.7 |
| *Basic research* | *14,431* | *14,700* | *14,816* | *2.7* |

[a]Includes conduct of R&D and R&D facilities.
[b]Includes DOD R&D and atomic energy defense R&D in DOE.

Source: *Issues in Science and Technology* (Winter 1996–1997).

*R&D expenditures are shifting toward nondefense needs, particularly health and human services.*

- Continuing support for basic research through NIH and NSF.
- Increasing technology-based educational initiatives.
- Coordinating cross-agency S&T endeavors through the National Science and Technology Council.[43]

The president's proposed S&T strategy emphasized nine principles for 1996 S&T budget priorities:

1. Peer review.
2. Human resources development.
3. Fundamental science.
4. Integrated defense and civilian research.
5. Integrating environmental objectives into other goals.
6. Cost-sharing partnerships.
7. Anticipatory R&D.
8. International cooperation.
9. Equity and diversity.[44]

These are all laudable objectives but do not address some of the serious issues affecting growth in the services, software, and intellect-based economy of the late 1990s. And the record on support for improved national databases and attacking environmental and health problems as markets has been poor to sporadic. The administration's $73 billion budget, as submitted to Congress, emphasized many important shifts in S&T emphasis—from military to civilian, from big science to small science, from energy development to environmental protection, and from physics to information and biology-based sciences—and a strong component of educational support. Only some were implemented. (See Table 11.3.) Chapters 12 and 13 will suggest the major lines of further shifts needed.

## SUMMARY

In any national technology strategy, private market mechanisms should be used to the extent possible. However, history shows that government actions have helped create trillions of dollars in new industries and innovation opportunities that otherwise would not have existed. Many of the nation's most successful industries today have benefited from such interventions. These include both generic policies (like interest rates, education, or standard setting) and very selective actions supporting emerging industries, public utilities, agriculture, mining and basic metals, railroads, airlines, energy, aircraft, software, computers, telecommunications, health care, education, biotechnology, and consumer products. To argue that these interventions have not created wealth is fatuous. The question is not whether governments should intervene but where and how. Experience suggests that governments have been most effective when they increase private market efficiencies, help create new freestanding markets, break down institutional barriers to innovation, extend corporate time horizons, and provide strong differential incentives for savers, innovators, producers, and learners. While not always efficient, these interventions have undoubtedly been highly effective in the past.

As populations increase, natural resources are depleted, urbanization grows, health and security problems expand, nature's recycling systems are overwhelmed, and complex new technologies are needed to solve problems, the need for effective government intervention is likely to expand. A determined effort will be required to prevent these needs from converting themselves into huge government bureaucracies. Many new demands will require government support in some form; without it, innovation and economic growth will suffer. The challenge and opportunity lies in approaching these new demands as what they are—public markets aggregating individual demands for a higher quality of life—and exploiting these new opportunities as extensions of the marketplace.

# 12

# National Technology Strategies: Creating Public Markets

Why are national strategies needed at all? Why not just leave the market alone and get government out of the marketplace? There are several important reasons:

- Unfettered markets frequently allocate national resources extremely poorly.
- Government actions often create entirely new public markets that generate large growth opportunities for the nation and for private companies.
- Government can support many classes of value-creating innovation that private markets rationally cannot.
- When properly implemented, government actions make private markets much more efficient and effective.

## OVERCOMING MARKET FAILURES

However successful private markets may be in many circumstances, they often allocate total economic and S&T resources poorly. Indeed, they can actually decrease innovation if not carefully modulated by government actions. This occurs in a number of situations.

## When Individual Buyers and Sellers Do Not Internalize All Their Transaction Costs

The most widely recognized failure occurs when buyers and sellers do not internalize all costs of their transactions. When automobile makers, fertilizer producers, metal producers, or packaging companies do not absorb the full costs of their products' disposal or use, their products will be overproduced (and underpriced) at the margin compared to other goods and services. Wealth arbitrarily goes to one set of producers at a genuine cost to others. Deduct the full property losses and clean-up costs of misused spray paint from the industry's profits and the net is a large negative value. Underabsorption of such industries' true costs unfairly discriminates against other goods, services, or alternate technologies that have fewer externalities. This kind of underpricing has long discriminated against services—which generally create fewer externalities than manufactures—for example, in favor of automobiles and against mass transit. The best remedy would be to force both producers and users to internalize all their relevant costs. But complications occur when it is difficult to charge each (producing or using) party directly for its costs or when it is more efficient to handle major externalities, such as building roads or removing wastes, collectively rather than individually.

Since all "externalities" for a single industry are "internalities" for the whole society, any distortions in allocation among industries will lower a nation's total efficiency and its standards of living. For example, if the whole nation must pay $3 billion to remove excess chemical fertilizer from farm wastewater, while a biodegradable fertilizer costs farmers only $2 billion, then consumers have given up $1 billion of their wealth to support uneconomic chemical production and agricultural practices. Each case of nonabsorption represents a unilaterally imposed industry tax on specific competing parties (and their product's consumers) without their approval. Under these circumstances, government can increase total societal gains versus costs by distributing costs more appropriately among producers and users.

Nonabsorption of externalities not only arbitrarily lowers competitive costs for the favored producers and prices for their customers (causing excess production of the uneconomic goods), it also decreases the incentives for innovation by both producers and users. Cost-reducing innovation is one of the frequently encountered benefits of well-conceived regulations that force internalization.[1] For example, many producers who used mercury in their processes when by-product wastes could be freely discharged into rivers found that they significantly lowered costs when they innovated to get rid of the mercury altogether. Regulations to reduce brown lung disease forced modernization, automation, and productivity improvements that helped competitiveness in the U.S. textile industry.[2] Enforced reprocessing of aluminum cans had similar benefits, as did the German refusal to allow dumping of the captured solid effluents from their central power stations into landfills. The latter created profitable new technologies for making lower-cost, better-quality wallboard for domestic construction and export. Such regulations are hardly onerous costs to the society. However, ill-conceived regulation can be very costly, as have been those for chlorine and organochlorine compounds.[3]

## When Individual Buyers Cannot Aggregate Demands Effectively

To create some markets, governmental bodies have to aggregate and dispense funds. The Highway Trust Fund, as a major example, allowed motorists to purchase transportation facilities they clearly could not buy individually. At the margin, the resulting "superhighway market" improved driving pleasure for millions, lowered national transportation costs, and decreased traffic accidents and deaths significantly. It also increased the markets for autos, trucks, gasoline, and spare parts. Similarly, governments have aggregated funds to satisfy demands for clean water supplies, pest controls, flood control, weather forecasting, air depollution, satellite launch systems, the Internet, and so on that individual parties could not have implemented on their own. All these created broad new innovation and market opportunities.

In other cases, government regulations aggregate individual demands and create or expand private markets with relatively little direct governmental expenditure.[4] For example, regulations of the FDA and the Department of Agriculture forced all companies to meet quality and safety standards that some producers would have rejected as too costly if they were not imposed on all players. These regulations aggregated consumer demands for purer and safer products, allowed responsible manufacturers to charge for these product features, and helped create the consumer confidence that is essential to the nation's profitable mass markets in foods, drugs, and household products. Few consumers today would like to return to an earlier age when charlatanism and unsanitary practices were common.

Properly structured, such interventions provide responsible goods and services producers with vastly expanded market opportunities they otherwise could not access.[5] In economic terms, they aggregate demands for safety or reliability features that consumers—at the margin—prefer as opposed to lower prices, greater risks, or other product features. Failure to recognize these demands becomes especially dire when an activity with relatively low cost to one party—either producer or user—imposes irreparable consequences on others. For example, builders of substandard housing, dams, or bridges (or the producers and users of guns, armor-penetrating bullets, or nerve gas) can increase their private gains by market transactions that later impose intolerable costs on others. A driver buying $20 of alcohol from a bar can impose death or dismemberment penalties on others not part of the transaction. Or children can be killed by inadequately packaged products. In these cases, regulations become methods of aggregating safety demands that market players would otherwise not respond to. In such instances, unfettered markets become an obscenity, not a desirable instrument of policy.

## When Established Institutions Have the Power to Constrain Innovation

Labor unions and their imposed work rules long thwarted innovation in many areas, as did the monopoly grants to communications, transportation, and electric power companies after these industries attained self-sustaining scale. If left in individual corporate hands, the large patent pools of Bell Laboratories and RCA could have substantially inhibited progress in the rapidly advancing electronics and telecommunications industries. By opening up these patent pools, the government released explosive potentials for millions of other innovators to create totally unexpected new markets, jobs, products, and services.[6] Similarly, the power of the highly integrated Big Three U.S. auto manufacturers for years encouraged oligopolistic behavior, significantly decreasing innovation, price, and quality benefits for U.S. automotive users. Only when new technologies and changed regulatory actions opened the market to new competitive possibilities did these firms extensively tap into the full innovation and value-added potentials that were available.

## When the Government Itself Is a Monopsony Buyer

A special case occurs when governments are the only potential buyers. War weapons, mass education, large dams, government buildings, intelligence technologies, municipal safety, and emergency systems are major examples. In these cases, policy mechanisms must replace the innovation generated by multiple competing customers' demands with surrogates that ensure highest value for the public rather than highest value for the power holders in government. Review panels, cost-benefit analyses, and open scrutiny of purchasing processes help overcome some of the inefficiencies in these markets. But cost-benefit analyses are often notoriously inaccurate. To be reasonably efficient, monopsony purchases generally require much more market-like incentives— like utilization cost sharing, voucher-value transfer, or tradeable quotas. Although monopsony markets are likely to be relatively inefficient, there are occasions when visionaries actually make them more effective than private markets operating alone might be. For example, the large public canal constructions at Suez and Panama championed by de Lesseps, the aircraft pioneering stimulated by General "Billy" Mitchell, and the radar, satellite, computer, and public health advances pushed by military, medical, and space visionaries all generated large increments of economic and social value much faster than private markets would have.

## When Risks Are Too Large for Individuals to Assume Safely

Because of excessive risks and long payoff times, private markets alone would probably not have created many of today's most advanced technologies as rapidly as government actions did. These include many space, biotechnology, system software, semiconductor, large computing, agricultural, public health, weather forecasting, environmental control, and advanced materials technologies. Large-scale impacts include the huge electric power, flood control, and water supply systems of the Tennessee, Colorado, and Columbia River basins; geosynchronous communications and global positioning systems; and, potentially, vaccines and drugs for devastating illnesses like cancer, Alzheimer's disease, ebola virus, or AIDS. In these cases probabilities of individual project success are too low, the need for interacting disciplines is too high, and times to payoff are too long for private companies to sponsor the needed integrated efforts. In such cases, governments can improve potential payoff-to-cost ratios by supporting a wider range of options, by extending benefits to a larger population, and in some cases by coordinating the various programs to lower total program costs. Since the real risk of these projects' achieving ultimate payoff is lower, so too should be the implicit and real interest rates used in their evaluation. And the public benefits the government can capture for the whole country legitimately justify investments that private companies would be unwise to undertake. When successful, such endeavors create whole new industries that otherwise would not exist.

## When There Are Large Intangibles That Cannot Be Valued

In some cases, very low-probability but high-impact events cannot be efficiently handled by markets—for example, the potential collapse of the ozone layer, earthquake damage, terrorist acts, war, nuclear meltdown, or ebola virus outbreaks. Similarly, the social costs of hackers disrupting air traffic controls or the banking system could be huge. The cost of such single events occurring could justify very large public expenditures for their prevention or correction, yet private market mechanisms could not reasonably be expected to provide needed resources. Government, in essence, creates a more efficient market to mitigate these fears through required insurance, anti-earthquake building standards, worldwide data-monitoring and intelligence collection, encryption research and network monitoring, emergency deployment units, environmental regulations, advanced health research, public health rules, earthquake or hurricane preparedness systems, military purchases, and so on. Government's attempts to deal with such legitimate fears have led to many major innovations and to very large but unmeasured security values to society.

## When Costs to Exploiters Do Not Increase As Resources Are Depleted

Another phenomenon, often called "the tragedy of the common," occurs when private individuals continue to benefit by exploiting a public resource at very low cost to themselves, until that resource becomes unavailable to anyone without prohibitive costs.[7] The two most startling current examples are the collapse of certain pelagic fisheries and the exploitation of the Ogallala Aquifer in the desert west of the United States. Because of overfishing that benefited individual parties, the formerly giant Norwegian, Canadian, and Grand Banks fisheries have been so depleted for many species that populations have dropped to 10% of their optimum levels and the fisheries will not recover their large economic potentials until fishing is substantially controlled.[8] Each party pumping the Ogallala Aquifer can benefit by using more water than would be economic if replacement costs were considered. Small personal gains (filling private swimming pools and irrigating heavily subsidized farms with Ogallala waters) can well lead to the long-term economic collapse of a major geographical region, America's semi-desert West.

• With a centrifugal pump and relatively shallow wells, a user can bring up 800 gallons of water per minute from the Ogallala Aquifer for only the cost of electricity for the pumps. People on barren grasslands found they could install self-propelled sprinklers which, through a quarter-mile-long pipeline with high pressure nozzles, could irrigate about 130 acres. Now these irrigated farms are sprinkled as green circles across the dry lands of the U.S. West, otherwise one of the poorest farming regions in the nation. Although the aquifer contains about 3 billion acre feet of water, at recent per capita rates of withdrawal it will be substantially depleted by 2025. While there is some disagreement, many geologists believe that much of this is "fossil water" from the Ice Ages and is not being replaced by snow or rainfall. Yet the cost of exploitation is so low that there is no incentive for any individual to stop pumping the water until it is depleted below replaceable levels.[9]

## When Secondary (or Public) Benefits Substantially Outweigh Private Benefits

No private individual or group of producers could probably have justified the risks, costs, and difficulties DARPA undertook in establishing the Internet because it would have been so difficult to get the institutional cooperation needed and to capture the benefits produced. Nevertheless, the potential benefits the Internet offers the public—through improved education, research, knowledge sharing, faster interactions, low-cost services access, and many billions of dollars in new market opportunities—clearly exceed its development costs by a massive margin. Similarly, secure worldwide electronic monetary systems, satellite weather forecasting, and access to libraries or databases provide public benefits immensely in excess of those capturable by any private party's developing, producing, or consuming such services solely for its own benefit.

Even when capturable at the national level, such benefits do not include the enormous peripheral benefits other countries can achieve by tapping into the systems. There are now at least 30 million Internet connections in 140 countries, with the number of users expected to be 150 to 200 million in the early years of the new century. Open software bidding systems, like GE's Trading Process Network (TPN) website, already allow smaller foreign suppliers to obtain bidding specifications and drawings rapidly and cheaply. Developing countries' suppliers can be brought up to date rapidly through these exchanges, helping the U.S. to support their economies through trade, not aid. GE says 15% of its TPN orders now go overseas. Within those countries, also, one can tap into the network and pose problems worldwide on an electronic bulletin board. Consequently, inventions do not have to be reproduced in every country or geographical area. For example, posting the question electronically, "How can one deal with a [particular] insect pest?" can lead to instant diffusion of knowledge, jumping over years in traditional invention and experimentation cycles for countries throughout the less developed world or in backwoods farm communities elsewhere. Although individual companies cannot capture the full benefits, such international leveraging can amplify the social benefits of non-market-driven innovations—and the value of the secondary markets they ultimately produce—well beyond those any private entrepreneur can realistically consider or capture.

## When Fairness Is More Important Than Immediate Cost

Goals and values other than economic cost-benefits dominate many transactions. For example, cost efficiency (up to a point) may be less important than reliability or fairness in court, educational, police protection, environmental, or health care systems. Similarly, a construction company's making another 1/4% on its ROI does not create social gain if the houses it builds quickly deteriorate into slums or deathtraps while it moves on to exploit unsuspecting victims in another town. Nor is a corporation's layoff of 40,000 people and the moving of its jobs into unregulated sweatshops along the Rio Grande (while increasing its CEO's salary to tens of millions of dollars) demonstrably desirable. The violence that drug lords inflict to increase their "efficiency" or to maximize their personal profitability-risk profiles may increase their industry's profits and satisfy identifiable demands, but few would regard the results as fair or socially optimizing. The society has a social interest (other than efficiency) in the type of outcome an action achieves. Some noneconomic goals are important in evaluating technology, innovation, and business performance at both the national and corporate levels. Fulfilling these is one reason for social control over some market decisions.

## In Important Areas of Life Quality

When all costs and benefits can be internalized within individual markets, market mechnisms tend to enhance individual freedom and choice, maximize innovation and net economic value produced, and come close to optimizing resource allocations. But often such conditions do not obtain. In fact, the greatest market inefficiencies occur in those very aspects of life that are most important to individuals' quality of life: their health, legal, personal safety, education, information access, water, air, catastrophe prevention, economic stability, safe housing, transportation, personal freedom, and recreational needs. It is extraordinarily unrealistic to argue that government should not have a role in these realms or in creating or aggregating markets that individual efforts alone cannot generate. As the world's population and complexity grow, there are likely to be more, not fewer, realms where public action is needed to create new and efficient markets. Developing and handling these demands as essential extensions of the market system may be the key to any real economic growth in the future.

## GOVERNMENTS CREATE NEW MARKETS

The kinds of market aberrations outlined above are important reasons for government intervention. But market misallocation is not the sole economic reason for such action. Contrary to much current dogma, any reasonable analysis will show that well-conceived public (or government) actions create large increments of economic growth. Properly constructed, such interventions create new public markets that are not merely transfers of resources from other demands.

Any opportunity, public or private, that calls forth previously uncommitted energies and resources can create growth. This is the essence of how real economic growth occurs in both the private and public sectors. If individuals work harder and buy an automobile, their private actions stimulate growth. If they and their neighbors jointly buy the same car for a car pool, they provide an equal direct stimulus. If 1,000 citizens buy a similar car as a public "school bus," they create the same direct sales, profits, and jobs. Yet they create an added benefit to the extent that this expenditure responds to a demand that private markets could not otherwise satisfy effectively. If the output (education) or satisfaction (convenience) benefits of the school bus are greater than those for the other private expenditures given up, the same investment increases total social value at the margin. Similarly, to the extent that publicly aggregated environmental, national security, public health or safety, or life quality demands add to existing private, household, or individual institutional demands, they will provide a genuine growth stimulus, regardless of whether the expenditures are private or public.

## Increasing Output Value Through Public Markets

Even when they merely substitute for certain private expenditures, public markets can increase real output values. This occurs whenever the public purchases are of higher relative value to the citizenry than the private items they could purchase for the same sum. For example, $10,000 jointly invested in a small town hospital's diagnostic equipment could have measurably more value to the townspeople whose life or health was saved (and to the town) than might the same sum privately spent on a new motorcycle. Even as insurance, the $5.00 the average person contributes to the diagnostic equipment could represent higher value received than if the same sum were spent to buy a videotape or CD recording. As people come to value life quality or environmental improvements more than many traditional products or services—as they often do in Europe, Canada, Austral-Asia, and Japan—equal resources and energies expended in such directions increase aggregate value produced even without an increase in total demand or resource inputs. Properly constructed public markets are simply extensions of private markets and choices.

Generally two conditions must be present for public markets to create real growth. First, there must be some underemployment of people and capital in the society. Given underinvested savings, underemployed people ready to work, unused technologies that could free people for other tasks, and undertrained and poorly managed workforces that produce less than they could, this condition is generally met. Second, the demand must be valid. Given comparable reinforcement for both public and private demands, people must want (or need) publicly generated life quality, safety, or environmental improvements (for example) more than other goods and services they could buy as individuals with the same resources. Although such preferences are hard to measure explicitly, they often can be determined within reason by market-like choice mechanisms or analytically by "indifference techniques" or relative rankings of possible alternatives. But for public markets to compete fairly in such surveys, they need the same degree of incentives, publicity, distribution access, sophisticated advertising, and sales support as competing private goods receive to influence potential purchasers.

## Markets, Not Costs

Granted these conditions, it is a major error to classify all expenditures for such things as sewage collection and treatment facilities, refuse disposal investments and services, health care facilities, plant or vehicular safety systems, freshwater supplies, recreation areas, educational systems, stack and exhaust decontamination devices, and so on as "national costs" to be borne by the country. This is a constant source of confusion in political discussions about environmental improvement. Only in the sense of other equally desirable growth opportunities forgone (if this actually happens) might this be true. But no one ever asks what such "alternative costs" are for snowmobiles, miniskirts, rock records, restaurants, sailboats, or third homes. These are simply regarded as markets—valid demands justifying the effort and resources needed to satisfy them. Conceptually, why should public markets be treated differently?

Monies effectively expended on needed equipment, construction, parts, overheads, or operating supplies for these markets both employ people and create desired output values just as private markets do. Such expenditures are no more social overhead costs to be derided by the society than the markets for fast automobiles, gasoline, movies, chic clothing, or safe athletic equipment are overhead costs. The people hired to provide park maintenance, health care, and education are no more national costs than the barbers, waiters, or dry cleaners who provide other desired private services. Do more hair stylists, at the margin, create more value than more teachers and health care professionals? The latter are simply people productively employed through different mechanisms to produce publicly consumed outputs.

The true nonmarket federal overheads are Medicaid ($82 billion), family welfare ($60 billion), military pensions and veterans' benefits ($53 billion), government employees' benefits ($40 billion), unemployment compensation ($26 billion), social security supplements ($24 billion), and farm price supports ($10 billion).[10] And some of these—like military and government employee benefits—may be simply unfunded payments for services already received.

Given the two prerequisites—of underemployed resources and valid demands—the true "national costs" of genuine public markets are considerably less than is touted. They are primarily the administrative or transaction costs of assembling and deploying the resources and the cost of overregulation—that is setting tighter or more rigid standards than are necessary to achieve the desired market effect. For example, the trihalomethane drinking water standard set in 1979 costs an estimated $200,000 per life saved, and restrictions on certain wood-preserving chemicals cost $6.3 trillion per life.[11] Such bureaucratically induced losses clearly need to be targeted. This is best done through market-like mechanisms. As in the private sector, each new person employed in an expanded field will create several new jobs in retailing, product, service, or other support fields. The taxes these people and their employers pay will easily cover the real overhead costs of collection, aggregation, and dispensing of funds to the marketplace.

Further, if work-competent people now receiving welfare were to perform such public tasks (receiving the same payments) instead, the net gains would be even greater; outputs could increase at no incremental cost. Add to this the innovative and economic stimulus of the markets themselves, generally higher employment and demand levels, and these markets can become not just self-sustaining but contribute to growth in other sectors just as any other primary markets do. For example, one wonders how well the U.S. economy would have performed over the past decade without a publicly stimulated health care market of over $1 trillion, growing at 15% per year.

## Data and Conceptual Anomalies

Why is it that we hear only of the "cost" of health care, environmental improvement, or occupational safety? In large part, the answer is that independent records of results exist, but benefits are never explicitly fed back into the national accounts. No credits appear against these expenditures for the increased outputs, employment, taxes, knowledge diffusion, or Keynesian or technological multiples they provide. *In fact, without these expenditures, the nation actually pays many very real life-quality and environmental costs and without receiving any of the market benefits afforded by solving these problems.*

The real costs of life quality degradation are actually being incurred but do not appear in the economic accounts. Inadequate housing and medical care mean people die earlier, are only partially productive, or are cared for by others whose efforts are not reflected in our national accounts. Underdeveloped public transportation and traffic control systems cost billions in personal delays, pollution, and equipment operating costs. Life risks are increased by inadequate safety controls, waste disposal, or air treatment systems. Polluted riverbeds, shorelines, and estuaries substantially reduce fishing, housing, and recreational values in nearby areas. And irreplaceable estuaries, farmlands, wetlands, forests, and national recreational areas are destroyed by uncontrolled resource exploitation. *It is doubly misleading that these genuine costs of inaction are not captured in the national accounts, yet the markets created to remedy them are considered costs.*

• From 1972 to 1993 American traffic fatalities dropped from 54,589 to 40,115, although there were 60 million more licensed drivers on the road collectively driving more than 1 trillion more miles per year. The average fatality rate per 100 million miles dropped from 5.5 in the 1960s to 1.7 today.[12] A combination of safety equipment, superhighways, lower driving speeds, and better enforcement of driving-while-intoxicated laws is largely responsible. Outputs of sulfur dioxide are down, and airborne lead has decreased by 90% in absolute terms.[13] Dangerously filthy rivers like the Hudson, "dead" lakes like Ontario, and destroyed beaches like those at Sydney, Australia, have regained much of their former aesthetic and utility value. But such benefits, repeated thousands of times over, appear nowhere in national economic accounts. Nor do the potentially huge, but currently unmeasurable, benefits that will probably accrue from governments' stimulating the chemical industry to cease production of ozone layer–destroying chlorofluorocarbons (CFSs).

These data and conceptual anomalies need systematic correction if we are to harness technology and innovation for maximum gain in the future. The *Annual Environmental Quality Report to the President* has repeatedly demonstrated that the benefits of environmental improvement, for example, are measurably greater than their costs.[14] The most thorough recent report on this topic suggests a positive payoff of about sixteen to one on environmental investments, not including other feedback and multiplier benefits.[15]

• This report, *The Benefits and Costs of the Clean Air Act 1970 to 1990,* estimates that benefits for that period outweigh costs by $6.4 trillion, with a 90% credible interval of $2.3 trillion to $14.2 trillion (1990 value dollars). This averages $20 in reduced health risks for each depollution dollar spent. Costs and benefits were based on a "no control" scenario (assuming no air controls were put in place since the 1970 act was passed) versus a "control" scenario based on documented evidence of depollution programs whether or not developed in response to the act. Between 1970 and 1990 there was a 40% emission reduction in sulfur oxide, 45% in volatile organic compounds, and 50% in carbon monoxide. Ozone concentrations decreased by 15%, airborne lead by 99%, and primary suspended particulates by 75%. Total estimated costs to achieve reductions were $436 million, but no credit was given for the effects of job growth in supplier industries, or the taxes paid by either the people employed in producing the results or the companies that sold materials, services, or equipment for them. Benefits were almost exclusively health benefits, primarily from reduced respiratory diseases, heart attacks, and lead damage to humans. None were included for pollution damage to crops, forests, waterways, buildings, or ecosystems.

Not recognizing such large benefits in public pronouncements and in the national accounts creates a totally false image of the real costs versus gains from life quality improvements as compared to industrial investments. While national accounts truncate with the collection of the "costs" of public markets without indicating any of their benefits, they set forth the value-added of the automobile, chemical, paper, energy, and agriculture fields (for example) without subtracting many of the very high real costs of injury, hospitalization, waste disposal, and environmental degradation these industries cause. For example, the cost of 43,000 deaths, 11 million tons of steel used, $110 billion in auto insurance premiums, $8 billion in auto disposal costs, and tens of billions of dollars in roads and pollution costs needs to be systematically subtracted from the auto industry's presumed contributions to the economy. There is a *multiple discrimination against public markets inherent in (1) their categorization as costs (not markets); (2) not reflecting the output values, jobs, taxes, secondary markets, and multiplier benefits they produce; and (3) not deducting from other industries' value-added the externalities they force on society.*

## Wrongheaded Opposition

In part because of data and analytical anomalies, public markets are often misunderstood and opposed by the very people who benefit most from them. For example, to clean up a river and the shorelines and beaches it affects requires sewage treatment plants, heat transfer units, improved storm drain and sewage systems, sophisticated monitoring equipment, and so on. The expenditures for sewage treatment plants (annualized) are approximately as follows: machinery and equipment, 26%; stone and clay products, 13%; metal products, 12%; other materials, 4%; and labor, 29%. Thus, water depollution creates multibillion dollar *markets* for steel and metal products, construction equipment, pumps and treatment equipment, meters, switches, wire, electronic controls, construction materials, glass, ceramics, bricks, mortar, plastics, and chemicals. OECD estimates these "equipment" markets for all depollution to be over $150 billion today, growing to over $220 billion by the year 2000. (See Figure 12.1.)

**FIGURE 12.1**
**Environmental Markets by Sector**

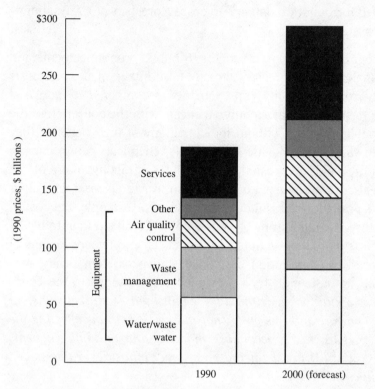

Source: Reproduced by special permission from "How to Make Lots of Money and Save the Planet, Too," *Economist*, June 3, 1995, p. 58.

*Environmental expenditures create multibillion dollar markets (not just costs) while re-ducing the actual costs society is paying for health care, property degradation, and loss of fishing, recreational, and property values as a result of pollution.*

Companies providing these materials and services obviously em-ploy people and generate profits from these markets. They pay taxes and increase demands for local consumer goods, and their compo-nent and supply requirements diffuse further to benefit suppliers in other industries.

• Consider the huge $1.1 trillion "cost" assigned to the U.S. health care industry. If considered as a public market—although admittedly currently inefficient—health care is really a large, growing, capital-in-tensive, high-technology, high-value-added industry providing good jobs, not just for those within the industry but for numerous supplier in-dustries. Patients clearly want (demand) its outputs. In addition to the

## FIGURE 12.2
## Health Care Spending per Person, 1994 (as % of GDP)

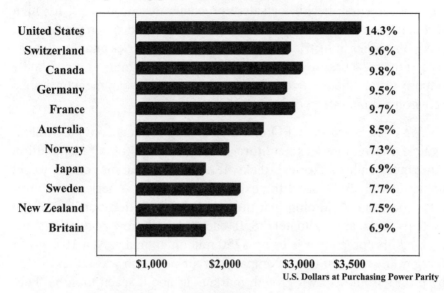

| | | |
|---|---|---|
| United States | | 14.3% |
| Switzerland | | 9.6% |
| Canada | | 9.8% |
| Germany | | 9.5% |
| France | | 9.7% |
| Australia | | 8.5% |
| Norway | | 7.3% |
| Japan | | 6.9% |
| Sweden | | 7.7% |
| New Zealand | | 7.5% |
| Britain | | 6.9% |

$1,000        $2,000        $3,000    $3,500

U.S. Dollars at Purchasing Power Parity

Source: Reproduced by special permission from *Economist*, August 3, 1996, p. 88.

*U.S. health care costs per person are higher than those of other advanced nations indicating inefficiencies, although in many areas the quality of U.S. health care is better than that of other nations.*

direct benefits patients receive, hospitals, clinics, outpatient, and special care units create huge continuing markets for construction, building supplies, and services. Medical services create further large markets for medical and dental equipment, hospital supplies, prosthetic and corrective devices, laboratory equipment and supplies, instruction materials, sanitary supplies, high-technology operating and life-support systems, and so on. All these supplier industries employ people and pay taxes. Both they and the health care units expand the markets for chemicals, plastics, textiles, basic metals, metal fabrication, production and construction equipment, measurement and test equipment, and so on throughout all of industry. Yet none of these benefits is registered or offset—in people's minds or in the national accounts—against the much-publicized costs of health care. The true problem is not the whole expenditure for health care, but that portion representing inefficient delivery. Calling all of these "costs" warps the political discussion of how much expenditure is appropriate and who pays for the "benefits" received. (See Figure 12.2.)

One would think that there normally would be broad support for such "growth industries." It is hard to imagine technological solutions to environmental, health, or safety problems that do not call for high technologies, metals, cement, chemicals, glass, and other products of myriad supplier industries. But such supplier industries and the companies in them—because of wrongheaded existing dogmas—often blindly oppose rather than actively encourage market development in public (environmental, safety, or health) sectors.

• We once heard the CEO of a diversified products company railing against the required expenditure of $15 million for air depollution equipment on his factories' stacks. It turned out that his company sold approximately 50% of all the exhaust systems for American automobile producers. Assuming that the exhaust depollution portions of the systems cost approximately $50 each, depollution regulations increased his company's sales by $250 million annually. At a 10% profit margin, the net cost to his company for air pollution was underwritten by profits from his own growth markets in about seven months. Further, since all competitive producers had to meet the same standards, his company was not put at a disadvantage, and the cost of his depollution devices could be passed on to consumers through modest price increases in autos. Even when confronted with such facts, however, the CEO ranted that "air depollution regulations are nothing but costs."

## Benefits to the Industries Regulated

When the actual results of creating markets through regulation are carefully analyzed, they are rarely as menacing as the opposition rhetoric makes them sound. Affected industries, of course, tend to exaggerate potential hardships. Cost estimates based on technologies available at the time of imposition are generally too high because innovations almost always quickly lower costs. If regulations use flexibly designed market mechanisms or reward higher performance achievements—as opposed to specifying particular technologies or existing best practices—innovators create solutions that generate both better outputs and lower costs far more than anyone could forecast at the time. For example:

• When the Occupational Safety and Health Administration (OSHA) issued new standards for workers' exposure to chemical formaldehyde, the industry argued it would cost $10 million per year to install vent systems. Instead, foundry suppliers modified their bonding resins, slashing the amounts of formaldehyde, at negligible costs to most firms, and actually making the U.S. industry more competitive.

• A Canadian company, Dynamotive Inc., is working on a combined process with Babcock and Wilcox to use rubbish in a pyrolysis process as a fuel for power plants. Using a new substance called BioLime in combination with this fuel and ordinary coal, the consortium can remove 95% of a power plant's sulfur oxide and most of its nitrogen oxide. The process also reduces the rubbish volume by 70%. If the process at scale can come in for less than $150 per ton, as experiments indicate it can, costs for both power plants and rubbish removal will drop.[16]

• When the town of Trenton, Michigan, refused to allow McLouth Steel to install bessemer converters in the early 1950s because they produced too much air pollution, McLouth went on a search for substitute low-cost processes. This led in 1954 to the first major U.S. installation of the basic oxygen process. When diffused through the steel industry, the cost savings and value gains from this profitable innovation alone would more than pay for the steel industry's highly touted air depollution costs.

Although not so dramatic in many cases, such impacts are widespread; yet they rarely enter executive or policy discussions about regulation. The OECD found that early expenditures on environmental regulations had strong positive impacts on economic growth, even as measured, in its member countries.[17] As in most other economic activities, however, one would expect marginal returns to be highest in early stages. But changed social attitudes and the continuing pressure of anticipated regulations have led many companies systematically to change their processes and product designs to lower "full product life cycle costs," in essence selling a new service (a cleaner environment) along with their traditional products.[18] Well-designed regulations create new markets, make existing markets more efficient, and increase total values produced in the long run. As Frances Cairncross, environmental editor of the conservative *Economist* magazine, notes, "Good environmental policy and good economics go hand in hand. . . . Higher income levels have proved in the last three decades to go hand in hand with a greater environmental concern and a willingness to spend a rising share of national income on environmental protection."[19]

## Enhancing Market Efficiencies

Unfortunately, for the past thirty years, it has been common to consider environmental costs as externalities, literally not in the economic reckoning.[20] The effect has been to seriously distort market efficiencies. Any reasonable theory says that properly pricing the factors of production leads to a more, not less, efficient economy and better use of resources. Many have feared that forcing internalization would cause mass movements of industries to less restrictive areas, but there is little empirical evidence that this is a dominating concern for companies making location decisions. Areas with among the most stringent regulations (California, Germany, New Jersey, and the Netherlands) have continued to grow. Other factors—such as closeness to supplies, markets, educational facilities, skilled labor, and transportation—tend to be much more important, especially as environmental standards approach common norms across geographical areas. This is a strong argument for negotiating regional (if not worldwide) standards in U.S. trade agreements. It is time to shift from a misleading "externalities" calculus to a focus on environmental concerns as just another demand element to be considered in developing efficient markets that encourage, rather than discourage, growth and innovation.

## CREATING PUBLIC MARKETS EFFECTIVELY

The critical question is not so much whether such public markets can have positive benefits but how to optimize that benefit in social and economic terms. Recent legislation has demanded specific cost-benefit analyses for any new environmental regulations—as if this were either a new or highly reliable answer to such issues. Well-made cost-benefit analyses may help avoid huge errors if they include the kinds of adjustments already noted. However, as in industry, they can be wildly inaccurate unless one includes the impact of constructive innovation and new market creation, once these forces are released.[21] Recognizing this, both economists and sensible policymakers are beginning to stress "market-like" incentive mechanisms, which, by creating new markets, generate higher-quality and lower-cost solutions to public problems. One of the inhibitors in developing such markets is that, like quality innovation in industry, their front-end costs seem so measurably apparent while their benefits are hard to quantify or assess.

Economists use two starting points in establishing the demand potential of a public market. One is direct: they ask people questions. The second is indirect: they try to create a real-world market in which interested parties buy and sell real or surrogate assets or solutions. The simplest questions in the direct approach are, "How much would you be willing to pay [to have a clean river, or a better highway system, or to maintain national parks]?" These can be refined by defining values for different levels of cleanliness, highway speeds, or park maintenance and access, and they can be checked against other market values by indifference curve techniques. Another survey technique asks, "What amount would you demand to allow someone to decrease these values by an equal amount?" Such surveys or "contingent valuations" have two benefits: they allow the introduction of psychic values for public goods as well as their measurable cost-reducing benefits, and they allow people who might be only indirectly affected to express their preferences. Interestingly, these willingness-to-pay and willingness-to-accept questions end up with a strong and consistent bias. People would demand between two and six times more to be willing to accept a loss in current quality-of-life levels than they would be willing to pay to achieve or improve these levels.[22] The modal value tends to be about four times as much.

The indirect method analyzes how people perform in an actual market situation—how much they actually do pay on average to vacation in a national park or to fish in a clean wilderness area rather than to picnic or fish locally. Similar calculations show how much a hectare of tropical forest yields if carefully harvested for its biological products ($9,000) as opposed to being used for cow pasture ($3,000).[23] In Kenya, the Amboseli Park produces annual earnings of $40 per hectare, a net profit of five times its most optimistic agricultural use. Such calculations, providing benchmarks for analyzing similar alternatives in other locations, are becoming widely used to influence policy on a more market-oriented basis.

## Market-Like Mechanisms: Tradable Quotas

The widest use of market-like mechanisms has been in the U.S. environmental arena, where "tradable quotas" have begun to establish market values for environmental actions in many areas. They have been unarguably successful in reducing Los Angeles's air pollution and preserving selected fisheries from overexploitation. When the action point of causation is identifiable and effective monitoring is feasible, tradable quotas can create market solutions that avoid many shortcomings of direct regulation, where standards are more often dictated by political power and by current technology limitations and tend to discourage long-term innovations that could go well beyond these standards. While properly set tradable quotas give innovative players a market stake in more stringent regulation, direct regulation causes offending companies or users to band against and strongly oppose any regulation. Further, when standards apply only to new installations (as they often have on new drugs or automobiles), they discriminate against the very results sought. If the new devices initially have higher prices, people stick with the older—more damaging—products longer than they would have; they scrap their old cars or processes later, not earlier.

The main benefits of market-like mechanisms are that they encourage innovation and reward those who act responsibly. They positively affect the decisions of many millions of users and entrepreneurs rather than just punish a few bad actors. Standards can be tightened on a pre-announced basis once technological advance curves can be calculated. The initial problems of introducing standards decrease because low polluters can sell the quotas they do not need while current polluters without large capital capabilities can buy time to comply. Auctioning off tradable quotas at the outset sets a realistic value on the cost of noncompliance, and buying back or freezing the total rights available can ensure desired future improvement across the entire system.

Another market alternative is to tax undesired actions on a unit purchase basis to increase their cost. Taxing effluents or externality producing products like cigarettes as their volume increases encourages all players to lower their amount. A unit tax set at a level where total revenue generated just offsets total externalities created will make the total market efficient and will provide incentives for both producer innovation and voluntary consumer choice of other more cost-effective products or services. Today's grandfathering of bad actors—old car owners or old plants that threaten communities with shutdowns if standards are enacted—does just the opposite. Unit taxes would encourage all in their own self-interest to comply more fully, while providing the funds needed to monitor actions and clean up past insults. Further, placing taxes on those who are currently or potentially costing the society for their support makes more economic sense than placing taxes on income makers who are implicitly increasing output values by selling fully costed services or products the society wants. In fact, since relatively small environmental use taxes (like carbon or gasoline taxes) raise large amounts of money, they could be used to decrease the level of personal income taxes if politicians saw merit in doing so.

Despite the clearly demonstrated benefits of using market-based mechanisms whenever possible, there are certain situations where actions should be directly regulated (through standards or banning) as the most efficient way of fulfilling the public interest. Examples include ensuring the quality of drinking water, enforcing sanitary standards in foods, prohibiting private sale of plutonium or weapons of mass destruction, and preventing hackers from disrupting the world financial markets. For most purposes, however, decentralizing decisions through public markets will be a more effective and efficient method for achieving desired results.

## Very Large Markets

In the United States, public markets now aggregate at least $2 trillion per year on a continuing basis, compared to a GNP of approximately $7.5 trillion. (See Table 12.1.) Further, government actions in the past have created (or guaranteed the initial demands for) new industries that later generated ongoing, freestanding markets of hundreds of billions of dollars per year (e.g., early cargo aircraft, high-octane gasoline, synthetic rubber, computers, software, penicillin, vaccines, semiconductors, advanced materials, satellite communications). The impetus given by large government projects or contracts has also created large new companies—as the Hoover Dam spawned Bechtel and the military and space programs launched TRW and Hughes Aircraft—which then went on as private enterprises to generate multiple billions of dollars per year

**TABLE 12.1**
**Major Public Markets,**
**1995 or Latest ($ billions)**

| | |
|---|---|
| Health care | 1,008 |
| Education | 508 |
| Public construction | 137 |
| Pollution abatement | 110 |
| Law enforcement | 110 |
| Sanitation and water supply | 57 |
| Federal transport | 38.6 |

Sources: (1) *PROPAC Report to Congress 1996*; (2) *Digest of Education Statistics, 1996*; (3) *Statistical Abstract of the United States 1996*; (4) *Bureau of Justice Statistics, 1996*; (5) *Survey of Current Business,* May 1995.

*Government-created public markets generate trillions of dollars of opportunities for private companies in civilian (nondefense) activities.*

in sales and exports to private domestic and foreign markets. Once these companies gained technological skills and satisfied the initial guaranteed demand, they were able to invest their own money, become familiar with various new markets' problems and potentials, introduce further product and technical-production solutions, and build profitable, growing businesses in other private markets. Yet none of these direct benefits or their supplier market gains are ever, even in retrospect, offset against the expenditures that enabled them.

When government properly structures its policies to stimulate innovation in these early markets, as it often has in recent years, it uses the same concepts (of competing designs, interactive testing, performance figures of merit, problem-solving incentives, and R&D-production continuity) that characterize innovative private marketplaces. The government consciously exploits the companies' own interests in later commercialization (as, for example, U.S. Air Force procurement and the multiagency small business industrial research and development (SBIR) grant programs have). Such approaches avoid the barriers to further development and exploitation that government self-production or in-house development so often created (in other countries and the U.S.) in the past. Market-like guiding mechanisms have become increasingly common in government-technical R&D and procurement as well as regulatory programs. To further this trend, there is no rational reason why the government's practices could not parallel industry's "core-competency-with-outsourcing" strategies. If a government agency is not best in world at producing something internally, its monitors can seriously consider forcing it to outsource the activity. Major benefits would accrue if this strategy were more visibly used across government agencies.

## ECONOMIC GROWTH DEMANDS EFFECTIVE PUBLIC MARKETS

Among the most important policies affecting innovation and economic growth in advanced economies today are those enabling people to learn, save, consume, and invest as groups. Private enterprise systems have proved marvelously adept at producing virtually anything individual customers are prepared to buy. But individuals cannot buy the roads, schools, police protection, health services, or depollution systems their families need. Without regional cooperation even cities or towns cannot develop the complete education, air traffic control, major transport, or waste disposal systems they need. Nor can entire states effectively develop the electric power, water resource, or environmental protection capabilities their populations demand. Private producers often have the technology and productive capacity to satisfy such whole system needs. What is missing are effectively structured markets to fulfill these demands. Archaic economic measurements, definitions of national wealth, and political institutions often make it very difficult for governments to act effectively in these spheres.

## Changing Terminology and Perceptions

Two of the most important changes needed in technology-economic strategy are (1) better definition and acknowledgment of the true costs and benefits that public markets create, and (2) establishment of more market-like mechanisms to channel demands, aggregate resources, and allocate costs in these "public market" or "aggregate demand" situations. Unless our current perceptions and analytical concepts are changed, intellect, technology, and wealth creation allocations will be substantially suboptimized.

Although no analytical system will be a perfect allocator, just as private markets systems are not, many social innovations made since the early passage of the 1970s' environmental and safety laws allow more effective distribution of costs and benefits among users and producers in individual public markets. Two large problems remain: (1) how to handle nuances of demand within a single market category (e.g., what is the optimum trade-off between particulate, gaseous, and noise outputs of an engine?), and (2) how to determine relative preferences among completely different public markets (such as health care, environmental improvement, transportation, national defense, public safety, energy independence, or public education). Political processes have been the traditional mechanisms for resolving social priorities and will doubtless continue to be the ultimate arbiter.

## Net Value Creation, Not Cost Minimization

However, a crucial element in making these allocations more effectively is the recognition by all parties that most preferences are values or aesthetically based, not simply cost optimizing. People do not "cost minimize" in their purchases of other items (e.g., automobiles, homes, shirts, theater tickets, vacations, furniture, foods, or other personal goods). If they did, Cadillac, Coca-Cola, Four Seasons, Disneyland, Maxim's, beachfront condos, and Louis Vuitton would have disappeared long ago. Similarly, people do not necessarily want clean rivers, unpolluted shorelines, clean air, police systems, education, or public recreational facilities because they "cost less." To demand that public expenditures or regulations must lower costs in order to be justified places an unrealistic and unfair burden on public markets. Improved life quality deserves the same emphasis in public markets as it receives in private markets.

There are giant biases now favoring private versus public markets. Today everyone can buy any trivial private product or service they want, and entrepreneurs are praised for creating ever more such opportunities daily. Yet we must question whether current concepts are truly optimizing allocations in a $7 trillion economy that creates such trinkets in profusion but where streets are unsafe, educational quality is declining, murders per capita are the highest in the world, public transportation systems are collapsing, millions of people are homeless, real family incomes are declining, 2.7% of the adult male population is in jail, and the highest causes of death among young adults are homicide and drugs. Until at least a comparable calculus is used between public and private markets—and both public leaders and the press begin to think about and explain the economics of public markets in a more cohesive fashion—these issues will not go away and misallocations will persist.

## Encumbrances to Allocation

Currently, the greatest encumbrances to objective public allocation are the inadequacies of current cost and benefit measurements and the interposition of strongly motivated, well-financed, special interest groups between voters and legislators. Tragically, political forces and constant misstatements about public markets are influencing actions counter to both these requisites for more productive allocation of resources. To date, Congress has refused to pass effective bills designed to decrease the impact of special interest financing; and the courts have overturned those that have passed, insisting that private rights (to do such financing) exceed the public's right to fairness in representation. Making the problem even worse, in 1995 the Congress began systematically dismantling programs whose purpose had been to provide more objective data. These include its own Office of Technology Assessment, the Bureau of Economic Analysis (BEA) of the Commerce Department, the President's Office of Science and Technology Policy, and many of the EPA's and Department of Interior's census-taking programs designed to provide baseline data—on wildlife populations and other natural systems—against which policymakers could assess the actual impacts of policies implemented. Even conservative, business-based journals like *Business Week* are joining the battle to reverse these damaging trends.[24]

Without objective data, powerful special interest groups can wreak unique havoc. Such interest groups often contribute valuable information and have a right to be heard, but the distortions they introduce through their implied (or actual) contributions and attacks during political campaigns distort market processes out of all proportion. In contrast to other advertisers there is no requirement for honesty in the lobbying campaigns of these groups and little social control over their activities other than bribery laws. No structure for national resource allocation will be effective until these distortions are eliminated. Because of these well-financed political efforts, public procedures and media presentations tend to exaggerate substantially the purported hardships of those potentially harmed (and to understate real gains) at the time decisions are made. If a market-creation and innovation-stimulating approach is taken, many purported costs often disappear altogether.

- The automobile industry fought against air bags for years. More recently it has sold air bags as desirable features. Vinyl chloride regulation forced the U.S. plastics industry to install automated technology that cut exposures and boosted productivity at a much lower cost. In 1990, utilities estimated the price tag for reducing sulfur dioxide emissions, causing acid rain, at $1,000 per ton. Yet technology improvements and, low-sulphur coal have lowered costs so much that the actual cost (as established by the purchase price for tradeable quotas) is only $140 per ton.[25] None of the original calculations included the benefits of innovation or economic growth from the new markets and jobs created in the depollution equipment and supplies markets.

Two major perversities in the misleading analyses these groups purvey are to accept the high cost and current performance of existing equipment as their standard and to argue—based on this wrong gauge—for less stringent standards that will delay, not spark, innovation for better technology. The result is the worst of both worlds: higher investments and costs for everyone and less effluent (or other externality) reductions in real terms.

## Referendum Voting as a Market Surrogate

Many have pointed to the opportunities of using information technologies for referendum voting on complex public choices. An auction mode of preference allocation has many attractions. If reasonable analytical and compromise processes could be introduced in the formulation of referendum items, the approach could work well, as it generally does in the smaller European countries. But experience suggests certain warnings in the U.S. culture.

• California's proposition voting provides some instructive insights. First, overly simplistic propositions can be designed by public relations specialists to appeal to a wide public without reflecting their true costs. Second, such propositions do not lend themselves to the kind of sophisticated political compromises that democratic legislative processes allow. All polities are more likely to be heard and understood in a legislative environment. The small wording changes that decrease disastrous consequences for minority interests often cannot be included in referenda. Third, and more important, the California approach does not force those who vote for certain consequences to be held responsible for raising the funds to achieve them. As a result, the proposition form of referendum is bankrupting many local communities trying to meet referendum demands, but deprived by other referenda (passed at earlier times) of the resources with which to accomplish the goals.

Until electronic referendum processes allow incorporation of all such factors, they appear unlikely to improve matters, except insofar as they allow a straw vote or ranking procedure concerning preferences. Often complex regulatory bargaining and evaluation infrastructures are essential to handle the technical details of compromise. The devils are always in the details. Two examples were setting standards for auto bumper heights and for 2-by-4-inch wood products, seemingly simple problems.

• No one company could have set bumper standards alone; each potential solution posed very different costs for each party. An acceptable compromise had to be reached among all players. Yet when achieved, bumper height standards increased safety for individuals, offered useful new targets for materials research, lowered accident costs for owners, and hence increased the industry's competitiveness against other industries. Similarly, the head of the Bureau of Standards found that changed 2-by-4-inch wood product standards, which would open many markets for competition and lower costs enormously, were very costly to implement in individual wood mills, communities where old standards were different, and accessory industries that depended on existing standards.

Given a set of decision rules, a computer that had no vested interest could easily calculate national optimizations among various policies in such situations, under any set of agreed-on trade-off rules. But different personal interests and costs, unequal political power relationships, and outmoded political structures often make such rationality impossible.

## Outmoded Decision Structures

A major complication creating allocation inefficiencies is the fact that today's national, state, county, and local governments' political boundaries were largely designed around the transportation and communication technologies available when each state came into the Union. Most important public problems now overlap different sets of these political units. Water problems may involve thousands of linear miles of a river system. Local transportation networks may embrace an entirely different contiguous area. Development of a hospital center may require coordination of still other local units, educational development yet another region, and so on. Existing smaller political units and decision centers—villages, precincts, towns and cities, counties, states—often cannot cope with today's group consumption problems. It is difficult for these units to (1) obtain the popular financial support to solve problems not conforming to their geographical boundaries; (2) standardize system, component, or building specifications to achieve mass production economies; (3) develop administrative units to oversee desired group expenditures and manage the operations of complex facilities on a regional basis; (4) and set priorities across individual programs among local, regional, or national groups.

Slowly, functional or problem-oriented regional authorities like riverbed commissions, regional air quality commissions, waste disposal authorities, transit authorities, school districts, and health centers have arisen to fill the void. But often without taxing authority, these units have been considerably less effective than they could be. If adequately supported by sophisticated databases, these ad hoc regional structures can suffice for a few decades. But in time, new, more decentralized, problem-oriented decision structures will have to arise within the country's political matrix. The analytical processes suggested here will be essential to the sensible development of these new structures.

## SUMMARY

Contrary to much current dogma, private markets alone do not create as much wealth or potential growth as a combination of private markets and well-conceived government policy. Private markets can be quite inefficient without effective government interventions to force parties to internalize their costs, aggregate marginal demands effectively, overcome institutional constraints to innovation, assume very large risks, enforce fairness and life quality rules on market participants, or capture secondary (or public) benefits that individual firms or consumers cannot capture.

However, such market inefficiencies are not the sole reason for government interventions. Governments can create "public markets" that stimulate growth and innovation beyond those provided by private markets. Once underway, these markets satisfy demands, create jobs, stimulate innovation, pay taxes, and generate wealth just as private markets do. The only difference is that they allow individuals to aggregate their demands for goods or services that private markets could not satisfy. When these conditions obtain—as they do in environmental, health care, catastrophe prevention, public health, police protection, and legal systems—they are natural extensions of the private market system, and to the extent possible they should be so structured.

Such public markets are not national costs to be abhorred. They are no more national costs than are the markets for automobiles, power boats, entertainment, and larger houses. Defining and dismissing these essential economic activities as "costs" misallocates resources on a significant scale. New mechanisms are needed (and are being developed) to make these public markets more efficient. National account data, public policy discussions, and economics presentations need to reflect this market reality. Unless perceptions are changed, nations will not be able to deal rationally and well with many of the important technological and growth challenges of the future.

# 13

# National Technology Strategies in a Services and Software World

Because of the inherent internal frictions, uncertainties, and political risks ever present in government and a market economy, national technology strategists have tended to focus on incremental changes in shaping their future domain.[1] However, in a few years' time a rapid series of physical, conceptual, and intellectual advances have produced changes in kind (rather than just in degree) in the modern policy-maker's and manager's tasks. In virtually all fields—foods, medicine, materials, environmental, services, and manufacturing—knowledge and its technological applications have grown at ever steeper exponential rates. Since the drivers of technology—demand, trained minds, individual component technologies' capabilities, and the interactiveness between technologies—are all growing exponentially, the trend is likely to continue. These changes are most apparent in the electronics, communications, information, and services worlds:

- Digital computing's cost-effectiveness has almost doubled every two years. Memory, computational speed, network, and peripherals (input-output) capabilities have dropped in price so dramatically that individuals now own computers and use networks that the Strategic Air Command would have coveted a few years ago.
- A growing $100 billion software industry now sells, for $25 to $50, user-friendly, over-the-counter software that whole divisions of IBM could not have produced in the early 1980s. As a result, senior

business managers now increasingly use computer and communication system capabilities to source and market internationally and to manage their complex tasks globally, despite their ignorance of the technology's inner workings.[2]

• The marriage of computation, display, and communication technologies is so seamless that the meaning of "distant" and "local" disappears when applied to information exchanges. Compressed gigabits of information fly across borders in a mere second at a cost of a few tenths of a cent, making worldwide interactive innovation and strategic outsourcing common.

• An exponentially growing number of highly trained research, system, production, marketing, and application talents now interact worldwide to create new basic research insights, product or process designs, and service system innovations at a rate never before imagined. Innovation and its risks are forever changed, as should be policies for domestic and international economic growth.

• A huge number (35 million in America alone) of relatively young, sophisticated computer "communicators"—not programmers—worldwide have become relaxed and competent in using networks and complex programs. Their network interactions are now creating "auto-catalytic" or "negative entropy growth," forcing economists and policymakers to rethink the very basics of education, trade policy, and economics.

## CHANGED APPROACHES TO TECHNOLOGY AND ECONOMIC POLICY

How do such facts change approaches to technology strategy at the national level? Until recently "technology" meant primarily physical devices and constructions and was considered an "error term" in the macroeconomists' production function.[3] Mainstream developmental economists still primarily focus on what a nation has in "objects" like factories, roads, power generation or lacks ("object gaps"), and relate these to policy through static equilibrium models concentrating on measurable physical assets. A new conceptual school of economists (including Paul Romer, Brian Arthur, Richard Nelson, and Paul Krugman) now focuses more on "idea gaps"—needs for intellectual, technological, and system infrastructures—and uses more dynamic, though often less formal, models. Balanced policy needs both approaches.[4] Increasingly, national intellectual, technology, and economic strategies must be integrated more specifically to support the rapidly developing services, software, and intellect-based economy of the future.

As the preceding chapters have suggested, there will never be a single, explicit, cohesive national U.S. strategy but rather many implicit strategies, with conflicts and compromises at the margins determining the overall balance and thrust. There seems little need for massive new government investments in R&D or physical infrastructures for the services-software age. Many elements of policy can be best exercised through private markets, generic interventions, and better-structured public markets. The chaos represented in private innovation has its analog in national policy that needs to be implemented primarily through disaggregated, competing, and collaborating entities. However, there is an overwhelming need for government to reinvigorate the nation's intellect-generating apparatus—its advanced research, public education, incentive, and national database infrastructures—in many areas. Further delays in these areas could rapidly diminish the nation's economic, military, and life quality standards. What are the most important elements affecting policy in this new technology-economic world?

## A SERVICES-SOFTWARE ECONOMY GROWING BALLISTICALLY

Tomorrow's economy will be at least 90% services: 70 to 80% directly in services industries plus another 60 to 70% of the product sector's 25% of GDP in intellectually based services like R&D, product design, logistics, marketing, and postsale services. Since 1993 the economy has produced a net of 8.5 million new jobs despite corporate downsizings costing 1.7 million jobs. Most of the new jobs were in services, and over half were in the top 30% of earnings.[5] All estimates also show future job demands will be primarily in high-education intellectually based services situations. (See Figure 13.1.)

A large and totally unpredictable element in this economy will be a huge new virtual marketplace of on-line activities. After its slow start as DARPANET, the explosive market-based growth of Internet and Web services and capabilities has come as a shock to many in the investment and management fields. A mad scramble is developing to graft economic activities, from purchasing goods to stock trading, onto the Internet backbone. Many of these will be new intellectually based services. Although its scale is uncertain, high growth is likely because Internet subscribers represent a carefully self-selected, intelligent, affluent market. Each customer owns, or has access to, a computer and communi-

**FIGURE 13.1**
**Job Growth in Services, 1990–2005**

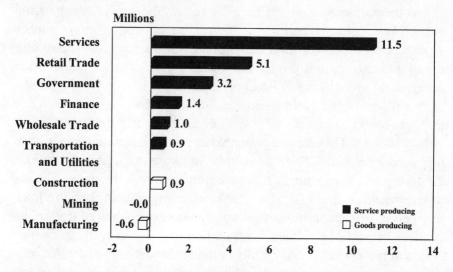

Source: "Projections of Employment by Occupation and Industry," *Handbook of Labor Statistics*, U.S. Department of Labor, Bureau of Labor Statistics, Government Printing Office, 1994.

*Virtually all job growth for the next decade will be in services.*

cation lines, is well educated, and is wealthy enough to support these services. Exponentially decreasing costs are allowing access to expand rapidly, making the Net even more attractive as a way to reach extensive markets.[6] Although early adopters in the virtual marketplace were usually academics, hackers, or computer enthusiasts, this is no longer true. Millions of children in elementary school, homemakers, businesspeople, medical professionals, farmers, sports enthusiasts, the homebound, and others now use the Net to solve their unique problems and to satisfy new needs.

Internet use has grown so much (70% in the last year alone) that it now clogs access lines to the telephone system. Vice President Gore's dramatic concept of an Information Superhighway is already a giant understatement. The Superhighway has become a profusion of attached side roads, businesses, hospitals, stores, schools, farms, communities, and specialized user systems. With little investment, growth has gone ballistic. The Net is now a whole self-sustaining virtual economy, growing auto-catalytically or with "negative entropy"; small energy and investment inputs, amplified through further innovative modifications, result in a huge positive feedback of value gains. Many traditionalists have assumed that the value of the Internet to society will come from its measurable direct transaction use, not merely through its existence. Yet many of the values it creates are hard to express in economic terms. A few economists like Paul Romer, Paul Krugman, and Nathan Rosenberg have begun to lay down some useful guidelines and caveats for thinking about this new economy.[7]

Unfortunately, national data collected about service activities are both skimpy and inaccurate. Much of the business, political, and press conversation about services is ill founded, and major policy errors result. This is especially true for international trade policies.

• There has been much attention to the nation's huge deficits in merchandise trade, but little recognition of the strong annual ($50–65 billion) positive balances in U.S. services trade, particularly with Japan. Numerous studies show that most large U.S. service industries—particularly the retail, wholesale, transportation, and communications industries—are substantially more productive than their Japanese or European counterparts.[8] Yet this comparative advantage is rarely pursued in U.S. trade negotiations as it should be. The United States is likely to gain far more from insisting that its large retailers (like Toys "R" Us, Wal-Mart, and Home Depot), fast foods restaurants, hotel chains, banks, package delivery, and communications companies have complete access to Japanese and East Asian markets than it will by insisting that private Japanese or Korean automobile companies buy U.S.-made parts in their home markets. Traditional thinking and poor data about the service sector interfere with the nation's taking advantage of its major strengths.[9]

## SERVICES IN MANUFACTURING AND INTERNATIONAL TRADE

This misplaced emphasis is especially tragic when one realizes how dramatically technology-based services are restructuring all manufacturing and international trade. The National Science Foundation's publication, *Science and Engineering Indicators, 1995,* did not even list the services industries' exports and imports in its data, despite U.S. technological preeminence in telecommunications, financial services, professional services, software, entertainment, and transportation trade.[10] The GATT did not seriously address services until the Uruguay Round, and most of its recommendations have yet to be implemented. Even these do not touch on some of the most important facets of services and intellect

**FIGURE 13.2**
**Invisible Exports as a Percentage of GDP, 1993**

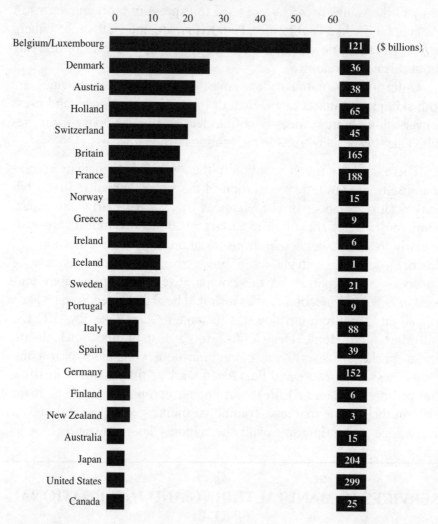

Source: Reproduced by special permission from "Financial Indicators: Invisible Trade," *Economist*, August 19, 1995, p. 93.

*The United States is the largest producer of invisible exports, but with greater emphasis could increase its potential sales significantly.*

as primary drivers in trade. Much of the intellectual value transferred in trade worldwide consists of unreported internal knowledge transfers within corporations, data or aural messages exchanged with external partners on networks, software support for products, or private-personal transfers of knowledge through specialists. Figure 13.2 shows the strong dollar position yet weak percentage of trade the United States enjoys in the approximately $2.4 trillion of "invisibles" trade now reported among countries.[11]

## Intellectually Based Services: Revolutionizing Manufacturing

Nationally the public's perception of the importance of the product sector is greatly exaggerated. Only 18% of employment is in manufacturing. Even then 65 to 75% of all manufacturing jobs—and a higher percentage of manufacturing value-added—are in service activities (like research, development, product design, process design, logistics, marketing, sales, distribution, accounting, personnel, legal, or MIS).[12] Most policymakers have yet to realize or face up to many of the implications. Intellectually based service activities, not manufacturing, are the nation's growth vector for the future. They create the highest value-adding and highest-paying jobs in the United States. Doctors, lawyers, consultants, entertainers, software designers, scientists, and engineers head the list. Recent studies show that middle managers who were downsized out of their non-value-adding jobs in manufacturing on average have improved their incomes in their new (dominantly services) jobs.[13] And virtually all new job growth in the United States has been in services, while less desirable product jobs have gone abroad.

To a large extent, manufacturing is now simply a series of service activities, linked together to create customer value in the form of a product output. Thinking about, or treating, manufacturing activities as significantly more important—or having higher value in job or output terms—than those in the service industries is a major conceptual error. Customers do not care whether a product feature is executed in software or hardware, nor is hardware-created productivity more important to an executive than marketing, design, advertising, software, or distribution-created productivity. *Fortune* magazine recognized this error in 1995 when—for the first time—it placed service industries and industrial companies together in its Fortune 500 statistics. Unfortunately, the misconception still dominates much of the nation's domestic and international policy thinking. The effects can be potentially devastating.

## Organizational Disaggregation and Outsourcing

Two of the most powerful trends in manufacturing today are organizational disaggregation and outsourcing. Both derive from the fact that the value chain of even the most seemingly vertically integrated corpo-

rations (like major oil companies) is primarily composed of intellectually based services activities. (See Figure 13.3.) Most services, like those
in multinational oil companies' value chains, can easily be transported
across geographical or corporate borders. Many therefore can be produced almost anywhere in the world, often at lower cost or with higher
value than any integrated company can produce them at its central locations. Combined with the improved capabilities other technologies allow
to manage, communicate about, produce, store, and transport goods
and services among remote locations, this has led to much greater international and domestic corporate outsourcing and to the geographical
disaggregation of internal organizations.[14]

If a company is not best-in-world in an activity (including both
value produced and transaction costs) and it produces that activity in-
house, it sacrifices competitive edge;[15] it can gain more by outsourcing
the activity.[16] U.S. companies alone perform over $200 billion of such
outsourcing today. Temporary and job-search employment groups have
become the fastest-growing sector of the U.S. economy, creating
899,000 jobs between 1990 and 1995.[17] Increasingly, companies
switch their sourcing to internal divisions or external sources in whatever country can produce the good or service most effectively. Such internal transfers now account for a large percentage (50 to 75%) of all
U.S. goods and services trade balances in most years.[18] As ever more industries follow this practice, they are making many traditional strategies
for economic and national technology development obsolete.

## International Outsourcing: Outmoding Old Policy Instruments

A company or nation wanting to participate in some industry's trade
growth—whether that growth be in the shoe, computer, oil, automobile, or other industry—no longer has to have its own production plants
in that industry. It can participate by developing some specialized intellectual capabilities (such as research, design, software, finance, or logistics) to best-in-world levels and selling these to other companies in the
industry, which integrate them into value packages appealing to specific
customer classes—as do Nike and Reebok (in shoes), Apple and Dell
(in computers), and Chrysler and BMW (in autos).[19] Some excellent
studies show that as these international suppliers innovate in developing
countries, they create large multipliers of benefits to their economies
through sharing challenges and knowledge with their suppliers, customers, and public S&T groups.[20] As international telecommunications

**FIGURE 13.3**
## Value Chain of Integrated Oil Companies

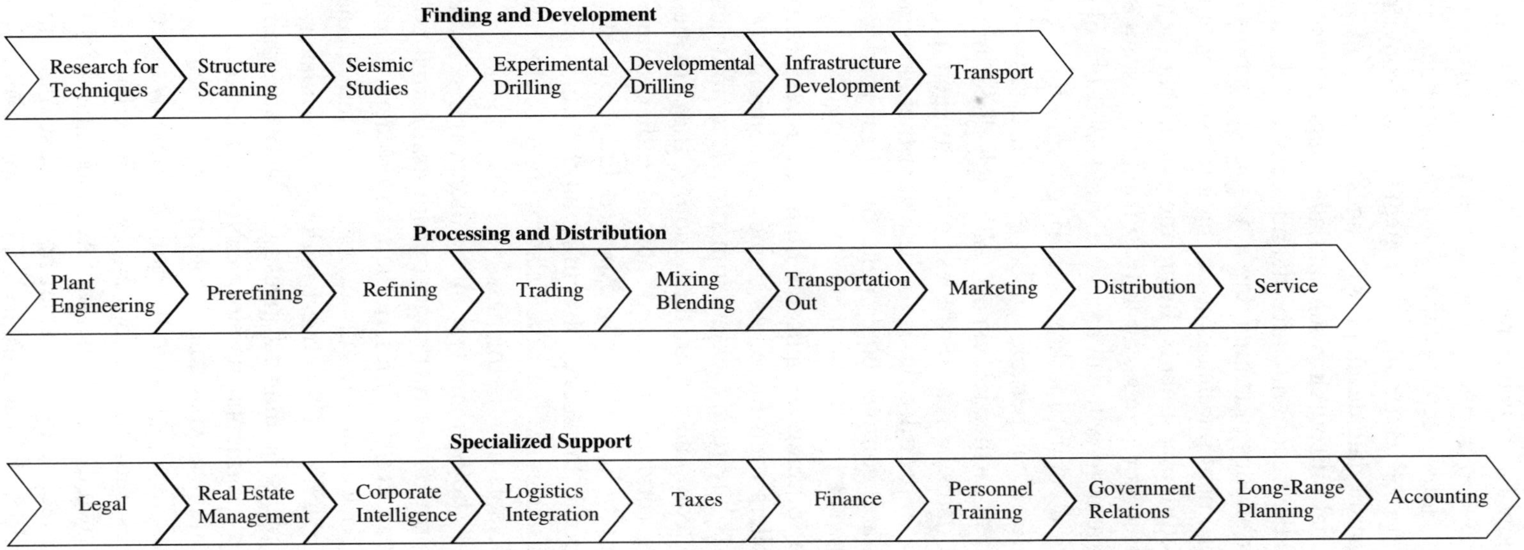

**Finding and Development**

Research for Techniques | Structure Scanning | Seismic Studies | Experimental Drilling | Developmental Drilling | Infrastructure Development | Transport

**Processing and Distribution**

Plant Engineering | Prerefining | Refining | Trading | Mixing Blending | Transportation Out | Marketing | Distribution | Service

**Specialized Support**

Legal | Real Estate Management | Corporate Intelligence | Logistics Integration | Taxes | Finance | Personnel Training | Government Relations | Long-Range Planning | Accounting

*The value chains of even the most integrated companies consist primarily of intellectually based services, which can be outsourced to suppliers anywhere in the world.*

costs drop below 10 cents per minute in the late 1990s, this outsourcing trade will expand even more,[21] having just the opposite effect to the "world without jobs" scenarios that some technophobes predict for developed countries.[22] But national strategies need some major adjustments to accommodate developing changes.

International outsourcing substantially alters the ways nations can best influence their economic growth and social development. The three most common modes of stimulating a national economy have been increasing government purchases, lowering interest rates, and making direct infrastructure investments. But to the extent that the primary seller of the purchased items (e.g., aircraft or trucks) outsources abroad, the resulting jobs and growth will also go abroad. Because of electronically integrated world capital markets, lowering domestic interest rates also means that foreign competitors can borrow at these rates, decrease their costs, and cause further job export. Although direct infrastructure investments (in dams or roads) are less prone to such aberrations, their developmental impact decreases to the extent that elements of the task (design, software, complex equipment, or oil for roads) are ultimately outsourced abroad.

Global outsourcing complicates domestic investment and technological multipliers even more. As domestic recipients of government-provided funds buy foods, entertainment, telecommunications, autos, or electronics equipment with their money, they frequently purchase products and services produced abroad rather than domestically. Hence, the multipliers normally expected for the domestic economy also move abroad. In theory, of course, all the funds eventually come back in increased trade, but time delays to impact can be much longer and less predictable than in the past.

Further, all the national and international transactions induced by policy are intermediated by people outside traditional policy circles—that is, securities, commodities, or monetary traders. As many countries from Mexico to Russia have discovered, these intermediaries' market judgments can completely subvert national policymakers' most politically rational plans or internal investment and development schemes. Bad economic judgments that formerly could be disguised in closed economic or monetary systems—or in large-deficit-spending countries—now quickly show up in the nation's borrowing costs, exchange rates, and prices. Although nations appear to have lost much direct control over their own destinies, market forces (because of the mobility services and their technologies enable) now impose much more discipline on political actions than domestic elections were ever able to enforce.

# INTERNATIONAL DEVELOPMENT STRATEGIES

Among the most important impacts of the services and software age is the capacity to compress development times and costs extensively through international innovation and production of products and services. Without innovation, economic growth is limited by physical resources available and (in an excess-capacity world) implicitly to marginal returns on capital invested. As physical product margins drop, the best way for a nation to break out of these marginal returns is to make better use of resources through innovation and direct connections to more advanced marketplaces.[23] Through software, innovators everywhere can be projected into any world marketplace or competitive situation. They can have instant access to the world's largest and most sophisticated marketplaces. No longer does an innovator in Southeast Asia have to invest in and build up distribution channels in the advanced markets of the world, as Honda or Sony once did. Computer or software innovators need only convince a Circuit City, Nintendo, or MCI of their product's merit, and they have instant sophisticated distribution. Textile or knit designers need only convince a J.C. Penney's or Benetton's buyer of their product's merit to achieve huge volume potentials. And biotech innovators need only to patent and publish to attract to their doorsteps a Lilly, Merck, Glaxo-Wellcome, or Hoffman-LaRoche with sophisticated worldwide production and distribution capabilities. Time cycles and first introduction risks are substantially reduced.

## Integrated World Innovation and Economies

Once a product is introduced and encounters real customer responses, constant detailed electronic feedback from the marketplace (about what features work or fail) lets innovators adapt their products to match the most current market perceptions. The implications of this feedback are straightforward. Since worldwide instant communications and competition interlink all economies in ways that make them totally interdependent, national strategies must be international in concept.

• Each night retail chains like Kmart, The Limited, Target, Computerland, Home Depot, Toys "R" Us, and Footlocker electronically aggregate their sales and profits for each product type nationally. They constantly experiment with new products and features in certain stores. They keep track of each detail of feature, size, color, style, and material. Using simple projection programs of current sales, these details provide the basis for replenishment orders to national or foreign suppliers. In the textile and software trades these literally become cutting or printing orders for Southeast Asia on the next day. Within four days or less, a wide-bodied aircraft takes off from Southeast Asia to the distribution depots of the major soft goods or computer chains, and stock is on the shelves a few days later.

Flexible manufacturing systems allow quick responses at the manufacturing level, and rapid cargo flights between foreign sources and U.S. markets mean that retail stocks stay current. The net result is that many of the investments, risks, and time lags for international innovation and diffusion have disappeared, and investors are more willing to invest internationally. Services and their technologies are forcing quick-cycle innovation practices on all industries. This trend will not change. U.S. innovators must compete immediately against other best-in-world competitors in each aspect of their value chain or lose the benefits of their innovations. This also means that successful foreign innovators will quickly tie into worldwide sources of technological and market knowledge to exploit their ideas. Since best-available technologies (for materials, components, parts, or ancillary services) may come from anywhere in the world, all innovators need to be tied into a worldwide network with access to these sources. The day of the insular inventor-innovator is dying, if not dead.

## Building Competencies, Not Making Investment Gifts

In the past, policymakers generally approached economic development as an investment issue, not as an intellectual development problem, and often these investments were regarded as gifts to achieve a political purpose. Sadly, operating under this conception, large amounts of capital have supported (or have been captured by) existing power structures, frequently with little benefit to the people the investment was intended to help.

• Examples of misappropriation abound in the lesser developed countries of the world as well in many U.S. programs. Waters from Bureau of Land Reclamation dams went primarily to large farmers and subsidized crops rather than to the smaller farms and towns they were intended to assist. Public housing projects enriched wealthy developers, while creating whole new slums for the cities and tenants. And inner-city welfare programs generated large bureaucracies and greater, rather than lesser, dependencies among their recipients. Results often reinforced the positions of power elites and decreased, rather than increased, the rates of progress that were possible.

In an electronically interconnected world, private capital will move to wherever competencies exist, provided public markets have built the infrastructures necessary to exploit and nurture these competencies. Development becomes primarily a question of building competencies and incentives throughout the society (and especially in the lesser developed portions of it) so that people can understand and tap into the capabilities available to them. Although the least developed areas of the world will also require large capital infusions at times for physical infrastructures (see Figure 13.4), using network concepts to connect local producers to the world can stimulate and diffuse innovations locally, shorten development times, and avoid many adverse appropriations. Early infrastructure investments shift into more decentralized, knowledge-based, entrepre-

**FIGURE 13.4**
**Net Long-Term Resource Flows to Developing Countries**

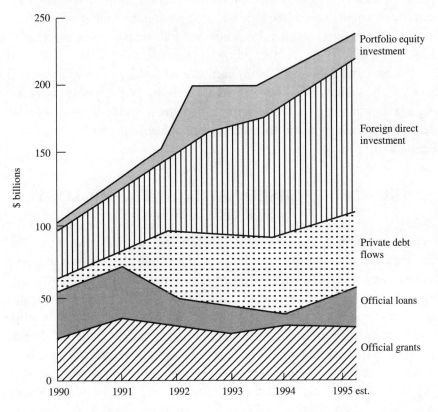

Source: Reproduced by special permission from "Finance and Economics: Shaken, But Not Stirred," *Economist,* March 16, 1996, p. 78.

*Private investment flows, facilitated by new technologies, provide the growing bulk of investments for emerging countries.*

neurial, services, telecommunications, network, and computer education approaches (versus traditional large factory, schoolhouse, book, and library directions). Economies of physical scale for both factories and most service entrepreneurs have tended to drop as technology advances. As the experiences of the "Asian Tigers," India, China, Chile, and even post-Stalinist Russia all suggest, progress is likely to be more highly diffused, locally relevant, and capturable by small groups or individuals than under prior schemes. New technologies can help lower investments in educational and communications infrastructures as nations leapfrog directly to wireless and fiberglass systems.

Many small local enterprises can develop production capabilities and connect directly to large sophisticated user centers, as do the software producers of India or Hokkaido, the fabric producers of Malaysia, the product design houses of Italy, the data inputters of the West Indies, the electronic game designers of Russia, or the physicists of China. A type of "industry cluster" development is becoming quite common, with groups of small, specialized firms cooperating in localized clusters. With proper infrastructures, local agricultural, textile (indigenous artisans in Vietnam), or boat-building entrepreneurs (yacht builders in Hong Kong and southern China) can take advantage of techniques and data widely available on the Net. Most striking is a Chinese workers' brigade that is using market pricing programs to guide its use of fertilizers on ground crops and to set feed, egg collection, and butcher times for its poultry flocks.

## KNOWLEDGE-BASED NATIONAL TECHNOLOGY STRATEGIES

Similar concepts can assist domestic technology-growth strategies. The first imperative for these strategies is a conceptual shift from traditional centrist command-control concepts to more decentralized, knowledge-building, network-interactive, high-diffusion, market-oriented strategies. This applies to both business and government. Unfortunately, both have built most of their practices around traditional allocation and control of physical assets models. This conceptual model was a major causative factor in the decline of most communist and socialist systems—as well as many large U.S. automobile, steel, railroad, consumer electronics, machine tool, and conglomerated companies. By contrast, the rapidly growing software, cable TV, entertainment, investment banking, microcomputer, pharmaceutical, biotechnology, publishing, and telecommunications industries have generally followed a knowledge-networking model. This model has powerful potentials and implications if applied systematically at the national level, both in the U.S. and elsewhere. The keys to progress become advanced research, education, people development, open access, incentives, knowledge diffusion, and empowerment. What national policies appear most relevant?

## Advanced Research

Most authorities agree that government expenditures on advanced research performed through universities are relatively inexpensive and offer extremely high intellectual leverages *if properly connected to user communities.* Zvi Griliches claims that much of the total factor productivity growth at the national level can be explained in terms of aggregate R&D spending.[24] Lichtenberg and others confirm this internationally.[25] However, many countries, like Britain and France, which heavily sponsored basic research but did not establish adequate connecting mechanisms to other institutions, did not fare nearly as well competitively as countries that sponsored less basic research but linked it better to applications. Basic research results, being widely published, cross borders easily and can be used by any competitor nation. But with proper linkages, university-based research also provides other significant benefits to the sponsoring nation:

- First resolution of the specific scientific problem at hand (e.g., does increased hemoglobin transport aid wound recovery?).
- Improvement of the quality of education (e.g., professors have more knowledge about oxygen transport and hemoglobin molecules and can better teach others about those concepts and their relationships to other knowledge frontiers).
- A better-trained body of students (e.g., people who can diffuse such knowledge into domestic organizations).
- New options for future scientific research and innovative products or services (e.g., improving the hemoglobin molecule or other substitute fluids through recombinant DNA techniques, finding better ways to produce it, or creating systems and devices for its production, distribution, and use).

A few breakthroughs from basic research occasionally open whole new industries and pay for the effort in perpetuity, as did Boyer and Cohen's interactions on recombinant DNA, Carruther's high polymer research, Fleming's antibiotic discoveries, Shockley and Bardeen's transistors, Townes's work on stimulated emission response, and Folkman's insights on angiogenesis. More often, however, basic research builds understanding piece by piece in ways that enrich the entire knowledge base of the country, strengthen capacities to work at the frontiers of knowledge and, most important, enable it to attract, lever, and exchange research information with leading intellectual sources throughout the world. The importance of less developed areas or countries having some minimum cadre of researchers cannot be overstressed. Even a few such people can serve as important coupling agents to tie the developing area into worldwide sources of information, methodologies, and specialized help.

## Open Access and Diffusion Systems

Well-indexed government publications, public library systems, and open databases leverage available knowledge at low cost through diffusion. These sources allow independent researchers to proceed more rapidly, avoid unnecessary duplication of effort, and exploit relationships both among the disciplines themselves and with problems that researchers might otherwise not even discern. Networks like the Internet are especially important in helping people find, exchange, and amplify diffuse knowledge. Network theory suggests that knowledge grows exponentially as it is shared across such networks.[26] The Internet has already revolutionized research methodology and pacing in many fields. Those not on the Net lose the stimulation, questions, and rapid verification of those sharing information from other fields. In many disciplines, professional publication dates have fallen so far behind the state of the art that no one can effectively participate in frontier research without network exchanges.

Open access systems enable an infinite number of minds to interact and create new combinations beyond any one person or group's current imagining. Two central characteristics of such network processes are that (a) no one can accurately predict ultimate outcomes and which industries they might affect, and (b) no individual or government can possibly control the sequences of interactions or limit their consequences to predetermined targets. Mathematicians have calculated that there are many trillions of different possible bit sequences on each 356-kilobyte diskette, and hence a comparable number of possible product outputs from it. In this kind of world, a command-and-control S&T strategy becomes meaningless, as does any possibility of really picking winners. In fact, the advent of huge, mind-sharing networks may finally lay to rest even the concept of picking winners.[27]

Winners are made, not picked. They are made by four formerly laborious processes: (1) exploring market needs and preferences, (2) creating or adapting products or services to match those needs, (3) modifying production processes to improve cost and quality, and (4) publicizing and diffusing results. The Internet is a powerful vehicle facilitating, shortening, amplifying, and supporting all these capabilities and enabling the kind of rapid, collaborative, worldwide innovation and diffusion that today's markets demand. From a societal viewpoint, such extended information access helps provide maximum benefits through diffusion to the widest possible range of students, scientists, technologists, users, and geographic locations. The leverage of diffusion is so powerful that providing information access, generating the requisite analytical and synthesis skills to use it, and empowering people to utilize such networks' knowledge—more than centrist funding and allocation procedures—will be the keys to future national science, technology, and innovation strategies. Although project funding will still be necessary to support long-term or complex solutions, the social value of these projects can be amplified if more rewards are shifted toward results achieved, disseminated, and actually used by others.

## Auto-Catalytic Growth Through Sharing and Feedback

A unique feature of a modern intellectual service economy is that once the substantial investment to develop a concept up to its first use has been made, the marginal costs of its reproduction (or dissemination) often drop to essentially zero, and the economic concept of decreasing marginal returns for these industries becomes obsolete. Such is the case of shrink-wrap software, pill-based medical cures, electronic funds transfers, electronically developed CASE/CAE/CAM designs, new financial securities or insurance concepts, or new modes of entertainment like CDs, movies, and videotapes. The potential leverages of very small intellect-based investments can be very high as others amplify their value by further modification, innovative use, and reposting of their results onto the network for others to use and modify. Thus each participant "auto-catalyzes" other nodes and amplifies value exponentially at relatively low investment cost. Such innovation is starting from an ever-higher knowledge base. Because of electronically based knowledge diffusion, high school students and college freshmen now deal with science concepts only an elite few understood a decade ago. And other teenaged Gates, Andressen, McCracken, Mullis, or Folkman prototypes with access to today's network knowledge bases are doubtless poised to create new Microsoft, Netscape, Sun, Cetus, or Amgen equivalents based on their knowledge and collaboration capabilities. No one can even faintly guess what their new concepts will be and what impacts they will have.

## Three Levels of Policy Support

Under these circumstances, the widest possible distribution of knowledge, analytical techniques, and system access will maximize benefits, provided there are proper incentives to carry the new concepts to market. Creating the knowledge skills to appreciate new concepts (small science) and opening network access for exchanges about them (diffusion)— rather than Japan's current approach of making huge investments in large research programs or physical assets (large science)—are likely to generate the greatest number of potential options for knowledge advance at lowest cost.[28] Providing incentives to harness these results and their secondary potentials through technological multipliers and worldwide diffusion can amplify benefits to extraordinary dimensions. Such results will require entirely different institutional arrangements, pricing systems, and exchange bases to promote efficient growth.

Economists have long used the terminology of private versus public "goods" to separate the appropriateness of market versus nonmarket interventions in policy. Richard Nelson has suggested how the two interrelate in the technology realm.[29] Paul Romer makes the further distinction of "rival" directly competing (VCRs or audio recorders) versus "nonrival" generic goods (like software bit strings or engineering principles) in which use by one person does not diminish the value of the goods remaining. He suggests three levels of support for these different economic subsets: government support and control of public goods, competition for rival goods, and voluntary industry support for nonrival or generic goods. For public goods, we strongly recommend allocation and development as public markets. For nonrival goods, Romer suggests that if an industry group agrees, government could levy a uniform tax on its products. The tax could support precompetitive research—as Sematech, Bell Labs, and EPRI have.[30] These frameworks are useful but do not address many of the profound issues posed by new software-network based innovation.

## Encouraging Private Software Innovation and Public Diffusion

A central problem of the new economy is that sophisticated use and further development of software innovations is often impossible without full disclosure of systems characteristics. Yet as soon as these are known, unscrupulous people can use or resell the basic software with little risk of being identified. Because rapid use of the latest knowledge is important to advance in many related areas, there are strong incentives to diffuse new software concepts rapidly and broadly.[31] But policing and collecting on fraudulent internal use of software is even more difficult than for industrial process infringements. Society benefits most when both protection and diffusion are possible.

Rapid innovation depends on innovators being rewarded for their efforts, and society benefits most as the general parameters of their innovations become known and others amplify and innovate specific features in their own self-interest.[32] Colin Gilfillan, founder of technology forecasting, underlined the awesome power of technological diffusion, once underway: "Once an innovation becomes known, thousands of inventions join it to give it a momentum and continuing force that becomes irresistible."[33] This amplification has been true of all great innovations from steam engines to biotechnology. It is much more rapid with software.

A major problem is how to reward innovators when software, once produced, can migrate so easily. On the Net, practices are emerging, as they have in consultants' publications, where the home page offers enough information to entice; but if a user wants really valuable information, there is more personal contact and a fee for encrypted use. Encryption can change as frequently as the seller chooses. Small-scale inventor-creators will generally need such intellectual property protection if they are to make their personally large initial investments, as will companies that have spent billions of dollars on large systems implementation. Statutory defenses to date have been hard to achieve; strong software patents are rare, although such applications are now swamping the system. And copyrights have been less than perfect defenses.[34] As in medical technologies, proprietary incentives pose major conceptual (and sometimes ethical) problems. Fortunately, economic and societal benefits come largely from diffusion of the software. And Atari, AT&T, and Apple's experiences suggest that even private interests are often better served by diffusion.

## New Threats and New Policy Needs

Unfortunately, diffusion can carry with it large negative potentials. A worldwide hacker culture exists that considers diffusion of software with minor modifications as a right—and as natural and legal as orally retelling the story of a good book. Hand in hand with diffusion come some gigantic new social threats—such as fraud, scurrilous libel, massive system disruptions, or creation of dangerous chemicals, potential disease agents, or weapons of mass destruction—that need to be controlled if society is to have any hope for survival. With an infinite number of potential alternative sources open to all participants, the best form of monitoring and control will be providing incentives for the many decentralized players on networks to detect and admonish bizarre behavior, actively anticipate potential problems, and disseminate information about destructive behaviors through some coordinating clearinghouse.[35]

A whole new class of social controls may be needed over those who—for their own amusement—try to destroy home records that may be irreplaceable, savings or retirement records whose loss could bankrupt families, electronic systems that protect air travelers, medical systems or records that protect secrets and save lives, production or customer records that mean livelihood for thousands, and so on. Never before has it been so possible, short of war and mass murder, to destroy so many lives so easily. Electronic protection may be the greatest innovation challenge in the new economy. Government investments in this area are clearly warranted to ensure equity and to lower total societal costs.

## Are Quasi-Monopolies Destructive?

One of the anomalies of software-based national technology strategies is that governments will probably have to grant some form of intellectual monopoly in order to generate technologies it hopes to be freely available to all. How well do such quasi-monopoly structures work? There have been constant concerns in the industrialized world that each new technology will be dominated by two or three of its early creators. This rarely happens. The natural state of any rapidly advancing technology sector seems to be a few large systems companies and a host of specialist features or applications companies. Both subgroups depend heavily on defendable intellectual property rights and tend to be quasi-monopolies competing for different segments of the market. Later, as a dominant technology emerges, there is a shakedown, with much consolidation and merging around those companies that have created de facto standards in the industry.[36] For a time the fortunate companies defend their positions through scale economies, distribution blocks, or superior information capabilities. Then follows another period of disaggregated company growth as these large companies become bureaucratized, and more innovative smaller companies focus on specialized aspects of the larger companies' value chains or on new technologies to replace their standards. Industries as diverse as pharmaceuticals, telecommunications, movies, television, electronic home appliances, airlines, automobiles, photography, financial services, and package delivery provide examples of this process.

Similar outcomes seem likely to occur in the international software world if countries enforce intellectual property rights even at the cost of quasi-monopolies. There are many counter-examples where socialist or populist dictatorship governments destroyed their own industrial sectors by refusing to protect intellectual property rights in fields like pharmaceuticals, agriculture and publication. Innovation either ceased or innovators took their concepts to countries where they would be rewarded. This can happen very easily in software innovations. Yet the rate of software piracy tolerated in many countries seems oblivious of such long-term effects. (See Table 13.1.)

As Romer has pointed out, permitting short-term technological quasi-monopolies is probably the most efficient way to promote innova-

**TABLE 13.1**
**Losses in Individual Nations from**
**Illegal Copying of Software, 1994**

|  | Loss ($ millions) | Piracy Rate (%) |
|---|---|---|
| United States | 2,877 | 35 |
| Japan | 2,067 | 67 |
| Germany | 1,875 | 50 |
| France | 771 | 57 |
| Brazil | 550 | 77 |
| Korea | 546 | 78 |
| Britain | 544 | 43 |
| Russia | 541 | 94 |
| China | 527 | 98 |
| Italy | 404 | 58 |

Source: *Business Week,* June 5, 1995, p. 4.

tion in rapidly advancing and highly diffuse industries like software, sensors, biotechnology, and services.[37] Larger companies' systems innovations seem to be naturally protected. Many studies show that attempts to pirate such systems and move them to other companies simply do not work, because operations are too dependent on other cultural, management, and innovation practices of the innovating company.[38] Such rigidities allow large companies to exploit their software advantages through secret art, while permitting benefits from enforced monopoly protection of innovations to be where they should be: with smaller enterprises.

## NEW DATABASES FOR A SERVICES AND INTELLECT-BASED SOCIETY

This kind of highly disaggregated, intellectually based economy requires a broad new set of measurements for effective self-guidance, public market development, and broad policy support. At the very apex, GDP, as measured by current techniques, misrepresents both progress and problems in many important economic sectors, especially those having to do with intellectual, service, and life quality outputs. Some of the most important concerns of society—the quality of housing, health care, education, transportation, justice, waste disposal, personal security, air, water, and recreation—are the very ones traditional economic measures handle least well, if at all.[39] In many countries—and cities of the United States—improved health services, recreational facilities, public transportation systems, educational opportunities, law enforcement, and environmental conditions could contribute much more to human well-being than higher measured GDP levels achieved through producing more gadgets and services for private consumption.[40]

Most macroeconomic measures and productivity paradigms, focusing on quantity and ignoring quality—were conceived during the agricultural-mechanical industrialization era. National accounts data about intellectual assets barely exist. No value is assigned to the Internet, for example. And data on business services are extremely misleading and contain major gaps.[41] Service industry productivity statistics cover only about 42% of service sector employment and only a limited range of industries. Units of output are difficult to define in many service industries. For some major service industries—notably banking and other financial services, education, health care, and government activities like police and fire departments—output is measured solely on the basis of input.[42] This assumption affects about 25 to 30% of the

$5 trillion services sector and makes productivity measurement in those areas almost meaningless.

## Defining Service and Technology Outputs

Measurement problems are multiplied by the fact that macroeconomic data do not capture many of the most important elements of service quality—for example, how well a hospital, airline, restaurant, hotel, or bank satisfies its customers.[43] This is especially true of those quality features most influenced by information and rapid-response technologies—features like complexity handling, timeliness, system flexibility, response times, reliability, safety, and accuracy. It is clearly meaningless to measure the number or dollar value of loans in banking without knowing the quality of those loans—or the number of airline miles traveled without knowing how long trips took, how safely, and with what delays. Similarly, the number of procedures performed in hospitals is useless without knowing how those procedures affected the health, morbidity, or longevity of patients. The same is true whether measuring outputs at the national or individual enterprise level.

Defining units of output poses major problems in many service industries, among them accounting, law, advertising, consulting, firefighting, or museum enterprises. How does one define output units for auditing, lawsuits, firefighting, or investment banking? One can measure total financial costs or outputs in some cases. However, without being able to define reasonable output units—or suitable deflators to convert dollar sales to a volume basis—how can one measure real output or productivity changes over several years? The answer is, poorly. has been a major source of confusion about the so-called "productivity slowdown" of the past decades.

## Pass-throughs to Other Sectors

Another major distortion is that, because of heavy competition, service enterprises often pass along many performance improvements—unrecognized by either corporate financial or macroeconomic measures—to customers or suppliers in other industries who may benefit enormously from them at no cost. Technology is moving so rapidly in some service sectors that it changes the nature of a sector's output radically within a few months or years. In these circumstances, it becomes difficult to use comparative macro-data to establish trends or measure national policy impacts meaningfully. For example, banks, telephone companies, wholesalers, product designers, airlines, supermarkets, advertising and travel agents provide much more complex, rapid, effective service than a decade ago; yet heavy competition has reduced their margins. Software's capabilities have also changed radically in the last two or three years. Many benefits from the improved outputs of these service industries now show up as enhanced capability for other sectors (including manufacturing). Two of many available examples will illustrate:

• McKesson Corporation, a $12.7 billion health care product producer and wholesaler, radically increased its services to customers during the 1980s. McKesson's drug wholesaling division began providing extensive computer support, accounting, layout and display, and price sticker services for its drug retailers and health provider customers. Many of these were previously extremely time-consuming and expensive operations for its customers. Yet McKesson saw wholesaling margins drop in its industry from about 7% to 3% over the past fifteen years. Although McKesson, and other wholesalers that followed, increased their service outputs significantly, competition did not allow them to capture these as higher profits or margins. Instead, they passed 4 percentage points of margin through to their pharmaceutical producers, retailers, and health customers.

• Travel agents today must complete in minutes arrangements they could not have handled in days, or in some cases weeks, only a decade ago. To optimize their load factors, airlines make an average of 175,000 fare adjustments a day and up to 600,000 on some days. Although these may help offset profit pressures in the airline industry, the frequency and complexity of travel itineraries, including worldwide travel and lodging arrangements, have increased by orders of magnitude. Yet agents' average commissions have held steady at between 7.5 and 9.5% on airline prices that have dropped in real terms since deregulation. Airlines are now trying to reduce this further.

## Outputs Overlooked

Standard databases also entirely overlook or fail to keep up with the advent of completely new services, like many currently being introduced on the Internet, in finance, or as new entertainment concepts. In financial services, information technologies have enabled huge transactions growth and have opened the way for a vast array of new products and services, from individually tailored loans and mortgages closed in thirty minutes, to international interest rate swaps and instant access to cash or loans in any world market. Daily, several trillions of dollars in financial (stock, bond, monetary, synthetic, hedging, and real property) transactions occur on various global financial networks. On these networks, new analysis techniques, financial instruments, and services offer customers much higher quality, variety, convenience, reliability, and accuracy than ever before. And access to global financial markets has decreased the cost of capital for U.S. companies and increased the potentials for individual investors to profit through a variety of new options. Yet such benefits are not reflected in the performance measures used for the financial services industry; rather, they are captured by customers or third parties, like governments or manufacturers, whose capital and transaction costs drop. But competitive pressures are such that the alternative for financial service providers is to go out of business.

Similarly, there are no effective measures of output value in the health care industry. At present, output value is assumed equal to costs. Yet new technologies and procedures allow cure of many formerly devastating diseases and traumas. They ameliorate the morbidity and pain of others, and they allow rapid handling of emergency cases in ways that save thousands of lives which would have been lost twenty years ago. None of these benefits is reflected in national economic accounts. It is clear, however, that despite complaints that "health care costs too much," few would want to return to an earlier era in which these potentials were not present. If the past investments made to achieve today's health, transportation, communications, and other miracles appeared in national accounts as "assets" for future use, it might become apparent that the retiring generation has left more assets than deficits; and some destructive political rhetoric might be mitigated.

## Disastrous Policy from Poor Data

All of these activities cry out for new sets of measures that can give better guidance. Various task forces—in the United States, GATT, the International Monetary Fund, OECD, and the UN—have suggested the nature of needed improvements.[44] None of these bodies yet has academically rigorous definitions or sufficiently refined granularity in its measurements to meet today's needs. But funding to achieve such benefits has neither been available internationally nor strongly enough supported domestically by the administration or Congress to do the job. Nor, interestingly, do the required financial reports of companies (on which national data rest) capture the full range of benefits these service enterprises offer. Some companies like General Motors, Sandia, and

Monsanto already issue extensive annual reports on nonfinancial aspects of their performance. Increasingly, it is becoming imperative to have certain critical nonfinancial measures of various industries' outputs, which can be linked to available financial measures, to answer relevant policy questions. While many such performance metrics already exist in arenas like health care, environmental improvement, communications, and transportation, they are rarely effectively integrated into national account databases or service industries' performance statistics.

## Restructuring Traditional Government Activities

Starting with these databases, many aspects of government will have to change to accommodate tomorrow's software- and intellect-dominated conditions. Decision structures of government itself will have to move from command-and-control bureaucracies toward market-type evaluations. Strong finance and control analytics will continue to be important when the government is buying for its own purposes. Increasingly, however, the most valuable assets and bases for agency power may be its data banks, communication systems, information accessibility, and responsiveness to user needs. The output of an agency will depend more on the use outsiders make of the agencies' information than on the impact it creates within the agency. The external uses of the DARPANET, NIH, EPA, National Weather Service, Commerce and Labor Departments, National Centers for Disease Control, Health Care Financing Administration (HCFA), GPS, and NASA satellite data are major cases in point. New methodologies must be found for calculating, crediting to the agencies, and perhaps selling the "network externality benefits" their systems create.

The private sector's experience is instructive. The most valuable assets of many large firms are their knowledge bases and information systems—typically software that embodies their true competitive edge. These include, among other things, their customer information systems (American Airlines or IBM), technology bases (3M or Intel), market databases (Dow Jones or TRW), operating software (Merrill Lynch or Federal Express), logistics (Boeing or McDonald's), product-marketing (Nike or Wal-Mart), distribution (AT&T or MCI), or concept implementation (Bechtel or Silicon Graphics) systems. Such information often has much greater value than the company's (or even the industry's) physical assets.

• In recent years, some companies providing public information about an industry—for example, *T.V. Guide* and *The Official Airline*

*Guide*—have sold for more than the asset value of any operating company in that industry at the time. Further, the sale, merger, or market price of successful information-based companies often exceeds their asset value by factors of three to seven, and stock market price-to-earnings multiples of 30 to 100 are common. Much of the difference lies in the value of the intellectual assets residing in the companies' databases and knowledge systems. (See Table 13.2.)

The government will still probably have to be a lead investor and development coordinator for some very large-scale electronic systems (like satellite communications) and those with long-term risks and very diffuse benefits (like the Internet). But its greatest contribution to social value will be in supporting access to and knowledge diffusion from these systems on the widest possible basis, especially to isolated areas and underdeveloped countries. From an investment viewpoint the government should facilitate diffuse private financings for the many decentralized ventures that will result from network innovations, rather than conceptualizing the problem as requiring major financial or R&D support for the Information Superhighway. If the government helps develop and break barriers to implementation of needed large systems—consciously designed with transparent structures and with sufficient access hooks for further innovation—private capital will minimize public costs and see to developing the multiple access points, failure-tolerant systems, and extensive linkages between innovators and markets that will maximize public gain.

## CAPITAL AND TAX POLICY SUPPORT FOR IT-BASED INNOVATION

Nevertheless, there are some broad policy moves that could greatly assist innovation and economic development through IT. Some would encourage further private investment in software. Others would encourage investment in other technologies IT supports. Others would provide infrastructures to help absorb employment dislocations that IT-based innovations will inevitably cause.

Most corporate accounting and national data practices now contain biases against software investments. Tax policies encourage companies to disguise or expense most software costs. Although such practices increase the tax shields from current IT investments, they lower apparent profits and result in a significant understatement of the enormous asset values of software, particularly in services companies. More important

**TABLE 13.2**
**Surplus or Intellectual Values of Largest Acquired Companies, 1987–1995**
**($ millions)**

| Transaction | Transaction Value | Book Value of Assets | Surplus or Intellectual Value | Transaction Value as % of Book | Date |
|---|---|---|---|---|---|
| Disney acquires Capital Cities/ABC | $19,000 | $4,404 | $14,596 | 431% | 1995 |
| First Bank acquires First Interstate | 10,300 | 4,154 | 6,146 | 248 | 1995 |
| AT&T acquires McGraw Cellular | 12,600 | -37 | 12,637 | (infinite) | 1994 |
| National Amusement acquires Blockbuster | 8,400 | 2,123 | 6,277 | 396 | 1994 |
| Matsushita acquires MCA | 6,274 | 2,340 | 3,933 | 268 | 1990 |
| MJR Holdings acquires First Interstate | 25,071 | 5,698 | 19,373 | 440 | 1989 |
| Bristol-Myers acquires Squibb | 12,656 | 1,485 | 11,170 | 852 | 1989 |
| Philip Morris acquires Kraft | 12,891 | 2,117 | 10,774 | 609 | 1988 |
| BP acquires Standard Oil (Ohio) | 7,995 | 3,160 | 4,835 | 253 | 1987 |

Sources: "Deals of the Year," *Fortune* magazine and *Mergerstat Review*, selected years.

*In market value terms, the intellectual value of companies outweighs their physical asset value by many times.*

from a policy viewpoint, categorizing software as an expense discriminates against such investments when investment tax credits or similar investment stimuli are established.

## Encouraging Savings and Investment over Consumption

With this notable exception, the basic macroeconomic and tax policies needed to support strong services and software activities are quite compatible with those desirable for a healthy manufacturing sector—not surprising when one understands the substitutability and interrelatedness of the two sectors. High among the national policies that would be most productive for innovation in either sector would be incentives to enhance capital formation, lower capital costs, and thus encourage long-term investments in technology. Innovation and productivity increases correlate highly with lowered capital costs. Low capital costs and high capital formation rates are stimulated by policies that selectively encourage savings and investment over consumption. Unfortunately, U.S. policies have run counter to both.

Total U.S. taxes actually take a lower percentage of GNP than those of their major trading partners. (See Figure 13.5.) The problem is their

**FIGURE 13.5**
**Government Receipts as a Percentage of GDP, 1995 (estimates)**

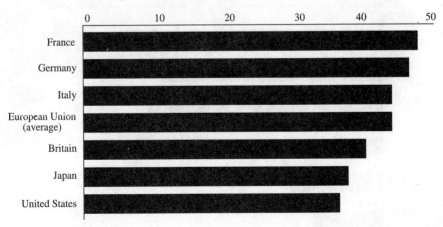

Source: Reproduced by special permission from "The Gloom Still Hovers," *Economist*, April 6, 1996, p. 43.

*In the United States taxes take a lower percentage of GDP than in other OECD countries. It is the structure of those taxes that discourages investment.*

structure. Current U.S. taxes are among the industrial world's most attractive for consumption and least attractive for long-term investors. (See Figure 13.6.) Income-based taxes account for 71.5% of all U.S. taxes, while indirect (property, goods, and services) taxes account for only 28.5%.[45] Since electronic integration of world capital markets has made a national policy of arbitrarily low average capital costs much more difficult to maintain, selectively lowering capital costs for longer-term investments (by requiring a three-to five-year holding period to obtain a lower capital gains tax) is one of the few ways American policy-

**FIGURE 13.6**
**General Consumption Taxes**

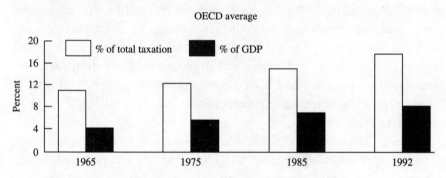

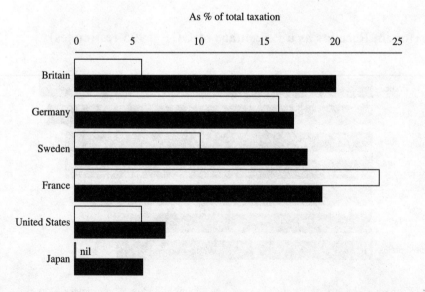

Source: Reproduced by special permission from "The Rise and Fall of VAT," *Economist,* April 19, 1995, p. 72.

*United States taxes on consumption are low compared to those of other major nations.*

makers can influence capital costs and savings to encourage longer-term investment.

Far from creating a tax break for investors, this might help redress the *multiple* levels of discrimination *against* savers and investors.[46] Investors must: first, pay taxes on their earned income before they invest it; second, have the corporation they invest in pay taxes on its returns; third, pay their taxes on the corporation's (after-tax) distributions when earned; fourth, forgo use of their income during the multiple years it is invested (implicitly dividing the total return by the number of years invested); then pay taxes on any capital gains they might make (not adjusted for the inflation tax already taken). The other selective mechanism the government has is direct investment. Historically, government-supported service infrastructure investments—starting with mail, road, canal, water, and transport systems, and expanding later into higher education, basic research, electric power distribution, and health care systems—have been major components in lowering private investment needs and in building technological and human capital bases for higher per capita income. These require better public market allocation mechanisms as discussed previously.

The well-documented shift from public investments to transfer payments has been one major reason for U.S. economic stagnation. Another is the large capital toll taken by the government's deficits and its refusal to release any social security funds for investment in the private sector. (Currently, all social security funds must be placed in treasury bonds.) Redressing the balance between true government investments and the portion of its expenditures spent on transfer payments could provide a large growth stimulus, especially if this reinvestment goes into such productive infrastructures as computer-literate education. Another redress would be to permit individuals to invest their component of required social security payments into higher-yielding private securities, thus directing trillions of dollars to higher-productivity uses. This subject is finally under serious discussion in the late 1990s.

## Regulation and Anticompetitive Activities

Services technologies have facilitated much wider ranges and more complex sets of cross-industry competition in the economy. Consequently, it is becoming ever less effective to stimulate investments or regulate on an industry or institutional basis (regulating banks or airlines as individual industries). In many cases (like trucking, railroads, banking, and telecommunications), more efficient market structures and full disclosure laws have already allowed deregulated competition to replace less efficient regulatory mechanisms. Because of cross-competition, whatever regulation remains is likely to be more equitable at a transactional level (establishing similar disclosure, safety, or insurance requirements for a particular transaction) regardless of which institution actually handles it, or at the functional level (establishing similar health, maintenance, environmental, safety, or electronics interface standards across all industries that might compete at a functional level). This becomes especially important as firms outsource many of their internal services, components, or parts. Without such regulation, they could simply externalize costs from their industries onto foreign countries or onto the public in a different fashion. Regulation at the institutional level (such as the Glass-Steagall Act) merely encourages disintermediation—that is, bypassing of the overregulated institution—as do any regulations that affect potential service outsourcing in the guise of job maintenance.

New forms of vertical integration through information networks, enabling retailers, distributors, manufacturers, and suppliers to tightly coordinate their efforts, may pose some new and complex regulatory issues. While lowering costs for consumers and generally increasing U.S. competitiveness, such systems also contain potentials for anticompetitive behavior—that is, market control through interlocking relationships. As long as a significant number of large-scale competitors exist at all levels of the value and selling chain, competition overcomes such problems. But government will have to monitor competitive behavior by new standards—across industry classes and by challenging whether the total effect of a large alliance will be to deny access to potential innovators, groups of buyers, or new competitive entrants.

## EDUCATION AND THE INTELLIGENT ECONOMY

In advanced countries, perhaps the most critical area for public concern is education for flexible employment and personal growth. Education is clearly a key resource in an intellectually driven service and software economy, and it is the best safety net in a changing employment situation. It is also the critical element in improving productivity and life quality in less developed countries. Many studies indicate that female education is the most important factor in improving infant mortality, family size and health, educational impacts, and hence economic development in these countries.[47]

Domestically, data indicate that the U.S. public education system, once among the world's strongest, has not been producing the kinds of skills needed to support this new economy. Test scores in mathematics and sciences experienced a long-term slide from earlier heights until 1995 provided some encouragement. However, current studies indicate the real problem is that K–12 education is not providing youth with the basic skills needed for the modern job market. The difficulty is largely that job skills for a middle-class income have increased much beyond those of the average high school graduate. Ninety percent of high school graduates could not meet the entry requirements at Ford Motor Company today.[48] The system's total production of scientists and engineers has not kept pace with the growth of international competitors. (See Table 13.3) The general quality of K–12 public education in many areas has been questionable. Numerous alternatives have been proposed to correct the now-apparent problems.[49] None as yet has sufficient support to be called an education policy.

Reformers nevertheless should be careful to apply any solutions selectively and experimentally at first. Although the country's basic education system seems to be performing less than adequately, its university and graduate systems remain the envy of the world. A large proportion (greater than 40%) of graduate science and engineering students in U.S. universities come from abroad. They do so because few graduate-level programs even in Japan or Europe enjoy the quality, discipline, support, and prestige of the best graduate schools in the United States. U.S. management schools are still considered the world's best, and U.S. corporate personnel training programs have been growing at an extraordinary rate. In combination with its developing infrastructures of computers, communications networks, and software, the United States has some great strengths on which to build for the future.

Fortunately, if developed properly, the national policies that support these technologies can simultaneously encourage a much more accessible, better-quality, total education system. Public K–12 education facilities should be looked at as critical nodes in developing both the information highway and a new educational infrastructure for the United States. In the past, free public schools and libraries were the critical elements in the education infrastructure. New policy emphasis should add greater availability and utilization of electronically based information throughout the system.

## Electronic Learning Potentials

Despite much discussion and their undoubtedly high potential value, electronic educational formats are still very experimental in most K –12

**TABLE 13.3**

## U.S. Scientists and Engineers Engaged in R&D by Country, 1965–1993 (in thousands)

|      | United States | Japan | West Germany | France | United Kingdom | Italy |
|------|------|------|------|------|------|------|
| 1965 | 494.2 | 117.6 | 61.0 | 42.8 | 49.9 | N/A |
| 1970 | 543.8 | 172.0 | 82.5 | 58.5 | N/A | 27.6 |
| 1971 | 523.5 | 194.3 | 90.2 | 60.1 | N/A | 30.9 |
| 1972 | 515.0 | 198.1 | 96.0 | 61.2 | 76.7 | 32.6 |
| 1973 | 514.6 | 226.6 | 101.0 | 62.7 | N/A | 33.3 |
| 1974 | 520.6 | 238.2 | 102.5 | 64.1 | N/A | 34.3 |
| 1975 | 527.4 | 255.2 | 103.7 | 65.3 | 80.5 | 37.9 |
| 1976 | 535.2 | 260.2 | 104.5 | 67.0 | N/A | 37.9 |
| 1977 | 560.6 | 272.0 | 111.0 | 68.0 | N/A | 39.7 |
| 1978 | 586.6 | 273.1 | 113.9 | 70.9 | 87.7 | 40.8 |
| 1979 | 614.5 | 281.9 | 116.9 | 72.9 | N/A | 46.4 |
| 1980 | 651.1 | 302.6 | 120.7 | 74.9 | N/A | 47.0 |
| 1981 | 683.2 | 317.5 | 124.7 | 85.5 | 95.4 | 52.1 |
| 1982 | 711.8 | 329.7 | N/A | 90.1 | N/A | 56.7 |
| 1983 | 751.6 | 342.2 | 130.8 | 92.7 | 94.0 | 63.0 |
| 1984 | 797.6 | 370.0 | N/A | 98.2 | N/A | 62.0 |
| 1985 | 841.2 | 381.3 | 143.6 | 102.3 | 97.8 | 63.8 |
| 1986 | 882.3 | 405.6 | N/A | 105.0 | 101.7 | 67.8 |
| 1987 | 910.2 | 418.3 | 165.6 | 109.4 | 101.4 | 70.6 |
| 1988 | 927.3 | 441.9 | N/A | 115.2 | 102.6 | 74.8 |
| 1989 | 949.3 | 461.6 | 176.4 | 120.7 | N/A | 76.1 |
| 1990 | N/A | 482.3 | N/A | 123.9 | 133.0 | 77.9 |
| 1991 | 960.4 | 491.1 | 240.8 | 129.8 | 131.0 | 75.2 |
| 1992 | N/A | 511.4 | N/A | 137.6 | 135.0 | 74.4 |
| 1993 | 962.7 | 526.5 | N/A | N/A | N/A | N/A |

N/A=not available

Sources: Science Resources Studies Division, National Science Foundation, *National Patterns of R&D Resources: 1992, Final Report,* NSF 92-330 (Washington, D.C.: NSF, 1992); and National Science Foundation, *Science and Engineering Indicators–1996.*

Notes: Data include all scientists and engineers engaged in R&D on a full-time basis with the following exceptions. Japanese data include persons primarily employed in R&D in the natural sciences and engineering, and the United Kingdom data include only government and industry sectors. The figures for Germany are for the former West Germany only; these data increased in 1979 because of increased coverage of small and medium-sized enterprises not surveyed in 1977, and data starting with 1979 were revised in 1988 using improved methodologies. The figures for France increased in 1981 in part because of a reevaluation of university research efforts.

**FIGURE 13.7**
**Social Returns for Investment in Education**

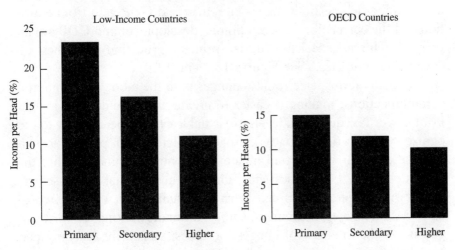

Source: "Schools Brief: Investing in People," *Economist,* March 26, 1994. Reproduced by special permission.
*Primary education pays high dividends in both low- and high-income countries.*

systems, but there is mounting evidence that children have the same high affinity for properly designed electronic learning that they have for games or languages. Experiments show that many slow learners in classroom situations can progress rapidly under the disciplined, but friendly, feedback from computers and gamelike devices as opposed to the authority and peer pressures of traditional classrooms. As the Armed Services and many companies have already demonstrated for more advanced education programs, quality of teaching can improve substantially through videotaped presentations, interactive learning simulations, and structured lessons on computers. At the basics level, television-based science and skills-training presentations are already well beyond the lecture capabilities of all but a few truly talented teachers. Many interesting computer-based arithmetic, spelling, and early reading programs can achieve better student responses than can most teachers—and they free teachers for more creative and targeted help sessions.

Although not well used in most areas of the United States to date, electronic approaches offer strong positive potentials if school systems, teachers, and administrators are willing to exploit them. The Clinton administration's proposed $2 billion Educational Technology Initiative is a jump start in extending these capabilities.[50] As hardware, networking, and software prices continue to plunge, wireless networks may allow less developed countries with well-educated elites, like India or China, to leap over some large educational infrastructure investments and training delays. Both the social return and GDP gain from education and the correlation between human development and GDP are impressive. This is especially true for primary education investments in developing countries. (See Figures 13.7 and 13.8).

In quality terms, electronics changes both the mode and content of communications, making it easier to create more memorable images. Printed words require two levels of virtual learning: the capacity to recognize symbolic (letter) patterns that associate with a particular word and the creation of a virtual image in the human mind of what that word describes. Electronics short-circuits these virtual processes and permits immediate, reinforced learning enhancement through words, color, visual images, movement, sound, dramatic lighting, or voice emphasis. As the intensity of images increases, so can the learning pace and the capacity to recall. Studies show that well-designed electronic learning programs like *Sesame Street* can have high impact on young learners. When interactiveness is added, the intensity and recall of the learning experience are even greater.[51] Graphic display capabilities of modern computers make it possible to show visual simulations of phenomena that are not directly observable, like a light wave diffracting around an edge, or surface phenomena at the atomic level. Computer graphics make these concepts much easier to understand and allow more students to participate directly in experiments changing various constants.

All this means probable shifts in the ratio between written and aural-visual learning, with corresponding efficiency improvements. Printed words are frozen on the page, immutable for time, and difficult to change or distribute widely. By contrast, electronic information can be updated constantly, modified for specific cultural settings, translated for various demographic purposes, and even modified by feedback. Since individuals learn best by different means—by experience, from observation, from print, by hearing, or from repetition—electronic literacy enhances the ability to match the medium to both the information offered and to its target audience. The capacity to modify the communication at the reception point can make education much more efficient, effective, and fun. And search software is increasingly being developed "to teach me what I need to know" for specific purposes. With its lead in computers per household, the United States enjoys some natural advantages. It already has 35 to 40 million households with interactive computer games, and numerous school systems have introduced

**FIGURE 13.8**
**Human Development Index, Country Ranking, 1992**

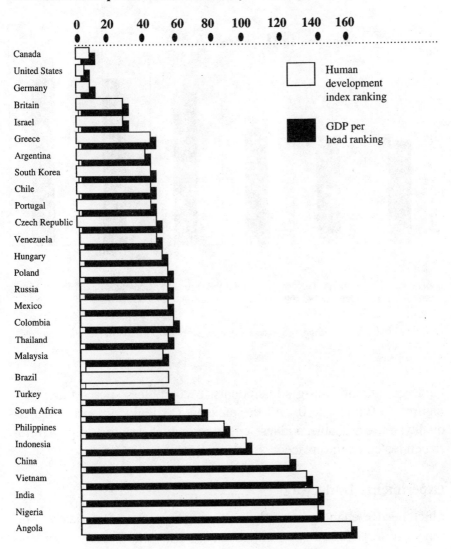

Source: Reproduced by permission from "Emerging-Market Indicators," *Economist*, August 26, 1995, p. 90.

*The United States Development Program Human Development Index (incorporating life expectancy, income, adult literacy, and educational enrollments) indicates a strong correlation between GDP and education. Canada and the United States ranked highest in the index rankings.*

**FIGURE 13.9**
**U.S. Households with Video Games and Computers (millions)**

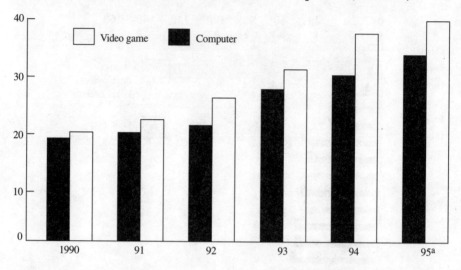

Source: Reproduced by special permission from"Will Your Next Computer Be a Tin Can and a Wire?" *Economist,* October 14, 1995, p. 76.
[a]forecast

*U.S. households have a large and expanding capability for participating in electronic education.*

kindergarten and first-grade students to computers successfully. (See Figures 13.9 and 13.10.) All these elements should support a higher-quality, more available, and less-costly education system as digital infra-structures come into place.

## Experiments Underway

Much needed change is already happening but not systematically. University professors are constantly amazed at the gap between the comprehension many students have of very complex ideas they have seen on television—about space, underseas, weather, politics, environmental, wildlife, physics, chemistry, or human health systems—and their ignorance of things they were supposedly taught in school—language, basic mathematics, geography, or history—all of which could be taught in child-fascinating form on interactive computer-television. Although there are substantial initial costs in training teachers, for the cost of a few textbooks every child could have an interactive, portable "learning game" computer. The cost of providing such devices has been dropping in real terms at about 30% per year, while the costs of education and re-

**FIGURE 13.10**
**Computers per 100 people, 1993**

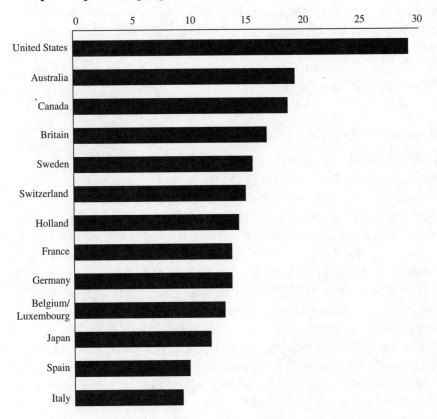

Source: Reproduced by special permission from"Technology and Unemployment: A World Without Jobs?" *Economist,* February 11, 1995, p. 22.
*The United States enjoys by far the highest penetration of computers for home and office use.*

placing books have been rising at 5 to 7% per year. Many experiments, both publicly and privately supported, are under way to exploit electronic potentials.

• Some teachers in suburban St. Paul have turned the Internet into a classroom teaching tool. With the support of the 3M Foundation and the University of Minnesota, they run two Web sites, Web 66 and Mustang, providing other teachers and educators with a place to share experiences and ideas. Their students have worked with counterparts around the world, contacting scientists, museums, and others globally. They note not only the enhanced interest this approach creates but that their students write better because "they are publishing for the world, not just writing for a teacher."[52] In the university sciences, a group of young graduate students, scientists, and post-docs has developed a virtual research center called BioMOO (for Multiple-user, Object Oriented). The center creates a virtual laboratory where researchers can share experiments, data, viewpoints, and techniques face to face in real time. The lab "occupants" need only a computer, software, and Internet connections to share the full facility.[53]

## Government or Private Action?

In developing countries most electronic education programs have been stymied by the high initial costs of electricity and telecommunications infrastructures. However, recognizing the potentials of large markets and a massive possible substitution of capital for labor in all education systems, private companies are beginning to provide the necessary infrastructures (software and hardware) as commercial ventures. Private investments in emerging countries grew from $41.9 billion to $172.9 billion from 1989 to 1994.[54] If host countries allow them to share adequately in profits, large consortia appear ready to invest in emerging-country infrastructures for basic telecommunications. (See Figure 13.11.)

One method by which the United States can participate for commercial profitability and with lowest cost nationally is to facilitate transfer of information *among* those nations where such privately supported installations do work well. Such cooperative arrangements are most productive when the developmental stage of the two countries is similar.

- India can benefit greatly from the experience of another highly populated, geographically dispersed, and low-earning-rate country like China. The United States government and U.S. companies have supported growth endeavors in both countries. In India, a satellite-based NICNET now allows anyone in government labs to connect with any others in India and to tap into worldwide sources on the same basis that a U.S. researcher could. The Indian National Scientific and Documentation Center has begun developing a database covering the nation's 1,000 technical and scientific libraries as well as 5,000 international journals.[55]

It seems clear that the value to a developing country's investing in creating its own telecommunication equipment, computers, or software is questionable and that its capacity to absorb information needs to be a major consideration in making technological support investments. The World Bank, the National Research Council of the United States, and

**FIGURE 13.11**
**Private Contributions to International Finance Corporation-
Sponsored Infrastructure Projects ($ billions)**

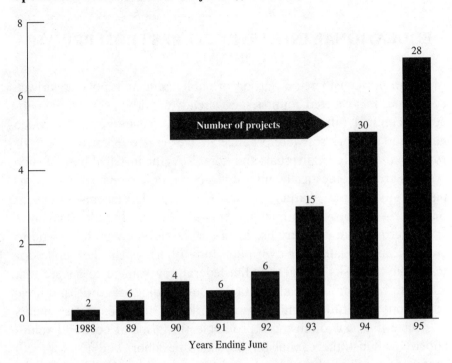

Source: Reproduced by special permission from"Finance and Economics," *Economist,* August 26, 1995, p. 62.
*If host countries allow reasonable opportunities for profits, private companies can ease the burdens of infrastructure investments for host countries.*

such volunteer organizations as Volunteers in Technical Assistance are engaged in major efforts to quantify the "knowledge-absorption" ability of various countries. When IT solutions do not match social capabilities, they tend to fail. When they do, the benefits are profound.

• The Internet allows people in developing countries like Jamaica, Barbados, and India to perform tasks ranging from entering credit card transactions, to translating technical papers, to establishing marketing cooperatives. In the United States much of the problem of finding jobs for welfare recipients revolves around young mothers who cannot realistically leave their children. Remote-access operations in services provide just the kinds of jobs they need. Carefully designed programs to teach these people what they need to know linked to local or national employers' needs have provided numerous permanent success stories.

Many of the opportunities for future economic development will call for the reconceptualization of society as a knowledge network and policies to support that concept.

## EDUCATIONAL INFRASTRUCTURES FROM PRIVATE COMPANIES

Although not considered a portion of public education policies, private companies in advanced countries are already providing substantial public educational infrastructures in their own self-interest. PC, video game, and network software producers have created massive decentralized capabilities for individuals and homes. As the installed base of such systems grows domestically, publishing-communications network companies—like Time Warner, News Corp., and Viacom–Simon & Schuster—are providing linkages between knowledgeable academics and entertainment software producers to develop new products and to enhance and update their own publishing offerings. In the public domain, the big tasks are: (1) for the federal government to ensure that adequate bandwidth and compatibility standards exist to tie all public educational institutions into such networks, (2) for local governments to realize that it is often more profitable (in terms of cost and value-added) to substitute capital for bureaucratic labor, and (3) for both groups to combine their powers and interests to break the substantial barriers to progress posed by educational bureaucracies and unions.

### From Teachers and Librarians to Information Agents

One critical factor is to change the way teachers and librarians perceive their roles. Without some way to locate, filter, organize, and summarize information, students (especially early learners) can be overwhelmed. Much of teaching has always been distilling vast amounts of information to a relevant core and then transmitting it effectively. Given the huge information bases now available on electronic networks, librarians, teachers, and scholars must essentially become information agents, helping to define and make information relevant to target audiences. Indexing programs—like Archie, Veronica, and the "web crawlers"—are an early starting point for this process. Nevertheless, one of the great challenges of educational policy will be to create an easily usable electronic cataloging system, allowing anyone in the electronic world to find any document, database, or needed information resource, as well as its related information sets, quickly and simply.[56] With so much information available, the capacity to interrogate it successfully will become a major creative skill for teachers to impart and an opportunity for innovators to provide new "smart" and adaptive solutions.

Along with these initiatives, there is a growing need for accepted open-format standards that enable still images, texts, video, and databases to be readily captured, cross-analyzed, and built upon. Extending existing copyright and patent laws to cover all electronic network exchanges is probably hopeless. Litigation is a very expensive remedial process, and litigation on software has already jammed available courts. There is a serious question as to whether standards allowing connection to these systems should be left completely to private discretion or established to ensure that conflicts of intention and interest can be resolved at minimum total (public and private) cost. Policymaking to create needed compromises between those who advocate free access and those who demand no unauthorized copying must proceed rapidly, before cumulative private investments and market interests make corrections too difficult or costly to contemplate.

• The model of the video rental and TV-movie industries is a useful starting point. Once a system for policing copyrights was established, TV stations were able to broadcast movies directly to homes. In addition, more than 50 million people also visited video rental stores weekly, rented over 100 gigabits of information each, paid only a few dollars, and began to create a $10 billion business with relatively little other formal regulation. Libraries already interconnect electronically, and lectures appear on transcontinental TV hookups for a fee. Extending such capabilities to public educational and other business realms should be feasible with reasonable oversight.

The problems are less technological than in the institutional-personal resistance realms. By breaking these resistances down, government actions and incentives could open the next wave of large public markets for advanced technology and provide a crucial intellectual infrastructure for the nation's future competitiveness.

## SUMMARY

The key parameters for strategy in the knowledge, software, and services age are (1) increasing general knowledge and access to S&T information, (2) lowering capital costs and facilitating venture investments, (3) improving educational infrastructures, (4) leveraging public and private investments together to provide better information diffusion domestically and internationally, and (5) developing public markets to deal with the inefficiencies and "white spaces" in private markets. If pursued properly, such intellectual development and network-growth policies will create very large output multipliers from the investments that initially stimulate them. As more people connect to the education system and the information networks supporting knowledge distribution, they will innovate new value-producing activities vastly in excess of those that can be foreseen by the original investors. This type of auto-catalytic or negative entropy economy provides a genuine hope for maintaining economic growth in a stimulating, exciting new mode. However, if policymakers stay with old product-driven, heavy investment, top-down command strategies, discouragement and stagnation are sure to occur.

Better education is clearly the linchpin of any sensible national strategy. The specifics of the right solution for a national education overhaul are well beyond our intended scope here. But it seems inevitable that, if consistent national leadership were applied, the same forces could overcome the U.S. public education malaise as overcame private companies' outmoded development practices and lack of productivity in the 1980s. Primary among these are (1) customer forces demanding better value, (2) social and technological changes creating a generation of young people unafraid of computers and comfortable in less-structured organizations, (3) business-technological entrepreneurs forcing new alternatives into rigidified and failing older institutions, (4) increasing outsourcing to and innovation from developing countries, (5) changed government rules to break barriers to progress, and (6) new technology-organization relationships that support totally different learning and work practices. With consistent policy support, these forces can change the face of education, the country, and the world within the decade. Countries that support education, intellectual, and economic development in the new mode are likely to be winners. Those that follow past practices or allow bureaucracies to rule development of their most important assets will pay a high price.

# Notes

## Introduction

1. See H. Itani, *Mobilizing Invisible Assets* (Cambridge, MA: Harvard University Press, 1987); G. Von Krogh, J. Roos, and K. Slocum, "An Essay on Corporate Epistemology," *Strategic Management Journal* (Summer 1994); S. Davis, "The Coming of Knowledge Based Business," *Harvard Business Review* (September–October 1994); J. Quinn, *Intelligent Enterprise* (New York: Free Press, 1992).

2. J. Quinn, P. Anderson, and S. Finkelstein, "Managing Professional Intellect," *Harvard Business Review* (March–April 1996), and "Leveraging Intellect," *Academy of Management Review* (Fall 1996) amplify these comments.

3. D. Montgomery and G. Day, "Experience Curves, Evidence, Empirical Issues," Report 85–101 (Cambridge MA: Marketing Science Institute, 1985); and D. Abell and J. Hammond, "Cost Dynamics and Experience Effects," *Strategic Market Planning* (Englewood Cliffs, NJ: Prentice Hall, 1979).

4. J. Quinn, "Microsoft (B) Case," in H. Mintzberg and J. Quinn, *The Strategy Process* (Englewood Cliffs, NJ: Prentice Hall, 1996).

5. Ibid. describes these practices in great detail.

6. I. Nakaka and M. Kenny, "Towards a New Theory of Innovation Management," *Journal of Engineering and Technology Management* 8 (1991); J. Hendry, "Barriers to Excellence and the Politics of Innovation," *Journal of General Management* (Winter 1989).

7. Specific examples are expanded at length in Quinn, *Intelligent Enterprise;* National Research Council, *Technology in the Service Society* (Washington, DC: National Academy Press, 1993); Quinn and Mintzberg, *Strategy Process;* S. Buckler, K.A. Zien et al, The Polaroid Invention and Innovation Research Project, 1993–1994; S. Buckler and K. A. Zien, "From Experience: The Spirituality of Innovation: Learning from Stories," *Journal of Product Innovation Management* (September 1996), and "From Experience: Dreams to Market: Crafting a Culture of Innovation," *Journal of Product Innovation Management* (July 1997).

8. J. Quinn in "Technological Innovation, Entrepreneurship and Strategy," *Sloan*

*Management Review* (Spring 1979), and "Managing Innovation: Controlled Chaos," *Harvard Business Review* (May–June 1985); and Zien and Buckler, in "Spirituality of Innovation" and "Dreams to Market," summarize these studies.

9. R. Moss-Kantor, *The Change Masters: Innovation for Productivity in the American Corporation* (New York: Simon & Schuster, 1983) is an excellent study of this sort.
10. Ibid.
11. H. Mintzberg, *Mintzberg on Management* (New York: Free Press, 1989).
12. J. Diebold, *The Innovators: The Discoveries, Inventions and Breakthroughs of Our Times* (New York: Dutton, 1990).
13. J. Jewkes, D. Sawers, S. Stillerman, *Sources of Innovation* (London: St. Martin's Press, 1958); A. Koestler, *The Sleepwalkers: A History of Man's Changing Vision of the Universe* (London: Hutchinson, 1959); T. Kuhn, *The Structure of Scientific Revolutions* (Chicago: University of Chicago Press, 1962). D. DeSola Price, "Of Sealing Wax and String," *Natural History* (January 1984).
14. A. D. Little Inc., *Barriers to Innovation in Industry* (Cambridge, MA: A. D. Little, 1973); Battelle Memorial Labs, *Science, Technology and Innovation*, report to National Science Foundation (Columbus, OH, 1973).
15. E. Von Hippel, *Sources of Innovation* (New York: Oxford Press, 1988).
16. Buckler and Zien, "Spirituality of Innovation."
17. E. Mansfield, *The Economics of Technological Change* (New York: Norton, 1968).
18. D. Teece, "Strategies for Capturing the Financial Benefits from Technological Innovation," in N. Rosenberg, R. Landau, and D. Mowery (eds.), *Technology and the Wealth of Nations* (Stanford, CA: Stanford University Press, 1992).
19. D. Schön, *Technology and Change* (New York: Delacorte Press, 1967).
20. I. Nonaka, "A Dynamic Theory of Organizational Knowledge Creation," *Organization Science* (February 1994), and "The Knowledge Creating Company," *Harvard Business Review* (November–December 1991).
21. A. Koestler, *The Act of Creation* (London: Hutchinson, 1964).
22. D. Schön, "Champions for Radical New Inventions," *Harvard Business Review* (March–April 1963); M. Maidique, "Entrepreneurs, Champions, and Technological Innovation," *Sloan Management Review* (Winter 1980); J. Howell and C. Higgins, "Champions of Technological Innovation," *Administrative Science Quarterly* (June 1990).
23. Quinn, *Intelligent Enterprise*, develops the implications of the "voluntary organization" in some depth; P. Senge, *The Fifth Discipline: The Art and Practice of the Learning Organization* (Garden City, NY: Doubleday, 1994), develops related concepts.
24. Quinn, "Managing Innovation: Controlled Chaos."
25. R. Dubin, *Theory Building* (New York: Free Press, 1968).

## Chapter 1. Executive Overview

1. Bureau of Economic Analysis. "The National Income and Product Accounts of the United States," series in the *Survey of Current Business*.
2. *Economist*, September 28, 1996, p. 25.
3. K. Sabbagh, *The Twenty First Century Jet* (New York: Scribner's, 1996).
4. J. Quinn, J. Baruch, and K. A. Zien, "Software-Based Innovation," *Sloan Management Review* (Summer 1996).

5. R. D' Aveni, *Hypercompetition* (New York: Free Press, 1994).

6. "How Does Your Economy Grow?" *Economist,* September 30, 1995.

7. M. Boskin and L. Lan, "Capital, Technology, and Economic Growth," in N. Rosenberg, R. Landau, and D. Mowery (eds.), *Technology and the Wealth of Nations* (Stanford, CA: Stanford University Press, 1992), analyze the key elements in this calculus.

8. J. Schumpeter, *The Theory of Economic Development* (Cambridge, MA: Harvard University Press, 1949), is his principal statement of these theories.

9. M. Abramovitz, "Resource and Output Trends in the U.S. Since 1870." *American Economic Review Papers and Proceedings* (May 1956); J. Kendrick, "Productivity Trends: Capital and Labor," *Review of Economics and Statistics* (August 1956); R. Solow, "A Contribution to the Theory of Economic Growth," *Quarterly Journal of Economics* (February 1956); J. Kindelberger, *Economic Development* (New York: McGraw-Hill, 1965); J. Dewhurst, *America's Needs and Resources: A New Survey* (New York: Twentieth Century Fund, 1965).

10. S. Kuznets, *Economic Growth of Nations* (Cambridge, MA: Harvard University Press, 1971); R. Solow, "A Contribution to the Theory of Economic Growth"; same author, "Technological Change and the Aggregate Production Function," *Review of Economics and Statistics* 39 (August 1957); same author, *Growth Theory: An Exposition* (Cambridge: Oxford University Press, 1988).

11. U.S. Department of Energy, Energy Information Administration, *International Energy Annual,* (Washington, DC: Government Printing Office, 1984).

12. R. Revelle, "The Resources Available for Agriculture," in *Food and Agriculture* (San Francisco: Freeman, 1976).

13. G. Mankiw, "The Growth of Nations," *Brookings Papers on Economic Activities* (Washington, DC: Brookings Institution, September 1995).

14. Ibid.

15. P. Romer, "Endogenous Technological Change," *Journal of Political Economy* 98, no. 5 (1990).

16. *Economist,* June 8, 1996, p. 19.

17. D. Jorgensen and R. Landau (eds.), *Technology and Capital Formation* (Cambridge, MA: MIT Press, 1989).

18. P. Romer and R. Barro, "Human Capital and Growth: Theory and Evidence," *Carnegie-Rochester Conference Series on Public Policy* (Spring 1990), develops the evidence rigorously and shows the influence of different government policies.

19. *Economist,* September 14, 1996, p. 26.

20. Interview by J. Quinn with G. Carr, former astronaut, now Senior V.P., Camus, September 1996.

21. D. Price, "The Scientific Establishment," in W. Nelson (ed.), *The Politics of Science* (New York: Oxford University Press, 1968).

22. J. Quinn, "National Planning of Science and Technology in France," *Science* 19 (November 1965).

23. See National Academy of Engineering, *Time Horizons and Technology Investments* (Washington, DC: National Academy Press, 1992); E. Hatsoupolis, P. Krugman, and L. Summers, "U.S. Competitiveness Beyond the Trade Deficit," *Science,* July 15, 1988; J. Poterba, "Comparing the Cost of Capital in the U.S. and Japan," *Federal Reserve Board of New York, Quarterly Review* (Winter 1991).

24. M. Reisner, *Cadillac Desert: The American West and Its Disappearing Water* (New York: Penguin Books, 1987), cites numerous specific examples of such misallocations.
25. P. Romer et al. have a series of papers on how technology and human capital affect growth: "Implementing a National Technological Strategy with Self Organizing Industry," *Breakout Papers on Economic Activity* (1993), pp. 345–399; "Idea Gaps and Object Gaps in Economic Development," *Journal of Monetary Economics* 32 (1994), and "Increasing Return and Long-Run Growth," *Journal of Political Economy* 94, 5 (1986), 1002–1037. Also note National Research Council, Computer Science and Telecommunications Board, *Information Technology in the Services Society* (Washington, DC: National Academy Press, 1994).
26. M. Baily and R. Gordon, "The Productivity Slowdown: Measurement Issues and the Explosion of Computer Power," *Brookings Papers on Economic Activity* (Washington, DC: Brookings Institution, 1988).

## Chapter 2. Software-Based Innovation

1. J. Kaiser, "A New Way of Seeing Proteins in Motion," *Science* (September 1994).
2. D. Weingarter, "Quarks by Computer," *Scientific American* 274 (February 1996): 116–120.
3. J. Marx, "A New Guide to the Human Genome," *Science,* December 22, 1995.
4. For examples and details, see J. Verity, "A Trillion Byte Weapon," *Business Week,* July 31, 1995; "IBM Backlog," *Computerworld,* October 11, 1993, pp. 1, 7; "Boeing Overhaul Taking Flight," *Information Week,* September 26, 1994, p. 18; and P. Anderson, *Conquest,* case (Hanover, NH: Amos Tuck School, 1996).
5. A. Aynbinder, "Nonlinear Analysis Can Improve Pipeline Design," *Oil and Gas Journal,* March 25, 1996, pp. 76–81.
6. J. Quinn and F. Hilmer, "Strategic Outsourcing," *Sloan Management Review* 35 (Summer 1994): 43–55; and G Bylinski, "The Digital Factory," *Fortune,* November 14, 1994.
7. D. Bartholemew, "Ford Retools," *Information Week,* April 1, 1996.
8. "Virtual Reality Comes to Design Reviews," *Machine Design,* April 4, 1996.
9. Many innovative new organizational forms depend heavily on software for their implementation. See J. Quinn, P. Anderson, and S. Finkelstein, "Leveraging Professional Intellect," *Academy of Management Executive* (August 1996).
10. J. Moore, "The Death of Competition," *Fortune,* April 15, 1996, pp. 142–144.
11. P. Roussel, K. Saad, and T. Erickson, *Third Generation R&D* (Boston: Harvard Business School Press, 1991).
12. P. Proctor, "Automatic Design Software," *Aviation and Space Technology,* April 8, 1996.
13. K. Sabbagh, *The Twenty First Century Jet* (New York: Scribner's, 1996).
14. J. Main, "Betting on the Twenty First Century Jet," *Fortune,* April 1992, pp. 102–104, 108, 112, 116–117.
15. T. Stadt, "Research Speeds Development," *R&D* (March 1996): 14–18.
16. For a description of the electronic processes and interactions with other fields that molecular designs in biotechnology require, see B. Werth, *The Billion Dollar Molecule* (New York: Touchstone Books, 1995); and H. Berendsen, "Bimolecular Dynamics Comes of Age," *Science,* February 16, 1996, pp. 954–955.

17. R. Leahy, "Asphalt Update," *Civil Engineering* (April 1996).

18. W. Gibbs, "Where the Wind Blows," *Scientific American* (December 1996), shows how remote sensing and massive computation can now forewarn ships of unusual wave conditions that could be life threatening.

19. J. Snow, "The Expanding Role of Industrial Design Software," *Automotive Production* (January 1966): 46–47.

20. M. Troscinski, "Real World Modeling Keeps Analysis Honest," *Machine Design*, March 31, 1996, offers multiple examples.

21. L. Randall, "The Magician," *Forbes*, March 11, 1996, pp. 122–128.

22. A. Mushegian and E. Koonin, *Proceedings of the National Academy of Sciences, USA* 93 (1996): 10268–10273.

23. "Computing: Networks and Modeling," *Science*, August 12, 1994.

24. "Looking for the Evidence in Medicine," *Science*, April 5, 1996, pp. 22–24.

25. E. Von Hippel, *Sources of Innovation* (New York: Oxford University Press, 1988).

26. D. Romanchik, "Virtual Instruments Meet Custom Test Needs," *Quality* (February 1996): 28–32.

27. J. Martin, "Are You As Good As You Think You Are?" *Fortune*, September 30, 1996.

28. P. Senge, *The Fifth Discipline: The Art and Practice of the Learning Organization* (Garden City, NY: Doubleday, 1994).

29. R. D'Aveni, *Hypercompetition* (New York: Free Press, 1994).

30. L. Kempfer, "The 'Wow' Factor," *Computer Aided Engineering* (November 1995): 24–32.

31. J. Quinn and M. Baily, "Information Technology: Increasing Productivity in Services," *Academy of Management Executive* 8 (August 1994): 28–51.

32. The National Research Council found attempts to build such megasystems among the most costly errors that large users had made in installing information technology. See National Research Council, *Information Technology in the Service Society* (Washington, DC: National Academy Press, 1994).

33. J. Pine, *Mass Customization: The New Frontier in Business* (Boston: Harvard Business School Press, 1993).

34. For an excellent overview of the generally available network software in early 1996, see "The Software Revolution," *Business Week*, December 4, 1995, p. 78.

## Chapter 3. Managing Software-Based Innovation

1. P. Romer, "Increasing Returns and Long Term Growth," *Journal of Political Economy* 94, no. 5 (1986) makes this argument as a strategy for the national economy.

2. "Software Industry Survey," *Economist*, May 25, 1966, p. 17.

3. B. Palsson, "What Lies 'Beyond Bioinformatics'," *Nature Biotechnology*, January 15, 1997.

4. M. Mitchell, "Taking the Data in Hand—Literally—with Virtual Reality," *Science*, August 12, 1994; "Computing: Networks and Modeling," *Science*, August 12, 1994; and W. Gibbs, "Where the Wind Blows," *Scientific American* (December 1996), outline many of these approaches.

5. "Computers That Think Are Almost Here," *Business Week*, July 17, 1995.

6. R. Lewin, *Complexity: Life at the Edge of Chaos* (New York: Macmillan, 1992); and

M. Waldrop, *Complexity: The Emerging Science at the Edge of Order and Chaos* (New York: Simon & Schuster, 1992).

7. *Business Week,* December 4, 1995, p. 78.
8. "The Property of the Mind," *Economist,* July 27, 1996, poses some interesting implications and alternatives.
9. F. Brooks, *The Mythical Man Month* (Reading, MA: Addison–Wesley, 1975);˙ S. Chan, "From Software Art to Software Engineering," *Engineering Management Journal* (December 1995): 23–27.
10. R. Moss-Kantor, *The Change Masters* (New York: Simon & Schuster, 1983); and J. Utterback, *Mastering the Dynamics of Innovation* (Boston: Harvard Business School Press, 1994).
11. J. Kotter and J. Heskett, *Corporate Culture and Performance* (New York: Free Press, 1992).
12. For a more detailed view of this process, see H. Mintzberg and J. Quinn, "Microsoft (B)," in *The Strategy Process* (Englewood Cliffs, NJ: Prentice Hall, 1996).
13. For further details on this process, see "Andersen Consulting (Europe)," in ibid.
14. *Phoenix SPI Reference Guide* (McLean, VA: Litton-PRC, April 1996), and J. Quinn interviews with PRC executives, December 1996.

## Chapter 4. Beyond Teams

1. A. Cambrosio and P. Keating, *Exquisite Specificity* (New York: Oxford University Press, 1995), demonstrates this in exquisite detail for the monoclonal antibody innovation.
2. We gratefully acknowledge the many major contributions of Philip Anderson and Sydney Finkelstein of Amos Tuck School to the development of this and the next chapter.
3. This structure derives from discussions with Goodloe Suttler, technical planning director of Analog Devices, Inc., around the concepts of TRIZ software.
4. "Sam Walton in His Own Words," *Fortune,* June 29, 1992.
5. W. Saporito, "What Sam Walton Taught America," *Fortune,* May 4, 1992.
6. S. Wheelwright and K. Clark, *Revolutionizing Product Development: Quantum Leaps to Speed, Efficiency and Quality* (New York: Free Press, 1992).
7. M. Schrage, *No More Teams: Mastering the Dynamics of Creative Collaborations* (Garden City, NY: Doubleday, 1989), pp. 32–33.
8. E. Gamow, *Thirty Years That Shook Physics: The Story of Quantum Theory* (Garden City, NY: Doubleday, 1965), offers many excellent examples.
9. I. Janis, *Groupthink* (Boston: Houghton Mifflin, 1982), sets forth many of the limits of teams, as do Schrage, *No More Teams;* H. Robbins and M. Finley, *Why Teams Don't Work: What Went Wrong* (Princeton, NJ: Pacesetter Books, 1995); and "The Trouble with Teams," *Economist,* January 14, 1995.
10. "A Virtual Lab That Turns Up Real-Life Designs," *Business Week,* November 13, 1995.
11. "Hot Property: Biologists Who Compute," *Science,* June 21, 1996, offers some interesting examples.
12. T. Hoffman, "Clorox Cleans Up Its Design Process," *Computerworld,* November 20, 1995, p. 81.

13. J. Quinn, P. Anderson, and S. Finkelstein, "Leveraging Professional Intellect," *Academy of Management Executive* (Summer 1996).

14. E. Hall, *Beyond Culture* (Garden City, NY: Doubleday, 1989).

15. This example is paraphrased from "Sam Walton, Wal-Mart, and the Discounting of America," in D. Gross, *Forbes Greatest Stories of All Time* (New York: Wiley, 1996).

16. Information on Boston Market from J. Quinn interview with CEO Scott Beck, December 1996.

17. A simple computer search brought forth ninety books on various aspects of team management published in 1995–1996 alone.

18. R. Miles and C. Snow, "Organizations: New Concepts for New Forms," *California Management Review* (Spring 1986).

19. R. Cyert and J. March, *A Behavioral Theory of the Firm* (Englewood Cliffs, NJ: Prentice Hall, 1963), and L. Sayles, *Managerial Behavior in Complex Organizations* (New York: McGraw-Hill, 1964), are among the early classics investigating this type of management.

20. F. Contractor and P. Lorange, *Cooperative Strategies in International Business* (San Francisco: Lexington Books, 1987); J. Lewis, *Partnership for Profit, Structuring and Managing Strategic Alliances* (New York: Free Press, 1990); T. Collins and T. Doorley, *Teaming Up for the 90's* (Homewood, IL: Irwin, 1991).

21. P. Drucker, "The Coming of the New Organization," *Harvard Business Review* (January–February 1988).

22. Schrage, *No More Teams.*

23. M. Wheatley, *Leadership and the New Science* (San Francisco: Berrett-Koehler, 1992).

24. P. Rabinow, *Making PCR* (Chicago: University of Chicago Press, 1995).

25. The theoretical and experiential basis for these observations comes from classic studies cited below; and from K. A. Zien's collaboration and participation with others in Margaret Wheatley and Myron Kellner-Rogers' "Berkana Dialogues," beginning in 1992.

26. R. Merton, "The Normative Structure of Science," in *The Sociology of Science, Theoretical and Empirical Innovations* (Chicago: Chicago University Press, 1942).

27. W. Given, *Bottom Up Management: People Working Together* (New York: Harper, 1949), and W. Ouchi, *Theory Z: How American Business Can Meet the Japanese Challenge* (Reading, MA: Addison-Wesley, 1981).

28. M. Wheatley and M. Kellner-Rogers, *A Simpler Way* (San Francisco: Berrett-Koehler, 1996).

29. Rabinow, *Making PCR.*

30. D. McGregor, *The Human Side of Enterprise* (New York: McGraw-Hill, 1960); R. Likert, *New Patterns in Management* (New York: McGraw-Hill, 1961); and C. Argyris, *Integrating the Individual and the Organization* (New York: Wiley, 1969).

31. M. Heidegger, *The Question Concerning Technology and Other Essays*, trans. W. Lovett (New York: Harper & Row, 1977).

32. P. Senge, *The Fifth Discipline: The Art and Practice of the Learning Organization* (Garden City, NY: Doubleday, 1990).

33. S. Buckler and K. A. Zien, "From Experience: The Spirituality of Innovation: Learning from Stories," *Journal of Product Innovation Management* (September 1996).

34. F. Shipper and C. Manz, *W.L. Gore and Associates, Inc., 1996,* case (Tempe: Arizona State University, 1996).

35. K. A. Zien and S. Buckler, "From Experience: Dreams to Market: Crafting a Culture of Innovation," *Journal of Product Innovation Management* (July, 1997).

36. "How to Kick the Mainframe Habit," *Business Week,* June 26, 1996.

37. "Zap, Splat, Smarts," *Business Week,* December 23, 1996, offers many current examples

38. I. Nonaka, "A Dynamic Theory of Organizational Knowledge Creation," *Organization Science* (February 1994).

39. K. Weick, *The Social Psychology of Organizations* (New York: Random House, 1979).

40. Schrage, *No More Teams.*

41. Philip Anderson brought this insight to our attention as he did for many other aspects of the technology, software, organizational interfaces. We are most grateful.

42. G. Arnaut, "Partners in a Virtual Workspace," *Information World,* December 16, 1996.

43. C. Perrow, "Accidents in High Risk Systems," in *Technological Studies* (Berlin: W. de Gruyter & Co., 1994), and S. Casey, *Set Phasers on Stun: True Tales of Design, Technology, and Human Error* (Santa Barbara, CA: Aegean Publishing Co., 1993), analyze the causes of many such failures.

44. I. Nonaka and H. Takeuchi, *The Knowledge Creating Company* (New York: Oxford University Press, 1994).

45. R. Stross, "Microsoft's Big Advantage: Hiring Only the Supersmart," *Fortune,* November 25, 1996.

46. Nonaka and Takeuchi, *Knowledge-Creating Company.*

47. I. Nonaka, "Toward Middle-Up-Down Management; Accelerating Information Creation," *Sloan Management Review* (Spring 1988), discusses the imperatives of such organizations.

48. Wheelwright and Clark, *Revolutionizing Product Development,* demonstrates how to organize for several different kinds of intensity in this collaboration.

49. R. Katz and T. Allen, "Project Performance and the Locus of Influence in the R&D Matrix," *Academy of Management Journal* (March 1985); and C. O'Reilly and M. Tushman, "Using Culture for Strategic Advantage: Promoting Innovation Through Social Control," in M. Tushman and P. Anderson (eds.), *Managing Strategic Innovation and Change* (New York: Oxford University Press 1996).

50. Nonaka and Takeuchi, *Knowledge-Creating Company.*

51. C. Bartlett and S. Goshal, "Release the Entrepreneurial Hostages from Your Corporate Hierarchy," *Strategy and Leadership* (July–August 1996).

52. Shipper and Manz, *W.L. Gore and Associates.*

53. W. Starbuck, "Organizations and Their Environments," in M. Dunnette (ed.), *Industrial and Organizational Psychology* (New York: Rand, 1976).

54. R. Lewin, *Complexity: Life at the Edge of Chaos* (New York: Macmillan, 1992).

55. R. Wesson, *Beyond Natural Selection* (Cambridge, MA: MIT Press, 1991).

56. Wheatley, *Leadership and the New Science.*

57. E. Mayr, *Systematics and the Origins of the Species* (New York: Columbia University Press, 1942).

58. I. Prigogine and I. Stenger, *Order Out of Chaos* (New York: Bantam Books, 1984).

59. S. Kauffman, "Escaping the Red Queen Effect," in *At Home in the Universe: The Search for Laws of Self Organization and Complexity* (New York: Oxford University Press, 1995).

60. Kellner-Rogers and Wheatley, "The Berkana Dialogues."

61. J. Forrester, *Industrial Dynamics* (Cambridge, MA: MIT Press, 1961).

62. J. Gleick, *Chaos: Making a New Science* (New York: Viking Press, 1987).

63. M. Kellner-Rogers and M. Wheatley, "Self Organizing: The Irresistible Future of Organizing," *Strategy and Leadership* (July–August 1996).

64. T. Amabile, "Motivational Synergy: Toward New Conceptions of Intrinsic and Extrinsic Motivation in the Marketplace," *Human Resource Management Review* 3, no. 3 (1993).

65. R. Kaplan and D. Norton, "Using the Balanced Scorecard as a Strategic Management System," *Harvard Business Review* (January–February 1996).

66. *Intellectual Capital: Power of Innovation* (Stockholm, Sweden: Scandia Corporation, 1996) explains that company's approach to this identity.

67. R. Howard, "Values Make the Company: An Interview with Robert Haas," *Harvard Business Review* (September–October 1990).

68. Wheatley, *Leadership and the New Science*, p. 44.

## Chapter 5. Motivating Creativity Toward Markets

1. A. Koestler, *The Act of Creation* (London: Hutchinson, 1964); and J. Diebold, *The Innovators: The Discoveries, Inventions, and Innovations of Our Times* (New York: Dutton, 1990).

2. S. Kaplan, *An Introduction to TRIZ: The Russian Theory of Problem Solving* (Southfield, MI: Ideation International Inc., 1996), G. Altshuller, *And Suddenly the Inventor Appeared: TRIZ, The Theory of Inventive Problem Solving* (Worcester, MA: Technical Innovation Center, 1996).

3. A. Choi, "Invention Machine's Software Wins Orders for Picking Brains of Inventors," *Wall Street Journal*, February 12, 1996.

4. A. Cambrosio and P. Keating, *Exquisite Specificity: The Monoclonal Antibody Revolution* (New York: Oxford University Press, 1995).

5. K. A. Zien and S. Buckler, "From Experience: Dreams to Market: Crafting a Culture of Innovation," *Journal of Product Innovation Management* (July 1997).

6. Edith Wilson, "Product Definition: Assorted Techniques and Their Marketplace Impact," Institute of Electrical and Electronics Engineers: Engineering Management Conference Report, 1990, pp. 64–69.

7. H. Mintzberg and J. Quinn, *The Strategy Process* (Englewood Cliffs, NJ: Prentice Hall, 1995).

8. We gratefully acknowledge the key contributions of Philip Anderson of Amos Tuck School for these and other major insights in this chapter.

9. R. Root-Bernstein, *Discovering* (Cambridge, MA: Harvard University Press, 1991).

10. R. Feynman, *Surely You're Joking, Mr. Feynman: Adventures of a Curious Character* (New York: Norton, 1984).

11. M. Tushman, P. Anderson, and C. O'Reilly, "Technology Cycles, Innovation Streams, and Ambidextrous Organizations," in M. Tushman and P. Anderson, *Managing Strategic Innovation and Change* (New York: Oxford University Press, 1997), describes the problems and essentiality for this kind of responsiveness.

12. P. Rabinow, *Making PCR* (Chicago: Chicago University Press, 1996).
13. Zien and Buckler, "From Experience: Dreams to Market."
14. E. Von Hippel, "Sticky Information and New Market Research Methodologies," *And Now for Something Completely Different: Really New Products,* Marketing Science Institute Conference, September, 1994.
15. D. Leonard-Barton, *Wellsprings of Knowledge* (Boston: Harvard Business School Press, 1995), amplifies this and practical approaches to linking innovators and users.
16. Zien and Buckler, "From Experience: Dreams to Market."
17. *Concept Engineering,* document 71 (Boston: Center for Quality Management, September 1992).
18. S. Buckler and K. A. Zien, "From Experience: The Spirituality of Innovation: Learning from Stories," *Journal of Product Innovation Management* (September 1996).
19. J. O'Toole, *Leading Change* (San Francisco: Jossey-Bass, 1996).
20. D. Schön, "Champions for Radical New Inventions," *Harvard Business Review* (March–April 1963).
21. J. Quinn, *Strategies for Change: Logical Incrementalism* (Homewood, IL: Irwin, 1980).
22. H. Mintzberg, "The Pitfalls of Strategic Planning," *California Management Review* (Fall 1993).
23. J. Quinn, "How to Evaluate Industrial Research Results," *Harvard Business Review* (May–June 1959), and *Yardsticks for Industrial Research* (New York: Ronald Press, 1959), develop multiple methodologies in detail.
24. K. Kelly, *Out of Control* (New York: Macmillan, 1994).
25. R. Frank and P. Cook, *The Winner Take All Society* (New York: Free Press, 1995).

### Chapter 6. Vision, Leadership, and Strategic Focus

1. J. Quinn, *Intelligent Enterprise* (New York: Free Press, 1992). Also see A. Deutschman, "The Managing Wisdom of High-Tech Superstars," *Fortune,* October 17, 1994; T. Stevens, "Converting Ideas into Profits," *Industry Week,* June 3, 1996; S. Buckler and K. A. Zien, "From Experience: The Spirituality of Innovation: Learning from Stories," *Journal of Product Innovation Management* (September 1996) and From Experience: Dreams to Market: Crafting a Culture of Innovation," *Journal of Product Innovation Management* (July 1997); all of whom make this point very clearly.
2. "Intel Corporation" and "Polaroid Corporation" Cases, in H. Mintzberg and J. Quinn, *The Strategy Process* (Englewood Cliffs, NJ: Prentice Hall, 1996).
3. N. Nichols, "Scientific Management at Merck: An Interview with CFO Judy Lewent," *Harvard Business Review* (January–February 1994): 89–90.
4. K. Inamori, "Respect the Divine and Love People," *Industry Week,* June 5, 1995.
5. K. A. Zien, "Market Leadership," *Sloan Management Review* (Spring 1996); and Zien and Buckler, "Dreams to Market."
6. C. Perrow, "The Analysis of Goals in Complex Organizations," *American Sociological Review* (February 1961), and T. Peters and R. Waterman, *In Search of Excellence* (New York: Harper & Row, 1983), provide classic theoretical and empirical statements of this phenomenon.
7. "Microsoft (B)," case in Mintzberg and Quinn, *Strategy Process.*

8. R. Cyert and J. March, *A Behavioral Theory of the Firm* (Englewood Cliffs, NJ: Prentice Hall, 1963); and Zien and Buckler, "Dreams to Market."

9. T. Levitt, "Creativity Is Not Enough," *Harvard Business Review* (May–June 1963) was an early recognition of this concept.

10. J. Martin, "Are You as Good as You Think You Are?" *Fortune,* September 30, 1996.

11. T. Steiner and D. Teixeira, *Technology in Banking* (Homewood IL: Dow Jones–Irwin, 1996.)

12. "Honda Motor Company," case in Mintzberg and Quinn, *Strategy Process.*

13. H. Mintzberg and F. Westley, "Visionary Leadership and Strategic Management," *Strategic Management Journal* (June 1989).

14. R. Fritz, *Creating* (New York: Ballantine, 1990.)

15. W. Bennis, *Leaders: Strategies for Taking Charge* (NewYork: Harper & Row, 1985).

16. For some practical methodologies for creating a vision see T. Stewart, "A Refreshing Change: Vision Statements That Make Sense," *Fortune* (September 1996).

17. *Prospectus: Genentech Corporation* (April 1976).

18. J. Kotter and J. Heskett, *Corporate Culture and Performance* (New York: Free Press, 1992), p. 11.

19. Buckler and Zien, "Spirituality of Innovation," refer to aligning "life-work with work-work."

20. R. Fritz, *The Path of Least Resistance* (New York: Ballantine, 1989).

21. S. Jönson and R. Lundin, "Myths and Wishful Thinking as Management Tools," in P. Nystrom and W. Starbuck (eds.), *Prescriptive Models of Organizations* (Amsterdam: North-Holland, 1977).

22. Buckler and Zien, "Spirituality of Organization."

23. Ibid.

24. P. Senge, "The Leader's New Work: Building Learning Organizations," *Sloan Management Review* (Fall 1990).

25. Buckler and Zien, "Spirituality of Organization."

26. M. DePree, *Leadership Is an Art* (Garden City, NY: Doubleday, 1989).

27. T. L. Smith, speech delivered at Eastern Nazarene College, Quincy, MA, 1948.

28. "Smart Management, Best Practices, Careers and Ideas," *Fortune,* September 30, 1996.

29. This structure is elaborated thoroughly in J. Quinn, *Strategies for Change: Logical Incrementalism* (Homewood, IL: Dow Jones–Irwin, 1980.)

30. National Research Council, *Information Technology in the Service Society* (Washington, DC: National Academy Press, 1994).

31. Portfolio planning first appeared in the guise of mission planning in the Department of Defense in the early 1960s and was adapted for industry by D. Smalter and R. Ruggles in "Six Lessons from the Pentagon," *Harvard Business Review* (March–April 1966).

32. C. Hitch, *Decision Making for Defense* (Berkeley, CA: University of California, 1965), provides the classic economic and managerial arguments for this approach. B. Henderson, *Henderson on Corporate Strategy* (Cambridge, MA: Abt Books, 1989), provides the widely accepted corporate management structure for financial portfolio planning.

33. R. Hayes and W. Abernathy, "Managing Our Way to Economic Decline," *Harvard Business Review* (July–August 1980), is the classic statement of why this happens.

34. C. Hitch, *Decision Making for Defense.*
35. J. Quinn and M. Baily, "Information Technology: Increasing Productivity in Services," *Academy of Management Executive* 8, no. 3 (1994), illustrates some of the consequences and ways to include alternative costs for some projects.
36. R. Hayes and D. Garvin, "Managing As If Tomorrow Mattered," *Harvard Business Review* (May–June 1982).
37. J. Hodder and A. Triantis, "Valuing Flexibility as a Complex Option," *Journal of Finance* (June 1990); R. Pindyck, "Investments of Uncertain Cost," *Journal of Financial Economics* 34 (1993); N. Nichols, "Scientific Management at Merck," *Harvard Business Review* (January–February 1994) L. Ankum, "A Real Options and Game Theoretic Approach to Corporate Investment Strategy Under Competition," *Financial Management* (Autumn 1993): all provide examples of advanced financial analysis approaches.
38. F. Prahalad and G. Hamel, "Strategic Intent," *Harvard Business Review* (May–June 1989).

## Chapter 7. Creating "Best-in-World" Capabilities

1. J. Bright, *Technological Forecasting for Industry* (Englewood Cliffs, NJ: Prentice Hall, 1968), was perhaps the first systematic presentation of this concept for guiding technological activities.
2. J. Fisher and R. Pry, *A Simple Substitution Model of Technological Change* (Schenectady, NY: General Electric, 1981).
3. R. Ayres, "Envelope Curve Forecasting," in Bright, *Technological Forecasting,* is the origin of this concept.
4. This idea was first developed in J. Quinn, T. Doorley, and P. Paquette, "Technology in Services: Rethinking Strategic Focus," *Sloan Management Review* (January 1990).
5. I. Ansoff, *Corporate Strategy: An Analytical Approach to Business Policy Growth and Expansion* (New York: McGraw-Hill, 1965), provided a structure that dominated this kind of thinking for decades. K. Andrews, *The Concept of Corporate Strategy* (Homewood, IL: Richard D. Irwin, 1980), is the classic restatement.
6. J. Quinn, *Intelligent Enterprise* (New York: Free Press, 1992), develops the concept of core intellectual competencies in depth.
7. D. Leonard-Barton, "Core Capabilities and Core Rigidities," *Strategic Management Journal* 13 (1992) illustrates some of the complexities as they apply to managing product development.
8. C. Prahalad and G. Hamel, "The Core Competence of the Corporation," *Harvard Business Review* (May–June 1990).
9. These strategies are amplified at length in Quinn, *Intelligent Enterprise.*
10. T. Steiner and D. Teixeira, *Technology in Banking* (Homewood, IL: Dow Jones–Irwin, 1996), provide excellent amplifications.
11. M. Porter, *Competitive Strategy: Techniques for Analyzing Industries and Competitors* (New York: Free Press, 1980).
12. J. Quinn and F. Hilmer, "Strategic Outsourcing," *Sloan Management Review* (Summer 1994).
13. J. Quinn, P. Anderson, and S. Finkelstein, "Leveraging Intellect," *Academy of Management Executive* (Summer 1996).

14. M. Moritz, *The Little Kingdom: The Private Story of Apple Computer* (New York: Morrow, 1984).
15. W. Davidson, "Apple Computer, Inc.," case UVA-BP 219 (Charlottesville: University of Virginia, Darden School Foundation, 1984).
16. Data produced by T. Doorley, Braxton Assoc., reproduced in Quinn, *Intelligent Enterprise.*
17. "Nike, Inc. Vignette," in Quinn, *Intelligent Enterprise.*
18. "Ford Team Taurus," case, in H. Mintzberg and J. Quinn, *The Strategy Process,* 3d ed. (Englewood Cliffs, NJ: Prentice Hall, 1996).
19. O. Williamson, "Transaction Costs," in *Economic Organizations: Firms, Markets and Policy Control* (New York: New York University Press, 1986).
20. R. D'Aveni and D. Ravenscraft, "Economics of Integration vs. Bureaucratic Costs: Does Vertical Integration Improve Performance?" *Academy of Management Journal* 37, no. 5 (1994).
21. J. Quinn, J. Baruch, and P. Paquette, "Exploiting the Manufacturing-Services Interface," *Sloan Management Review* (Summer 1988).
22. J. Quinn, T. Doorley, and P. Paquette, "Beyond Products: Services-Based Strategies," *Harvard Business Review* (March–April 1990).
23. Interviewed by J. Quinn for National Research Council, *Information Technology in the Service Society* (Washington, DC: National Academy Press, 1994).
24. J. Martin, "Are You As Good As You Think You Are?" *Fortune,* September 30, 1996.
25. T. Amabile, "Motivational Synergy: Toward New Conceptions of Intrinsic and Extrinsic Motivation in the Marketplace," *Human Resource Management Review* 3, no. 3 (1993).
26. S. Buckler and K. A. Zien, "From Experience: The Spirituality of Innovation: Learning from Stories," *Journal of Product Innovation Management* (September 1996).
27. R. Noyce, "Creativity by the Numbers," *Harvard Business Review* (May–June 1980).
28. Martin, "Are You As Good As You Think You Are?"
29. J. Quinn, P. Anderson, and S. Finkelstein, "Managing Intellect: Getting the Most from the Best," *Harvard Business Review* (March–April 1996).
30. National Research Council, *Information Technology.*

## Chapter 8: Matching Strategies, Structures, and Incentives

1. D. De Sola Price, "Of Sealing Wax and String," *Natural History* (January 1984).
2. J. Fisher and R. Pry, "A Simple Substitution Model of Technological Change," Monograph, General Electric Co., Schenectady, NY, 1981; and R. Ayres, "Envelope Curve Forecasting," in J. Bright, *Technological Forecasting in Industry and Government* (Englewood Cliffs, NJ: Prentice Hall, 1968), were the first to document such analyses.
3. T. Hughes, "The Inventive Continuum," *Science* 84, p. 83.
4. Harold Rosen, quoted in *Fortune,* September 17, 1996, p. 158.
5. J. Quinn, "Managing Innovation: Controlled Chaos," *Harvard Business Review* (May–June 1985).
6. R. C. Dean, "The Temporal Mismatch—Innovations' Pace vs. Management's Time

Horizon," *Research Management* (May 1974); Battelle Memorial Laboratories, *Science, Technology and Innovation,* Report to the National Science Foundation (Columbus, OH, 1973).

7. De Sola Price, "Of Sealing Wax."

8. J. Watson,*The Double Helix* (New York: Athenaeum, 1968), offers an excellent narrative of many crucial events in this sequence.

9. F. Schonfeld, "The New Biotech Boom: A Star Is Born," *Fortune,* January 13, 1997.

10. R. Kaplan, "The Effects of Management Payouts on Operating Performance and Value," *Journal of Financial Economics* 24 (1989) 217.

11. H. Mintzberg, *Mintzberg on Management: Inside Our Strange World of Organizations* (New York: Free Press, 1989).

12. H. Mintzberg, "The Innovative Organization," in H. Mintzberg and J. Quinn, *The Strategy Process,* 3d ed. (Englewood Cliffs, NJ: Prentice Hall, 1996), p. 680.

13. J. Carlzon, *Moments of Truth* (Cambridge, MA: Ballinger, 1987).

14. M. Loeb, "How to Grow a New Product Every Day," *Fortune,* November 14, 1994.

15. "Honda Motor Co." case, in Mintzberg and Quinn, *Strategy Process.*

16. "TCG, Ltd./Thermo Electron Corp," case, in Mintzberg and Quinn, *Strategy Process,* describes two starburst companies' strategies and structures in detail.

17. D. McClellan, *The Achieving Society* (Princeton, NJ: Van Nostrand Press, 1961), and G. Bylinski, *The Innovation Millionaires* (New York: Scribners, 1976), offer some specific and interesting insights on entrepreneurial motives.

18. T. Kidder, *The Soul of a New Machine* (Boston: Little, Brown, 1981), refers to this as "playing pinball."

19. P. Smith and D. Reinertsen, *Developing Products in Half the Time* (New York: Van Nostrand, 1991), is perhaps the best reference on this point.

## *Chapter 9. Middle Management: The Basics*

1. W. Bennis, Leaders: *Strategies for Taking Charge* (New York: Harper & Row, 1985).

2. H. Mintzberg, "Strategy Making in Three Modes," *California Management Review* (Winter 1973).

3. H. Mintzberg and A. McHugh, "Strategy Formation in Adhocracy," *Administrative Science Quarterly,* no. 30 (1985): 160–197.

4. J. Marsh, J. Olsen, and S. Christensen, Ambiguity and Choice in Organizations (Bergen, Norway: Universitetsforlaget, 1976).

5. "The Press of New Business," *Business Week*, January 15, 1996, describes the nature and pace of change and how it affects major firms.

6. "Sony Corporation," case in H. Mintzberg and J. Quinn, *The Strategy Process,* 3d ed. (Englewood Cliffs, NJ: Prentice Hall, 1966).

7. S. Helgesen, *The Web of Inclusion* (Garden City, NY: Currency-Doubleday, 1995), develops this idea in depth.

8. "Intel Corporation," case, in Mintzberg and Quinn, *Strategy Process;* G. Moore, "Intel—Memories and the Microprocessor," *Engineering Management Review* (Winter 1996).

9. D. Nathanson and J. Cassano, "Organization Diversity and Performance," *Wharton Magazine* (Summer 1982).

10. J. Bourgeois and K. Eisenhardt, "Strategic Decision Processes in High Velocity Environments," *Management Science* (July 1988).

11. For a fuller development of planned flexibility, see J. Quinn, *Strategies for Change* (Homewood, IL: Dow Jones–Irwin, 1980).

12. "Honda Motor Co.," case, in Mintzberg and Quinn, *Strategy Process*.

13. J. Diebold, *The Innovators: The Discoveries, Inventions, and Breakthroughs of Our Times* (New York: Dutton, 1990); D. DeSola Price, "Of Sealing Wax and String," *Natural History* (1984).

14. R. Hayes and D. Garvin, "Managing As If Tomorrow Really Mattered," Harvard Business Review (May–June 1982); National Academy of Engineering, *Time Horizons and Technology Investments* (Washington, DC: National Academy Press, 1992).

15. T. Stewart, "3M Fights Back," *Fortune*, February 5, 1996.

16. J. Jewkes, D. Sawers, and R. Stillerman, *The Sources of Innovation* (New York: St. Martin's Press, 1958); and Battelle Laboratories, "Science, Technology, and Innovation": Report to National Science Foundation, Columbus, OH, 1973, are the two classic studies on this subject.

17. J. Quinn, "Innovation and Corporate Strategy," *Technology in Society* 7 (1986): 263–279.

18. "Xerox (A), Intel Corporation, and Sony Corporation: Innovation System," cases, in Mintzberg and Quinn, *Strategy Process*.

19. M. Cusamano, *The Factory Approach to Large Scale Software Development: Implications for Strategy, Technology, and Structure*, monograph MITJSTP 88-04 (Cambridge, MA: MIT, 1988).

20. Diebold, *The Innovators*.

21. J. Quinn, "Technological Innovation, Entrepreneurship and Strategy," *Sloan Management Review* (Spring 1979), details the reasoning further.

22. Calculations by Victor McGee, Amos Tuck School, Dartmouth College, 1985, suggest that for all possible communications interactions, the number increases as $2^{(n-1)} - 1$.

23. T. Allen and S. Cohen,"Information Flow in R&D Labs," *Administrative Science Quarterly*, no. 14 (1969), establish the very high leverage of such gatekeeper activities in technology organizations.

24. A variety of classic and useful examples appear in R. Miles and C. Snow, "Organizations, New Concepts for New Forms," *California Management Review* (Spring 1986); K. Harrigan, *Strategies for Joint Ventures* (Lexington, MA: Lexington Books, 1985); J. Lewis, *Partnership for Profit Structuring and Managing Strategic Alliances* (New York: Free Press, 1990); and S. Urban (ed.), *European Strategic Alliances: Comparative Strategies in the New Europe* (Cambridge, MA: Blackwell Publishing, 1992).

25. M. Maidique, "Entrepreneurs, Champions, and Technological Innovation," *Sloan Management Review* (Winter 1980).

26. T. Peters and R. Waterman, *In Search of Excellence* (New York: Harper & Row, 1982).

## *Chapter 10. The Politics of Science*

1. F. Bacon, *Novum Organum*, pt. 2, *Instauratio Magna* (London: J. Billium, 1620).

2. I. Newton, *The Mathematical Principles of Natural Philosophy* (London: B. Matte, 1729).

3. K. Popper, *Conjectures and Refutations: The Growth of Scientific Knowledge* (New York: Basic Books, 1962); K. Popper, *The Logic of Scientific Discovery* (New York: Basic Books, 1959).

4. J. Platt, "Strong Inferences," *Science,* October 15, 1964.

5. B. Russell, *An Inquiry into the Meaning of Truth* (New York: Norton, 1940), suggests other definitions of truth; J. Bronowski, *Science and Human Values* (New York: Harper & Row, 1956); A. Kaplan, *The Conduct of Inquiry* (San Francisco: Chandler Publishing, 1964); M. Polyani, *Personal Knowledge: Toward a Post-Critical Philosophy* (New York: Harper & Row, 1962), *Knowing and Being* (Chicago: University of Chicago Press, 1969); and T. Kuhn, *The Structure of Scientific Revolutions* (Chicago: University of Chicago Press, 1970).

6. Kuhn, *Structure.*

7. G. Homans, *The Human Group* (San Diego, CA: Harcourt Brace Jovanovich, 1950).

8. J. Lamarck, *Philosophic Zoologique: Exposition des Considerations Relatives à l'Histoire Naturelle des Animaux* (Paris: Balliere, 1830), is the most often discussed of these.

9. H. Selye, *From Dream to Discovery* (New York: McGraw-Hill 1964).

10. G. Harris, *Neural Control of the Pituitary Gland* (London: Edward Arnold, 1955).

11. C. Darwin, *The Structure and Distribution of Coral Reefs* (1842), *A Monograph on Fossil Lepadidae or Pedunculated Cerripedes of Great Britain* (1854), *A Monograph of the Fossil Balanidae and Verrucidae of Great Britain* (1854), *Monograph on the Various Contrivances by Which Orchids Are Fertilized by Insects* (1862), and *On the Origin of Species by Means of Natural Selection, or the Preservation of Favored Races in the Struggle for Life* (London: J. Murray, 1860).

12. N. Wade, *The Nobel Duel* (Garden City, NY: Doubleday, 1981).

13. J. Kemeny and L. Snell, *Mathematical Models in the Social Sciences* (Cambridge, MA: MIT Press, 1972).

14. Bronowski, *Science and Human Values,* specifically comments on the identification of patterns as a major step in knowledge creation.

15. C. Darwin, *The Descent of Man, and Selection in Relation to Sex* (London: J. Murray, 1871).

16. R. Guillemin, "Hypothalamic Control of the Anterior Pituitary: Study with Tissue Culture Techniques," *Federation Proceedings* 14 (1955): 211. M. Saffran and A. Schally, "The Release of Corticotrophin by Anterior Pituitary Tissue in Vitro," *Canadian Journal of Biochemistry and Physiology* 33 (1955): 408.

17. A. Einstein, *Essays in Science* (New York: Philosophical Library, 1934), p. 36; A. Koestler, *The Act of Creation* (London: Hutchinson, 1964); and Kaplan, *Conduct.*

18. G. Harris and D. Jacobsohn, "Functional Grafts of the Anterior Pituitary Gland," *Proceedings of the Royal Society,* ser. B, 139 (1952): 263.

19. S. Zuckerman, "Control for the Pituitary Function," *Nature* 178 (1956): 442.

20. R. Lewin, "Science News . . . Two Part Series," *Science,* August 12, 19, 1983.

21. Harris and Jacobsohn, "Functional Grafts."

22. A. Schally et al., "Purification of Thrytropic Hormone Releasing Factor from Bovine Hypothalamus," *Endocrinology* 78 (1966): 726; R. Guillemin et al., "Nouvelles Données sur la Purification de l'Hormone Hypothalamique THS—Hypophysiotrope, TRF," *Compte Rendus des Seances de l'Academie des Sciences* 262 (1966): 2278.

23. J. Haldane, *The Causes of Evolution* (London: Harper and Bros., 1932); T. Dobzhansky, *Genetics and the Origin of Species* (New York: Columbia University Press, 1941); E. Mayr, *Systematics and the Origins of the Species,* (New York: Columbia University Press, 1942).

24. E. Von Hippel, "The Dominant Role of the User in Semiconductor and Electronic Process Innovation," *IEEE Transactions on Engineering Management,* vol. *EM24* (1977).

25. H. Gruber, *Learning and Strategic Product Innovation: Theory and Evidence for the Semiconductor Industry* (New York: North-Holland, 1994); T. Amabile, *The Social Psychology of Creativity* (New York: Springer-Verlag, 1983); R. Bruce, "Determinants of Innovative Behavior: A Path Model of Individual Innovation in the Workplace," *Academy of Management Journal* 37 (1994).

## Chapter 11. National Technology Competitiveness

1. A. Schonfield, *Modern Capitalism* (New York: Oxford University Press, 1965), was a pioneer piece on how economic and other policy mechanisms support the modern market economy.

2. N. Gingrich, *To Renew America* (New York: HarperCollins, 1995), and "Over-Regulating America," Economist, July 29, 1996; J. Carey, "Industrial Policy or Industrial Folly," Business Week, May 17, 1993.

3. H. Ergas, "Does Technology Policy Matter?" in B. Guile and H. Brooks, *Technology and Global Industry: Companies and Nations in the World Economy* (Washington, DC: National Academy Press, 1987).

4. B. Bartlett, "The Case for Dynamic Scoring," Wall Street Journal, July 30, 1996.

5. "Industry Policy . . . The Nation Needs a Plan to Nurture Growth," *Business Week,* April 6, 1992.

6. V. Bush, *Science: The Endless Frontier* (Washington, DC: National Science Foundation, 1945).

7. A. Weinberger, "Criteria for Scientific Choice," *Minerva* (Winter 1963).

8. National Academy of Engineering, *U.S. Leadership in Manufacturing* (Washington, DC: National Academy Press, 1983), was the first in a series of competitiveness conferences, studies, and publications in the 1980s.

9. U.S. Department of Commerce, *Report of Advisory Committee on Industrial Innovation: Domestic Policy Review for the President of the United States* (Washington, DC: Government Printing Office, 1979).

10. M. Borotsky, "Trends in U.S. Technology," American Scientist (January–February 1975).

11. S. Cohen and J. Zysman, "Why Manufacturing Matters: The Myth of the Post Industrial Economy," *California Management Review* (Spring 1987).

12. Z. Griliches, "Research Costs and Social Returns: Hybrid Corn and Related Innovations," *Journal of Political Economy* (October 1958), and "The Search for R&D Spillovers," *Scandinavian Journal of Economics* (Supplement) (1994).

13. J. Servan-Schreiber, *The American Challenge* (New York: Athenaeum, 1968).

14. J. Schmandt, "U.S. Science Policy," in *Science Policies of Industrial Nations* (New York: Praeger, 1975).

15. "White House Science: Hail and Farewell," *Science,* March 30, 1973.

16. Notably the power bases built up by key figures on the Armed Services, Space, Public Works, Atomic Energy, and Health, Education and Welfare committees of the 1970s.

17. L. Cohen and R. Noll, *The Technology Pork Barrel* (Washington, DC: Brookings Institution, 1991).

18. E. F. David, "Introductory Remarks," in G. Strasser and E. M. Simmons (eds.), *Science and Technology Policies* (Cambridge, MA: Ballinger, 1973).

19. J. Walsh, "Truman Era, Formative Years for Sciences Policy," *Science* (January 1973).

20. Weinberger, "Criteria," is the classic statement of this position.

21. J. Schumpeter, *The Theory of Economic Development* (Cambridge, MA: Harvard University Press, 1949).

22. S. Kuznets, *Economic Growth of Nations* (Cambridge, MA: Harvard University Press, 1971).

23. J. Quinn, *Intelligent Enterprise* (New York: Free Press, 1992).

24. U.S. Congress, Office of Technology Assessment, *Electronic Enterprises: Looking to the Future* (Washington, DC: Government Printing Office, 1994).

25. R. Nelson, "What Is Commercial and What Is 'Public' About Technology and What Should Be?" in N. Rosenberg, R. Landau, and D. Mowery (eds.), *Technology and the Wealth of Nations* (Stanford, CA: Stanford University Press, 1992).

26. R. Nelson, "Government Support of Technological Progress: Lessons from History," *Journal of Policy Analysis and Management* (Summer 1983).

27. E. Von Hippel, *Sources of Innovation* (New York: Oxford, University Press, 1987).

28. M. Dertouzas, R. Lester, and R. Solow, *Made in America* (Cambridge, MA: MIT Press, 1989).

29. J. Quinn, "Monetary Policy, Heavy Hand on Technology," *Technology Review* (June 1974).

30. D. Bernheim and J. Shoven, "Comparing the Cost of Capital in the U.S. and Japan," in Rosenberg, Landau, and Mowery, *Technology and the Wealth of Nations*, explains the complications.

31. G. Hatsoupolis and S. Brooks, "The Gap in Cost of Capital: Causes, Effects, Remedies," in R. Landau and S. Jorgenson (eds.), *Technology and Economic Policy* (Cambridge, MA: Ballinger, 1986).

32. W. Kester and T. Leuhrman, *Cross Country Differences in the Cost of Capital* (Boston: Harvard Business School Press, 1991); and R. Zelinski and N. Holloway, *Unequal Opportunities* (Tokyo: Kodansha International, 1991).

33. "Survey of Capital Markets: Special Report," Economist, September 7, 1991.

34. Notably the studies made by McKinsey and Co. Global Research Group, 1992, and National Academy of Engineering, 1988–1992; Office of the President of the United States, Commission on Competitiveness, 1990–1992.

35. National Academy of Engineering, *Time Horizons and Technology Investments* (Washington, DC: National Academy Press, 1991).

36. P. Romer, "The Origins of Endogenous Growth," *Journal of Economic Perspectives* (Winter 1994).

37. M. Reisner, *Cadillac Desert: The American West and Its Disappearing Water* (New York: Viking, 1986), p. 500.

38. R. Repetto, "Deforestation in the Tropics," *Scientific American* (April 1990).

39. J. Frey and H. Ide, *A History of the Petroleum Administration for War* (Washington, DC: Government Printing Office, 1946).
40. B. Brooks and A. Dunstan, *The Science of Petroleum,* vol. 5, p 2 (New York: Oxford University Press, 1955).
41. C. Phillips, Jr., *Competition in the Synthetic Rubber Industry* (Cambridge, MA: Harvard University Press, 1948); and G. Babcock, History of the United States Rubber Company (Bloomington: Foundation for the School of Business, Indiana University, 1966).
41. J. Wennberg, "Unwanted Variations in the Rules of Practice," *Journal of the American Medical Association,* March 13, 1991; Center for Evaluative Clinical Studies, Dartmouth Medical School, *The Dartmouth Atlas of Health Care* (Chicago: American Hospital Publishing Company, 1996).
42. "Clinton R&D Achievements Tilt Toward Technology," *Science,* February 23, 1996.
43. "1996 U.S. Science Policy," *Science,* June 3, 1995.

## Chapter 12. Creating Public Markets

1. J. Carey and M. Regan, "Are Regs Bleeding the Economy?." *Business Week,* July 17, 1995.
2. Ibid.
3. P. Abelson, "Chlorine and Organochlorine Compounds," *Science,* August 26, 1994.
4. J. Quinn, "Public Markets: Growth Opportunities and Environmental Improvement," *Technology Review* (June 1974), provided an early statement of these concepts and the data then available.
5. J. Quinn, "The Next Big Market: Environmental Improvement," *Harvard Business Review* (September–October 1971), suggests how such markets would operate.
6. J. Quinn, "National Policies for Science and Technology," *Research Management* (November 1977), gave a history of successful and unsuccessful U.S. government interventions in supporting technology development.
7. G. Hardin, "The Tragedy of the Commons," *Science* (March 1969).
8. M. Barinaga, "Biologists Sort the Lessons of Fisheries Collapse," *Science,* May 27, 1994.
9. M. Reisner, *Cadillac Desert: The American West and Its Disappearing Water* (New York: Viking, 1986).
10. *Economist,* January 28, 1995.
11. R. Hahn, *Risks, Costs, and Lives Saved* (Cambridge: Oxford University Press, 1996).
12. National Safety Council, *Accident Facts, 1995 Edition* (Washington, DC, 1995).
13. *Motor Vehicle Pollution: Reduction Strategies Beyond 2010* (Paris: OECD, 1995).
14. Office of the President of the United States, *Annual Report of the Council on Environmental Quality* (Washington, DC: Government Printing Office, various years).
15. Environmental Protection Agency, *The Benefits and Costs of the Clean Air Act 1970 to 1992,* preliminary report (Washington, DC: Government Printing Office, July 1996).
16. "Environmental Technology: Muck and Brass," *Economist,* April 27, 1996.
17. OECD, *Environment and Economics* (Paris, 1984).

18. National Academy of Engineering, *Technology and Environment* (Washington, DC: National Academy Press, 1989), offers a superb taxonomy of approaches for this.
19. F. Cairncross, *Costing the Earth* (Boston: Harvard Business School Press, 1996).
20. "Over-Regulating America," *Economist,* July 29, 1996.
21. T. Beardsley, "Death by Analysis," *Scientific American* (November 1995).
22. D. Pearce and K. Turner, *Economics of Natural Resources and the Environment* (London: Harvester Wheatsheaf, 1990).
23. C. Peters, A. Gentry, and R. Mendelsohn, "Valuation of an Amazonian Rain Forest," *Nature,* June 29, 1989.
24. "Good Numbers Are Worth a Great Deal," *Business Week,* August 21, 1995.
25. Carey and Regan, "Are Regs Bleeding the Economy?"

## Chapter 13. National Technology Strategies in a Services and Software World

1. J. Quinn, *Strategies for Change: Logical Incrementalism* (Homewood, IL: R. D. Irwin, 1980), explains the logic of this form of strategy formulation.
2. This fact is often treated as alarming, despite the fact that CEOs in textiles do not know how polymer threads are spun or how a laser cutter works; few CFOs could ever have explained how an adding machine works; nor can the many who daily rely on radios, telephones, or automobiles describe how these devices work in more than the vaguest detail.
3. "Understanding Economic Growth," *Economist,* May 25, 1996.
4. P. Romer, "Idea Gaps and Knowledge Gaps in Economic Development," *Journal of Monetary Economics* (December 1993).
5. "Why More Looks Like Less," *Economist,* April 27, 1996, p. 26.
6. "The War of the Wires," *Economist,* May 11, 1996.
7. N. Rosenberg, R. Landau, and D. Mowery (eds.), *Technology and the Wealth of Nations* (Stanford, CA: Stanford University Press, 1992), and P. Romer, "Increasing Returns and Long Term Growth," *Journal of Political Economy* 94, no. 5 (1986), offer some superb insights.
8. McKinsey Global Institute, *Services Sector Productivity* (New York: McKinsey & Co., 1994).
9. L. Von Wantoch, "Services—Especially Business, Professional, and Technical—Are a Success Story of U.S. Trade Balance," *Business America* (August 1994).
10. National Science Foundation, *Science and Engineering Indicators, 1993* (Washington, DC: Government Printing Office, 1995).
11. "Financial Indicators," *Economist,* August 19, 1995.
12. Office of U.S. Trade Representative, *U.S. National Study on Trade in Services* (Washington, DC, 1983); T. Vollmann, "The Effect of Zero Inventories on Cost," in *Cost Accounting for the 1990s: The Challenge of Technological Change* (Montvale, NJ: National Association of Accountants, 1986).
13. J. Aley, "Where the Laid Off Workers Go," *Fortune,* October 30, 1995.
14. R. Coase, *The Firm, the Market, and the Law* (Chicago: Chicago University Press, 1988).
15. J. Quinn, T. Doorley, and P. Paquette, "Beyond Products: Services-Based Strategies," *Harvard Business Review* (March–April 1990).

16. J. Quinn and F. Hilmer, "Strategic Outsourcing," *Sloan Management Review* (Summer 1994).

17. J. Aley, "Where the Jobs Are," *Fortune,* September 18, 1995.

18. "An Ownership-Based Disaggregation of the U.S. Current Account 1982–1993," in U.S. Commerce Department, *Survey of Current Business* (Washington, DC: Government Printing Office, October 1995).

19. Quinn and Hilmer, "Strategic Outsourcing."

20. M. Chui, P. Levine, and J. Pearlman, "Innovation, Imitation, and Growth in a Changing World Economy," *London Business School Economic Outlook* (May 1996).

21. "The Death of Distance: Special Survey of Telecommunications," *Economist,* September 30, 1990.

22. J. Rivkin, *The End of Work* (New York: Putnam's, 1995), is a typical doomsday prediction.

23. P. Romer, "Ideas and Things: The Concept of Production Is Being Retooled," *Economist,* September 11, 1993; and "Two Strategies for Economic Development," *World Bank Research Observer* (1992): 63–115.

24. Z. Griliches, "Productivity Puzzles and R&D: Another Explanation," *Journal of Economic Perspectives* 2 (Fall 1988).

25. F. Lichtenberg, *R&D Investment and International Productivity Differences,* Working Paper 416 (Cambridge, MA: National Bureau of Economic Research, 1992).

26. Depending on the interactions assumed, potential knowledge grows either factorially as $n!$ or $2^{(n-1)} - 1$ where $n =$ nodes.

27. "Let the Digital Age Bloom," *Economist,* February 25, 1995.

28. "Big Science Is Booming in Japan," *Science,* 271 (February 1996).

29. R. Nelson, "What Is Commercial and What Is Public About Technology and What Should Be?" in Rosenberg, Landau, and Mowery, *Technology and the Wealth of Nations.*

30. P. Romer, *Implementing a National Technological Strategy with Self Organizing Investment Bonds,* Brookings Papers: Microeconomics 2, (Washington, DC: Brookings Institution, 1993).

31. E. Mansfield et al., *The Production and Application of New Industrial Technology* (New York: Norton, 1977).

32. R. Merges and R. Nelson, *A Limiting or Encouraging Rivalry in Technological Progress: The Effect of Patent Scope Decisions* (Berkeley: Center for Research and Management, University of California, 1992).

33. C. Gillfillin, "A Sociologist Looks at Technical Prediction," in *Technological Forecasting for Industry and Government* (Englewood Cliffs, NJ: Prentice Hall, 1968).

34. R. Evenson, "Patents, R&D, and Invention Potential: International Evidence," *American Economic Review* (May 1993).

35. Some authors suggest this kind of voluntary self-monitoring on networks can result from the sense of connectedness that community cooperation engenders. F. Capra and D. Steindl-Rast, *Belonging to the Universe* (New York: HarperCollins, 1991.) Also, "Ethics Is How We Behave When We Decide We Belong Together" in M. Wheatley and M. Kellner-Rogers, *A Simpler Way* (San Francisco: Berrett-Koehler, 1996).

36. J. Utterback, *Mastering the Dynamics of Innovation* (Boston: Harvard Business School Press, 1994).

37. P. Romer, "Origins of Endogenous Growth," *Journal of Economic Perspectives* (1994).

38. J. Quinn, S. Finkelstein, and P. Anderson, "Leveraging Intellect," *Academy of Management Executive* (Summer 1996).

39. P. Krugman, "Monetary Policy: Stable Prices—Just Say No," *Economist,* August 31, 1996.

40. "Different Roads to Development," *Economist,* August 19, 1995.

41. Z. Griliches, "The Search for R&D Spillovers," *Scandinavian Journal of Economics* (Supplement) (1991).

42. M. Baily and R. Gordon, *The Productivity Slowdown: Measurement Issues and the Explosion of Computer Power,* Brookings Papers on Economic Activity (Washington, DC: Brookings Institution, 1988).

43. Ibid.

44. Many groups have been working on this issue, including the Rees Committee of the National Research Council, the Presidential Economics and Statistics Initiative (Raskin Initiative), Financial Accounting Standards Board, and task forces in the Bureau of Labor Statistics and Commerce Department.

45. *Economist,* February 4, 1995, p. 18.

46. "How Governments Can Stop Taxing Those Who Save," *Economist,* January 21, 1995.

47. "Different Roads to Development," *Economist,* August 19, 1995, p. 35.

48. R. Murnane and F. Levy, *Teaching the New Basic Skills: Principles for Educating Children to Thrive on the New Economy* (New York: Free Press, 1996).

49. "NSF Takes Leap into School Reform," *Science,* October 23, 1994, describes one of the larger proposed endeavors.

50. "Clinton's R&D Achievements Tilt Toward Technology," *Science,* February 23, 1996.

51. N. Gross, "Creating Worlds," *Business Week,* December 23, 1996, reports on a number of such studies in the refereed journals.

52. Interview by K. A. Zien with H. G. Owen, 3M Creative Services, re: Chris and Steve Collins's Internet education work, March 22, 1996.

53. "Cyberspace Offers Chance to Do Virtually Real Science," *Science,* May 13, 1994.

54. "Going with the Flows," *Economist,* January 28, 1995.

55. B. Margla, "India Expands Electronic Research Network," *Science,* March 18, 1994.

56. "Turning an Info-Glut into a Library," *Science,* October 7, 1994; and "Indexing the Internet," *Science,* September 8, 1995.

# Index

Aavid Thermal Technologies, 54–55, 68–69
AAW. See Arthur Andersen Worldwide (AAW)
Abramovitz, M., 34
Adaptec, 63
Adhocracies, 17–19, 222, 224, 226–37, 251–60, 288
Adobe Systems, 63, 96
Advanced research, 357–58
Advanced skills, 2, 3, 5, 19
Advanced Technology Group, Microsoft, 166, 184
AEC. See Atomic Energy Commission (AEC)
Aeronet, 127
Aetna, 7
"Affinity diagram," 153
Aggressor company technique, 192
Agnoter, 127
Agriculture, 22, 23, 28, 282, 285, 306, 307, 320
Agriculture Department, 287, 305, 311, 316
Air Force, 336
Airline industry, 86–87, 366. See also specific airlines
Aligned purpose, 122–24, 155, 170
Alles, J., 123
Alliance model of behavior, 117
Altair, 32
Alternative cost analysis, 182–83
Altshuller, G., 142

"Ambassadors," 133
America Online, 63
American Airlines, 30, 65, 71, 83, 86–87, 89, 201, 368
American Express, 83, 86, 87, 192, 201, 211
American Management Systems, 96
American Standard, 92, 236
Ames Research Center, 127
Amgen, 196, 238
"Amoeba management practice," 165
AMR, 108
Analog Devices, 153
Andersen Consulting, 95, 99, 108
Andersen Notes system, 90
Andersen Worldwide. See Arthur Andersen Worldwide (AAW)
Anderson, P., 150
Anderson Windows, 58
ANET, 8, 90
Apple Computer, 32, 57–58, 128, 133, 203–04, 208, 350, 361
Apple DOS, 203
Apple II, 203
Applets, 72, 91
Applied research, 47
Aquinas, T., 268
Archie, 384
Argyle Diamonds, 25
Argyris, C., 122
Army Corps of Engineers, 285
Arthur, B., 344

Arthur Andersen Worldwide (AAW), 8, 90, 99, 130, 201
Ascend Communications, 63
Asea-Brown-Boveri, 50
"Asian Tigers," 356
Astra-Hässle, 164
Asynchronous organizations, 126–28
AT&T: acquisition of McGraw Cellular by, 370; auto catalysis and, 77; Bell Labs of, 6, 97, 170, 192–93, 193n, 201, 231, 252, 317, 360; "black box performance criteria" at, 192–93, 193n; cellular phones produced by, 71; competitors of, 201; core competencies and, 201; databases of, 85; diffusion and, 361; figures of merit at, 192–93; intellectual preeminence of, 201; intellectually based services of, 25; large-scale systems at, 231; and leveraging value creation, 57; market orientation of, 252; monitoring programs and, 99; and smallest replicable units, 71; software developed by, 368; top management at, 163; UNIX distribution by, 97
Atari, 361
Atomic Energy Commission (AEC), 286, 287
Auto catalysis, 77–80, 344, 359–60
Autodesk, 63, 96
Automobile industry, 182, 282, 294. *See also* specific companies
Avery, S., 173
Avery Dennison, 173
Awards. *See* Rewards for innovation

Babcock and Wilcox, 331
Bacon, F., 267
Baldrige Awards, 305
BancOne, 192
"Bandit teams," 110–11, 119
Bankers Trust (BT), 167–68, 192
Banks. See Financial services; and specific banks
Barbados, 383
Barings Bank, 228
Basic research, 46–47, 233, 357–38. See also Science
BEA. See Bureau of Economic Analysis (BEA)
Bear Stearns, 199
Bechtel, 11, 30, 108, 201, 226, 335, 368
Beck, S., 116–17

Bell Atlantic, 133
Bell Laboratories, 6, 97, 170, 192–93, 193n, 201, 231, 252, 317, 360
Benchmarking, 188–90
Benneton's, 89
Bennigan's, 88
"Best-practices resource map," 167
BioMOO (Multiple-user, Object Oriented), 382
Biotechnology, 47, 54, 56, 71, 80, 82–83, 143–44, 149–50, 198, 199, 221–22, 233, 283, 294. *See also* Health care; and specific companies
"Black box performance criteria," 192–93
Blackbird software, 184
Blockbuster, 370
BMW, 350
Boeing: and airlines' difficulties, 305; Darwin data used by, 127; diffusion and, 50; intellectual preeminence of, 201; as large-system technology producer, 231; 777 aircraft project of, 53–54, 119, 258; software system of, 30, 51, 53–54, 65, 68, 108, 368
Bolt Beranek and Newman, 153
Bootleg projects, 249
Bose, 153
Boston Chicken, 116–17, 245
Boston Market, 116–17, 121, 245
Boston University Medical School, 149–50
Bottlenecks, breaking of, 247–49
Boyer, H., 143, 169–70, 221, 357
BP, 370
Brain hormones, 270–76
Braniff, 87
Brazil, 363, 379
Bristol-Myers, 370
Britain: basic research in, 357; bond interest rates in, 301; computers per 100 people in, 381; employment in services in, 24; government receipts as percentage of GDP in, 371; human development index in, 379; investment versus economic growth in, 298; invisible exports as percentage of GDP, 348; losses from illegal copying of software in, 363; R&D in, 376; savings and investment in, 299, 300; taxes in, 372
Bronowski, J., 268
BT. *See* Bankers Trust (BT)
Buffon, G., 270

Buick, 236
"Build-and-bust" experiments, 94, 113–14
"Builds" and "way points," 223–24
"Build-test-drive" coordinating mechanism, 98, 114
Burchill, G., 153
Bureau of Economic Analysis (BEA), 338
Bureau of Land Reclamation, 285, 306, 354
Bureau of Standards, 340
Burgus, R., 271

CAD/CAM. See CAE/CAD/CAM
CADD, 79
Cadence Design Systems, 96
CAE/CAD/CAM, 29, 48, 51, 53, 54, 58, 176, 359
Cairncross, F., 331
California, 332, 340
CAM. See CAE/CAD/CAM
Cambrosio, A., 144
Canada, 35, 298, 299, 331, 348, 379, 381
Capability maturity model (CMM), 101
Capital: as growth factor, 35–36; for information technology (IT)-based innovation, 369, 371–74; Keynesian multipliers and, 37; technology and, 35–36;venture capital, 61, 96, 184, 302, 303. See also Investment
Capital Cities/ABC, 370
Capital costs, 292–93, 296
CASE, 98, 99–100, 359
Cataloging and classification in science, 270–71
Census Bureau, 33
Center for Quality Management, 153
Cetus, 121, 122
Champions, 17, 134, 148, 240, 249, 259–60
Change: emergent process in, 154–55; intervention points in, 157; as managed, not haphazard, system, 155–56; partial, tentative, and experimental processes in, 156–57; prerequisites for, 154; process focus for collaborative change and innovation, 154–57; resistance to, 16, 138. See also High innovativeness toward markets; Independent collaboration; Innovation
Chaos: focus and, 220; hypercompetition and, 32–33; innovation and, 93, 136–37, 220; management of, by mid-dle managers, 220–26; product development program (PDP) concept, 224, 225; in scientific knowledge building, 18–19; self-organizing systems and, 136–39; survival and, 136; systemic order despite process chaos, 137–38
Chaparral, 138, 190–91, 293
Chemical engineering, 113
Chemineer, 69
Chevron, 167
Chile, 356, 379
China, 356, 363, 378, 379, 382
CHIPS, 76
Chrysler, 209, 210, 350
Circular interdependent organizations, 118–20, 130–33
Cisco Systems, 63
Citibank, 82
Citicorp, 201
Clean Air and Water Acts, 286, 297, 326–27
Clinton administration, 310–12, 377
Clorox Company, 114
Clothing design, 73, 92
Club Med, 152, 170
CMM. See Capability maturity model (CMM)
CNN, 86
"Coatracks of talent," 248
Cochrane Collaboration, 56–57
Cognitive knowledge, 2, 3, 5, 19
Cognoter, 127
Cohen, S., 143, 221, 357
Colab, 127
Colabra, 73
Collaboration. See Independent collaboration
Command-and-control strategies, 39, 40
Commerce Department, 33, 286, 308, 311, 338, 368
Common bond and independent collaboration, 115–21
Compaq, 29
Competition: chaos and hypercompetition, 32–33; lateral competition, 201, 202; measures of international competitiveness, 295; national technology competitiveness, 279–313; U.S. competitiveness problems, 293–95. See also Deregulation; Government regulation
Competitive edge versus strategic risk, 205
"Competitive paranoia," 155, 245

Complexity of innovation, 13–14

Complexity theory, 136–37

Computer Associates International, 63, 96

Computer industry. *See* specific companies

Computer-aided software engineering (CASE), 98, 99–100

Computerland, 353

Computers: government support for, 282; initial public offerings from 1980–1996, 62; innovation in hardware, 64; microprocessors as direct and indirect multiplier, 37–38; per 100 persons, by country, 381; profits from software versus hardware, 29; time horizons for computer industry, 294; in U.S. households, 378, 380; Von Neumann's conception of, 145. *See also* Technology; headings beginning with Software; and specific companies

Computervision, 96

Compuware, 96

"Concept Engineering," 152–54

"Conceptual controls," 138

Confrontation and trust, 246–47

Conquer, 83

Conquer and Selling Chain, 47

"Conscious storytelling," 172

Consensus model of behavior, 117

Constructive confrontation and trust, 246–47

Consumption versus savings and investment, 371–73

"Contingent valuations," 333

Continuous flow processes, 54–55

Copyrights, 361, 385

Core competency strategies: characteristics of core competencies, 196–200; customer focus and, 197–98; defining core competencies, 194, 196; and flexible long-term skill platforms, 199–200; focus on a few critical activities, 196–97; focus on skill or knowledge sets, not products, 197; intellectual power important in, 200; and leveraging unique intellect in value chain, 198–99; preeminence and, 201; strategic focus and analysis for, 200–01; value chain and, 193–94, 193n, 195, 198–99

"Core-competency-with-outsourcing" strategies, 194, 203–12

COSMOS II, 77

Cost-benefit analyses, 332

Costs: alternative costs, 182–83; capital costs, 292–93, 296; of education, 380–81; to exploiters not increasing as resources are depleted, 319–20; fairness as more important than immediate cost, 321; of health care, 328–29; of outsourcing, 207–08; outsourcing as innovation leverage, not short-term cost reduction, 208–10; public markets and, 323–27, 337–38, 342; transaction costs, 315–16

CPM (critical path management), 64

Cray, S., 81

Cray Research, 197, 234

Cray 2 computers, 248

Creation of knowledge, 9–12

Creativity: motivated creativity, 2, 3, 5, 19; and new knowledge creation, 9–10. *See also* High innovativeness toward markets; Innovation

Crick, F., 221

"Criterion functions," 84

Crystal Awards, 157, 214

CSC, 101

CSC Index, 95

CTO ("chief tormenting officers"), 245

Culch bag approach, 142–43

Customers: core competencies related to, 197–98; innovations made by, 148–49; interactive customer design, 49, 73, 92; and market orientation and interactiveness, 252–54; needs information from, 147–49; software-based innovation in customer interaction, 47, 49; user- based innovation and virtual shopping, 60. *See also* High innovativeness toward markets

Cycle time of innovation, 53–54, 221, 222

Daiwa banks, 228

DARPA, 254, 320

DARPANET, 79, 345, 368

Darwin, C., 270–74

Darwin, E., 270

Darwin design system, 127

Data: disastrous policy from poor data, 367–68; from government agencies, 368; inadequacy of economic and technological data, 276, 338–39, 364–65; on public markets, 325–27; sorting and visualizing data, 124–25

Database and model access system, 65
Databases: of companies, 368–70; creation of, in scientific research, 269–70; in developing countries, 382; disastrous policy from poor data, 367–68; of government agencies, 368; for services and intellect-based society, 364–69, 370. *See also* headings beginning with Software
DEC, 254
Deep knowledge, 130
Deere and Co., 82
Defense Department, 284, 311, 397n31
Delays in innovation, 15
Delegation, 174
Dell, 350
Demand potential of public markets, 332–33
Deregulation, 304, 305, 374
Description in science, 269–70
Design and evaluation software, 54–55, 68–69
Design to requirements (support systems), 100–01
DESIGN/1, 99–100
Developing countries, 32, 320–21, 353–56, 374, 376–78, 382–84. *See also* specific countries
Development: government elimination of barriers to, 307–10; "industry cluster" development, 356; software-based innovation in, 47–48. *See also* Economic development; R&D; Software development
Dewhurst, J., 34
Differentness, not sameness, 143–144
Diffusion: definition of, 3; encouragement by government of public diffusion, 360–61; global outsourcing and, 30–32; lateral diffusion and learning, 167–68; and national technology policy, 290–91; national technology strategies for, 358–61; negative potentials of, 361–62; open access and, 358–59; and problems of rewards for software innovators, 361; relationship with science, 274–76; of scientific-technological knowledge, 276–77; software and, 78–79; software-based innovation in, 50
Direct and indirect multipliers, 37–38
Disaggregated organizations, 21, 29–30
Discovery: definition of, 3. *See also* Innovation; Invention
Disney, 164, 231, 370
Djerassi, C., 254
DNA, 221
DOA. *See* Agriculture Department
Dobzhansky, T., 274
DOD. *See* Defense Department
DOE. *See* Energy Department
Dom, 91–92
Dominant market share-oriented companies, 233–34
Dow, 69
Dow Jones, 368
Downsizing. *See* Outsourcing
Du Pont, 69, 134, 210
Dynamotive Inc., 331

Eastern Airlines, 87
Eastman Kodak, 82
ECHO, 50, 83, 132
Economic development: as building competencies, not making investment gifts, 354–56; "industry cluster" development, 356; integrated world innovation and economies, 353–54; international development strategies, 353–56
Economic growth: national income, 20, 22, 345–47, 364–65, 371; public markets and, 336–41; services-software economy and, 345–47; versus investment, 298. *See also* Economic trends
Economic paradigms: changing traditional economic paradigms, 33–40; direct and indirect multipliers, 37–38; growth and productivity factors, 34, 35–36; impacts of scale and affluence on, 39–40; Keynesian multipliers, 37, 38; outmoded economic measures and models, 40–41; public economic values, 40–41; rational approach to technology, 38–39; technology for quality of life, 34, 36; technology multipliers, 37
Economic policy: changed approaches to, 344–45; education and intelligent economy, 374–84
Economic trends: chaos and hypercompetition, 32–33; global outsourcing, 21, 30–32; intellectually based services, 20–25; national income, 20, 22, 345–47, 364–65, 371; overcapacity worldwide, 21, 25–28; radically disaggregated organizations, 21, 29–30;

Economic trends *(cont.)*
    services-software economy, 345–47;
    software, 21, 28–29. *See also* Eco-
    nomic development; Economic growth
Economost, 76, 77, 83, 222, 250
Edison, T., 37, 275
EDS, 95, 101
Education and training: computers and
    video games per household in U.S.,
    378, 380; computers per 100 people,
    by country, 381; cost of, 380–81; in
    developing countries, 374, 377–79,
    382–84; educational infrastructures
    from private companies, 384–85; elec-
    tronic education programs, 375,
    377–84; experiments in, 380–82; gov-
    ernment or private action for elec-
    tronic education programs, 382–84;
    government support for, 283; as
    growth factor, 36; human development
    index by country, 379; importance of,
    374, 386; information agents and,
    384–85; intelligent economy and,
    374–84; priorities for, 386; roles of
    teachers and librarians, 377, 384–85;
    skills value versus training expendi-
    tures, 4, 5; social returns for invest-
    ment in, 377; U.S. public education
    system, 374–75; U.S. university and
    graduate education systems, 375
Educational Technology Initiative, 377
Edward Marshall Boehm, 236
Effects software module, 143
Einstein, A., 274
Electronic education programs, 375,
    377–84
Electronic protection, 361–62
Embedding. *See* Sharing and embedding
Emergent process, 154–55
"Empathic design," 152
Employment: in agriculture, 22, 23; de-
    mand for IT-competent people, 158; in
    goods sector of economy, 22, 23, 349;
    labor as growth factor, 35; raw materi-
    als prices relative to real wages, 26; in
    services sector of economy, 20, 22, 23,
    24, 345, 346; in software program-
    ming, 75; temporary and job-search
    employment groups, 350
Encryption, 361
Endangered Species Act, 297
Energy Department, 286, 287

Engine design, 65–66
England. *See* Britain
Enhanced results with software, 55
EntreMed, 222
Entropy, 76–77
"Envelope curves," 191
Environmental issues, 82–83, 283, 286,
    297, 315–16, 323–28, 330–35, 339
Environmental Protection Agency (EPA),
    83, 311, 368
EPA. *See* Environmental Protection
    Agency (EPA)
EPRI, 360
Erlich, H., 121
Etzioni, A., 122
"Eureka" phenomenon, 17
Europe: bond interest rates in, 301; com-
    puters per 100 people in, 381; general
    consumption taxes in, 372; government
    receipts as percentage of GDP, 371;
    human development index in, 379; in-
    vestment and savings in, 292, 298–300;
    invisible exports as percentage of GDP,
    348; losses from illegal copying of soft-
    ware in, 363; post–World War II econ-
    omy of, 303; R&D in, 376; referendum
    voting in, 340; universities in, 303,
    375. *See also* specific countries
European Union, 371
Evaluation software, 54–55
Evaluations of performance, 135, 138,
    157, 228
Excel, 76, 81, 166, 184
Expandability of intellect, 7–9
Experimental hypothesis testing, 267–68,
    273–74
Exploration in science, 269–70
Exponentiality: of intellect's growth, 4–6;
    of software innovation, 77–78
Exports, 295, 348
Externalities, 315–16, 331–32
Exxon, 68, 201

FAA. *See* Federal Aviation Administration
    (FAA)
Failures, 40, 127–28, 252–53, 255,
    305–06, 314–22
Faloona, F., 121
Fanatics and innovation, 17
Fast cycle innovation, 53–58, 222
FDA. *See* Food and Drug Administration
    (FDA)

Federal Aviation Administration (FAA), 253, 305–06

Federal Express, 85, 164, 170, 192, 201, 368

Federal Reserve, 285

Feynman, R., 148

Fidelity Investments, 121, 201

Fidelity Securities, 7

Figures of merit: and aggregate of thrusts equal to strategic intent, 183–85; aggressor company technique for setting, 192; and alternative costs, not just incremental gains, 182–83; analytical methods for setting, 191–92; benchmarking versus, 188–90; definition of, 179, 187–88; development of, 152, 174; establishment of, 190–92; and overall financial targets, 179–85; and overriding pure financial rankings, 181–82; portfolio of thrusts and, 180, 181; rate of return (ROR) and, 181–82; theoretical limits analysis for setting, 191–92; winning with, 192–93

Financial services, 7, 67, 82, 89, 167–68, 197–98, 213, 283, 294, 305, 366–67. *See also* specific companies

Financial targets, 179–85

Firefly, 124–25

First Bank, 370

First Financial Management, 63

First Interstate, 370

Fisher, G., 188–89

Fisher, R., 274

Fisher-Pry forecasting technique, 191

Flat, externally leveraged organizations, 258–59

Flexibilities: long-term skill platforms, 199–200; outsourcing and, 211–12; resources to break barriers, 247–49

Flexible manufacturing systems (FMS), 176

Fluent, Inc., 54–55, 68–69

FMs. See Flexible manufacturing systems (FMS)

Folkman, J., 221–22, 259, 357–58

Food and Drug Administration (FDA), 221, 308, 309, 316

Food production. *See* Agriculture

Footlocker, 353

Ford Foundation, 306

Ford Motor Company: competitors of, 201; core competencies and, 201; Development group at, 182; diffusion and, 50; Edsel and, 253; entry requirements of, not met by high school graduates, 375; identity-creating information and, 138; intellectually based services of, 25; outsourcing at, 210; software system of, 30, 48, 68; Taurus-Sable project at, 147, 206–07, 240, 258; Team Taurus, 119–20, 147, 257

Forecasting techniques, 191

"Formal" strategic planning, 155

FotoMat, 200

France: basic research in, 357; computers per 100 people in, 381; employment in services in, 24; government receipts as percentage of GDP in, 371; investment versus economic growth in, 298; invisible exports as percentage of GDP, 348; losses from illegal copying of software in, 363; post–World War II economy of, 39; R&D in, 376; savings and investment in, 298, 299, 300; taxes in, 372

Franklin Mint, 236

Frito-Lay, 170, 211

Frogdesign, 203

Galvin, R., 188

"Gatekeepers," 133, 258

Gates, B., 98, 170, 184, 248

GATT, 310, 347, 367

Gaussian curve, 191, 220

GDP. *See* Gross domestic product (GDP)

GE, 25, 185, 201, 320–21

Gelfand, D., 121, 122

Gell-Mann, M., 270

Genentech, 163, 164, 169–70, 170, 196, 214, 234

General Agreement on Tariffs and Trade (GATT), 310, 347, 367

General Mills Restaurants Group (GMR), 86, 88

General Motors (GM), 173, 201, 367–68

Genesis, 83

Genesis Grant, 251

Genetics, 270–75

Gen-Rad, 153

Germany: bond interest rates in, 301; computers per 100 people in, 381; economy after world wars, 285; employment in

Germany *(cont.)*
  services in, 24; government receipts as
  percentage of GDP in, 371; human development index in, 379; investment versus economic growth in, 298; invisible
  exports as percentage of GDP, 348;
  losses from illegal copying of software in,
  363; R&D in, 376; regulations in, 332;
  savings and investment in, 35–36, 298,
  299, 300; subsidies for coal mining in,
  307; taxes in, 372
Ghoshal, S., 134
GI Bill, 286, 303
Gibraltar, 184
Gilfillan, C., 361
Gillette, 16, 148
Global trends. See International trends;
  and specific countries
GM. *See* General Motors (GM)
GMR. *See* General Mills Restaurants
  Group (GMR)
GNP. *See* Gross national product (GNP)
Goals: change process and goal congruence, 155; definition of, 174; demanding goals set by middle management,
  245–46; goal congruence, 122–24,
  155, 170; independent collaboration
  and goal congruence, 122–24; multiple
  goals, 174; in technology strategy,
  174–75
"Gold badge" groups and projects, 119,
  130, 228, 250
Goods: private versus public goods, 360;
  "rival" versus "nonrival" generic goods,
  360
Goods sector of economy: employment
  in, 22, 23, 349; national income from,
  22; overcapacity worldwide, 21,
  25–28; and pass-throughs from services sector to, 365–66; prices of commodities and manufactured goods, 27;
  raw materials prices relative to real
  wages, 26; services in manufacturing
  and international trade, 347–52
Gore, A., 138, 246, 346
Gore, B., 123, 134
Gore, N.L., & Associates, 121, 123,
  134–35, 164, 256
GoreCom, 134
Gosling, J., 253
Gould Corporation, 246
Government activities: restructuring of,

368–69. *See also* Government regulation; Government-industry strategies;
  and headings beginning with National
Government deficits, 373
Government-industry strategies: Clinton
  administration and, 310–12; and elimination of barriers to development,
  307–10; expenditures creating perpet-
  ual support polities, 306; extending
  time horizons, 291–301; generic interventions supporting private markets,
  281, 284; government assistance to
  long-term industries, 282–83, 295–96;
  government-supported innovation,
  279–84; historical guidelines on,
  289–91; impacts on government functions, 299–301; incentives from government, 301–12; industrial policy,
  280–84, 295–97; market mechanisms
  and, 290; negative government impact
  on time horizons, 297–99; past U.S.
  technology strategies, 284–289; and
  perverse subsidies, 306–07; successes
  in, 279–80; and technology's perceived
  role in national growth, 289; time horizons and, 291–301; two- to four-year
  industries, 296–97; and U.S. competitiveness problems, 293–95; and use
  and diffusion, 290–91
Government regulation, 286, 330–32,
  334–35, 339, 373–74
Government-supported innovation,
  279–84
GPS, 368
Great Britain. *See* Britain
Griliches, Z., 287, 357
Gross domestic product (GDP), 345,
  348, 371–72, 378, 379
Gross national product (GNP), 22, 40,
  280, 335, 371
Grove, A., 50–51, 129, 247, 248
Guillemin, R., 271, 272, 273

Haas, R., 138
Haldane, J., 274
Half-measures, avoidance of, 138–39
Harley-Davidson, 246
Harreld, B., 245
Harris, G., 270, 272–73
HBO & Co., 96
HCFA. See Health Care Financing Ad-
  ministration (HCFA)

Health and Human Services Department, 311

Health care, 149–50, 283, 294, 306, 309–10, 323, 325, 328–29, 367. *See also* Biotechnology; and specific companies

Health Care Financing Administration (HCFA), 368

Heidegger, M., 122

Heskett, J., 170–71

Hewlett, W., 189

Hewlett-Packard (HP), 68, 110, 136, 146–50, 164, 176–77, 185, 189, 211, 234, 253

Hierarchies, destruction of, by software, 80

High innovativeness toward markets: and caring why, 147–49; culch bag approach and, 142–43; and differentness, not sameness, 143–44; and emerging organizations and results, 154–55; guidelines on, 157–60; and hierarchy-free software networks, 150–51; intervention points and, 157; key elements for, 141–49; as managed, not haphazard, system, 155–56; and partial, tentative, and experimental processes, 156–57; process focus for collaborative change and innovation, 154–57; and solutions and uses in waiting, 144–46; and structuring user interactions and participation, 146–47; and systematically attacking white spaces, 149–54; "white space" technique and, 149–54. *See also* Innovation

Highly disciplined procedures (legacy systems), 101–03

Highway Trust Fund, 316

Highways, 55, 316

Hoff, T., 37, 143, 254

Hoffman-LaRoche, 233, 238

Hokkaido, 356

Holland. *See* Netherlands

Home Depot, 347, 353

Honda, S., 257

Honda Motor Company, 108, 168, 176, 197, 201, 228, 248, 256

Hong Kong, 356

"Hooks". *See* Software "hooks"

"Horizontal company," 203

Hormones, 270–76

HP. *See* Hewlett-Packard (HP)

HP Medical Products, 152

HTML, 66, 72, 76, 81, 90

HTTP, 127

HTTP/HTML, 66

Hughes Aircraft, 335

Hughes Electronics, 234

Human development index, 379

Human Genome Project, 47, 56, 71

Hypercompetition and chaos, 32–33

Hypothalamic-releasing hormones, 270–76

Hypothesis proposal, 272–73

Hypothesis testing, 267–68, 273–74

IBM: competitors of, 201; core competencies and, 201; as dominant market share-oriented company, 233; intellectually based services of, 25; Johnson-effect devices developed by, 253; phase-out of printers at, 181; R&D division of, 181; revenue data not available, 95; software system of, 368; technology strategy of, 176; top management at, 251; Watson Research Center at, 46–47

Ibuka, M., 189–90, 191, 245, 246, 257, 259

ICI (Imperial Chemicals Industries) Polyester, 123–24

"Idea gaps," 344

Ideation International Inc., 142–43

"If hit, win" techniques, 192

Illegal copying of software, 363

Illinois Institute of Technology, 210

Imperial Chemicals Industries (ICI) Polyester, 123–24

Implementation. *See* Middle management

Inamori, K., 165

Incentives: company incentives for innovation, 135–36, 138, 157, 212–14, 228, 237–42; government incentives, 301–12; middle management and, 228, 237–42; for software innovators, 361; top management and, 157, 212–14

Income: household savings as percentage of disposable income, 300; national income, 20, 22, 40

Incremental gains, 182

Independent collaboration: and aligned purpose, 122–24; and avoiding suboptimization and half-measures, 138–39;

Independent collaboration *(cont.)*
and chaos and self-organizing systems,
136–39; and developing a common
bond, 115–21; dictates of collaboration, 111–12; and differences of individuals, 128–29; and evaluations of
performance, 135, 138; examples of,
108, 121; guidelines on, 157–60; incentives and rewards for, 135–36, 138;
and levels of innovation, 108–11;
process analogs and, 107–08; and psychological and work interconnections,
134–35; and questioning of need for
arbitrary structure, 132–33; and rich
and profuse networks of relationships,
128–36; software backbone of,
108–12, 139–40, 144–46; and software development as innovation paradigm, 112–15; and superabundant
information, 124–28; and swimming in
user's environment, 151–54; and tacit
versus specialist knowledge, 129–30;
three-level independent collaboration
structure, 130–33; within bureaucratic
organization, 138–39
Indexing programs, 384–85
India, 32, 38, 356, 378, 379, 382, 383
Indian National Scientific and Documentation Center, 382
"Indifference techniques," 323
Indirect and direct multipliers, 37–38
Individual inventor-innovators, 95–97
Industrial policy, 280–84, 295–97
"Industry cluster" development, 356
Information: asynchronous organizations
and superabundant information,
126–28; intellectual values of largest
acquired companies, 369, 370; maximizing information availability and use,
158; open access to, and diffusion,
358–59; sharing of, at Kao, 131; and
sorting and visualizing data, 124–25;
superabundant information and innovation, 124–28; virtual organization
and superabundant information,
125–26. *See also* Data; Knowledge
Information agents, 384–85
Information-based companies, 368–70
Information technology (IT): capital and
tax policy support for IT-based innovation, 369, 371–74; demand for IT-
competent people, 158; federal

government's underinvestment in,
305–06; impact of IT software, 45–46;
initial public offerings from
1980–1996, by business sector, 62;
strategies for, 176. *See also* Software;
Software- based innovation; Technology; and other headings beginning with
Software
Informix, 63, 96
Inland Steel, 293
Innovation: adhocracies and, 17–19; analytical structures and, 17–19; capital
and tax policy support for IT-based innovation, 369, 371–74; changing traditional economic paradigms on, 33–40;
characteristics of, 12–17; complex nature of, 13–14; continual, pulsing, and
organic innovation, 165–66; cycle time
of, 53–54, 221, 222; definition of, 3; direct and indirect multipliers and, 37–38;
economics of, 90–92; fanatics or champions for, 17; fast cycle innovation,
53–58, 222; government-supported innovation, 279–84; information technology (IT)-based innovation, 369,
371–74; integrated world innovation
and economies, 353–54; integration of
innovation subsystems, 68–73; Internet
model of, 76–80; intuition and tacit
knowledge for, 17; inventive solutions,
109; levels of, 108–11; lucky "accidents" involved in, 254–55; mistakes in,
due to scale, 40; along multiple dimensions, 164–65, 254–55; national encouragement of software innovation,
360–61; need-oriented nature of,
15–16; nonlinear progress in, 15; opposition to, 16, 138; probabilistic nature
of, 13; process focus for, 154–57; questions about interrelationships involving,
1; radical inventions, 109; resistance
created by, 16; service innovations characteristics, 23–25; simple solutions,
108–09; software development as innovation paradigm, 112–15; spurts, delays, and setbacks in, 15; system
solutions, 109; technology multipliers
and, 37; time-consuming nature of, 14;
totally new phenomena, 109; unpredictability in, 254–55; user-based innovation, 60, 72–73, 81–82, 89–90;
worldwide virtual innovation, 60–61.

*See also* High innovativeness toward markets; Software-based innovation
Innovation Workbench, 143
Insiders software system, 133
Integrated Tactical Warning/Attack Systems Support (ISISS), 79
Integration: benefits of more fully integrated systems, 93–94; of innovation subsystems, 68–73; vertical integration, 374
Intel: Architecture Labs at, 51; commonly held culture at, 138, 247; constructive confrontation and trust at, 247; core competencies and, 199, 201; databases of, 65; demanding goals at, 245; development of new personal computer by, 50–51; employees of, 6; figures of merit and, 189; impact of microprocessor developed by, 37–38; innovation along multiple dimensions at, 164; innovators at, 128; management of, 248; market research and, 252; performance of, 293; recognition system at, 214; value-added systems and, 50–51; vision of, 170
Intellect: changing traditional economic paradigms on, 33–40; characteristics of, 4–9; definition of, 3; expandability of, 7–9; exponential growth of, 4–6; and firm's ability to attract best talent, 6; focus on, in software development, 112–13; intellectual values of largest acquired companies, 369, 370; leveraging unique intellect in value chain, 198–99; new databases for services and intellect-based society, 364–69, 370; organizational structures and, 10–12; questions about interrelationships involving, 1; redefining intellectual processes in management of software-based innovation, 92–94; ROE (return on intellect), 24; and sharing and embedding of, for knowledge growth, 6–7; skills value versus training expenditures, 4, 5
Intellectual property rights, 362–63, 385
Intellectual value of companies, 369, 370
Intellectually based services, 20–25
"Intelligent enterprise," 203
Interactive customer design, 49, 73, 92
Interactive sales tool, 59
Interactive simulations, 125
Interest rates, 299–300, 301

Interfaces, 66
Interior Department, 311, 338
Intermediate size operating systems, 98
Internal Revenue Service (IRS), 305–06
International Finance Corporation, 383
International Monetary Fund, 367
International trends: development strategies, 353–56; food production, 28; outsourcing, 21, 30–32, 350, 352; overcapacity of goods, 21, 25–28; population, 28; trade, 304–05, 332, 347–52; virtual innovation, 60–61. *See also* specific countries
Internet: auto catalysis and, 77–80; as classroom teaching tool, 381–82; DARPA's development of, 254, 320; destruction of hierarchies by, 80; in developing countries, 383; diffusion and, 78–79, 359; downloading software from, 90–91; and economics of innovation, 90–92; elimination of "solution and use" mismatches by, 145–46; fees for software publicized on home pages, 361; globalization and, 31, 383; growth of, 345–47; hybrid cycles and, 242; as innovation model, 60, 76–80, 90–91; market research not able to predict user response to, 40; Netscape on, 92; new threats and new policy needs for, 361–62; not included in data on intellectual assets, 364; open systems and, 79–80; revenue from Internet software, 77, 78; search and agent software systems for, 66; smallest replicable units and, 71; and user-based innovation and virtual shopping, 60, 72, 81; BioMOO virtual laboratory on, 382. *See also* World Wide Web
Intervention points in innovation, 157
Intranets, 89–90, 145
Intuit, 96
Intuition, 2, 3, 17, 19
Invention: definition of, 3; inventors as pack rats, 142; software as inventor, 56; software facilitating, 142–43. See also Innovation
Invention Machine Corp., 142–43
Inventive solutions, 109
Inverted organizations, 11, 226–28
Investment: encouragement of, over consumption, 371–73; international development and, 354–56; savings and, 299, 371–73; social returns for investment in

Investment *(cont.)*
    education, 377; venture capital, 61, 96,
    184, 302, 303; versus economic growth,
    298
IRS. *See* Internal Revenue Service (IRS)
ISISS. *See* Integrated Tactical
    Warning/Attack Systems Support
    (ISISS)
Israel, 32, 39, 289, 291, 379
IT software. *See* Information technology
    (IT) software
Italy, 298, 299, 348, 356, 363, 371, 376,
    381

Jamaica, 383
Japan: bond interest rates in, 301; capital
    costs in, 292; color copier developed
    in, 136; computers per 100 people in,
    381; constructive confrontation and
    trust in, 246; consumer products com-
    panies in, 50, 131–32; electronics in-
    dustry in, 189–90, 246, 250;
    employment in services in, 24; govern-
    ment receipts as percentage of GDP,
    371; graduate education in, 375;
    Honda facilities in, 201; human rela-
    tions staffs in, 133; incentive changes
    in, from 1950s-1970s, 284; industrial
    and technological development in, 32,
    289, 291; investment versus economic
    growth in, 298; invisible exports as
    percentage of GDP, 348; losses from il-
    legal copying of software in, 363;
    post–World War II economy of, 39;
    R&D in, 376; savings and investment
    in, 35, 292, 298, 299, 300, 301; skunk
    works in, 257; software industry in,
    38; steel industry in, 190; taxes in,
    372; trade policies of, 304–05, 347.
    *See also* Kao Corporation; Sony Cor-
    poration
Java, 8, 66, 72, 73, 76, 81, 90, 91, 96,
    127, 253
Jet Propulsion Laboratory, 79
Jiro, K., 153
Job-search employment groups, 350
Jobs. *See* Employment
Jobs, S., 128
Johnson, K., 257
Johnson and Johnson, 201
JPL, 6
Justice Department, 308

Kao Corporation, 30, 50, 83, 108, 119,
    131–32
Kaplan, A., 268
Kapor, M., 129
Kauffman, S., 83
Keating, P., 144
Kellner-Rogers, M., 122
Kelly, K., 157–58
Kendrik, J., 34
Kennedy, J. F., 284
Kenya, 333
Keynesian multipliers, 37, 38
Kihara, N., 190, 257
Kindelberger, J., 34
KJ methodology, 153
Kmart, 353
Knowledge: advanced skills, 2, 3, 5, 19;
    anomalies in scientific knowledge spec-
    trum, 276–77; chaos in development of
    scientific knowledge, 18–19; character-
    istics of intellect, 4–9; cognitive knowl-
    edge, 2, 3, 5, 19; creation of scientific
    and technological knowledge, 9–12;
    deep knowledge, 130; and expandabil-
    ity of intellect, 7–9; exponential growth
    of, 4–6; intellectual values of largest ac-
    quired companies, 369, 370; levels of,
    2, 3, 5, 19; motivated creativity, 2, 3, 5,
    19; new knowledge creation, 9–10;
    open access to, and diffusion, 358–59;
    professional knowledge, 2–9, 19; ques-
    tions about interrelationships involving,
    1; sharing and embedding of, for
    growth, 6–7; software leverages for,
    2–4; specialist knowledge, 129–30;
    synthesis, 2, 3; system understanding,
    2, 3, 5, 19; tacit knowledge, 17,
    129–30, 133; trained intuition, 2, 3,
    19; types of, 2. *See also* Information
Knowledge-based national technology
    strategies, 356–64
Knowledge diffusion. *See* Diffusion
Korea, 32, 190, 363, 379
Kotter, J., 170–71
Kraft, 370
Krugman, P., 344, 347
Kuhn, T., 268
Kuznets, S., 34
Kyocera, 164–65, 176, 226, 234

Labor as growth factor, 35. *See also* Em-
    ployment

Labor Department, 368
Lamarck, J., 270
Land, E., 164
Land as growth factor, 35
Landsat, 77
Large integrated systems, 99–100
Large-scale systems, 11
Large-system technology producers, 231–33
Lateral competition, 201, 202
Lateral diffusion, 167–68
"Lattice" unstructure, 134–35, 138
"Lead user method," 151–52
Leadership: characteristics of effective leaders, 244–51; essence of, 172–74; vision and, 168–74. *See also* Middle management; Top management
Learning. *See* Education and training
"Learning game" computers, 380–81
Learson, V., 250–51
Legacy system, 101–03
Legends about company, 172–73
Leonard-Barton, D., 152
Less developed countries, 32, 320–21, 353–56, 374, 377–79, 382–84. *See also* specific countries
Levi Strauss & Co., 138
Lewent, J., 164
Lewin, R., 136
Libraries and librarians, 384–85
Lichtenberg, F., 357
Liebhaber, R., 209
Life quality, 34, 36, 321–22
Life-work connection with work-life, 123–24, 171
Lightnin, 69
Likert, R., 122
The Limited, 49–50, 353
Limited volume or fashion companies, 234, 236
Lincoln Electric, 138
"Line" hierarchy, 227
Litton-PRC, 79, 101–03
Lockheed, 257
Lotus, 129
Lucas, G., 56

Mac OS, 65, 203
Malaysia, 356
Malpractice suits, 309
Management of software-based innovation: benefits of more fully integrated systems, 93–94; and capturing experience and explaining why, 94; changes in software innovation organizations, 80–83; critical issues in, 74–75; database and model access system, 65; definition of, 94; design to requirements (support systems), 100–01; highly disciplined procedures (integrating and improving legacy systems), 101–03; individual inventor-innovators (small, discrete applications), 95–97; and interacting subsystems, not megasystems, 66–68; interfaces, 66; Internet model of innovation, 76–80; monitoring programs (large integrated systems), 99–100; and new economics of computing, 90–92; object orientation, 71–72, 73, 83–92; and priesthood of mathematicians, 80–81; and redefining intellectual processes and organizations, 92–94; and self-learning software systems, 82–83; small interactive teams (operating systems), 98; software-centered design and, 75–76; software development management, 94–95; software (process) engines, 65–66; three critical systems for, 64–66; user-innovators and, 81–82. *See also* Middle management; Software-based innovation; Top management
Managing chaos, 220–22
Mandelbrot, B., 83
Mansfield, E., 16
Manufacturing: organizational disaggregation and outsourcing in, 349–50; services in, 347–52. *See also* Goods sector of economy
Manufacturing engineering, 48
Markem Machine Company, 147
Marker, R., 221
Market failures: costs to exploiters not increasing as resources are depleted, 319–20; established institutions with power to constrain innovation, 317; fairness as more important than immediate cost, 321; government as monopsony buyer, 317–18; individual buyers and sellers unable to internalize all transaction costs, 315–16; individual buyers unable to aggregate demands effectively, 316–17; large intangibles which cannot be valued, 319; life quality and, 321–22;

Market failures *(cont.)*
national technology strategies for overcoming, 314–22; risks too large for individuals to assume safely, 318–19;
secondary (or public) benefits outweigh
private benefits, 320–21
Market orientation and interactiveness,
252–54
Market research, 252–53
Markets: biases favoring private versus
public markets, 338; government-in-
dustry strategies and, 290; govern-
ment's creation of new markets,
322–32. *See also* Public markets
Maruta, Y., 132
Mastercard, 87
Matsuo, H., 271
Matsushita, 138, 196, 197, 211, 233, 370
Maxim Integrated Products, 63
Maxus, 91, 92
Mayo Clinic, 6, 201
Mayr, E., 274
MBNA, 213
MCA, 370
MCC, 82, 308
McDonald's, 49–50, 368
McGraw Cellular, 370
McGregor, D., 122
MCI, 77, 86, 97, 164, 192, 208, 209,
368
"McIntel" approach, 164
McKesson Corporation, 83, 89, 222,
250, 366
McKinsey & Company, 6, 20, 201, 228
McLouth Steel, 331
McNealy, S., 248
Medicine. *See* Biotechnology; Health care
Megasystems, 66–67, 391n32
Mendeleyev, D., 270
Mercer Management Consulting, 173–74
Merck, 5, 163, 164, 182, 196, 197, 201,
233, 238, 308
Merrill Lynch, 5, 30, 65, 108, 256, 368
Merton, Robert K., 122
METHOD/1, 99–100
Michigan, 331
Microsoft: Advanced Technology Group
at, 166, 184; competitive paranoia at,
245; competitors of, 201, 204; core
competencies and, 201, 204, 212;and
cycle time for innovation, 222; employ-
ees of, 6; figures of merit and, 192; "if

hit, win" techniques of, 192; incentive
systems in, 214, 237; independent collaboration at, 121; and innovation
along multiple dimensions, 164; intellectual preeminence of, 5, 201; inverted organizational strategies in, 228;
and leveraging value creation, 58; management of, 248; market orientation of,
253; multiple companies within, 166;
revenues and profits of, 29, 63, 96;
small interactive teams at, 98, 99; software system as integral part of, 30,
108; technology strategy of, 174–75;
time horizons and, 240; vision of, 170;
Windows from, 65, 72, 76, 166, 184,
222, 240; Word from, 81, 166, 184
"Microsoft or Nintendo effect," 91
Middle management: adhocracies and,
222, 224, 226–37, 251–60; "builds"
and "way points," 223–24; characteristics of effective leaders, 159,
244–51; and constructive confrontation and trust, 246–47; demanding
goals set by, 245–46; direct access to,
249–50; and flat, externally leveraged
organizations, 258–59; and flexible resources to break barriers, 247–49; and
focus and chaos, 220; incentive systems and, 228, 237–42; and managing
chaos, 220–22; and market orientation
and interactiveness, 252–54; multiple
development approaches and, 254–55;
objective performance shoot-outs and,
255–56; and product development-
product life cycles, 222, 238–42; protected time horizons and underground
activities, 250–51; recognition of innovators by, 245–46; and rewards for
champions and experts, 259–60; roles
and responsibilities of, 219, 242–43,
260–61; and skunk work units,
256–58; and somewhat orderly tumult, 222–26; venture teams and, 260.
*See also* Top management
"Middleware," 124
Millstein, N., 143
Minimum replicable unit level, 70–72,
86–87
Minnesota, 381–82
Mintzberg, H., 155, 224
Mission statements, 169. *See also* Vision
MIT, 82, 153

Mitchell, B., 318
MITS, 32
MJR Holdings, 370
Monitoring programs, 49–50, 99–100
Monopsony purchases, 317–18
Monsanto, 368
Moore, G., 128, 164, 170, 189
Morgan Stanley, 6, 199, 212
Morita, A., 246, 249, 257
Mortgage industry, 197–98. *See also* Financial services
Mosaic, 66, 72, 91, 96
Motivation: for high innovativeness toward markets, 141–60; incentive systems, 135–36, 138, 157, 212–14, 228, 237–42; for independent collaboration, 135–36, 138; motivated creativity, 2, 3, 5, 19; performance measurement and recognition systems, 157, 212–14
Motorola, 71, 92, 110–11, 119, 188–89, 199, 201, 236, 245, 252, 293
Moulènex, 211
Movie industry, 56
Mrs. Fields, 86
MS-DOS, 184
Mullis, K., 121, 143
Multiple companies within the company, 166
Multiple, discrete, freestanding product lines, 234, 235
Multipliers: auto catalysis and, 77–80, 344, 359–60; changes affecting, 343–44; direct and indirect multipliers, 37–38; Keynesian multipliers, 37, 38; open access and diffusion systems, 358–61; services-software economy, 345–47; technology multipliers, 37. *See also* Information technology (IT); Services sector of economy; and Software headings
Myhrvold, N., 166, 184

NASA, 38, 51, 82, 127, 286, 287, 311, 368
National Academy of Engineering, 298–99
National Academy of Sciences, 285
National Aeronautics and Space Administration (NASA), 38, 51, 82, 127, 286, 287, 311, 368
National Amusement, 370
National Centers for Disease Control, 368

National Defense Education Act, 286, 303; *see also* GI Bill
National Environmental Supercomputing Center, 83
National income, 20, 22, 345–47, 364–65, 371. *See also* Economic development; Economic growth; Economic trends; Gross domestic product (GDP); Gross national product (GNP)
National Institutes of Health (NIH), 56, 82, 286, 287, 305, 368
National Rental Car, 89
National Research Council, 382, 391n32
National science and technology policy, 265–67, 276–77, 287–89, 310–12, 344–45, 367–68
National Science Foundation (NSF), 286, 305, 311, 347
National strategies: government-industry strategies, 279–313; industrial policy, 280–84, 295–97; and politics of science, 265–78; science and technology policy, 265–67, 276–77, 287–89, 290, 310–12, 344–45. See also National technology strategies
National technology strategies: advanced research, 357–58; auto-catalytic growth through sharing and feedback, 359–60; benefits to industry regulation, 330–31; changed approaches to, 344–45; creation of public markets, 314–42; disastrous policy from poor data, 367–68; education and intelligent economy, 374–84; effective public markets needed for economic growth, 336–41; encouragement of private software innovation and public diffusion, 360–61; and encumbrances to public allocation, 338–39; and enhancement of market efficiencies, 331–32; and inadequacy of economic and technological data, 276, 338–39; and intellectual values of largest acquired companies, 369, 370; international development strategies and, 353–56; key parameters for, 385–86; knowledge-based strategies, 356–64; levels of policy support, 360; need for, 314; new databases for services and intellect-based society, 364–69, 370; new threats and new policy needs in, 361–62; open access and diffusion systems, 358–59; and outmoded decision

National technology strategies (*cont.*)
structures, 341; overcoming market failures, 314–22; past successes, 284–89; quasi-monopolies and, 362–64; and restructuring traditional government activities, 368–69; services in manufacturing and international trade, 347–52; trends affecting, 343–44
National Weather Service, 82, 368
Navigator, 66, 72, 76, 81
Navstar, 77
Need-oriented nature of innovation, 15–16, 147–49
Negative entropy, 77, 344
"Negative entropy growth," 344
Nelson, R., 344, 360
Netherlands, 298, 299, 332, 348, 381
Netscape, 77, 91, 92, 201, 212
Netscape Communications, 90
"Network externality benefits," 368
Network innovation strategies, 228–30
Network model of behavior, 117
Network ("spider's web") organization, 11–12, 228–30
Networks: and high innovativeness toward markets, 150–51; independent collaboration and, 128–36; network innovation strategies, 228–30. *See also* Internet; Intranets; and specific networks
New Jersey, 332
Newport News, 293
News Corp., 384
Newton, I., 267
"Next-bench technique," 146
NextStep software, 114
NICNET, 382
NIH. *See* National Institutes of Health (NIH)
Nike, 68, 108, 196, 197, 201, 204, 208, 350, 368
Nintendo Co., 25, 38, 97, 214, 237, 253, 257
*No More Teams* (Schrage), 111
Nolen, W., 250
Nonlinear progress in innovation, 15
"Nonrival" generic goods, 360
NovaCare, 11, 30, 50, 108, 163, 226
Novell, 63, 96
*Novum Organum* (Bacon), 267
Noyce, R., 128, 164
NSF. *See* National Science Foundation (NSF)

Nucor, 190

"Object gaps," 344
Object orientation, 71–72, 73, 83–92
Objective performance shoot-outs, 255–56
Observation in science, 269–70
Occupational Health Acts, 286
Occupational Health and Safety Act, 297
Occupational Health and Safety Administration (OSHA), 330
OECD. *See* Organization for Economic Cooperation and Development (OECD)
Office of Technology Assessment, 338
Ogallala Aquifer, 319–20
Ohga, N., 257
OLE, 73, 184
Olive Gardens, 88
*On the Origin of Species* (Darwin), 272
One-off job shops, 236
Open access systems, 358–59
Open systems, 79–80
Operating systems development, 98
Opposition to innovation, 16, 138
Oracle, 63, 66, 96, 212
Orbital Engines, 25, 249
Organization for Economic Cooperation and Development (OECD), 33–34, 304, 327, 331, 367, 372, 377
Organizational structures: adhocracies, 17–19, 222, 224, 226–37, 251–60; "amoeba management practice," 165; asynchronous organizations, 126–28; basic research companies, 233; circular interdependent organizations, 118–20, 130–33; destruction of hierarchies by software, 80; determinants in choice of, 10–11; dominant market share-oriented companies, 233–34; flat, externally leveraged organizations, 258–59; incentives and, 228, 237–39; independent collaboration, 107–40; independent units or teams within bureaucratic organization, 138–39; intellect and, 10–12; inverted organizations, 11, 226–28; large-scale systems, 11; large-system technology producers, 231–33; "lattice" unstructure, 134–35, 138; limited volume or fashion companies, 234, 236; multiple companies within the company, 166; multiple, discrete, freestanding product

lines, 234, 235; network innovation strategies, 228–30; network ("spider's web") organization, 11–12, 228–30; one-off job shops, 236; "paperweight" organization form, 168; process analogs for, 107–08; questioning of need for arbitrary structure, 132–33; radically disaggregated organizations, 21, 29–30; redefining of, in management of software-based innovation, 92–94; software as integral part of, 11–12, 30, 125–26, 228–30; "spider's web" organization, 11–12, 228–30; starburst strategies, 230–31; state-of-the-art technologies, 234; teams, 107, 117, 128, 132; three-level independent collaboration structure, 130–33;virtual organization as real organization, 125–26. *See also* Middle management; Top management

OSHA. *See* Occupational Health and Safety Administration (OSHA)

OST (objectives, strategies, and tactics) system, 185

O'Toole, J., 154

Outputs: increase in output value through public markets, 323; of services, 365–67; of technology, 365

Outsourcing: "core-competency-with-outsourcing" strategies, 194, 203–12; and faster better innovation, 210–11; as innovation leverage, not short-term cost reduction, 208–10; internal and external transactions costs for, 207–08; international outsourcing, 21, 30–32, 350, 352; and leveraging innovation through, 203–12; in manufacturing, 349–50; and maximizing efficiency, flexibility, and stability simultaneously, 211–12; questions concerning, 207–08; strategic outsourcing and handling vulnerability, 204–07

Overcapacity worldwide, 21, 25–28

PAL. *See* Process Asset Library (PAL)

Pan Am, 87

"Paperweight" organization form, 168

Parametric Technology, 63, 96

"Partner objects," 71

Patents, 50, 385

PAW. *See* Petroleum Administration for War (PAW)

Paychex, 63

PCR. *See* Polymerase chain reaction (PCR)

PDP. *See* Product development program (PDP) concept

"Pediatrician" technical specialists, 260

People's Express, 228

Pepsico, 211

Performance evaluations, 135, 138, 157, 228

Performance measurement and recognition systems, 157, 212–14

Performance shoot-outs, 255–56

PERT (program evaluation and review technique), 64

Petroleum Administration for War (PAW), 308

Pharmaceutical industry, 113, 221–22, 238, 282, 294, 308, 309, 366. *See also* specific companies

Philip Morris, 370

Phoenix process, 101–02

Physical prototype comparisons, 256

Pilkington, A., 250, 254

Pilkington Bros., 163, 210, 250, 253

Polanyi, M., 268

Polaroid Corporation, 153, 164, 185, 251

Policies in technology strategy, 175. *See also* Economic policy; Industrial policy; National science and technology policy

Pollution. *See* Environmental issues

Polymerase chain reaction (PCR), 121, 143, 151

Poppa, 270

Popper, K., 267

Population trends, 28

Portfolio of commitments, 179, 180, 183–85, 250, 397n31

Positive entropy, 76–77

Power Objects, 60, 81

PRC, 95, 101–03; *see also* Litton-PRC

Predictions software module, 143

Preeminence, 201

President's Office of Science and Technology Policy, 338

Pricing systems of software, 91–92

*Principia Mathematica* (Newton), 267

Principle software module, 143

Private versus public goods, 360

Probabilistic nature of innovation, 13

Process analogs, 107–08

Process Asset Library (PAL), 102

Process focus for innovation, 154–57
"Process masters," 167
Process (software) engines, 65–66
Procter & Gamble, 211
Product development–product life cycles, 222, 238–42, 295–97
Product development program (PDP) concept, 224, 225
Professional knowledge. *See* Knowledge
Profit sharing, 123, 214
Profits and human values, 166–68
Programs in technology strategy, 175
"Protector" for new product, 240
Prototype comparisons, 256
Psychological and work interconnections, 134–35
Public economic values, 40–41
Public markets: biases favoring private versus public markets, 338; changing terminology and perceptions needed for, 337; creation of, 314–42; data and conceptual anomalies on, 325–27; def-inition of, 41; demand potential of, 332–33; economic growth and, 336–41; and encumbrances to public allocation, 338–39; increasing output value through, 323; market-like mech-anisms for, 333–35; "national costs" of, 323–25, 337, 342; and net value creation, not cost minimization, 337–38; and outmoded decision struc-tures, 341; and referendum voting as market surrogate, 339–41; survey techniques for, 332–33; tradable quo-tas and, 333–35; very large markets, 335–36; wrongheaded opposition to, 327–30
Public versus private goods, 360

Q ratios, 212
Quality of life, 34, 36, 321–22
Quasi-monopolies, 362–64

R&D: command-and-control strategies for, 39, 40; federal government expen-ditures for, 286, 287, 311; productivity growth and, 357; software-based inno-vation in, 47–48; U.S. scientists and engineers engaged in, by country, 376; worldwide budget for, 258. *See also* Development; High innovativeness to-ward markets; Innovation; Science

Rabinow, P., 151
Radical inventions, 109
Radically disaggregated organizations, 21, 29–30
Rate of return (ROR), 181–82, 212
"Rational analytical" process, 155
Raychem, 133, 136, 199, 253
RCA, 317
REA. *See* Rural Electrification Agency (REA)
Recognition systems, 135–36, 138, 157, 212–14, 228
Red Lobster, 88
Reebok, 350
Referendum voting, 339–41
Regis McKenna, 203
Regulation by government, 286, 330–32, 334–35, 339, 373–74
Reinventing Government team, 246
Repetto, R., 307
Replicable units, 70–72, 86–87
Research. *See* R&D; Science
Resistance to change and innovation, 16, 138
Resumex, 133
Retailing, 85, 294, 353–54
Return on intellect (ROI), 24, 321
Return on physical assets (ROA), 24, 246
Rewards for innovation, 135–36, 138, 157, 212–14, 237–42, 259–60, 361
Ringii decision-making process, 257
Risks: strategic outsourcing and, 204–07; strategic risk versus competitive edge, 205; too- large risks for individuals to assume safely, 318–19
"Rival" versus "nonrival" generic goods, 360
ROA (return on physical assets), 24, 246
Rocketdyne, 234
Rockwell, 127
ROI (return on intellect), 24, 321
Romer, P., 344, 347, 360, 363–64
ROR (rate of return), 181–82, 212
Rosenberg, N., 347
Rubbermaid, 11, 121, 176, 226, 228, 253
Rural Electrification Administration (REA), 37, 39, 285
Russell, B., 268
Russia, 38, 356, 363, 379

SABRE, 71, 76, 83, 86–87
Sachs, J., 129

Saiki, R., 121
Sales tools, 59
SALP AG, 96
Sandia, 367–68
Saritch, R., 248–49
SAS Institute, 11, 96, 138, 226, 228
Saturn 5 program, 51
Savings, 298–301, 371–73
Scanning unit techniques, 146–47, 149
Schally, A., 271, 272, 273
Scharf, S., 121
Schrage, M., 111
Schumpeter, J., 34, 289
SCI, 201
Science: advanced research in, 357–58;
    applied research in, 47; basic research
    in, 46–47, 233, 357–58; cataloging
    and classification, 270–71; chaos in
    development of scientific knowledge,
    18–19; as continuous, tumultuous
    contingent process, 268–69; creation
    of database in, 269–70; creation of
    scientific and technological knowl-
    edge, 9–12; definition of, 3; experi-
    mental hypothesis testing, 267–68,
    273–74; hypotheses proposal in,
    272–73; manipulation for a purpose
    in, 274–76; national science policy,
    276–77, 287–89, 290, 310–12; ob-
    servation, exploration, and descrip-
    tion, 269–70; politics of, 265–78;
    relationship with technology, 274–76;
    search for generalized patterns in,
    271–72; simplistic view of, 266–67;
    subsystem relationships in, 271–72;
    synthesis in, 274; taxonomy develop-
    ment in, 270–71; types of valid scien-
    tific processes, 267–76; U.S. scientists
    and engineers engaged in R&D by
    country, 376; university-based re-
    search in, 357–58
*Science and Engineering Indicators, 1995*,
    347
Science policy, 276–77, 287–89, 290,
    310–12, 367–68
"Screen" tests, 223
SEC. *See* Securities and Exchange Com-
    mission (SEC)
Securities and Exchange Commission
    (SEC), 284
Self-learning software systems, 82–83
Self-organizing systems: chaos and,

136–39; guidelines on, 158
Selye, H., 270
Sematech, 308, 360
Semmelweis, I., 271
Senge, P., 122
Services: definition of, 22; in manufac-
    turing and international trade, 347–52;
    new databases for, 364–69, 370
Services sector of economy: characteris-
    tics of service innovations, 23–25;
    defining outputs for, 365; definition of
    services, 22; in different countries, 20,
    24; employment in, 20, 22, 23, 24,
    345, 346; growth of services-software
    economy, 345–47; income from, 20,
    22, 40; intellectually based services,
    20–25; measurement problems re-
    garding, 364–68; object orientation
    and, 84–85; outmoded economic
    measures and models of, 40–41; out-
    puts from, 365–67; outputs over-
    looked in, 366–67; and pass-throughs
    to other sectors, 365–66; productivity
    statistics on, 364–65; quality mea-
    surement in, 365; transaction values
    in services, 23, 25; world trade in ser-
    vices, 31, 40
Setbacks in innovation, 15
"Shadow stock," 214
Shamlin, S., 110
Sharp Electronics, 30, 119, 130, 131,
    226, 228, 250, 256
Shiba, S., 152–53
Shoot-out system, 255–56
Shopping. *See* Virtual shopping
Siberia, 35
Silicon Graphics, 30, 38, 56, 79, 164,
    201, 368
Silicon Junction software, 79
Sim, 91, 92
Simple solutions, 108–09
Simulations, 83, 125, 149–50
"Simultaneous design" process, 207
Singapore, 32
Six Sigma quality target, 188
Skills value versus training expenditures,
    4, 5
Skunk works, 69–70, 98, 256–58
Small discrete applications, 95–97
Small interactive teams, 98
Smallest replicable units, 70–72, 86–87
Social security funds, 373

Software: as backbone of independent collaboration, 108–12, 139–40, 144–46; as critical ingredient, 51–52; for design and evaluation, 54–55, 68–69; diffusion and, 78–79; economic trends and, 21, 28–29; enhanced results with, 55; in fast cycle innovation, 53–58; fees for software publicized on Internet, 361; illegal copying of, 363; impact of, 19, 21, 28–29, 42, 45–46, 51–52, 61–63, 73; information technology (IT) software, 45–46; as integral part of organizational structure, 11–12, 30, 125–26, 228–30; as inventor, 56–57; as leverages for knowledge, 2–4; and leveraging value creation, 57–58; limitations of, 70; markets and industries largely facilitated by, 52; national encouragement of software innovation, 360–61; network ("spider's web") organization, 11–12, 228–30; object-oriented software, 71–72, 73; open systems, 79–80; pricing systems of, 91–92; revolution in, 46–52; self-learning software systems, 82–83; services-software economy growth, 345–47; technology strategy and, 176; types of, 2. *See also* other headings beginning with Software
Software AG, 96
Software "applets," 72, 91
Software-based discipline and culture, 114–15
Software-based innovation: in applied research, 47; in basic research, 46–47; changes in software innovation organizations, 80–83; database and model access system, 65; design and evaluation software, 54–55, 68–69; and destruction of hierarchies, 80; in development, 47–48; diffusion and, 50, 78–79; dominating all aspects of innovation, 46–51, 61–63; enhanced results and, 55; fast cycle innovation, 53–58; and identification of opportunities interactively, 58–61; impact of information technology (IT) software, 45–46; integration of innovation subsystems, 68–73; and interacting subsystems, not megasystems, 66–68; in interactive customer design, 49, 73, 92; interactive sales tool, 59; inter-

faces, 66; and leveraging value creation, 57–58; management of, 61, 64–68, 74–103; in manufacturing engineering, 48; markets and industries largely facilitated by software, 52; and new economics of computing, 90–92; in new value-added systems, 50–51; object orientation, 71–72, 73, 83–92; open systems, 79–80; in post-introduction monitoring, 49–50; and priesthood of mathematicians, 80–81; and self- learning software systems, 82–83; and smallest replicable units, 70–72; software-centered design and, 75–76; software as critical ingredient, 51–52; software as inventor, 56–57; software (process) engines, 65–66; user-innovators and, 72–73, 81–82, 89–90; value creation and, 50–51, 57–58; virtual shopping and user-based innovation, 60; virtual skunk works and storerooms, 69–70; worldwide virtual innovation, 60–61. *See also* Management of software-based innovation
Software "buttons," 89
Software-centered design, 75–76
Software development: "build-and-bust" physical experiments in, 94, 113–14; "build-test-drive" coordinating mechanism for, 98, 114; computer-aided software engineering (CASE), 98, 99–100; design to requirements (support systems), 100–01; focus on intellectual content in, 112–13; highly disciplined procedures (integrating and improving legacy systems), 101–03; individual inventor-innovators (small, discrete applications), 95–97; as innovation paradigm, 112–15; management of generally, 94–95; Microsoft approach to, 6; monitoring programs (large integrated systems), 99–100; small interactive teams (operating systems), 98; and software-based discipline and culture, 114–15
Software Engineering Institute, 101
Software "hooks," 30, 57–58, 66, 71, 77, 84, 140
Software industry: design to requirements (support systems), 100–01; employment in, 75; government support for, 282; highly disciplined procedures

(integrating and improving legacy systems), 101–03; individual inventor-innovators (small, discrete applications), 95–97; initial public offerings from 1980–1996, 62; investment of venture capital in, 61, 96; monitoring programs (large integrated systems), 99–100; profits in, 29; revenue from, 75, 77, 78, 343; small interactive teams (operating systems), 98; time horizons for computer industry, 294; top companies from 1980–1996, 63, 96. *See also* specific companies
Software integration. *See* Integration
Software networks. *See* Internet; Intranets; Networks
Software (process) engines, 65–66
Software Process Improvement Plan (SPIP), 101
Solectron, 63
Solow, R., 34
Sony Corporation: core competencies and, 196, 197; demanding goals at, 246; diffusion and, 32; figures of merit at, 189–90; innovation along multiple dimensions by, 164; management of, 249; market orientation of, 253; market research and, 252–53; multiple development approaches at, 255; outsourcing by, 211; recognition and incentives at, 157, 214, 245; resistance to change in, 16; skunk works at, 257; technology strategy of, 176; time horizons and, 222, 239; vision of, 170
Special interest groups, 338, 339
Specialist knowledge, 129–30
Spider software system, 133
"Spider's web" (network) organization, 11–12, 228–30
SPIP. *See* Software Process Improvement Plan (SPIP)
SQL, 66
Squibb, 370
Standard Oil (Ohio), 370
Starburst strategies, 230–31
State-of-the-art technologies, 234
State Street Boston, 7, 192, 196, 197, 199–200
Sterling Software, 96
Steuben Glass, 236
Storerooms. *See* Virtual storerooms
Storytelling about company, 172–73

"Stovepipe" systems, 101
Strategic focus, 200–01, 212. *See also* Strategies; Vision
Strategic Highway Research Program, 55
Strategic planning, 155
Strategic risk versus competitive edge, 205
Strategies: core competency strategies, 193–202; goals in, 174–75; information technology (IT) strategies, 176; model of, 175; most effective innovation strategies, 177; policies in, 175; programs in, 175; technology strategy of company, 174–79. *See also* National strategies; National technology strategies; Technology strategies
Strategy implementation. *See* Middle management
Suboptimization, avoidance of, 138–39
Subsidies from government, 306–07
Subsystem relationships in science, 271–72
Succession biogenetics, 270–75
Sun Microsystems, 8, 25, 30, 50, 68, 108, 124, 164, 201, 248, 253
Sun Network, 124
Sun Paperless Reporter, 124
SunDans software, 124
Sunguard Data Systems, 96
Superpave, 55
Support systems designed to requirements, 100–01
Survey techniques for public markets, 332–33
Swanson, R., 169–70
Sweden, 298, 372, 381
SWIFT, 77
Sybase, 96
Syntex, 221, 254
Synthesis, 2, 3, 274
"System builds," 223
System solutions, 109
System understanding, 2, 3, 5, 19
Systems Engineering Group, Bell Laboratories, 192–93, 193n

Tacit knowledge, 17, 129–30, 133
Tactical action programs (TAPs), 185
Taligent, 73
TAPs (tactical action programs), 185
TAPS (Trades and Processing System), 199

Target, 353

Taurus team, 119–20, 147, 257

Taurus-Sable project, 147, 206–07, 240, 258

Taxes, 303, 304, 334, 360, 369, 371–74

Taxonomy development in science, 270–71

TCP/IP, 72, 90

Teachers, 377, 384–85. *See also* Education and training

Team Taurus, 119–20, 147, 257

Teams, 107, 117, 128, 132, 260

Technological failures, 40, 127–28, 252–53, 255, 305–06

Technological forecasting techniques, 191

Technology: capital and, 35–36; changing traditional economic paradigms on, 33–40; creation of scientific and technological knowledge, 9–12; defining outputs for, 365; definition of, 3, 344; education and training and, 36; government-industry strategies, 279–313; historical development of, in U.S., 284–289; impact of, on growth and productivity gains, 34, 35–36; initial public offerings from 1980–1996, 62; labor and, 35; land and, 35; manager's ignorance of inner workings of, 343–44, 406n2; national technology competitiveness, 279–313; national technology policy, 276–77, 287–88, 310–12, 344–45; for quality of life, 34, 36;questions about interrelationships involving, 1; rational approach to choice of, 38–39; relationship with science, 274–76; as "residual" in traditional economic paradigm, 33; role of, in national growth, 289; technology multipliers, 37; U.S. scientists and engineers engaged in R&D by country, 376. *See also* Information technology (IT); Software headings

Technology multipliers, 37; *see also* Government-supported innovation

Technology policy, 276–77, 287–88, 310–12, 344–45, 367–68. *See also* National technology strategies

Technology strategies: historical development of, in U.S., 284–91; of innovative companies, 174–79; need for national technology strategies, 314; for overcoming market failures, 314–22. *See*

*also* Information technology (IT); Software headings

Teerlink, Richard, 246

Telecommunications Act of 1995, 308

Telltabs, 63

Temporary and job-search employment groups, 350

10X goal, 188–89, 252

Tennessee Valley Authority, 37

Test equipment software, 58

Texas Instruments, 148, 185, 189, 260

Theoretical limits analysis, 191–92

Thermo Electron Co., 230

Thermos, Inc., 152

Thinking Machines, 167

"Thoughtware," 211

3Com, 63

3D Pharmaceuticals, Inc., 113

Three-level independent collaboration structure, 130–33

3M: bootleg projects at, 249; core competencies and, 197, 201; databases of, 368; decision making about innovation at, 249; failures at, 16; incentives at, 136, 214; independent collaboration at, 121; intellectual preeminence of, 201; market orientation of, 253; multiple, discrete, freestanding product lines at, 234; outsourcing by, 211; overhead projector program at, 172; portfolio mechanisms at, 185; protected underground activities at, 251; self-selected champions and successful projects at, 148; technology strategy of, 176, 177

3M Foundation, 381

Time-consuming nature of innovation, 14

Time horizons: capital costs, government and, 292–93; extension of, 291–301; incentives and, 238–42; by industry, 294; negative government impacts on, 297–99; protected time horizons and underground activities, 250–51

Time Warner, 384

Tokyo Electric, 203

Top management: characteristics of successful innovation managers, 159, 163–64, 187; and continual, pulsing, and organic innovation, 165–66; core competency strategies and, 193–202; direct access to, 249–50; as dream spinners and legends, 171–72; and essence of leadership, 172–74; figures of merit and, 179, 181–85, 187–93; and innovation along multiple dimensions, 164–65; and lateral diffusion and learning, 167–68; and leveraging innovation through outsourcing, 203–12; and multiple companies within the company, 166; and performance measurement and recognition systems, 157, 212–14; portfolio of commitments and, 179, 180, 183–85; and profits, human values, and innovation, 166–68; support for change and innovation by, 155–56, 163–64, 185–86, 214–15; technology strategy and, 174–79; as "tie-breaker," 133; vision and, 168–74. *See also* Middle management

Toshiba, 254

Total quality management (TQM), 109

Totally new phenomena, 109

Toxic Substances Act, 297

Toyota, 92, 236

Toys "R" Us, 199, 347, 353

TPN. See Trading Process Network (TPN)

TQM, 109

Tradable quotas, 333–35

Trade policies, 304–05, 332, 347–52

Trading Process Network (TPN), 320–21

Traffic safety, 326

"Tragedy of the commons," 319

Training. See Education and training

Transaction costs, 315–16

Transfer payments, 373

Transportation Department, 311

Travel agents, 366

Trilogy, 47, 83

TRIZ, 142

Trust and constructive confrontation, 246–47

TRW, 201, 335, 368

T-shaped skills, 129–30

Turbotax, 76

Tushman, M., 150

TVA, 285

TWA, 87

Underground activities, 250–51

United Kingdom. *See* Britain

United Nations, 34, 367

U.S./Israel Binational Industrial Research Foundation, 229–30

U.S. Sprint, 173

University-based research, 357–58

University of Minnesota, 381

UNIX, 76, 79, 97

Upjohn, 210

UPS, 201

Uruguay Round, 347

User-based innovation, 60, 72–73, 89–90, 148–49

USSR, 279

Vale, W., 271

Value chain, 193–94, 193n, 195, 198–99, 349–50, 351

Value creation: intellectual values of largest acquired companies, 369, 370; object orientation and, 87–89; public markets and, 337–38; and software-based innovation, 50–51, 57–58

Vanguard Investments, 192

"Velcro balls," 84, 140

Venezuela, 35, 379

Venture capital, 61, 96, 184, 302, 303

Venture teams, 260

Veronica, 384

Vertical integration, 374

"Vertical mixing," 164

Viacom–Simon & Schuster, 384

Video games, 378, 380

Video simulations, 149–50

Vietnam, 356, 379

Viraldi, L., 119

"Virtual collaboration spaces," 148

"Virtual corporation," 203

"Virtual culch bag," 143

Virtual innovation, 60–61

"Virtual instruments," 58

Virtual laboratory, 382

Virtual organization, 125–26

Virtual reality models, 150

"Virtual reality" representation, 125

Virtual shopping, 60

Virtual skunk works, 69–70

Virtual storerooms, 70

"Virtual workgroup," 114

Visicalc, 96

Vision: aligned purpose and, 122; and essence of leadership, 172–74; excitement and, 171–72; and glittering sense of purpose, 169; and innovation leaders as dream spinners and legends, 171–72; and pragmatism, not bland abstractions, 169–71; questions concerning, 169; top management and, 168–74

Visual Basic, 60, 73, 184
Visual software models, 125
Volunteers in Technical Assistance, 383
Volvo, 181
Von Hippel, E., 151
Von Neumann, J., 83, 145

W. L. Gore & Associates, 121, 123,
    134–35, 164, 256
W. R. Grace, 173
Wages, 26. *See also* Employment
Wal-Mart: common bond and, 116; iden-
    tity-creating information and, 138; inno-
    vation along multiple dimensions at,
    164; innovation level of, 110; intellectual
    preeminence of, 201; market orientation
    of, 253;post-introduction monitoring by,
    49–50; software system as integral part
    of, 30, 85, 108, 368; top management
    at, 163; trade policies and, 347
Walton, S., 110, 116, 253
"Waterline" principle, 123
Waters from Land Reclamation, 354
Watson, J., 221
Watson Research Center, IBM, 46–47
"Web crawlers," 384
Weick, K., 126
Weiden and Kennedy, 204
Wesson, R., 136
West Indies, 356

"We-they" attitude, 123
Wheatley, M., 122, 136, 139
"White space" technique, 149–54
White, T., 121
WIIFM ("What's in it for me?") ratio,
    16, 307
Windows, 65, 72, 76, 166, 184, 222, 240
Winning, processes involved in, 358–59
Wisewire, 124–25
Word, 81, 166, 184
Work-life connection with life-work,
    123–24, 171
World Bank, 382
World Wide Web, 60, 66, 67, 72,
    77–78, 80, 81, 91, 124, 242, 345. *See
    also* Internet
"Wow factor," 59
Wozniak, S., 128
Wright, S., 274
WYSIWIS (What You See Is What I
    See), 127

Xerox, 136, 259
Xerox PARC, 127

Yahoo, 66, 72
Yamauchi, 257

Zona Research, 90
Zucherman, H., 111